When the State Winks

RELIGION, CULTURE, AND PUBLIC LIFE

RELIGION, CULTURE, AND PUBLIC LIFE

Series Editor: Katherine Pratt Ewing

The resurgence of religion calls for careful analysis and constructive criticism of new forms of intolerance, as well as new approaches to tolerance, respect, mutual understanding, and accommodation. In order to promote serious scholarship and informed debate, the Institute for Religion, Culture, and Public Life and Columbia University Press are sponsoring a book series devoted to the investigation of the role of religion in society and culture today. This series includes works by scholars in religious studies, political science, history, cultural anthropology, economics, social psychology, and other allied fields whose work sustains multidisciplinary and comparative as well as transnational analyses of historical and contemporary issues. The series focuses on issues related to questions of difference, identity, and practice within local, national, and international contexts. Special attention is paid to the ways in which religious traditions encourage conflict, violence, and intolerance and also support human rights, ecumenical values, and mutual understanding. By mediating alternative methodologies and different religious, social, and cultural traditions, books published in this series will open channels of communication that facilitate critical analysis.

After Pluralism: Reimagining Religious Engagement, edited by Courtney Bender and Pamela E. Klassen

Religion and International Relations Theory, edited by Jack Snyder

Religion in America: A Political History, Denis Lacorne

Democracy, Islam, and Secularism in Turkey, edited by Ahmet T. Kuru and Alfred Stepan

Refiguring the Spiritual: Beuys, Barney, Turrell, Goldsworthy, Mark C. Taylor

Tolerance, Democracy, and Sufis in Senegal, edited by Mamadou Diouf

Rewiring the Real: In Conversation with William Gaddis, Richard Powers, Mark Danielewski, and Don DeLillo, Mark C. Taylor

Democracy and Islam in Indonesia, edited by Mirjam Künkler and Alfred Stepan

Religion, the Secular, and the Politics of Sexual Difference, edited by Linell E. Cady and Tracy Fessenden

Boundaries of Toleration, edited by Alfred Stepan and Charles Taylor

Recovering Place: Reflections on Stone Hill, Mark C. Taylor

Blood: A Critique of Christianity, Gil Anidjar

Choreographies of Shared Sacred Sites: Religion, Politics, and Conflict Resolution, edited by Elazar Barkan and Karen Barkey

Beyond Individualism: The Challenge of Inclusive Communities, George Rupp

Love and Forgiveness for a More Just World, edited by Hent de Vries and Nils F. Schott

Relativism and Religion: Why Democratic Societies Do Not Need Moral Absolutes, Carlo Invernizzi Accetti

The Making of Salafism: Islamic Reform in the Twentieth Century, Henri Lauzière

Mormonism and American Politics, edited by Randall Balmer and Jana Riess

Religion, Secularism, and Constitutional Democracy, edited by Jean L. Cohen and Cécile Laborde

Race and Secularism in America, edited by Jonathon S. Kahn and Vincent W. Lloyd

Beyond the Secular West, edited by Akeel Bilgrami

Pakistan at the Crossroads: Domestic Dynamics and External Pressures, edited by Christophe Jaffrelot

Faithful to Secularism: The Religious Politics of Democracy in Ireland, Senegal, and the Philippines, David T. Buckley

Holy Wars or Holy Alliances: The Return of Religion Onto the Global Political Stage, Manlio Graziano

WHEN THE STATE WINKS

The Performance of Jewish Conversion in Israel

MICHAL KRAVEL-TOVI

COLUMBIA UNIVERSITY PRESS *NEW YORK*

Columbia University Press
Publishers Since 1893
New York Chichester, West Sussex
cup.columbia.edu

Library of Congress Cataloging-in-Publication Data
Names: Kravel-Tovi, Michal, author.
Title: When the state winks: the performance of Jewish conversion in Israel / Michal Kravel-Tovi.
Other titles: Religion, culture, and public life.
Description: New York: Columbia University Press, 2017. | Series: Religion, culture, and public life
Identifiers: LCCN 2017011282 | ISBN 9780231183246 (cloth: alk. paper) |
ISBN 9780231544818 (e-book)
Subjects: LCSH: Conversion—Judaism. | Jewish converts. | Jews—Identity. | Zionism.
Classification: LCC BM645.C6 K73 2017 | DDC 296.7/14095694—dc23
LC record available at https://lccn.loc.gov/2017011282

Columbia University Press books are printed on permanent and durable acid-free paper.
Printed in the United States of America

Cover design: Noah Arlow

In loving memory of my dear friend Liat Kastiel z"l (1973–1997). Liat planned to study anthropology. She was perceptive about people and had a talent for putting the world into words. She would have made a wonderful ethnographer.

Contents

Acknowledgments

Writing a book involves the unavoidable pleasure of accumulating debts. Both large and small, these debts give a tangible sense—names, faces, conversations, and places—to what generosity is all about. They remind us of the extent to which an endeavor as personal as writing a book depends on the efforts of so many people. My book is no different. In the classrooms at the Hebrew University of Jerusalem, where, back in the 1990s, I first understood that I wanted to become an anthropologist; in the offices of my mentors, where I was always given the space to articulate my ideas (as tentative and fragile as they were); and, finally, in my kitchen, where I sit now writing these acknowledgments, and where I wrote much of this book, with my partner and boys around, I have grown fortunate enough to owe so much to so many people.

I began my undergraduate studies with the intention of becoming a psychologist. However, due mainly to an inspiring encounter with Tamar El-Or and Yoram Bilu, who would later become my mentors, I changed my plans. Each in their own way, Tamar and Yoram sparked my interest in the ethnography of Jewish life. They soon became role models and have remained a source of wisdom. Tamar taught me why ethnography matters and how it allows scholars to write creatively. Yoram provided intellectual guidance, expressed confidence in my work, and allowed me to carve out my own path. For me, he exemplifies how modesty can go hand in hand with fame and shrewd scholarship. The Memorial Foundation for Jewish Culture and the

Mandel Scholion Interdisciplinary Research Center in the Humanities and Jewish Studies at the Hebrew University of Jerusalem provided financial support for this project. As a fellow at the center, and a member of the research group on religion and education, I benefited from a vibrant and stimulating academic setting during the critical early stages of this project.

I was fortunate to join the University of Michigan's Frankel Center for Judaic Studies as a postdoctoral fellow during Deborah Dash Moore's tenure as the center's director. I hope she knows how much I value her generosity to junior scholars, her high standards for scholarship, and the political and disciplinary open-mindedness of her approach to Jewish studies. At the Frankel Center I also met my dearest (and undoubtedly funniest) colleague and friend, Vanessa Ochs. Vanessa was the first among several supportive colleagues to "demand" that I rework my dissertation into a book manuscript. It is hardly original to describe Jennifer Robertson as a generous colleague and adviser. Many have written this about her, and they are right. I thank her for pushing me to write this book. At Michigan I was also fortunate to meet Josh Friedman, then a PhD candidate in anthropology and now a wonderful young anthropologist. As a talented editor, colleague, and friend, Josh has helped me sharpen my skills as an Israeli author writing ethnography for non-Israeli audiences. The traces of our ongoing dialogue exist throughout the pages that follow, and I look forward to reading his own book.

I am blessed with wonderful colleagues at Tel Aviv University. Ofra Goldstein-Gidoni was an exceptional chair when I joined the Department of Sociology and Anthropology, and she is a large part of why the department has become a home for me. My profound thanks go out to other dear colleagues as well, including Yehuda Shenhav, Adriana Kemp, Khaled Furani, Dan Rabinowitz, Hadas Mandel, Nissim Mizrachi, and Hana Herzog, who have always offered generosity and support. The bright students and research and teaching assistants with whom I have worked at Tel Aviv University always remind me why I chose academia and why I believe in ethnography, despite its contingencies and pitfalls. Two of these students, Maayan Shtendel and Thalia Thereza Assan were helpful and dependable resources in the writing process—the first by reading through most of the manuscript and organizing the reference list, and the second by indexing the book. I am indebted to both.

I cannot thank my close and beloved friends enough—Kinneret Lahad, Inna Leykin, Sigal Ozeri, Vered Kara, Sarit Brook, Ma'ayan Eitan, Ilana Blumberg, and Avi Shoshana—for their encouragement and invaluable support, including during the writing process. My writing group—Adam Klin-Oron,

Ari Engelberg, Rachel Werzberger, and Dana Kaplan—read early versions of several chapters and articles and contributed their challenging, productive critiques. Nissim Leon, Matthew Hull, Marcy Brink-Danan, Ronen Mandelkern, Yael Zerubavel, Carol Kidron, Yulia Lerner, Shaul Kelner, and Tomer Persico responded to ideas presented in lectures or early versions of chapters and offered helpful comments. Helene Furani edited several chapters wholeheartedly and professionally.

At Columbia University Press Karen Barkey embraced this project from the outset as the then editor of the Religion, Culture, and Public Life series. She has been particularly kind, encouraging, and supportive. I also thank Anne Routon for her wisdom in handling the review process, and Susan Pensak for her professional handling of the book's production. Miriam Grossman answered every query I raised, and Michael Simon copyedited the book with particularly impressive care and attention. I want to thank the reviewers of the manuscript: Don Seeman (who disclosed his name to me) and the other reviewer, who remains anonymous. In their close reading of the manuscript and their thoughtful comments, they enhanced the book and pushed me to sharpen some of my descriptions and arguments. The Israel Institute supported the publication of this book.

I'm grateful to my interlocutors in the field, mostly converts and conversion agents, for their willingness to accept my ethnographic gaze in settings shot through with suspicion and during delicate moments of their lives. I cannot thank most of them by name, but I hope they see their experiences reflected in the pages that follow and perhaps even recognize themselves. I did my best to reciprocate their trust and I do not take it for granted.

My beloved mother, Dorit, supported each and every step on my path to becoming a scholar. I know it is cliché to write about unconditional motherly love, but sometimes clichés are true. One of the benefits of building a life with my partner, Yoel, was getting my in-laws, Isabel and Carlos Tovi, in the deal; their profound care and support are always significant and were crucial through fieldwork and the writing of this book. Most of all I have depended on the everyday love and patience of Yoel. Although I was the one to write the book, it has in many respects been a joint venture. And finally, our boys, Eviatar and Shauli, who by now know a thing or two about monographs, academic publishers, and tenure committees (enough to decline my gentle encouragement that, one day, they might pursue a similar path). During the final few months of the writing process, they concluded that "Ima [mother] really must finish this book." So I did.

When the State Winks

Prologue

The Naked Truth on Tel Aviv's Beaches

JEWISH CONVERSION (*giyyur*) in Israel has always been a highly politicized and publicly contentious issue. Given Israel's weak separation between state and religion, as well as its Jewish self-definition, state institutions have historically maintained the prerogative to regulate conversion. However, since the late 1980s, in response to the mass influx of non-Jewish immigrants (*olim*; lit. "ascendants") from the former Soviet Union (FSU), the state's involvement in Jewish conversion has both expanded in scale and grown in complexity. These processes have transformed the role of conversion in public Israeli life. Today Jewish conversion in Israel is a national mission. National concerns about intermarriage, the Israeli collective's blurred boundaries, and, ultimately, questions about Israel's future as a Jewish state all inform this mission.

This book tells the story of how and why Israel has engrossed itself in both encouraging and managing the conversion of non-Jewish FSU immigrants. It explores the political circumstances, bureaucratic arrangements, and moral implications of this contested state policy. The paradoxes underwriting this policy ground my ethnographic and analytical focus. In particular, the book focuses on the incongruity between inclusive national aspirations and exclusive rabbinic gatekeeping practices and, relatedly, between collective, population-related concerns and procedures that focus on the religious conduct and sincerity of individuals. The ethnography that follows traces the macropolitical and micro socio-institutional dynamics that have emerged from Israel's reliance on rabbinic tools to actualize its national mission of conversion. These tools require Israel's conversion agents to focus on the religious observance of individuals, even if the state's primary concerns lie elsewhere.

The protagonists in this ethnography include both conversion candidates and state conversion agents. Most of the candidates are young, secular Israeli women from an FSU background who must navigate the institutional processes of state conversion. The conversion agents hail mostly from religious Zionist circles and are caught between the contradictory demands of their nationalist and religious commitments. These agents consist of rabbis, policy makers, bureaucrats, religious judges, and educators. During three years of ethnographic research (2004–2007), I engaged conversion candidates and conversion agents where they engaged each other—in the pedagogic, bureaucratic, and ritualistic settings that organize the conversion process under the auspices of the state. I met them at the conversion school (*ulpan*), where Jewish teachers provide candidates with a basic Jewish education and expose them to Jewish practice; at the rabbinic courts of conversion, where rabbinic judges rule on converts' applications; and at the ritual baths (*mikvaot*), where candidates whose applications were endorsed at the rabbinic court immerse themselves in water (undergoing *tvilah*) and become Jews according to Jewish law (*halakha*). All of these encounters taught me a great deal about how, in their everyday lives, these differently positioned individuals manage the incredible challenges generated by Israel's contradictory conversion policy.

To illuminate the core tensions that concern the protagonists of this book, it is instructive to begin with an alternative conversion policy route suggested in the early 2000s by a prominent Orthodox Zionist rabbi: the enactment of conversion en masse. The plan, which was immediately rejected by other rabbis and policy makers, completely disregarded the dominant *halakhic* understanding of conversion as the sincere commitment of individuals to religious observance. Instead, this rabbi insisted upon the existence of a national demographic crisis, thus justifying in its name a quick, single act of mass conversion. Because his proposal, oriented toward collective, national goals, threatened to render hollow the conversion ritual, sapping it of both personal agency and religious sincerity, it had no chance of being widely embraced. As a religious ritual, it sounded not only overly thin; it also seemed too direct, too crude, and too naked a demonstration of the state's national stakes in Jewish conversion. In that respect, his policy recommendation, and its aftermath, offers a productive point of departure for understanding the conversion system at the center of this book: one that is formally dedicated to the sincere religious conversion of individuals, but ill suited to address its pressing national goals.

The rabbi, Rabbi Yoel Bin-Nun, laid out his manifesto in a 2003 article published in the Israeli magazine *Eretz Acheret* under the provocative headline "Mass Conversion Must Be Carried Out." It was not the first time he had delivered this message. In the tone of an ostracized prophet of doom, Rabbi Bin-Nun urged the public to listen to what he had been saying for some time: that large-scale non-Jewish immigration from the FSU had created a real national catastrophe and now required an emergency response. The "disaster," as he called it, was imminent.

He reminded his audience that the many non-Jewish immigrants who arrived in Israel did so under the generous auspices of the Israeli repatriation law (the expanded Law of Return) and as a fulfillment of the grand Zionist scheme of return to the promised land. Even though the state does not recognize these non-Jewish immigrants as Jews—that is, according to the matrilineal principles that govern Israel's system of Jewish identity—it has nonetheless absorbed them as Israeli citizens under the privileged, and politically sacred, category of *olim*. These immigrants frequently identify and pass as Jews and, in general, are well integrated into Jewish Israeli society. Because of these factors, Rabbi Bin-Nun implicitly argued, non-Jewish FSU immigrants do not just actualize a fundamental Zionist script and fortify Israel's Jewish majority; they simultaneously threaten the boundaries of the Jewish population (as defined in Israel by the Orthodox rabbinic establishment) and unavoidably sabotage Israel's ongoing Zionist struggle to secure a Jewish majority. Conjuring dark images of impending doom, Rabbi Bin-Nun positioned these non-Jewish FSU immigrants between the Zionist dream and its downfall, depicting a scenario that begins with the immigrants' social integration and intermarriage with Jewish Israelis, and ends with nothing less than the loss of Jewish sovereignty:[1]

> Worst of all, Jews will not only become a minority in Greater Israel—that's already happening now—Jews will become a minority even in a contracted, shrunken State of Israel. The Jewish State might even turn into a Jewish autonomy, viable only by the grace of foreigners. The elders of the ultra-Orthodox

> [*Haredi*] community will mock us and claim: "We told you so! After all, the writing was on the wall!" All the enemies of Israel will rub their palms together in glee: The Palestinians, the radical Muslims, the anti-Semites of Europe, and the devout Christians.[2]
>
> (Bin-Nun 2003)

The emergency measures proposed by Rabbi Bin-Nun mirrored the enormity of the horror he described. His conclusion was clear: the State of Israel must summon the political courage to carry out the mass conversion of non-Jewish FSU olim. He argued that the current state conversion system—manifested in the broad network of conversion institutions operating for some two decades under the aegis of the state—had failed to meet the portentousness of the moment. Certainly, Rabbi Bin-Nun acknowledged, the extant system had some degree of merit. After all, the state's conversion efforts have been informed by the Zionist imperative to convert non-Jewish olim on a large scale. In particular, his colleagues in the rabbinic conversion courts, Orthodox rabbis like himself, perform what he deemed "sacred work" (ibid.) on behalf of the Israeli state, while stretching what they perceive to be the limits of Jewish conversion laws.

But the conversion system, he went on to argue, simultaneously undermines prospective candidates and undermines itself, because of its meticulous, unrealistic focus on religious obligations. Insofar as the work of conversion agents depends on the converts' "acceptance of the commandments" (*kabalat hamitzvoth*)—that is, in the rabbis' interpretation, adherence to a specific Orthodox lifestyle—the conversion procedures undermine the state's own goals. The sociological profile of FSU immigrants only highlights the conversion policy's basic dysfunction. Rarely inclined toward religion, and generally blending into secular Jewish Israeli social milieus, these non-Jewish olim are hardly good candidates for a religiously oriented conversion process. This is why Rabbi Bin-Nun pressed the state rabbinic institutions to favor an exceptionally lenient halakhic policy that would permit the state to dramatically ease (if not totally eliminate) the requirement that candidates accept the commandments. To justify such a policy both publicly and rabbinically, he pointed to the precedents in halakhic literature for minimizing the centrality of accepting the commandments and stressed that in the current emergency situation, Israel's rabbinic authorities do not have the luxury of a less dramatic response.

A few years later, in 2006, at a public conference on conversion, which I attended, Rabbi Bin-Nun distilled the essence of his notably lenient halakhic approach into a concrete action plan:

> I want to talk about how we should cope with a mass multitude of gentiles, those who are not Jewish by halakha but nevertheless live amongst us. Maimonides states that anyone who is circumcised and has undergone ritual immersion [tvilah] is retroactively a convert. This is not to be undertaken a priori, but it is valid retroactively. I have been arguing for fifteen years that the current situation in Israel is one that requires retroactive judgment. A priori, the question would be whether or not to have brought non-Jews into the country in the first place, and my answer is that we must be much more careful and strict than we are today. Our situation is one of retroactive judgment because non-Jewish immigrants are already here. Those who pose stringent conditions on conversion make light of the Jewish character of Israel, and open the gate to assimilation. I propose that we convert everyone in an act of mass conversion. We will create an impressive, moving ceremony on the eve of the Day of Atonement [Yom Kippur] or on the Festival of Weeks [Shavuoth] on the beach in Tel Aviv. Everyone will call out together "Hear O Israel" [Shma' Yisrael], "We will do and obey" [*Na'ase venishma*], then sign a document before an authorized rabbinic court, and that's it. We should do this recurrently for 10–20 years, and solve the problem. When I first introduced this idea, everyone looked at me as if I were crazy. Why? Because conversion is, as you know, an individual, personal matter . . . [but] if we really want to solve the problem, we need to scale up, and therefore avoid insisting that non-Jewish olim accept the commandments but, rather, inform them that they already have. We need to do all this as quickly as possible.[3]

At the conference, Rabbi Bin-Nun addressed a primarily religious-Zionist (i.e., Orthodox) Jewish audience and thus had little need to explain the concepts he used. He correctly assumed they already knew that the decisive acts of conversion, halakhically speaking, consist of circumcision (for men) and ritual immersion (for both men and women). He also knew that even if his listeners were not familiar with Maimonides's writing on conversion, they would certainly be aware of the generic halakhic distinction between a priori situations (what is permitted or prohibited before an action) and retroactive ones (what is considered legitimate after the deed). Maimonides's interpretation of conversion provided Rabbi Bin-Nun with an approach that made full use of ritual immersion's performative effect: authorizing conversion to Judaism. For Israel's rabbinic authorities, this approach could both circumvent the polemical halakhic debate over the converts' religious observance and provide a realistic solution given the profile of potential FSU converts.

What makes Rabbi Bin-Nun's idea so compelling is how, as a solution to a perceived national emergency, it simply rendered the religious sincerity and personal agency of potential converts immaterial. As one can see from Avi Sagi and Zvi Zohar's account of the rabbinic literature on conversion (2007), Rabbi Bin-Nun is not the first Orthodox authority to compromise religious ideals in order to adapt Jewish law to Jewish modernity and secularity. Yet Rabbi Bin-Nun's approach, which radically nullified the individual convert, represented a remarkably dramatic subjection of Jewish religious law to considerations of communal policy. For Rabbi Bin-Nun, the national desire to identify and tally the olim as (halakhic, "kosher") Jews took precedence over the religious work that these immigrants should ideally perform as conversion candidates. Instead of counting one individual convert after another, as they slowly accumulate in the files of government ministries, Rabbi Bin-Nun offered a solution numerically appropriate to the massive nature of the disaster he perceived. This is why he envisioned the mass of bodies joining the Jewish body politic. This is also why, in his portrayal of the conversion ritual, acceptance of the commandments was transformed from a personal commitment of individuals into a mere echo uttered by a faceless crowd formulaically repeating the required oaths and prayers.

The scene of a crowd ritually immersing itself in the sea during critical days in the Jewish calendar evokes constitutive biblical myths,[4] including the moment when the Jewish people's covenant with God was first established at Mount Sinai. Rabbi Bin-Nun's imagined scene foregrounds the primacy of the collective Jewish experience and one of the central myths of Jewish nationalism. By referencing such powerful, existential Jewish moments, the scene symbolically counters a second archaic image that Rabbi Bin-Nun invoked—one hardly alien to contemporary Israel's alarmist political discourses. In this alternative image, multitudes of Israel's enemies gather from near and far in anticipation of the Jewish state's inevitable collapse. In Zionist terms, these two images stand in opposition: the first represents redemption, the latter apocalypse. Who among you, Rabbi Bin-Nun implicitly asked his audience, will not choose redemption?

Yet at the conversion conference, the audience treated Rabbi Bin-Nun's address as little more than an amusing curiosity—an idea more or less beyond the pale of legitimate discourse. Unlike other discussions that aroused heated debate among those who packed the yeshiva auditorium's seats, the rabbi's words were met with quiet murmurs, a few dismissive hand gestures, and scoffing smiles. "If only it were possible," a woman sitting next to me whispered to her companion; "if only he were right." Her friend responded angrily: "Does he think that people are just tea bags you dip in water?" A number of rabbis and public figures who sat together with Rabbi Bin-Nun on the panel briefly argued with him, but the idea was simply so anomalous that it seemed unworthy of the effort.

It is not that Rabbi Bin-Nun's copanelists embraced a different understanding of the national crisis that, they felt, non-Jewish FSU immigration had precipitated. Nor did they disagree with his insistence upon the urgent need for formal, state-authorized policies to address the problem. On the contrary, most of them were just as concerned about the numbers of non-Jewish olim and their extensive integration within Jewish-Israeli society. But despite this shared anxiety, all of the speakers adhered to a halakhic rabbinic model that foregrounded the religious agency of individuals.

Rabbi Israel Rosen, a prominent Zionist rabbi and one of the central architects of Israeli conversion policy, clearly illustrated the common resistance to Rabbi Bin-Nun's idea of mass conversion. Writing for a popular religious magazine, Rabbi Rosen contended: "There are some Orthodox pontificators . . . who dream about large-scale group conversion—ritual immersion in the Jordan River or the Sea of Galilee, like in the Ganges, a proclamation 'He is God,' and presto, Jews! There is no such thing and never was. The concept of conversion is individual by definition, and is connected to personal existence and to internal experience. . . . [Mass conversion] is a waste of time and money. [It's] a wasteful illusion" (Rosen 2006:37).

Historically speaking, conversion to Judaism contains both individualistic and collective dimensions. On the one hand, the vast corpus of halakhic literature, beginning with the Talmudic period, engages repeatedly with cases of individual candidates for conversion. In these discussions, debates about the volition and motivation of individuals—what we, anachronistically, might describe in terms of identity, subjectivity, and agency—reappear from time to time. On the other hand, collective, and at times enforced, conversion to Judaism is documented in prerabbinic periods. During the

Hasmonean regime, for example, the Jewish community forcibly incorporated the Idumaeans and Ituraeans. In contemporary cases, sociopolitical circumstances that pertain to the conversion of entire groups, as well as collectively applied bureaucratic arrangements in Israel, mediate the conversions of those who wish to join the Jewish fold. Such is the case, for example, in the immigration and conversion (or "return to Judaism") of the Bnei Menashe of India or the Feres Mura of Ethiopia.

Even when individuals undergo conversion, one should not dismiss the act's collective implications. Individual converts join a community and a nation, and the representatives of the Jewish collective (i.e., rabbis, leaders of the community, and state bureaucrats) govern that process. An entire nation shares the God with whom Jewish converts are supposed to form a lasting and exclusive relationship. Furthermore, conversion allows the individual convert to participate in the public life of the Jewish people: to marry fellow Jews, to testify in a rabbinic court, and to join (and be counted in) religious practices (e.g., for *minyan*, the quorum of ten Jewish adults required for certain Jewish practices).[5]

Despite all these dimensions of collectivity, most, if not all, contemporary canonical approaches to Jewish conversion, in Orthodoxy and all other major religious denominations, take individual converts as their essential unit of reference. Moreover, in line with modern perceptions of the self, Jewish conversion is often perceived as a deep, meaningful process intertwined with intention and volition (Buckser 2003; Lichtenstein, Feldman, and Wolowelsky 1990; Porton 1994; Weiss 1996; Weiss and Silverman 2000). Rabbi Rosen's assertion should be read in light of this modern, individualized interpretive framework. Across a wide array of textual and ethnographic representations, Jewish conversion is depicted as a process involving a significant reworking of personal and social identity, a process in which a person resituates him- or herself in the world and actively develops new understandings, experiences, and family customs. Whether the process of conversion is conceptualized in terms of *identity*, *soul*, or *consciousness* (to note only a few of the terms to which I was exposed during my research), it is clear that it amounts to more than just a body immersing itself in water. The Jewish convert is not a tea bag.

This monograph departs from the failure of Rabbi Bin-Nun's proposal. It begins with the acceptance by most Israeli rabbis and policy makers that, while conversion policy should be wielded to address a dire national problem, the most direct solution of mass conversion is simply unthinkable. The chapters that follow tell a story of the institutional relationships and political consequences that have unfolded from an individual-centered and religiously informed conversion procedure—one that has become instrumental to, and instrumentalized toward, national, collective goals.

I demonstrate how the actors that animate the national mission of state-sponsored conversion manage the burden of these discrepancies. They do so by subtly and collaboratively crafting performances of sincerity. Both conversion agents and converting subjects depend on these performances, which allow state agents to reaffirm their own authority as arbiters of religious sincerity while simultaneously managing the unruly sociopolitical reality they must accommodate. For the conversion candidates, these performances provide highly complex, but manageable, scripts. Those scripts allow them to become Jewish—in the eyes of their fellow Israeli citizens, Israeli law, and Israel's state bureaucracy.

Introduction

Taking Winking Seriously

We Both Came in Jeans

IT TOOK ME a moment to recognize Moran and a little longer to understand why.[1] At first glance, she looked exactly the same. Her hair was long and thin, as before, and her face was pretty and makeup-free, like I remembered from the conversion class (*ulpan*). But there was something else about her now. It perhaps sounds a bit cliché, but there was something freer about her. And it certainly seems funny in retrospect that I failed to recognize her because she wore blue jeans. How much difference can blue jeans make? But she did look more comfortable, even from afar, and the blue jeans did make a difference; embarrassingly, but also instructively, I only recognized her when she approached me.

It had been six months since I'd last seen Moran. I first met her while she was studying in the conversion ulpan, the first and longest stage of the state conversion process. Moran had since completed her conversion requirements. After effectively finishing the ten-month ulpan, she was invited to a hearing of the rabbinic conversion court regarding her conversion application. Her hearing was a success, and she soon underwent immersion in the ritual bath—the final and decisive act of conversion. A few months later she received the certificate of conversion and was registered as a Jew in the population registry.

She has been in Israel for quite a few years, fourteen to be exact, since immigrating (making *aliyah*; lit. "ascension") to Israel from Ukraine at the age of eleven. She came with her parents under the extended Israeli law of repatriation, a law that since 1970 has granted the right of entry and "return" not only to those recognized as Jews but also to people of Jewish ancestry and their spouses. Moran's grandfather—the only halakhically recognized Jew in her family—never made it to Israel.

Moran received Israeli citizenship upon her arrival. She grew up in the mostly Jewish Gush Dan metropolitan area (of greater Tel Aviv), was educated in the public Jewish-Israeli school system, and served in the army. If you saw her, you would never realize that she is not a Jewish Israeli. You would not even necessarily pick up on her Ukrainian background. She adopted a common Hebrew name, she speaks beautiful Israeli Hebrew with only the faintest trace of an accent, and she is knowledgeable about Israeli politics.[2] Like most Jewish Israelis she celebrates both religious and civil Jewish holidays (Shoham 2014), and like many FSU immigrants, she is proud to be Israeli and cannot imagine a future elsewhere (Leshem 2008). But in spite of all these meaningful testaments to her national, cultural, and social Jewish Israeli belonging, the state only recognized Moran as a Jew when she completed the Orthodox conversion process.

Throughout most of the conversion ulpan, Moran consistently wore a skirt or a dress, her arms always covered by long shirt sleeves extending below her elbows. As an anthropologist, I also took care to dress according to the modesty code that the three male Orthodox teachers had introduced to the class of mostly young women. But now, six months later, only a short walking distance from the ulpan, we both allowed ourselves to show up in jeans.

"We both came in jeans," I wrote in my field notes a few hours later, after returning from the café where I interviewed Moran. This sentence would reappear more than once in my notebook, following the interviews I conducted with Moran's conversion course classmates. It described what was clearly visible—that indeed, we often wore jeans. But it also signified my own feeling, a feeling of free and open conversation, "talking in jeans," between us who could formerly meet only in skirts. I had not always been sure that I wanted or would even be able to interview Moran. While I had successfully established a rapport with many women in the conversion class, I could appreciate Moran only from a distance. That distance, to be sure, was of her making. She maintained it even in situations that seemed to afford the possibility of more intimate conversation—for example, when I drove her home one evening after class. I could tell even then that she felt guarded around me, saying little and speaking in a somewhat reserved tone. But at the café, during an interview that lasted three hours, her speech flowed, and I was glad we were "talking in jeans."

We met in the center of Tel Aviv on the Purim holiday. "Some day we picked for this interview," she said, gesturing toward the adjacent street alive with the sounds of the city's traditional Purim parade. Those sounds, occasionally picked up by my audio recorder, highlighted the irony of our meeting: that precisely when Jews in Israel don costumes in the carnivalesque spirit of the Purim tradition, I met Moran when, as she put it, she "wasn't masquerading anymore."

The story of my encounter with Moran captures the politics of performance and sincerity that are at the heart of my ethnographic account of Israel's Jewish conversion policy. Insofar as this account is rooted in the paradoxes that structure Israeli conversion policy at the macrolevel (as I briefly described in the prologue), the vignette with Moran provides a personal glimpse into how these paradoxes shape the lived experience and interpersonal dynamics of the conversion process at the microlevel. One of the central arguments of this book is that in order to understand how both conversion candidates and state agents handle, individually and jointly, the contradictory forces of the conversion policy, we need to better understand the mundane preoccupations, among those on both sides of these relationships, with issues of sincerity, role-playing, and suspicion. My meeting with Moran after she had been freed from such preoccupations epitomizes this core argument.

Nevertheless, there is certainly a risk involved in opening this ethnography about the conversion of non-Jewish FSU immigrants with the story of Moran's conversion. Hers is precisely the kind of story that is likely to feed the simplistic public and bureaucratic discourses that portray conversion as an elaborate ruse—discourses that this book explores but also complicates. These popular representations depict conversion candidates as only masquerading—not really intending to commit to the halakhic lifestyle they promise to maintain; their observance of Sabbath laws, kosher dietary restrictions, the modesty code, and family purity laws, these popular discourses maintain, lasts only the duration of the conversion process. The ubiquitous assumption is that conversion is merely about formality and that these converts put on an act for the rabbinic bureaucratic establishment, taking advantage of the conversion track for the sole purpose of obtaining official Jewish recognition.

This recognition is inconsequential for matters of immigration and naturalization, a reality reflected in the fact that Israel grants non-Jewish olim citizenship upon their arrival. But Jewish recognition is crucial for personal status matters (i.e., marriage, divorce, and burial) that are handled by the Orthodox rabbinic establishment. Non-Jewish citizens who seek to marry Israeli Jews or simply wish to marry according to Orthodox standards must attain Jewish recognition. State Orthodox conversion is the primary means of doing so.[3]

In relation to Moran, critics might emphasize how, just six months after the conversion process, she had already traded in her skirt for jeans. Or they might point out how she openly shares with an ethnographer stories that must differ in spirit from those she told the conversion agents. Indeed, her stories to me were different—like the one about how much she hated wearing skirts, and how one day, only a few months into the conversion process, she already felt she "couldn't take it anymore." Pulling out jeans and a tank top from her dresser, she put them on and walked outside, her face shielded by sunglasses and a wide-brimmed hat in case, god forbid, someone might recognize her on the street. Or her story about the day she immersed herself in the *mikveh* (ritual bath), a story that also features blue jeans. She abhorred the mikveh experience. She had arrived there depleted and angry, wracked with ambivalence about the whole process. Other converts sometimes shared with me the excitement and joy they felt about the symbolic meaning of rebirth and repair and the ceremonial experience of being accepted into the national fold; Moran felt none of this. Instead, apologizing for the graphic depiction, she described being forced to submerge herself "in that pee water" ("sorry, the water was just warmish for some reason") and then explained that what followed was the happiest day of her life: "After immersing myself in that 'amazing' mikveh, I left the place, went straight home to shower, and went out for the first time in a long while in jeans and a T-shirt. I was so happy. I felt so liberated, as if I had shed a building, eighty tons dropped from my shoulders. I didn't have to put on sunglasses and wear a wide-brimmed hat. A huge joy, what can I say, a huge joy."

But a suspicious reading of Moran's story would obscure the subtle, nuanced details that shape the conversion experience, and, as I will argue, the conversion performance, of so many converts in less dichotomous ways: as deeply complicated engagements unfolding in a gray area that blurs truths and lies, sincerity and deception—mixing skirts with blue jeans.

On Winks and Lies

The perception that converts from FSU backgrounds (henceforth "FSU converts") lie during their conversion process permeates Israeli public spheres. The Israeli press, social media, and even the protocols of Israeli parliamentary committees all reinforce the idea that state conversion could very well amount to an elaborate sham. These public debates are polyphonic, encompassing an array of ideological voices. Jewish Israeli citizens of all religious orientations, including secular Jews, traditional Jews, religious (Orthodox) Jews, and ultra-Orthodox Jews;[4] liberals seeking to separate religion from state and their opponents who support state intervention in religious life; FSU immigrants who underwent conversion and those who openly refuse to do so; and groups identified with lenient and others with stringent approaches to halakha—all these interlocutors, for various reasons, look upon the extant state conversion policy with suspicion. In the less public domains of the conversion debate, like the social contexts where the conversion process actually takes place, the concepts of sincerity, deception, and lies constitute the chief obsessions of all parties involved. During my fieldwork, this is what everybody talked about.

These kinds of preoccupations are not unique to the case of FSU converts in Israel. Concerns about converts' honesty, purity of intention, and trustworthiness—that is, about whether they might be motivated less by religious intentions and more by political or material interests—animate a broad range of conversion contexts. In the Israeli setting the case of Feres Mura immigrants from Ethiopia offers the most immediate parallel to the situation of FSU immigrants. As Don Seeman documented, mutual suspicion animates the relationship between the Feres Mura and the Israeli state. On the one hand, state gatekeepers suspect Feres Mura immigrants of cynically using Jewish conversion to flee oppression and poverty in Ethiopia. On the other hand, the immigrants themselves suspect that Israel's rabbinic establishment has sought to trick them into conversion (Seeman 2010).

What makes these public and bureaucratic discourses of suspicion so compelling in the context of state-sponsored conversion of FSU immigrants is the fact that, quite often, they treat conversion agents as complicit in the insincerity of converts. In particular, these discourses bear directly on the state conversion agents who, rather than exposing liars, help maintain the performances of converts.

Of course, FSU converts do not escape blame. The "Russians" (as FSU immigrants are commonly called) are described as both post-Soviet subjects who know a great deal about deceiving state authorities (see also Fialkova and Yelenevskaya 2006) and as fundamentally atheist subjects who lack any authentic religious inclination.[5] But for the most part, the suspicious public discourses of conversion blame the complicated Israeli political situation for the conversion candidates' lies. These discourses reference the structural conditions, political circumstances, and rabbinic authorities who force—but also enable—FSU conversion candidates to become impostors.

"Why do I need to go through hell and lie?" asked a former Israeli who immigrated from the FSU as a child, in a news article about non-Jewish "Russian" olim who later emigrated (*yardu*; lit. "descended") from Israel. "In all conversion cases," she continued, "women lie to the rabbinic court. Not one woman I know intended to observe the commandments, even though the point of conversion is to become religious. Conversion creates armies upon armies of liars, and they stand together and laugh about it" (Edelman 2014). In contrast, ultra-Orthodox rabbis, who insist on sincere and lasting commitments to religious practice as the central condition of conversion, accuse Orthodox Zionist conversion agents of making a mockery of halakha in the name of their Zionist ideology.

Speaking from quite different religious and political perspectives, liberal Orthodox rabbis and religious academics share a growing public criticism of the rabbinate. They argue that its harsh conversion policy simply leaves conversion candidates no other choice but insincerity and thus institutionalizes deceit within the conversion process. These critics describe conversion as a process of self- or mutual deception. As Yedidya Stern, the vice president at the Israel Democracy Institute and a religious public intellectual, writes: "In practice, most non-Jewish olim are not interested in religious observance, they consider themselves to be joining a nation, not a religion. They don't want to be different from the secular Jewish majority in Israel, and don't understand why they must fulfill a requirement that most Jews don't. The result is that in order to convert they must wear a mask. The path into Judaism and full integration into the Jewish nation passes through a lie." (Stern 2011:19)

During a 2008 conference on conversion at the Israeli Democracy Institute, which I attended, Rabbi David Stav, a well-respected liberal Zionist rabbi known for his critical stance on the extant state conversion policy sharply articulated a similar concern, which I recoded in my field notes: "There is a disagreement: 60%, 70%, maybe even 90% of converts do not observe the commandments. So who are you cheating? Judging by the outcomes, who is cheating whom? Are they cheating you? Or are you cheating them?"

This public, polyphonic critique of the conversion process is often expressed through the metaphor of winking. In an article entitled "The Renewed Polemics of Conversion," published in a journal of Jewish thought devoted to the issue of conversion, Rabbi Dr. Yehuda Brandes (2008) who, like Rabbi Stav, is identified with the liberal Orthodox camp, coined the term *wink-wink conversion*. Brandes writes that Zionist Orthodox rabbis in the rabbinic conversion court are bound by dual loyalties: to Jewish law and to their national responsibility. Because of this article's public resonance (see Abraham 2009; Edrei 2010; Rosen 2010), it is worth citing at length Rabbi Brandes's description of the outcomes of this duality:

> [As a result], a middle way has emerged, one which officially requires acceptance of the yoke of commandments but tolerates the fact that many of the converts do not sincerely intend to fully accept them. This intermediate approach is well known to teachers in the conversion ulpans and to the conversion candidates themselves. The latter know that when they stand in front of the court they will have to answer its questions in a manner that makes them appear as though they seriously intend to observe the commandments. The rabbinic court ignores the high likelihood that the vast majority of these converts do not intend to join religious society and adopt a fully-observant lifestyle, and both parties are thus satisfied . . . this approach is extremely harmful, not only to halakha but also to the conversion process. The converts understand that in order to join the Jewish faith they must collaborate in a process of lying and self-deception which is

> encouraged by the rabbis—an entire gang that has banded together for a kind of trickery and sophistry that lacks both integrity and decency.
>
> (Brandes 2008:93)

Subsequently, Rabbi Brandes describes state conversion as a system in which the agents and subjects of the rabbinic conversion court exchange winks. He denounces the moral stance of this system and suggests some halakhic alternatives. Winking constitutes a system in his mind because of its grounding in a mutually agreed-upon and institutionalized arrangement: the rabbinic judges wink at the converts and invite them to wink back.

Winking Relations and the Conversion Performance

This book draws on the metaphor of wink-wink conversions in order to analytically conceptualize the tense, institutional relationships that emerge between the agents and subjects of Israel's state-sponsored conversion policy. By attributing analytical significance to the winking metaphor, I would like to distance myself from the popular, cynical association between winks and lies and from the sharp distinction between sincere converts and impostors. My central critique is not only that the conversion process constitutes a complex human experience that cannot be confined to a binary logic of truth and falsity—a point already suggestively argued in the literature on religious conversion (see Seeman 2003, 2010). Nor would I, as an ethnographer, presume to know how to discriminate between truths and lies, a position that would problematically situate me "above" the social reality I investigate. Most of all, such a distinction does not help us understand the institutional relationships that are the subject matter of this book.

I develop the idea of *winking relations* in order to understand how the Orthodox representatives of the Israeli nation-state and FSU conversion candidates perform the impossible. How, despite the extant tensions that characterize state conversion policy—tensions between population policy and individual identity work, between national goals and religious technologies, between inclusive and exclusive politics of belonging, and, finally, between the Orthodox rabbinic establishment and Israeli citizens from secular backgrounds—how in the context of all of these contradictory conditions, the conversion policy is realized and experienced in everyday life. At the heart of this book, then, lies an ethnographic riddle. Several of the following chapters unpack the various dimensions of this riddle by pointing to the winking relations that permit both sides to achieve their shared goal: to facilitate and undergo conversion.

As an anthropologist, I take winking quite seriously. For those familiar with Geertz's (1973) canonical writing, winking represents the paradigmatic example of what interpretive ethnography, and anthropology more generally, is all about. For my purposes, winking indexes a central problem that the protagonists of this book confront—a problem of contested interpretation. The notion of winking allows me to trace how state agents and conversion candidates manage this problem in and through their mundane socio-institutional interactions. In the most basic sense, winking (which famously differs from blinking or parodying a wink; ibid.:6–7) is the transmission of a nuanced message. As such, it is an interactive gesture that takes place within a social situation and invests it with another layer of meaning. A wink is expressed in bodily and verbal signals, potentially creating a reflexive moment in which the participant seems to break from the social situation in order to comment upon it or deliver information about it to someone else. Winking contains an "as if" quality and signals an equivocal understanding about what is actually going on here. It indicates that what is being said might have an additional meaning, that it reflects only a partial truth, and that much has gone unsaid. By winking, individuals can create a shared understanding and invite each other to collaborate in the production of refined meaning.

In my own analytical use of this concept, I place primary emphasis on the everyday transmission of messages between conversion agents and candidates within their mundane encounters. The concept of winking underlines the fact that what transpires between the agents and subjects of state conversion policy is a sophisticated, creative system of double messages regarding the expectations placed on conversion candidates as well as the stakes of conversion policy for state agents—and the state itself. Equally important, in my account I emphasize the mutual, collaborative nature of winking relations. At a higher theoretical level this concept allows us to think analytically about these nuanced yet central features of sociability that are embedded in varied contexts of institutionalized relations between the state and its subjects, in Israel and beyond.

This book makes the case that dramaturgical principles organize winking relations between conversion candidates and conversion agents. This argument complements my earlier argument about the centrality of the politics of sincerity in the mundane operations of Israel's conversion policy. As I will show throughout this book, these two dimensions develop symbiotically as a way to practically handle the contradictory features of state conversion policy.

When I argue that dramaturgical principles organize winking relations, I mean that converts learn to manage impressions and play roles in order to pass as proper converts. This terminology draws heavily on Erving Goffman's dramaturgical perspective on social interaction (see Goffman 1959, [1963] 1986, 1971, 1974). Taking theater as his key metaphor, Goffman offers a microsociological understanding of how people, like actors, perform their identities and roles on stage in front of audiences. To the extent that everyday situations can be compared to interactions between actors and audiences, their success depends on an agreed-upon definition of the situation as well as on the boundaries between front stage, backstage, and off-stage domains.

Going against the popular notion of wink-wink conversions, in which converts blatantly learn how to lie and feign piety, I will show that converts learn from teachers, rabbis, and other bureaucrats how to present a persona sufficiently worthy of conversion despite, but also precisely because of, the public and rabbinic suspicion toward them. They do so by investing themselves in the management of what I call *conversion performances*—performances that will diminish bureaucratic suspicion and thus help evade the public designation of "wink-wink conversions."

If it is true, as Rabbi Brandes writes, that conversion candidates "know that when they stand in front of the court they will have to answer its questions in a manner that makes them appear as though they seriously intend to observe the commandments" (Brandes 2008:93), then how do they know this? Who teaches them their role as converts? How are they assisted in the staging, direction, and presentation of their personas? And what does it take for them to perform these personas correctly? Because these winking relationships are dialogical, I ask not only how the candidates learn to present believable personas to conversion agents but also how, throughout these dramaturgical processes, conversion agents present their own professional personas to candidates, and whether candidates believe them.

This book is concerned with the mechanisms, practices, and tensions involved in the presentation of selves in the everyday life of Israel's conversion policy. It is precisely my use of Erving Goffman's (1959) *The Presentation of Self in Everyday Life* (where he most thoroughly developed his dramaturgical framework) that allows me to conceptualize winking relations as relations that transcend a binary distinction between sincere and false conversion presentations. For Goffman the distinctions between front stage and backstage do not parallel distinctions between truth and falsehood.

Because performances take place at all times, even when the performer does not strategically intend them, role playing should be understood in terms much broader than simply lying. In other words, to say that someone plays a role is not to say that he or she is pretending. Goffman places human behavior on a dynamic continuum between sincerity and cynicism, between a person who believes his or her own performance and one who does not. Regions defined as backstage do not necessarily contain a greater inner truth about a person; they do not constitute a space in which the "real" person behind the mask is exposed but merely express another layer of that person.[6]

To a certain degree, the title *The Presentation of Self in Everyday Life*, like Goffman's extensive writing on the individual's management of impressions, is misleading, because the individual is not the sole unit of Goffman's analysis (Burns 1992:25). Goffman is equally interested in individuals whose performances represent institutions, official social roles, or collectives. And he also writes extensively about the presentations of teams and groups. As we shall see, conversion candidates learn to present their own selves, but they are also implicated in the performances of an array of other actors: romantic partners, Jewish families that host converts throughout the process, teachers, rabbinic judges, and many others. The agents of the conversion policy, for their part, embody their own selves, but they also embody the institution they work for, the Israeli state, and religious Zionism—the ideological stream to which they belong and in the name of which they participate in the conversion project.

Goffman writes that actors, audiences, and teams cooperate closely, if often subtly and unofficially, to sustain the management of impressions and the definition of situations. In so doing, they all aim to prevent disturbances that might cause social situations to break down. Goffman's writing on teamwork helps illustrate a somewhat counterintuitive ethnographic phenomenon that emerged during my fieldwork—that winking relations between conversion agents and candidates have collaborative dimensions. Alongside the strident politics of suspicion that underwrite many of their interactions, conversion agents and candidates collaborate in their mutually dependent efforts to prevent the conversion performance from collapsing. In particular, even as conversion agents continuously interrogate and question the sincerity and trustworthiness of conversion candidates, they also help shape the persona and orchestrate the performance that candidates are in the process of making.

Goffman's work reveals that Israel's conversion policy produces not cynical wink-wink conversions but instead morally loaded and deeply engaged "win-win conversions" for both the representatives and national subjects of the state. This argument explains the various subtle forms of collaboration that I trace throughout this book. Both conversion agents and conversion candidates have stakes in the success of the conversion performance. Conversion allows the state to secure the boundaries of the Jewish-Israeli collective while also increasing its numbers. The fact that, as surveys show,[7] most FSU immigrants do not seek to undergo conversion only sharpens the conversion agencies' efforts to succeed with the relative few who do seek out conversion. In addition to addressing sociodemographic issues, Israel's engagement with conversion articulates the key principles of kinship, relatedness, and, ultimately, the moral economies of Jewish solidarity on which the state relies. Engagement with Jewish conversion allows Israel to reinforce its ideological claims as a Jewish nation-state, particularly as those claims bear on the relationships Israel fosters with its actual and potential national subjects in Israel and the diaspora respectively. Finally, the state's involvement in conversion reaffirms Israel's identity as the primary arbiter of symbolically loaded Jewish issues, thus helping to consolidate its central role as a sovereign Jewish polity.[8]

The conversion candidates, for their part, wish to use conversion to regulate their belonging within Israeli society and to the Jewish state. For many of them this regulation is a necessary correction to a historical injustice that pushed them, halakhically, outside the Jewish fold—a correction with material and symbolic power to help them rectify their damaged civic status. Conversion allows non-Jewish olim not only to receive religiously endorsed services by state institution (i.e., marriage, divorce, and burial) but also to be identified socially and bureaucratically in the same way they identify themselves.

This corrective politics of belonging is clearly gendered. Because, as stated earlier, Jewish belonging in Israel is determined according to matrilineal principles,[9] conversion enables only women to transmit a secure Jewish identity to their future children (Hacker 2009).[10] Not surprisingly, most of the converts in Israel today are women.[11] The stakes, then, are high for both sides of the conversion encounter—so high that each becomes enmeshed in a relationship of mutual dependence. As I will show, these relationships hinge on the conversion performance.

In order to explicate the broad implications of the ethnography that follows, I turn, in the next four sections, to related fields of sociopolitical and theoretical scholarship. My own account is embedded in these scholarly fields, which consist, most importantly, of political anthropology, the anthropology of religion, performance studies, and Jewish studies. I first survey the historical development of Jewish conversion across a range of Jewish contexts, including the Israeli setting. I then lay out the main theoretical contributions of this book: the theorization of religious conversion as a biopolitical policy and the dramaturgical perspective as a lens through which to consider the socio-institutional relationships formed by and within the state.

Jewish Conversion

The term *conversion* is somewhat inadequate for discussions of Jewish giyyur. Its shortcomings derive from its inherent Christian bias (see Gooren 2014); while the term emphasizes religious experience, manifestations of faith, and transformations of the heart, giyyur foregrounds daily praxis, religious law, and the reorganization of daily life. Giyyur does not, of course, disregard belief or spirituality entirely but instead frames them as outcomes of compliant religious practice entailed in one's covenant with God. Relatedly, whereas a Christian convert joins a confessional community, a Jewish convert joins a group constituted by kinship. Because of its inherent Christian biases, the term *conversion* fails to capture the ethnonational meanings that form an inseparable part of Jewish identity. As Rogers Brubaker writes in relation to this inseparability, "The [Jewish] nation is imagined as composed of *all* and *only* those who belong to a particular religion" (Brubaker 2012:9; emphasis in original).

The biblical concept of a Jewish convert (*ger;* lit. "sojourner") indexes dimensions of foreignness. Placeless or landless, a ger is one who takes up permanent residence in a foreign city or does not belong to the people of Israel, although he or she may be a native in the land of Canaan (Rosenbloom 1978). Either way, the biblical concept describes a marginal social position that calls for distinct ethical, social, and civic treatment by Jews (Ratzabi 2001).

Under the Hasmonean polity this concept was drastically altered. Nonnative groups could (or were required to) become Judean through two emerging models of conversion: political citizenship and religious change (S. Cohen 1999:105). Only in the rabbinic era would a ger become someone who had formally converted to Judaism by attaching himself to the God of Israel (there were no female converts early in the rabbinic period; ibid.:218). The latter meaning became possible after the Judeans returned to Judah from the Babylonian exile, a political experience that required them to stress the religious, and hence mutable, aspects of their identity (S. Cohen 1983; Porton 1994; Samet 1992). It was only then that the word *giyyur* appeared in the nominal form.[12]

During the Second Temple period Jewish communities developed conversion ceremonies: circumcision for males to physically mark membership in the covenantal community; a declaration of acceptance of commandments before a judicial court (comprising three men who represent the community); and, finally, ritual immersion for both sexes to symbolize the transition between the convert's old identity and his or her new one as a Jew (Finn 1997). When the Temple existed, animal sacrifice was also required (Segal 2014). Over time, then, the conversion process took the shape of a ritual microcosm that brought together the constitutive moments of the nation's birth and its mythical covenants with God—such as the ritual immersion before the giving of the Torah at Mount Sinai and the circumcision of Abraham, who is often described as the first convert. By establishing these rituals, the rabbis attempted to prescribe social order by fixing boundaries that had hitherto been ambiguous and permeable (Samet 1992, 1993). Whereas in prerabbinic eras conversion had marked a personal and chaotic process, in the second century CE the rabbinic sages introduced set standards, verifiable criteria, and public supervision (S. Cohen 1999:218).

To this day the threefold conversion ritual constitutes the gateway into Judaism. The largest and most powerful Jewish denominations today (including the Orthodox, Conservative, and Reform Movements) uphold a variation on this ritual pattern. All include circumcision (or *haṭafat dam*; lit. "drawing a drop of blood"), ritual immersion, and acceptance of the yoke of the commandments (however those commandments are understood by different denominations).

Alongside the broad agreement among Jews on this threefold conversion ritual, the relationships between its components have always been a source of profound controversy in the rabbinic literature. Avi Sagi and Zvi Zohar (2007) trace the concurrent existence, from late antiquity to contemporary times, of two rabbinic paradigms regarding this issue, arguing that they offer distinct, even contradictory, perspectives on the meaning of giyyur. According to one paradigm, the acceptance of the commandments is the core criteria for valid conversion (see also M. Finkelstein 2006), while the other paradigm emphasizes the bodily rituals that frame giyyur as an act of rebirth into the kinship-based Jewish collective.[13] In the sixteenth century the great canonical code of Jewish law, the *Shulchan Aruch*, attempted to settle the issue. However, it left the meaning of "the acceptance of the commandments" unclear.

Indeed, among the three ritual components of conversion, "acceptance of the commandments" is the least understood and the most volatile. The halakhic (Talmudic and post-Talmudic) literature on this concept is marked by polyphony and vagueness, thereby inviting interpretation and controversy among rabbis and scholars: What exactly does the convert accept when he or she accepts the yoke of the commandments? Does one declare this acceptance aloud or in silence? Is the acceptance of the commandments an outcome of conversion or a prerequisite thereof? Must a convert's motivations be religious in nature to be treated as valid by rabbis, or should they be assessed independently in keeping with what the convert actually embraces during the process? Does the acceptance of the commandments require a commitment to full observance or just an understanding that full observance is obligatory and that violation can lead to divine punishment? And does the rabbinic court only inform the convert of the required commandments, or must it also determine whether she or he is indeed observing them (S. Cohen 1999; Sagi and Zohar 2007)?

During the Middle Ages, when political prohibitions against Jewish conversion rendered it a marginal phenomenon, these questions stimulated only hypothetical halakhic disputes. But in the modern era halakhic discussions about the nature of "the acceptance of the commandments" assumed particular urgency. From the middle of the eighteenth century, as emancipation in Europe enabled social and romantic connections between Jews and non-Jews, Jewish communities and leaders were forced to confront often divisive issues of Jewish identity, assimilation, and intermarriage.

Conversion is intricately linked to these questions. Because eighteenth- and nineteenth- century Jewish communities were both numerous and dispersed, and because Jewish modernity and secularity manifested themselves differently in various communities, rabbinic attitudes to conversion were far from uniform. These attitudes reflected a variety of ideological and pragmatic positions toward the shifting circumstances of the Jewish experience (Edrei 2010, 2013; Ellenson and Gordis 2012). Rabbis were divided over how to synthesize policy considerations with interpretations of conversion laws (Sagi and Zohar 2007). In particular, they argued over which option constituted the lesser evil: should they stringently interpret the halakhic requirements, even at the price of shrinking the Jewish community, or should they sacrifice halakhic stringency in order to include intermarried couples and "save" the Jewish community?

Jewish modernity presented the possibility of not only a secular identity but also a national one, thereby dividing the two anchors of Jewish identity (religion and ethnicity) and consequently further complicating the discussion of conversion. In the context of the Zionist revival, especially after the establishment of Israel, questions about the meanings of "the acceptance of the commandments" were entangled with questions about whether conversion entails, primarily, an entry into the Jewish nation or into the Jewish religion. These entangled questions linger throughout the sociopolitical history of conversion to Judaism in Israel, including the contemporary context of the national mission.

Jewish Conversion in Israel

The problem of conversion in Israel is chronic, periodically erupting in the form of legal, political, and bureaucratic crises (see Waxman 2013). This volatile dynamic is anchored in the fact that Israel is both a secular democracy and a Jewish state, combining civil laws and Jewish legal principles. Since the establishment of Israel in 1948 conversion has been perceived as a principal matter for the state—a domain the state is naturally entitled to govern. Hence, state institutions both secular (i.e., the Parliament [*Knesset*] and the Supreme Court) and religious (i.e., the rabbinic establishment) have addressed the issue, crafting different halakhic and civil conversion policies. As I will describe in chapter 1, debates over the religious requirements of conversion have emerged regularly among chief rabbis and other halakhic arbiters. These debates have also crystalized in the context of broad, public discussions about Israel's identity as a Jewish state and the loaded question of "Who is a Jew?"[14] Both symbolically and practically, this loaded question has profound national and public significance. It bears on the self-definition of the state and connects, in important ways, to a variety of issues, including immigration, naturalization, civil registration, and personal status matters.

To begin with, one of the central domains in which the question of "Who is a Jew?" has been most contentious is that of personal status issues of Israeli citizens. To the extent that Israel lacks a separation between religion and state (circumstances that were institutionalized by the secular-religious status quo arrangements),[15] Israel does not permit strictly civic, nonreligious channels for marriage, divorce, and burial. Rather, religious communities (e.g., Jewish, Muslim, and Christian), under the adjudication of their respective religious courts, govern these matters.[16] The immediate political repercussion of this legal arrangement is that Jews and Palestinians cannot intermarry in Israel. Within the Jewish context it also means that a person whom the state Orthodox rabbinic establishment does not recognize as halakhically Jewish cannot marry another Jew and cannot be buried in Jewish cemeteries.[17] The Spousal Covenant Act (passed in the Knesset in 2010), which was initially intended to allow non-Jewish FSU immigrants to marry in Israel, never managed to provide this population with a secure civil marriage alternative. As Fogiel-Bijaoui (2013) demonstrates, the act in its current, weakened manifestation ended up allowing those olim, categorized as "lacking religious affiliation," to marry only others classified under the same rubric—an outcome that lead to its widespread rejection by those it was meant to serve.

Another key legislative domain that has historically been marked by controversy over the question of "Who is a Jew?" is the Law of Return. In its initial instantiation (1950) the law was understood as a repatriation law. Intended to enshrine the return of a persecuted and dispersed minority to its homeland, the law foregrounded notions of Jewish solidarity and kinship-based commitments. The law's first provision, according to which "every Jew has the right to come to this country as an *oleh* [singular of olim]" validated the perception that all Jews everywhere maintained an irrefutable eligibility to be members of the Jewish national home in Israel.

But who may be defined as Jewish in the Jewish state? Is a person's subjective definition of a Jew sufficient for him or her to be recognized as such by the state, as secular politicians demanded, or must one qualify according to halakhic criteria, as religious leaders required? During the first decade of statehood, lacking established legal criteria for determining a person's Jewish identity for the matter of the Law of Return (and in practice, for the sake of registering in the population registry), the Orthodox ministers of the interior took the liberty of determining the issue. Already in the 1950s this situation precipitated political and coalitional crises, which led David Ben Gurion, Israel's first prime minister, to adopt the position that halakhic criteria must serve as the unifying normative and legal basis for determining Jewish identity in Israel (Ratzabi 2001). In 1960 it was decided for the first time that in Israel, a "Jew" would be a person who was born to a Jewish mother and did not belong to another religion or a person who had converted according to halakha (Neuberger 1998:84).

Over the years several exceptional legal cases involving the question of "Who is a Jew?" pushed these symbolic struggles to their extremes. Such was the "Brother Daniel" case, about a Christian minister born to a Jewish family, who had survived the Holocaust, converted to Christianity, become a priest, and later sought to immigrate to Israel under the Law of Return. These struggles also animated the "Shalit" case, in which a Jewish-Israeli father sought to have his children, born to a non-Jewish woman, registered in the population registry as members of the Jewish nation but not belonging to any religious group.[18]

In 1970, as an outcome of the political storm precipitated by the Shalit case, Israel amended the Law of Return. The revision both broadened and narrowed the dimensions of the law: on one hand, it made clear that the term *Jewish* referred to the recognized halakhic definition; on the other hand, it expanded the pool of those eligible for immigration and citizenship under the law so as to include immigration of intermarried families. In the framework of the expansion spouses, children, and grandchildren of a Jew became eligible for the right of return, as did the spouses of children and grandchildren (provided that the Jewish person did not willingly convert from Judaism to any other religion).[19] Morally justified as a counterweight to the Nazis' Nuremberg laws (which were applied to Jews up until the generation of the grandchild), this expansion gained actual demographic significance only two decades later in the context of the mass waves of non-Jewish immigration from the collapsing Soviet Union. In this context, the Law of Return gradually lost its near-sacred status, and groups from both the political left and right grew increasingly willing to revisit it (Gavison 2010; Ilan 2005). Foregrounding the ills of the amended law, the critics have pointed to its racial overtones (as it implicitly but clearly privileges the immigration of "non-Arabs"), its automatic coupling of immigration and naturalization, and, finally, its paradoxical implications for Zionist definitions of the Israeli state (i.e., the arrival of non-Jews).[20]

The amendment of the Law of Return intentionally preserved ambiguity about what would be deemed a valid conversion. In particular, it left unclear whether halakhic conversion is mandatory for the purpose of both return and civil registration. This deliberate ambiguity was politically productive, in that it allowed secular and religious parties alike to push through the amendment while avoiding direct confrontation with its conflicting implications. But this ambiguity also lay at the heart of the coalitional and political crises of the ensuing decades. In particular, the amendment's ambiguity conflicts with the Religious Community (Conversion) Ordinance according to which the heads of the various religious communities are solely authorized to grant conversion certificates and determine their validity.[21] In the Jewish context, given the Orthodox monopoly that sustains the link between religion and state in Israel, the understanding that slowly evolved within the Ministry of Interior was that the representative of Orthodox Judaism (the chief rabbi of Israel or the president of the Supreme Religious Court) would be in charge of giyyur.

Over the years, the legal lacuna surrounding the criteria for valid conversion gave rise to a growing demand for recognition of alternative modes of religious conversion.[22] Interestingly, the demand for secular giyyur remained a marginal issue.[23] The struggle over recognition has created unstable relationships between the Israeli state (in particular, the Orthodox rabbinic establishment) and diasporic Jewish communities (especially in the United States, where the Reform and Conservative denominations represent the majority of Jews). In 1997 Benjamin Netanyahu, then in his first term as prime minister, convened the Ne'eman Committee to address these issues and formulate a unified conversion procedure. The committee assembled public figures from the three main religious denominations and proposed, as a compromise, the separation of the legal process of conversion (which would remain under Orthodox control) from the pedagogic preparation process (which would be more pluralistic). Despite the stormy debates over the committee's recommendations, the Israeli government eventually adopted this basic principle and established in 1999 the Institute of Jewish Studies (colloquially known as the Joint Institute or Mali [a Hebrew acronym for the "Institute of Jewish Studies"]), as a state-authorized conversion school. Mali is one of the central research arenas of this book.

Since the 1990s the state's involvement in conversion has undergone a fundamental institutional transformation. Conversion not only continues to be a highly polemic issue in the public and legislative spheres; it has also become an institutional "field," or bureaucratic apparatus, teeming with operational activity. Already in the 1970s, the religious arms of the state had taken initial steps in this direction. But as I shall describe in detail in chapter 1, only since the late 1980s, in response to mass non-Jewish FSU immigration, has Israel established conversion as a means of Zionist population policy. The book traces the historical circumstances, institutional processes, and discursive formations of this development. In addition, it unpacks the everyday institutional encounter—replete as it is with winks—between state agents of conversion and its subjects.

Religious Conversion, Biopolitics, and the Nation-State

In keeping with contemporary anthropological writing on religious conversion, this book builds on the understanding that historical, ideological, cultural, national, and material forces all shape the spiritual relationships between converts and the divine. This understanding requires that scholars of conversion attend to the systems of power, regimes of truth, and political entities that both shape and are shaped by the religious dynamics of conversion. What might today seem an obvious argument about the political dimensions of religious phenomena was once a major theoretical departure, one audacious for its time, from William James's ([1902] 1985) canonical work, which emphasized the epiphanic moment of conversion. Far from the

Jamesian model, which struck deep roots in psychology and religious studies, leading sociological models (i.e., Lofland 1977; Lofland and Stark 1965) emphasized social dynamics and life circumstances over a radical Pauline transformation. Yet these sociological models overlooked the political dimensions of religious conversion—a scholarly lacuna that gave rise to alternative, more critically attuned research. In this vein, the past two decades have witnessed the emergence of a new theoretical vocabulary for the discussion of religious conversion in political terms. Concepts such as nationalism, citizenship, colonialism, and racialization are now central to how anthropologists and other scholars theorize religious conversion (Austin-Broos 2003; Keane 2002; Van der Veer 1996). This book adds the concept of *biopolitics* to this vocabulary.

This research trajectory does not ignore the actual experiences and practices of individual converts (e.g., Özyürek 2014; Roy 2013). However, this literature on religious conversion understands the modern state as a crucial political framework even when conversion focuses on individuals. The importance of the state lies in the connections it fosters between subjectivity and bureaucratic practices and between ethnonational and religious identity politics. Whether religious converts realize a new affiliation with a religious minority or a religious majority, they redefine and disturb the taken-for-granted nature of these connections (Viswanathan 1998). Depending on its direction, religious conversion is read either as a departure from the national consensus or as an act of incorporation into it (Gellner 2005; Kravel-Tovi 2015; Marzouki 2013; Özyürek 2009a).

Given these political sensibilities, it is not surprising that modern nation-states—including secular democracies—often take active roles in regulating conversion to and from religious minority groups. To note only a few examples, such involvement is starkly illustrated in Indonesia, a constitutionally secular state, which extends citizenship only to individuals who belong to one of the few official religions (Spyer 1996), and requires conversion for official endorsement of interfaith marriages (Connolly 2009). Such involvement is also evident in Turkey, where conversion is understood as a threat and source of pollution to the state's homogenized national body. These national anxieties are demonstrated by the secular Turkish legal system, which upholds exclusionary policies toward converts who defy the hegemonic equation of Turkishness with Islam. For example, communities of Christian converts are denied official recognition of their minority status

(Özyürek 2009b), and descendants of forcibly Islamized Armenians who attempt to return to their roots are denied state permission to adopt Armenian names (Özgül 2014). In India the conversion of Hindu individuals and groups to both Islam and Christianity disrupts the delicate balance that the secular state tries to maintain between religious communities. It also undermines the essentialized link between being Indian and Hindu. As a result, both nationalistic Hindu movements and various arms of the Indian state pursue legislative and governmental initiatives to restrict potential conversions (Fernandes 2011; Menon 2003).[24]

As my brief historical discussion of conversion in Israel illustrates, Israel can easily be included in the list of states where the politics of conversion intersect with the politics of the nation-state (see also Egorova 2015; Seeman 2003, 2010). But as this book will make clear, the contemporary conversion policy in Israel foregrounds the extraordinary institutional political involvement of the nation-state in religious conversion. As such, this case study raises fresh ethnographic and analytical possibilities. These possibilities, I argue, arise from the fact that in Israel the religious conversion of citizens has become a Zionist, nationally informed biopolitical policy.

Because the concept of biopolitics has been reworked, retheorized, and expanded within a variety of theories and research contexts, it is important to use it carefully. In the chapters that follow, I more thoroughly flesh out its ethnographic and analytical utility in this specific study. But for the time being, suffice it to say that biopolitics productively elucidates Israel's conversion policy because it highlights the population-related ambitions and commitments that drive it. In other words, conversion is biopolitical in that it constitutes a domain of practice through which the state engages with questions, anxieties, and ideals concerning its population. In this sense, state conversion is not directed at the religious subjectivity of non-Jewish FSU olim per se; rather, in deploying a proconversion policy (targeted, as I will show, at a specific cohort of non-Jewish immigrants), the Israeli state attempts to secure the boundaries of the Jewish collective and influence the reproduction of Jewish-Israeli families. Through the cumulative demographic effects of the conversion of individual citizens, ideally as many as possible, the Israeli state hopes to shape the composition, size, and boundaries of the national population.

This biopolitical policy is embedded in moralities of Jewish solidarity, return, and relatedness. It has been developed under the powerful ideological discourse of the national mission with its underlying kinship-based commitments. As such, it has entailed the mobilization of administrative systems as well as the allocation of substantial funds from government budgets.[25] *National* and *mission* each carry a double meaning in the context of the conversion of FSU olim. *National* refers to the Zionist ideological principle that informs the project, as well as the process of nationalization that has brought conversion under the auspices of state institutions. *Mission* denotes both a calling and sense of urgency, as well as a "missionary" attitude, oriented to FSU immigrants with the intention of expanding the number of converts within this population. Those invested in this national mission act according to their moral and ideological commitments to olim, fellow citizens, and the state, commitments that they themselves maintain as dedicated national subjects of the Jewish state. Hence, conversion constitutes an institutional domain in which both converts and conversion agents are preoccupied with their relationship to the state and the Jewish-Israeli fold.

Religious conversion is probably not the first domain that comes to mind when we think of biopolitics. As the contemporary academic work on biopolitics reveals, scholars more commonly investigate issues like reproduction, health, biotechnology, criminality, and other biologically related fields in which the state exercises its political power. Indeed, when we take Michel Foucault's writing as a point of departure, framing the national mission of conversion in terms of biopolitics hardly seems intuitive.[26] The further we move from Foucault, who more than anyone is identified with this concept, toward thinkers like Hannah Arendt and Giorgio Agamben (see Campbell and Sitze 2013), who reformulated the concept in different directions, the less intuitive biopolitics becomes. Nevertheless, I suggest that state conversion policy in Israel is a biopolitical mission aimed at managing individuals by virtue of their potentially full inclusion within the ethnonational population.

Foucault describes how since the eighteenth century, *population* has become a salient category or field of knowledge and intervention in relation to which the new governmental craft of modern power developed. He identifies a historical shift in which government no longer prioritized the disciplining of the individual body but instead started to concern itself with the management and regulation of the social body: "After a first seizure of power over the body in an individualizing mode, we have a second seizure of power that is not individualizing, but, if you like, massifying, that is directed not at man-as-body but man-as-species" (Foucault [1976] 2003:243). Through statistical forms of knowledge, the population became a knowable, imaginable, and forecastable object. Once the management of the population became a goal, the individual became a means or a potentially productive force whose daily affairs are politically "useful." Indeed, one of the complexities shaping Israel's proconversion policy is the fact that the conversion of individuals—as a process focused on their religiosity—is of political use.

I gradually became cognizant of the political usefulness of converts as I listened to conversion agents. When they advocated for the national mission, these agents focused primarily on the population: the population of non-Jewish FSU immigrants and the Jewish population in Israel as a whole. Their preoccupation with population was marked by an intensive engagement with numbers, in particular with numerical calculations, forecasts, goals, and failures. In a state where demographic data feed existential anxieties (in general, and vis-à-vis the Palestinian population in particular), and demography is hallowed as a field of political knowledge, one should not make light of what this obsessive concern with national numbers can teach us about conversion.

Since the late 1980s the Israeli state has aimed to convert as many non-Jewish FSU immigrants as possible. In fact, while the moral and ideological commitments of Jewish return apply to all immigrants to Israel, the national mission is oriented toward a very particular subset of FSU converts: young non-Jewish women who are usually first- or second-generation Israelis. Because of their life courses—as young, female Israeli citizens who offer the potential of marriage and family making with Jewish men—they pose a particularly grave threat to the boundaries, unity, and size of the national population. The assumption is that their significant and growing numerical presence in Israel could lead to widespread intermarriage, or alternatively, to the formation of separate Jewish communities that will not intermarry or envision themselves as part of a united imagined community. If prior to conversion these non-Jewish women are considered an internal threat to Zionist demography and national unity, then in their postconversion state they become an instrumental productive force in the nation-building project. They will likely marry Jews and build Jewish families; their children will be Jewish. To a great extent, it is this political use that their conversion offers the state.

Bureaucratic recognition is central to that political usefulness. The aim of Israel's conversion policy is not to better connect FSU immigrants to Jewish-Israeli culture. Nor does it aim to moderate the "non-Jewish effect" of FSU immigration on public and consumerist spaces in Israel (as manifested, for example, in the many "Russian" shops decorated for Christmas and selling pork; see Ben-Porat 2016). Furthermore, it does not seek to address the social and welfare issues, which social scientists have associated with more recently arrived populations of non-Jewish FSU youth, including poverty, at-risk behaviors, social alienation (see discussion in Zaslavsky and Horowitz 2007), and even rare displays of anti-Semitism (Galili 2003). Instead, the conversion policy focuses on those already living, in many significant ways, as Jewish Israelis, but who are not halakhically recognized as such. Conversion constitutes a process that will allow the state to identify—that is, classify, count, and document—these people as Jews. Yet these national, bureaucratic, and biopolitical goals can only be achieved by engaging individual conversion candidates in personal processes centered on their religious observance. How, then, do Israel's religious Zionist gatekeepers utilize meticulous rabbinic procedures, in which individuals are asked to accept the commandments, to achieve these collective, national goals? How is this done?

Dramaturgy and the Anthropology of the State

"How is it done?" I posed this question to Rabbi Dvir, a rabbinic judge, as we sat in the hearing room during a break. I asked it in reference to a discussion Rabbi Dvir and two of his colleagues had had earlier that morning with a conversion candidate. The conversion candidate, a non-Jewish FSU immigrant, had described her struggles as an Israeli citizen from a Jewish home who is not considered Jewish according to halakha: "I have to become Jewish although in a way I feel like I already am Jewish." The judges had responded sympathetically, conveying their desire to help her bridge this gap. I asked Rabbi Dvir whether he thought it was possible that this convert sought out religious conversion but did not necessarily want to live as a religious Jew. "It stands to reason," he answered. "Do you think it's possible," I continued, "that she only accepts the religious way of life because it's a condition for conversion?" "I assume that's possible," he responded. "So how is it done?" I asked, by which I meant, how does he (and all other conversion agents) manage to believe, accept, and authorize candidates under circumstances that are so unlikely to foster religious transformations? Despite my question's ambiguity, Rabbi Dvir seemed to understand my meaning. His response was compelling: "Given that the halakha cannot be changed, the only wiggle room we have is in reality—not in halakha."

Based on the scholarly and rabbinic controversy surrounding conversion, as already described, some might argue that Rabbi Dvir is wrong to assume that the halakhic literature on conversion provides rabbis insufficient wiggle room to deal with historically pressing problems of national significance. In fact, several former chief rabbis in Israel established precisely these kinds of contextually sensitive halakhic conversion policies, which took into account broader political and national considerations.[27] I know Rabbi Dvir was familiar with alternative, less stringent approaches within Orthodoxy for defining what it means for a convert to accept the commandments. More instructive, though, for my ethnographic purposes here, is the second part of his answer. It illuminates the freedom to maneuver that he feels within the socio-institutional reality of the conversion procedure he and his colleagues both create and attempt to govern.

This freedom, I demonstrate throughout this ethnography, builds on interactive and highly creative dramaturgical relationships that conversion agents establish with conversion candidates. By pointing to these mundane dramaturgical relationships—the winking that implicates both sides of Israel's conversion project—this book contributes to the anthropological literature on the state.

Though anthropologists entered into the growing, multidisciplinary scholarship on the state rather late (around the 1990s), their contribution has been profound. In particular, anthropologists have offered a unique analytical perspective by focusing on the routine ways in which state power operates, as well as the lived experiences involved in both the production and replication of the meaning of the state. Anthropology's attention to everyday state practices stems not only from the methodological notion that ethnography can render intelligible what might not even be visible in quantitative and deductive research. It departs also from a more ambitious theoretical objective: to study the everyday dynamics of the state precisely because it is there, within everyday practice, that the state is given life, sense, and meaning. Indeed, turning research attention to the minute details of state institutional labor has produced valuable analytical insights into bureaucratic procedures, thereby exposing the decentered, fluid, and labyrinthine nature of state political power.[28]

The absence of a dramaturgical perspective on the state is surprising. In light of the scholarly interest in everyday bureaucratic practices, and given the recognition of the social relations that these practices create (see Thelen, Vetters, and Von Benda-Beckmann 2014), one would expect to find in the anthropology of the state microsociological approaches such as dramaturgy. It is not that the notions of performance, drama, appearance, representation, and theatricality are missing from this literature. They are not. But they are only thinly and sporadically employed, mostly in the context of state rituals (see Geertz 1980; Handelman 2004) or in reference to the performativity of state practices.[29] Too little has been written about the techniques of impression management employed by bureaucrats in relationship to their "clients" or about the divisions between the front and backstage realms that structure bureaucratic work (Buur 2001; K. Ferguson 1984).

This book, by contrast, more thoroughly mobilizes a dramaturgical perspective as a theoretical lens through which to understand the relationship between states and individuals. My goal here is not merely to argue that within the intricate, decentered spaces of the state—as in any other place, the early Goffman would maintain—people present themselves and manage impressions. Rather, the dramaturgical perspective in this context foregrounds "the syntax of social interaction" (Burns 1992:24–25) between states and citizens, and makes clear the tremendous effort both sides invest in the maintenance of their often tense, if not wholly paradoxical, relationship. The dramaturgical perspective allows us to recognize the precariousness and creativity that characterize the everyday interactive engagements of and with state institutions. It allows us to consider how political power is enacted by placing the burden of performance on real people working and constituting their identities within state institutions.

I did not enter the field intending to apply a dramaturgical perspective to conversion. Rather, like the framework of biopolitics and the metaphor of winking, it emerged inductively from my research. The framework of dramaturgy is grounded in how my interlocutors in the conversion field spoke (mostly about each other) and in how they interacted with one another. These two spheres of activity did not align; when conversion agents and candidates spoke in the language of dramaturgy, they engaged in a political discourse of suspicion. When they acted and interacted in dramaturgical fashion, they collaborated in subtle ways that evaded both suspicion and clear-cut boundaries between true and false performances.

When agents of conversion articulated their suspicion, they used terms like *act*, *theater*, and *actors*. These figurative words indexed colloquial meanings associated with the lexicon of performance (e.g., "lying," "impersonation," and "deception"). Although conversion agents used these terms derogatorily, as they questioned and evaluated the sincerity of the candidates' conduct, the dramaturgical practices that unfolded between the two sides revealed the intricate, collaborative nature of their relationship. For example, conversion teachers consistently emphasized to their students that conversion is ideally a deep, life-changing religious process. But by means of subtle "winking" gestures they also communicated in class that they were, in fact, primarily interested in preparing candidates for their forthcoming conversion performance at the rabbinic court. To offer another example, conversion teachers sharply criticized deceptive candidates and empty conversion performances (describing them as "acts" or "theater"). Yet they simultaneously taught their students to play roles and manage impressions: to graft legible signs of proper converts onto their persona. Often these dynamics demanded that teachers compromise ideals of sincerity, minimize their suspicion, and even sometimes knowingly overlook signs of insincerity.

The rabbis in the conversion court also winked at candidates. From the outset the conversion court functioned as a disciplinary and judicial setting. While these features were indeed central to the sociality of court dynamics, "softer," collaborative dramaturgical dynamics informally unfolded there as well. Court agents clearly engaged in interrogative practices and suspicious discourses in an attempt to expose "performers"; but they also helped conversion candidates manage their fragile performances. The dramaturgical collaborations that marked these conversion performances were laden with interdependencies and comitragic moments that sometimes bordered on the absurd. Such performances remind us that, as much as conversion candidates need the state in order to be considered Jewish, the Israeli nation-state also needs converts in order to produce and reproduce its own Jewishness—its political reality as a Jewish state.

The Ethnography of State Conversion Policy

> How naturally we entify and give life to such. Take the case of God, the economy, and the State, abstract entities we credit with Being, species of things awesome with life-force of their own, transcendent over mere mortals. Cleary they are fetishes, invented wholes of materialized artifice into whose insufficiency of being we have placed soulstuff. Hence the big S of the State.
>
> —Michael Taussig, *The Magic of the State*

The current book is an ethnographic study of the state, or more precisely, it rests on the premise that the transition from a big *S* (State) to a little *s* (state) can be productively realized through ethnographic research. The state that appears in this monograph is not an abstract entity that exists as a self-sufficient whole. It is not a natural or magical entity that is simply "out there" but rather an assemblage of agents, mechanisms, institutions, ideologies, and discourses under whose auspices conversion policy takes place.[30] In my work the state emerges most powerfully not within grandiose spectacles or "big politics" but in the lives of those who experience it, idealize it, and choose to speak and act in its name. Based on extended ethnographic fieldwork (2004–2007), this book reveals the everyday dynamics of what we too easily and mistakenly think of as "the State." Hence the small *s* of the state.

The aggregate of agents, mechanisms, institutions, ideologies, and discourses that appear in this book constitutes a state that is dispersed, decentered, and ridden with conflict. To be sure, an extended ethnographic study is hardly necessary to show that the state that governs the Israeli conversion policy is far from a coherent whole. A daily newspaper would suffice. There one finds headlines describing the vicious struggles among conversion institutions or between them and other state institutions. But to understand the "policy world" of Israel's Jewish conversion project (Shore and Wright 2011)—that is, the practices, experiences, and cultural meanings that frame and give it form—one needs ethnography. The central goal of this monograph is not to determine why Israel's national mission is failing or to offer practical solutions to address this failure.[31] Instead, like other anthropological studies of policy worlds (e.g., Feldman 2005; Wedel et al. 2005:34), I wish to understand what people do in the name of this policy, what discursive structures and moral schemes justify it in the first place, and how it is imagined and experienced by all sides of the policy encounter.

Unlike many ethnographic research fields, which possess no inherent quality that defines them thematically or empirically (Gupta and Ferguson 1997), the institutional field of state conversion is, in fact, an actual field unto itself. It is a field "out there in the world," because the Israeli state made it one. Certainly, the boundaries of this statist institutional field reflect a degree of ambiguity, as Timothy Mitchell (1991) argued and as many anthropological studies have demonstrated; specifically, the boundaries between state and society can be seen as porous. Yet state conversion still operates as a discrete institutional field in the sense that it contains specific sites in which the conversion process materializes. Therefore, it was relatively easy for me to identify where to conduct ethnography: in the conversion classes, in the special rabbinic court of conversion, and in the ritual bath—the three institutional locations where agents of conversion and conversion candidates encounter each other.

The conversion ulpan is where conversion candidates and conversion agents first meet. Most of the state agents in this setting are professional educators, usually employees of the Ministry of Education or of the Jewish Agency of Israel, and are not part of the rabbinic conversion establishment. Alongside the bureaucratization processes that accompanied the establishment of a proconversion policy during the 1990s (as I will detail in chapter 1), the conversion ulpan was transformed from an optional stage to an obligatory stop on converts' paths to the rabbinic court. With the exception of a small number of conversion candidates still tutored in private by rabbis (because of language barriers, for example), conversion education is typically conducted in organized programs. These programs are often offered by Mali, the central governmental body responsible for teaching conversion candidates and recognized since 2008 as a special executive arm of the government for matters of conversion preparation.[32] The Ministry of Education as well as several private (but state authorized) associations provide alternative options for conversion programs.

This book focuses on Mali, an institute that holds classes throughout Israel, usually in community centers or synagogues, in several languages (primarily Hebrew and Russian). Mali is also in charge of the much contested state-organized conversion program established in the Israeli army (formally the Israeli Defense Force, or IDF).[33] During ten months in

2005–2006 I conducted participant observation in a classroom located in a bustling downtown section of Tel Aviv. Held in such a central location, this class enabled candidates from all Tel Aviv suburbs to attend. In this class as well as in a class in southern Israel that I observed less frequently (in 2004–2005), all of the teachers were religious Zionists; four out of five were men. The class, conducted in Hebrew, usually met two evenings a week for three hours per session and was attended by some twenty-five students, all but one of whom were women. Most students had immigrated to Israel from the FSU as children and were in their twenties and early thirties. Two or three male Israeli partners of conversion candidates also joined the sessions.

I attended all sessions and joined the class for field excursions, social events, and a Sabbath weekend. Eventually I became friends with some of the converts. In addition, I accompanied most of them during various stages of their court procedure. Because Mali is a nationwide institutional body, it organizes pedagogic workshops for teachers (which I attended) and publishes textual training materials (to which I had access). Fieldwork at Mali helped me gain converts' trust, allowing me to conduct in-depth interviews that were relatively relaxed and candid.

The second site is the Special Rabbinic Court of Conversion, an institution that was revived in the 1990s in the context of the bureaucratization of the national mission. As a legal arena, the rabbinic court constructs relationships between state agents and conversion candidates that differ markedly from the prolonged encounters that unfold in the ulpans; encounters there are brief, distant, and hierarchical, though not always starkly so. Similar to the conversion ulpan, these encounters are also gendered; all court agents are male while most candidates are female. Many of the conversion rabbinic judges are trained educators or community rabbis and are accustomed to treating converts with kindness and sensitivity.[34] Generally speaking, the procedure at the conversion court is made up of a number of brief meetings, organized during different points within the conversion process. The first occurs early in the process, when candidates submit their conversion application, and the court representative first opens their conversion file. This initial meeting is followed by an additional meeting closer to the end of the conversion course, and then by a final hearing of the rabbinic court (including, sometimes, repeated hearings).

During my 2005–2006 fieldwork I observed dozens of hearings at the conversion court and dozens of encounters between two court representatives and conversion candidates. I focused on five tribunals operating in the center and south of Israel located in four different cities. I was permitted to document, but not record, the hearings. During most of the hearings I tried to write down what was said in as much detail as possible and, during breaks between hearings, to complete parts of the discussion that I remembered. The candidates that I observed at the court came from diverse sociocultural backgrounds. They had immigrated to Israel from an array of different countries, although the significant majority of them were from the FSU. They arrived from various conversion ulpans (those mentioned earlier), but especially from Mali. Some I had met previously during my fieldwork at Mali's conversion ulpans. At the court I not only observed the hearings but also witnessed the routine work of the rabbinic judges and court representatives. For example, I was present in the hearing rooms during preliminary discussions of the rabbinic panel regarding the conversion candidates and during internal discussions after candidates had been asked to leave the room. Sometimes I ate lunch together with the judges or stayed behind to converse with them at the end of the day's hearings. Later, I also interviewed several of them.

To complete the conversion process, conversion candidates attend the ritual bath. The rabbinic court holds the authority to decide the conversion case. Neither the rabbinic court that governs the mikveh (composed of three male mikveh attendants [*balanim*]) nor the female mikveh attendant (*balanit*), all of whom observe the ritual immersion (of female converts), are permitted to alter this decision. But from a halakhic point of view, it is actually ritual immersion in the mikveh that constitutes the decisive phase of conversion.[35] After a ritual immersion document is signed and approved, both the rabbinic conversion court and the chief rabbi's representative authorize the whole process and the Conversion Administration issues a certificate of conversion, which the head of the Conversion Administration signs.[36] Only when this bureaucratic procedure has been completed is a convert allowed to register as a Jew in the Israeli population registry.

Since Jewish law considers ritual immersion for conversion to be a juridical act, it must take place before sunset, unlike female immersion for the purposes of cleansing and purification after menstruation, which takes place after sundown. Usually, mikvehs used for purification are also used for conversion (female converts are advised not to schedule their ritual immersion during their menstrual periods). Women's immersion for conversion is first performed naked in the presence of a female mikveh attendant, and then in a gown covering the body in the presence of three male mikveh attendants (who are not necessarily ordained rabbis).[37] Several mikvehs are open for the immersive rituals of conversion all over Israel. The mikveh that I observed is located in the center of Israel, and in summer 2006 I observed dozens of immersions (of women, only during the second part of the *tvilah*, when converts wore the gown). I also spent time with the female mikveh attendants and with conversion candidates in the waiting rooms.

Numerous textual materials that I gathered over the last decade (2004–2015) have significantly augmented my fieldwork in these three institutional sites. These materials reflect the dynamics of the impassioned public discourses that surround and constitute state conversion policy. A broad array of actors from the state conversion apparatus and civil society—rabbis, educators, bureaucrats, academics, policy researchers, politicians who represent FSU immigrants, non-Jewish Israeli citizens, converts, and many others—participate in these discourses. The public locations in which they occur also vary, ranging from Knesset committees to public conferences and seminars, art galleries, and media and social media platforms.

Passing as a Secular Jewish Ethnographer

The problem of access is an integral part of many ethnographic projects in which the anthropologist "studies up"; that is, studies the middle and upper end of the social power structure (Nader 1969). Textual materials are usually kept in archives and offices, to which entry is restricted; the social processes in which the ethnographer is interested often unfold within sites overseen by gatekeepers; and admission to them requires that one navigate an unpredictable system of permissions. Unsurprisingly, the problem of access weighed on me, too. But beyond the frustration and sometimes amazement that this problem provoked, the barriers I encountered taught me a great deal about the state, precisely because diverse groups of people both erected and removed these barriers in its name. When gatekeepers spoke in the name of the state, they opened, closed, and then reopened the field to me. At times, their understandable desire to contest the vociferous public critiques directed at their institutions worked in my favor. After all, giving entry to academics and other potentially critical outsiders creates a sense of an open organizational culture marked by dialogue and self-reflectiveness. I had the impression that the gatekeepers of the conversion institutes sought to avoid the perception that they had something to hide, and, even if some had misgivings about my presence, in a certain sense they could not permit themselves to say no.

So they said yes. But their yes frequently turned out to be a hollow and conditional response that involved a great many no's along the way—these, too, in the name of the state. For example, the argument for privacy (of either the conversion candidates or the conversion agents) recurred often during my fieldwork, usually as a justification for denying me access. It was used to turn me away from many sites (seminars for rabbinic judges, closed meetings of senior officials in the Conversion Administration, meetings of the interministerial committee of conversion) and to block me from access to certain texts (especially conversion files). I never took for granted the ethnographic opportunities I did receive.

The privacy of the state was a perpetual methodological hazard. Abrams ([1977] 2006:114) theorizes "state privacy" as a powerful ploy the state uses to remain immune to criticism. Like Abrams, I often took this argument as a cheap, overused trick employed for the purposes of exclusion. Such was the case with Rabbi Ron, the person in charge of conversion tvilah, who told me openly that "due to the personal privacy of converts, which the state is under obligation to protect, I cannot grant you permission to observe the immersions conducted in the mikveh"; but then he added that he was sorry about this early decision because I actually "seemed OK to him."

Yet I grew sympathetic to the privacy argument, even while regarding it as a threadbare slogan, and even though I knew it was I who would pay the price for it. My sympathy deepened the more I learned about the complexities that the conversion policy created for its agents. In the volatile field in which these agents worked—one highly scrutinized by rabbinic authorities, government agents, and the media—my gaze was an additional burden. As a woman, a secular Jew, and an academic, I was clearly a suspect to them, and for good reason.[38] Learning to appreciate the precarious situation of rabbinic judges, I came to understand and accept their suspicion of me. While I assume that the politics of suspicion are integral to Jewish conversion in various social and historical contexts (including in diasporic communities), through fieldwork I experienced the particular sensibilities that inform suspicion in the context of the national mission.

In a field mediated so deeply by these politics, it is not surprising that establishing rapport with my interlocutors (on both sides to the conversion policy encounter) depended upon small gestures and tokens of trust: on secrets shared with me in corridor talks, candid moments of openness, and disclosures qualified as "not for citation." The silences and half-truths to which I was exposed resembled the silences and half-truths that many anthropologists confront during fieldwork. From a methodological perspective, there was nothing inherently unique or interesting about them. But in the case of Jewish conversion in Israel, these silences and half-truths formed an inseparable part of the dynamics of the field rather than being merely part of my ethnographic relationships (see also Seeman 2010:101–102). I often wondered whether I was being told the truth and offered an honest performance. Ironically, these doubts were quite similar to those that concerned my interlocutors in their engagements with each other.

One way in which I attempted to deal with the politics of suspicion that surrounded me was to contrast my ethnographic work with journalistic work. In a volatile field such as conversion, the statement "I am not a journalist" tended to put people at ease. The documentary films on conversion broadcasted on Israeli television during my fieldwork became, in this context, a foil against which I could positively highlight my own research as a project with different goals. This strategy was of particular importance in my relationships with the rabbinic judges. To the extent that judges were seriously concerned about these films—scornfully dismissing their producers as ignorant secular Israelis—they grew more interested in the representations that my "not journalistic" gaze would yield.

At the rabbinic court I was asked to enter the hearings as a "fly on the wall." But this ideal, long ago discredited in anthropology, also had little validity in the rabbinic courtroom. Although I spent most of my time in the corner, quietly documenting what unfolded, I was by no means invisible. In a way, my visibility weighed more on rabbinic judges than on candidates. This difference was organized in part by the layout of the courtroom—by the fact that I was asked to sit in a corner behind candidates but within the visual field of rabbinic judges. But it also emerged from the fact that candidates were so goal oriented and focused on their interactions with the rabbinic judges that I was simply irrelevant to them.

The mikveh offered a completely different setting. Although I was still insignificant in the eyes of converts, I felt far more visible and intrusive. To begin with, the architecture of the mikveh chamber reinforced the power relations between (female) converts, who immerse themselves in water, and the three male ritual bath attendants who, literally, oversee them while standing on the edges of the small square-shaped pool. Even if we put the issue of modesty aside, an issue that in fact has prompted profound critiques among feminist Orthodox women (see Farkash 2013; Knesset 2013; Tikochinsky 2008), it is impossible to overlook such a stark form of patriarchal power over women.[39] Before instructing female converts how to immerse themselves and what prayers to recite, the male ritual bath attendants often asked them a few brief questions, usually related to their conversion experience. As the converts lifted their eyes to address the attendants' queries, the latter looked downward into the bath as they listened to converts and oversaw the ritual. It often proved impossible for converts to see above the judges' shoes. In an attempt to remove myself from this disturbing situation, I tried to minimize my presence by moving outside the convert's field of vision. After attending dozens of rituals, I ultimately decided to spend more time in the waiting room.

My ethnographic presence in both the rabbinic court and the ritual bath had its own ethical implications. Despite the general permission granted to me by senior officials to conduct research at both sites, I made sure to ask each conversion candidate individually for his or her permission. Only a few conversion candidates refused my request to observe the hearings in their case or to observe their ritual immersion. Yet one cannot ignore the fact that I approached candidates when they were clearly vulnerable, nervous, and stressed. Similarly, during the hearings at the rabbinic court, because I was already seated in the courtroom, the court representative or the rabbinic judges took it upon themselves to ask the conversion candidates for permission on my behalf ("she is not part of the court; she is from the university," they often assured the converts). For a long time I was troubled by the possibility that in such circumstances, the candidates could not really say no.

My ethnographic work turned out to be multisited, and the interactions in which I was involved as I crossed from one site to the next sparked my dramaturgical imagination and sharpened the emerging analytical framework of the study. In Goffmanian terms, the fieldwork unfolded in arenas that served as front and backstages for each other. In a field that involved the management and concealment of information as well as intensive preoccupations about truths and lies, each side sought out knowledge about the other—and I knew something about all sides. My participation in each site granted me a measure of social power: the rabbinic judges took interest in the conversion ulpans, while the conversion candidates and teachers positioned me as an expert on the rabbinic court. I became what Goffman (1959) would call the "middle [wo]man" who is exposed to both sides and expected to keep everyone's secrets. For example, I was familiar with how the candidates prepared themselves for their performances in the rabbinic court, the pedagogic work performed by conversion teachers in advance of the court hearings, and the discussions that rabbinic court agents held before and after their meetings with converts.

The process of managing my ethnographic persona—an integral part of any research engagement—was a morally loaded one. This process provoked daily questions about my multiple and potentially contradictory commitments: What side was I on? To whom did I tell what, and what did I talk about with whom? Who heard only half-truths from me, and to whom did I reveal nothing at all? For better or worse, I had no doubt that my commitments to converts took precedence over my commitments to conversion agents. Therefore, in several cases I shared with converts what conversion agents said about them but never cooperated with conversion agents when asked to share incriminating information. I participated in court discussions only on the infrequent occasions when I was asked for an opinion that I felt, if withheld, would be to the detriment of the convert.

During my academic training in anthropology, empathy occupied a special place among the array of emotions that should ideally regulate ethnographic work. Not compassion, not feelings of justice, not even curiosity; empathy—that's what we discussed most. During the preliminary stages of my fieldwork, I was seriously concerned that I would fail to be adequately empathetic. As a secular Jewish-Israeli woman armed with negative prejudices about rabbinic, state, and male bureaucratic systems, I feared that I would completely lack ethnographic empathy for state bureaucrats and rabbinic judges. Luckily, and much to my surprise, this was not the case. The conversion court agents whom I observed were impressive, pleasant, cordial people—good conversationalists and incisive in their thinking. I liked, respected, and even empathized with many of them. Contrary to what I had predicted, I met conversion agents who displayed sensitivity, humanity, and flexibility toward conversion candidates. Of course, there were less admirable conversion agents, people whose behavior more closely reflected the stereotypes I brought with me to the field; and there were moments when I flinched in my seat. But generally the conversion agents I met were careful, to the best of their ability, to avoid abusing their positions of power. Even the analytical framework I developed over the course of my research, concerning the fundamental tensions that entangle conversion agents in impossible relationships, led me to develop empathy not only for state privacy but also for those state agents who shoulder the paradoxical burdens of the nation-state's conversion policy—and of the conversion performance.

Overview of the Book

The connections I draw between the conversion policy's sociohistorical processes, its socio-institutional dynamics, and lived experiences underwrite the structure of the ethnography. These connections essentially organize the book into two thematic sections: the conversion mission (chapters 1 and 2) and the conversion performance (chapters 3 through 5).

The first chapter describes how and why Jewish conversion in Israel has become a national mission, presenting the institutional, ideological, rhetorical, and moral processes involved in that transformation. I show how Israel has organized Jewish conversion into an institutional field of Zionist biopolitical policy—a channel for population intervention through which Israel strives to maintain its moral economies of return and kinship while producing and reproducing itself as Jewish.

In the second chapter I explore the relationship between state-run conversion and religious Zionism. I focus on the lived experiences and everyday moralities of those calling and called to carry out the state's conversion policy. I trace how by expressing a shared commitment to the national mission of conversion, the religious Zionist community reworks its symbiotic, if fraught, relationship with the state.

In chapter 3 I analyze my encounters with both conversion agents and candidates where they first encounter each other: in the state-run conversion school. There they begin to collaboratively create winking relations, as conversion teachers transmit conflicting messages about the meanings of conversion as a religiously sincere process. I show how pedagogic preparation molds conversion into an elaborate performance, or what I call "a rite of passing," full of nuanced dramaturgical gestures and collaborations as well as educational and moral compromises.

Chapter 4 unpacks the dramaturgical interactions that entangle conversion court agents and candidates in a contradictory process. Working from a position of uncertainty, court agents employ strategies conveying both suspicion and trust. On the one hand, they meticulously interrogate the legible signs of religious observance that conversion candidates perform. On the other hand, court agents tacitly help conversion candidates sustain believable performances of sincerity—a process that reciprocally fosters agents' trust in converts' performances. By examining exceptional cases of conversion, this chapter shows the interdependent investments of court agents and candidates in preventing conversion performances from breaking down.

Chapter 5 addresses a critical question that preoccupies conversion candidates as they move through their conversion process toward the decisive moment at the rabbinic conversion court: how can they narrate their biography and conversion process in a way that lends credibility to their conversion performance? Drawing on ethnographic material gathered in the conversion school and rabbinic court, as well as in interviews with (already certified) converts, this chapter traces the interactive scripting process that provides conversion narratives their shape. I show how, in narrating significant personal change, candidates learn to tread a fine line of emphasizing national belonging while neither exaggerating nor instrumentalizing the religious element of their story. I argue that, ultimately, the conversion narratives affirmed by conversion court rabbis lie precariously on this fine line and do not emphasize the drama of religious repentance.

The epilogue discusses the book's theoretical contributions regarding winking, emphasizing the phenomenon's place within the Jewish state and within state bureaucracies more generally. In the Israeli context, I suggest that scholars consider how winking helps constitute the often tension-laden encounters between state Orthodox institutions and a predominantly secular Jewish population. Ultimately, winking permits the state to save its Jewish face. Extending beyond the Israeli context, the epilogue also builds on the importance scholars of the state have assigned to the visual domain. Specifically, it complicates the extensive literature focusing on how the state exercises its power by seeing its citizens—through mundane disciplinary gazes and anxiety-laden practices of terror surveillance, as well as government policies that enhance the legibility of populations. Alongside analysis of these practices, winking relations call attention to the nuanced, interactional alliances involved in the making of both state power and state subjects.

PART 1

The Conversion Mission

ONE

National Mission

THE CONCEPT OF a national mission pervades public Israeli discourse. Water conservation, road improvement, and Jewish settlement on the perimeter of the Gaza Strip, as well as the integration of the Arab sector into the labor market—these represent only a sample of the issues recently defined by Israeli politicians or government bureaucrats in terms of a mission. A national mission is not necessarily a Zionist mission. Rather, the "national" qualifier signals the mission's urgency for the Israeli public and state.[1] Despite its conceptual thinness, the trope of the national mission helps mobilize relevant publics and resources, thus placing what might otherwise be marginal issues at the center of the public agenda.

This chapter tells the story of how and why Jewish conversion has become a national mission. In so doing, it presents the institutional, ideological, rhetorical, and moral processes involved in the construction of Israel's conversion policy. My main argument is that, under the rubric of national mission, Jewish conversion has come to constitute a morally loaded Zionist biopolitical policy—an institutional channel for population policy through which the Jewish state strives to produce and reproduce the Israeli nation as Jewish.

Conversion policy in Israel became popularly identified as a national mission in 2003, when Ariel Sharon, then prime minister, used the concept to characterize the conversion of non-Jewish FSU olim. In fact, the expansion of the state's involvement in the conversion of newcomers from the

FSU had already begun in the early 1990s, in the wake of increased rabbinic concern over non-Jewish immigration from these regions. This initial expansion, it should be noted, already represented a significant departure from earlier conversion policies.[2]

Genealogy of the National Mission

To appreciate the significance of a secular political leader like Sharon elevating religious conversion to a top national priority, we must look back to the state's early history. During Israel's first decade of existence, David Ben Gurion, the state's first prime minister and an outspoken secular leader, rejected any attempt to establish a state apparatus that would manage conversion. From a policy perspective Ben Gurion did not feel that conversion was a particularly pressing issue. With little more than a few thousand non-Jewish family members of olim (mainly war refugees from Poland and Russia), there were relatively few people to convert. More importantly though, Ben Gurion ideologically opposed the idea that Israel, as a liberal democracy, should play a role in determining its citizens' religious preferences. Indeed, in the 1950s, in the absence of a religiously informed registration policy, people who were not halakhically Jewish could simply define themselves as Jews and register as such. In the spirit of secular Zionism, Ben Gurion generally preferred to encourage the quotidian sociological processes of national assimilation over the adoption of explicit religious, halakhically informed conversion procedures. In so doing, he implicitly favored a biblical model of conversion over a rabbinic one (Fisher 2013a).

Ben-Gurion's secular Zionist approach was politically defeated in the late 1950s in the context of the first parliamentary dispute over the question "Who is a Jew?" Ultimately, after consulting with about fifty prominent leaders from the Jewish world, Ben Gurion embraced halakhic criteria for the sake of Jewish recognition and registration in Israel. During the 1960s the state's political and administrative authorities interacted little with converts. Israeli governments did not concern themselves with conversion policy, nor did they encourage non-Jewish citizens to convert. On the contrary, they allowed all official state dealings with converts to be handled exclusively by the Chief Rabbinate—a state-authorized religious body whose suspicions about the religious sincerity of conversion candidates was well known (Fisher forthcoming).[3] The rabbinate was not particularly inclined to conduct conversions of non-Jewish spouses of Israeli Jews or of the children of intermarried couples. The rabbinate also insisted that the regional rabbinic courts (a state system that governs marriage, divorce, and other family-related issues for Israeli Jews) would exclusively handle conversion requests. Moreover, the rabbinate instituted a stringent halakhic policy, disregarding alternative, more lenient halakhic approaches (Edrei 2010, 2013).

The person most associated with a shift away from stringency in Israel's conversion policy is Rabbi Shlomo Goren, the chief rabbi of the IDF and later Israel's chief rabbi. Rabbi Goren, who espoused a Zionist statist (*mamlakhti*)[4] ideology and justified a more flexible approach to halakha in its name, regarded conversion as one of the moral prerogatives of state institutions. Instead of focusing on the religious earnestness of potential converts, he emphasized their national worthiness. From his Zionist perspective immigrants sought—and were entitled—to join the Jewish collective in Israel. It was therefore the state's responsibility, he argued, to fully integrate its non-Jewish citizens and soldiers—those who had already fulfilled important Jewish commandments by immigrating and displaying their willingness to sacrifice, perhaps even their lives, for the sake of the state. He believed that under these circumstances the halakha can and should permit a more compassionate and inclusive conversion policy. Relying on lenient rabbinic approaches that had emerged in diasporic contexts out of communal policy considerations (see introduction), Rabbi Goren underscored the importance of conversion within the unique context of a sovereign Jewish state.[5]

In the 1960s, during Rabbi Goren's tenure, the IDF provided for the first time ad-hoc religious conversions to non-Jewish soldiers who wished to convert during their military service (Fisher 2013a, 2013b). These conversions were relatively liberal and less halakhically rigorous. In this way, under the aegis of the army's religious courts Rabbi Goren managed to circumvent the conservative policies of the rabbinate. In the 1970s, in response to both a sharp rise in the number of non-Jewish volunteers in the kibbutzim (and a concomitant rise in the number of intermarriages with Israeli Jews) and the first waves of immigration from the Soviet Union, including intermarried families, Rabbi Goren concluded that these steps were insufficient.[6] As his personal assistant recounted to me about those years, "Rabbi Goren lost sleep over the issue of conversion" and was determined to change a rather reactive policy into a more established and proactive one.

To accomplish this goal he institutionalized the conversion process. For example, prior to the 1970s, preparation for conversion was undertaken in private tutorial settings without any institutionalized infrastructure or pedagogic oversight; conversion candidates simply studied for several months with rabbis, whose rates and curricula varied considerably (Hameiri 1997). During the 1970s, after Rabbi Goren created a nationwide network of conversion classes, the curriculum was standardized and students began conducting their preparatory studies in groups. Furthermore, the authority to make rabbinic decisions concerning conversion applications was transferred from the regional rabbinic courts to the special conversion courts under the direct aegis of Rabbi Goren. These conversion courts were staffed by religious Zionist rabbis who favored a more welcoming approach to converts—a position that was diametrically opposed to that of the ultra-Orthodox rabbinic judges who presided over most of the regional rabbinic courts.[7]

During the 1980s the conversion ulpans Rabbi Goren established retained their basic format. However, the special conversion courts he founded eventually succumbed to political pressure from the ultra-Orthodox rabbinic authorities, under which they came to function in only a limited capacity. Under these circumstances the regional rabbinic courts became once again the primary institutions in charge of authorizing conversion, with municipal chief rabbis occasionally working alongside them (Sheleg 2004b). It was on this modest bureaucratic scaffold that the state Conversion Administration would develop during the 1990s.

The Paradoxes of Return

> Sorry I made *aliyah*, I was seven. They didn't tell me at the airport that *goyim* can't sign on.
>
> The ID card is blue
> The heart is white
> Just don't touch a *talis* [prayer shawl], you are not from here!
>
> —Alexa Anastasia Yermolov, "Up to Here"

The collapse of the Soviet Union at the end of the 1980s created a precious opportunity for Israel to fulfill its Zionist scheme of return while substantially increasing its Jewish population. The state pursued various diplomatic channels to seize this opportunity. It encouraged immigration via its national institutions in the Soviet Union (e.g., the Jewish Agency) and channeled immigrants to Israel, even at the cost of confrontation with other states that offered alternative destinations for immigrants (Yonah 2005, 2008).[8] However, the Soviet Union's collapse turned out to be a double-edged sword. FSU immigration did indeed allow Israel to celebrate its self-conception as a homeland for Jews in need, and it precipitated a significant increase in Israel's Jewish population. But it also resulted in Israel's absorption of many non-Jewish citizens, mostly family members of halakhically Jewish olim. Altogether, some 270,000 to 350,000 non-Jewish immigrants have arrived in Israel under the expanded aegis of the Law of Return (see introduction).[9] To be sure, when Israel expanded the Law of Return in 1970, the government was already aware of the challenge that the mass immigration of intermarried families from the Soviet Union posed to Jewish unity and demography. But only the Soviet Union's collapse two decades later would transform this hypothetical scenario into a concrete reality that demanded a response.

The non-Jewish olim represent a significant and growing proportion of the approximately one million immigrants that have arrived from the FSU since the end of the 1980s. Some of these immigrants have a Jewish family background but are not considered Jewish according to Orthodox halakhic criteria. Some have more distant Jewish relatives (e.g., Jewish grandparents), while some have no Jewish background at all (e.g., spouses of the grandchildren of Jews). A minority of immigrants identify as Christians.[10] Despite these stark differences, the Central Bureau of Statistics classifies all non-Jewish, non-Christian FSU immigrants as "lacking religious classification" and groups them under the expansive rubric of "others" (together with "non-Arab Christians" [i.e., Christian olim] and others with unrecognized religious affiliations).

The relative proportion of non-Jews among the total number of FSU immigrants has increased consistently, from around 20 percent during the initial waves of immigration between 1990 and 1995 to 40–70 percent since the end of the 1990s (A. Cohen 2006:34). Each year some ten thousand non-Jews join the Jewish collective in Israel: some six thousand through immigration and some four thousand by virtue of their birth to non-Jewish mothers (Fisher 2015:44).

The massive FSU immigration under the revised Law of Return created a paradoxical state of affairs. Ironically, the law that epitomizes Israel's

Zionist ideology precipitated demographic developments that challenge the Zionist vision. Even if the Law of Return embodies the Zionist conviction that Israel should gather the world's Jewish diasporic communities within a national homeland, in its revised, post-1970 instantiation it made Israel less Jewish. And even if the expanded law is in line with what Rogers Brubaker (1996) calls "nationalizing nationality" and is geared toward securing a Jewish majority vis-à-vis the Palestinian minority in Israel, what it achieved at most is a "non-Arab" state (Lustick 1999). In these ways, FSU immigration has simultaneously fortified and undermined Israel's ongoing Zionist project for sovereignty, demographic supremacy, and Jewish cultural hegemony in the state.

Of course, non-Jewish immigration under the Law of Return applies to more than just those arriving from former Soviet states. During the last two decades non-Jewish olim have come from a number of other countries, especially Argentina and France. However, because of its unprecedented scope, non-Jewish immigration from the FSU has had by far the most dramatic impact on Israel's conversion policy. Non-Jewish olim split, in fact, Israel's bureaucratic logic—the taxonomic logic that shapes the Israeli nation-state (Handelman 2004)—by separating two sacred classificatory systems: the Law of Return and the rules of halakha. In this respect, by virtue of their problematic belonging in Israel, non-Jewish immigrants violate and "contaminate" the category of Jewish identity.

From a Zionist perspective the Law of Return offers newcomers a mode of belonging that is both profound and essential.[11] It is based on a potent religionational script that revolves around the "ingathering of the exiles" (*kibbutz galuyot*). Framed by narratives of historical justice and mythic return, the Law of Return embodies the notion of aliyah—as opposed to the more general notion of immigration (Zucker 1989)—and distills the ethnonational logic of Israel as a Jewish state. Its revision in 1970 does not disrupt this logic but rather expands it. In its expanded form the law preserves the preference of kinship logics over the right of territory, as non-Jewish olim join Israel through their family connections to the Jewish ethnos. Based on their family ties, non-Jewish immigrants enter the national fold through its most privileged entrance.

At the same time, from a halakhic perspective non-Jewish olim are excluded from the nation. Since in Israel halakha enjoys hegemonic status with respect to both the management of personal status matters of Jews and their registration in the population registry, non-Jewish olim remain outside the boundaries of the national fold. The exclusionary consequences of these institutional arrangements cannot be overstated. In addition to the fact that such arrangements deny basic civil rights to a significant proportion of Israel's population (no small matter for a state that claims to be a liberal democracy), they also bear on fundamental symbolic questions about kinship and relatedness (who is married to whom, and who is buried next to whom). Indeed, it is within these kinds of bureaucratic—and symbolically loaded—arenas that the modern nation-state regulates the belonging of its others and defines its core self (Handelman 2004; Herzfeld 1993).

Augmenting this paradoxical reality is the fact that considerable segments of FSU non-Jewish olim subvert the halakhic definition of their identity. Many of those whom the state defines as non-Jews do in fact define themselves as Jewish—in terms of origin and identity. This self-definition is premised to a large extent on the logic of Soviet bureaucracy. The Soviet regime preserved Jewish nationality as a separate rubric in internal passports and constructed Jewish identity as an ethnic rather than a religious category. Both the Soviet government and society adhered to a patrilineal system of recognition (e.g., by relying on the father's surname; Kimmerling 2004:414); therefore, the children of fathers with Jewish surnames were perceived as Jewish. Similarly, the fact that the Jewish aliyah agencies have actively courted potential olim has contributed to their Jewish self-identification. I was told as much by Sveta, one of the students at the conversion ulpan: "The State of Israel considered me Jewish and invited me to make aliyah—so I just assumed I was Jewish." But as Sveta (like many of her classmates) discovered after arriving in Israel, in an important way Israelis and the Israeli state regarded her as a gentile. The verses cited at the opening of this section capture this sense of simultaneous inclusion and exclusion. Holding her blue ID card, a document attesting to her Israeli citizenship, but grasping also her status in Israel as a *goya*—a highly derogatory term for a non-Jew, one with exclusionary halakhic implications—Alexa Anastasia Yermolov, an Israeli citizen and young poet, details her painful position (Kropkin 2015).

Further deepening the Law of Return's paradoxical implications is the fact that non-Jewish FSU immigrants undergo what Asher Cohen (2006) calls "sociological conversion." To some extent these immigrants embody Ben Gurion's vision from six decades earlier (Fisher 2013a): they integrate into Jewish-Israeli society without undergoing any formal rite of conversion. Although the population registry defines these citizens as "others," on many social levels their otherness is invisible. They share social networks with family members and friends who are bona fide Jews and blend into all settings and sectors of Jewish-Israeli society (Yakobson 2010). If we can say that they belong to an ethnic enclave, theirs is a cultural, linguistic, and consumerist one that preserves its "Russian" distinctiveness; it is surely not a "non-Jewish enclave."[12]

Non-Jewish FSU immigrants are clearly unmarked by external signs of otherness like skin color or language that might distinguish them from other FSU olim as non-Jews. Furthermore, they might be taken as stereotypically Jewish in appearance, and they tend to pass as Jews or simply as Russians. They might have Jewish surnames, celebrate Jewish civil religion, and, as mentioned earlier, define themselves as Jewish. As Danny, a teacher at Mali told me: "It's not written on their forehead, so how can one tell if someone is a Jew? Sometimes you hear a family name that sounds very Russian, very non-Jewish—but the person turns out to be Jewish; or, take Schwartz—it sounds Jewish—but no. You think you know but you can't know."

The otherness of second-generation non-Jewish immigrants, and of immigrants who arrived as children, is especially invisible. With Jewish surnames, only slight Russian accents (or even none at all), and a command of Israeli Hebrew, second-generation FSU immigrants (whether halakhically Jewish or not) sound perfectly Israeli. As Shmuel Yeselzon, during his tenure as the administrative head of the Conversion Department in the Prime Minister's Office, expressed in a parliament committee session: "We should say it upfront. They are not immigrants any more. We are talking here about complete Israelis" (Knesset 2013). Moreover, those citizens who wish to conceal their non-halakhic status in social settings do so with relative ease. Many of the conversion candidates I met in the conversion class did precisely that. In their daily lives they did not bring up their status in conversation, they avoided answering questions about their Jewish identity, and they often lied about it. After 2002, following the High Court decision to remove the "nationality" rubric from Israeli ID cards, passing as Jews became even easier.[13]

In the most basic and quotidian sense, the sociological conversion of non-Jewish FSU olim disrupts the mundane "Jewish 'epistemologies' or ways of knowing" (Glenn and Sokoloff 2010:3) by which Israelis determine who is Jewish. The social assimilation of non-Jewish olim brings those questions about Jewishness that are usually taken up in juridical and other formal state arenas into the mundane realm of everyday life, where they sometimes become the concrete source of social discomfort.

In the 2013 electoral campaign, the Sephardic (*Mizrachi*) ultra-Orthodox movement Shas (acronym in Hebrew for "Sephardic Keepers of the Torah") capitalized on this discomfort.[14] One Shas campaign television commercial depicts a Mizrachi (but not ultra-Orthodox) Jewish bridegroom under a wedding canopy with his stereotypically Russian bride: tall, blond, and with an exaggerated Russian accent. The television audience watches as he realizes not only that his wife is non-Jewish but also that she is undergoing an instant conversion at that very moment. The ritual is sealed when a nearby fax machine, installed under the wedding canopy as a gift from the FSU immigrant party Yisrael Beytenu (lit. "Israel Is Our Home"), prints the conversion certificate. The groom, in shock, asks his bride, "Wait a minute, you're not Jewish?" "Now I am," she responds confidently. The commercial mocks the state conversion process, presenting it as an empty bureaucratic act—a wink-wink conversion (Brandes 2008); it might be real on paper, but not for the groom who wishes to live, as the Shas party promises, in a "state with a [Jewish] soul."

The commercial sparked outrage across the Israeli public sphere. Secular and liberal Jews, mostly but not exclusively Russian-speaking young adults, were the most outspoken, critiquing it as a politically motivated act of racial incitement. Shas quickly took the commercial off the air, but public outcry soon stimulated a lively and amusing spate of viral memes on the Internet. For example, an image titled "Shas and the City" (punning on *Sex and the City*) appeared along with screen grabs from familiar movies captioned with the refrain "Wait a minute, you're not Jewish?!"[15]

Interestingly, the secular critique of the television commercial led to online discussions about subsequent claims by female Israeli citizens from FSU backgrounds that they were subjected to similar discriminatory and racist comments from seemingly liberal, secular Jewish-Israeli men. In this sense, Shas's campaign, frequently written off by critics as religious

Figure 1.1 “Wait a minute, you’re not Jewish?!” Can I Get a Falafel Facebook page, 2013. Photo from *Star Wars: Episode IV: A New Hope* (1977), directed by George Lucas.

Figure 1.2 “Wait a minute, you’re not Jewish?!” Aviv Mussai Facebook profile, 2013. Photo from Titanic (1997), directed by James Cameron.

obscurantism, seems in fact to have tapped into more deeply rooted (if often unspoken) national anxieties about the invisible otherness of non-Jewish olim. That these anxieties focus on women comes as no surprise.

Often defined by the oxymoronic label “non-Jewish Jews” (A. Cohen 2006; A. Cohen and Susser 2009), non-Jewish FSU immigrants and their descendants undergo sociological processes that allow them to bypass the rabbinic gatekeepers of the national collective.[16] In so doing, they present the

Figure 1.3 "I'm not Jewish." "Frankly, my dear, I don't give a damn." John Brown Facebook Profile, 2013. Photo from *Gone with the Wind* (1939), directed by Victor Fleming.

Israeli state with a contradictory, illegible, and ambivalent identity. The proconversion policy that the state has elaborated since the 1990s is an institutional attempt to deal with the anxieties engendered by such an identity. This policy signals both a symbolic war against the ambivalence embodied in the "other within" (Bauman 1991, 1992) and, as we will see later, a practical struggle against the sociodemographic implications of the collective's blurred boundaries.

Nationalization

Beginning in the late 1980s, in anticipation of mass immigration from the FSU, the Israeli chief rabbis began to plan for the large-scale, systematic conversion of non-Jews. Their preparation was largely motivated by bureaucratic considerations—that is, by the desire to standardize and centralize an institutional field that had previously been managed in a rather unregulated and decentralized manner. "We realized we had a problem," a former assistant of Rabbi Bakshi Doron, then chief Sephardic rabbi, told me, "and we realized that we wanted to solve the problem systemically, so that not every random group of municipal rabbis would convert whoever showed up on their doorstep. We wanted to put things in order."

The state took the first substantive steps toward bureaucratization in 1995, when it created the nationwide Conversion Administration (Min'hal Hagiyyur), which reinstituted the special rabbinic conversion courts (previously established by Rabbi Goren) and standardized halakhic and administrative requirements. It was decided that the court would only receive conversion candidates after they had studied in one of the conversion ulpans recognized by the Conversion Administration, and only after their progress had been assessed by the court representative. These new measures initially involved the service of nongovernmental civic agencies, in particular the Zomet Institute (*zomet*, a Hebrew acronym for "Teams of Science and Torah"), which ran the Conversion Administration for four years. The bill for this work, to be sure, has always been covered by the state conversion budget—which increased over a decade to annual amounts numbering in the tens of millions (A. Finkelstein 2013:10).[17]

The state was quick to legitimate the new Conversion Administration by drawing on a national logic. The issue of conversion, then, was nationalized in two senses: first through the state's bureaucratic appropriation of processes that had not been entirely under its control, and second by anchoring these bureaucratic processes in national ideologies and moralities. This second sense of nationalization helps highlight the Zionist logics behind some of the many organizational reforms that have shaped the Conversion Administration. These logics were in play in 1995, for example, when the Zomet Institute, with the support of the rabbinate, appointed Zionist rabbis who favored relatively lenient approaches to conversion as conversion judges. These logics were also reflected in 2003 and 2004, when then prime minister Sharon decided to once again wrest authority over conversion matters from the regional rabbinic courts. To do so, he placed the revitalized rabbinic conversion courts under the auspices of the new Conversion Administration (Ma'arach Hagiyyur) within the Prime Minister's Office, appointing Rabbi Haim Druckman—a leading religious Zionist rabbi, known for his mamlakhti, Zionist approach to conversion—at its head.

This deliberate recasting of roles and institutions signaled an ideological attempt to subject the halakhic issue of conversion to what state officials perceived as a national calling pertaining to the entire collective. As previously noted, already in the 1970s Rabbi Goren had instituted similar reforms on a lower scale, signaling that Jewish conversion in Israel should be viewed through two frameworks: halakha and Zionism.[18] This is how Rabbi Haim

Iram, a senior staff member at Mali, described the rationale of these reforms in a religious Zionist online newspaper: "The reason that the Prime Minister decided to transfer the Conversion Administration to the Prime Minister's office was that they wanted to convey the message that the state has an interest in conversion, and that it's not only a concern of the religious population. . . . The point was not to detract from the power of the Chief Rabbinate, but rather to make clear that conversion was something that concerned the entire people of Israel" (Toker 2012).

The intensive involvement of national institutions and nonreligious government ministries in the administration of conversion should be understood in the same manner. Needless to say, these bodies did not marginalize or replace rabbinic authority. Israel's chief rabbi still oversees the halakhic dimensions of the official conversion procedure (see Amar 2006) and maintains authority over the head of the Conversion Administration with regard to all matters of halakha. But various nonreligious bodies now operate in concert (though often in tension) with rabbinic agents and manage the administrative dimensions of the conversion policy. These bodies include the Prime Minister's Office, the Jewish Agency, the Ministry of Immigration and Absorption, and the IDF.[19] The fact that institutions like the IDF and the Jewish Agency engage with the issue of conversion has imbued it with an indelible Zionist aura. Even the transfer of the Conversion Department from the Prime Minister's Office to the Ministry of Religious Services in 2014 did not undermine these symbolically potent Zionist connotations. After all, this move took place at a time when the ministry was controlled by the religious Zionist party Habait Hayehudi (lit. "the Jewish Home"), which explicitly promotes Zionist approaches to conversion. In early 2016 the Conversion Department was reincorporated into the Prime Minister's Office.

To be sure, these processes of nationalization have not been wholeheartedly embraced by the Israeli public. Far from it. The nationalization of conversion has consistently provoked intense opposition from both ultra-Orthodox groups, which acknowledge the problems of assimilation and intermarriage but blame the Conversion Administration for too aggressively pushing its national agenda, and liberal Orthodox groups, which demand a stronger, more direct pursuit of the national mission. Both critiques demonstrate that the "national" dimension of the national mission hardly indexes a consensus about a solution. Rather, the discourse of the national mission nationalizes precisely by drawing together various Zionist publics, both religious and secular, who agree about the urgent need for corrective intervention.

The Time Calls for Conversion

> Conversion is not only a human need for many of the new immigrants, it is a need of our times, a national, existential matter of the highest level.
>
> —David Bass, "Giyyur and the Acceptance of the Commandments: Theory and Practice"

In bureaucratic, public, and even academic discourse, the national problem of non-Jewish FSU immigration represents a state of emergency. It is not akin to what Carl Schmitt ([1921] 2014, [1922] 2005) and Giorgio Agamben (2005) describe as a "state of exception"—in which sovereign power places individuals outside the law while exposing them to "bare life."[20] Nor is it a state of emergency in the sense of a system of legal arrangements through which states grant themselves broad (some might say draconian) powers.[21] Rather, by "emergency" I mean to invoke what Raymond Williams and Michael Orrom (1954) would call a "structure of feeling"—a mood of crisis or lived experience of emergency to which Israelis, or Jews in Israel, have grown accustomed. As Danny Kaplan argues, in Israeli collective perceptions of time, circumstances of emergency are likely to be experienced as morally superior to ordinary life (Kaplan 2009:333); as such, they are ritualized and tend to resonate with the notion of the sacred.

The state of emergency described by Israeli officials, experts, rabbis, and even scholars of Jewish conversion is related to the unprecedented scope of real and potential intermarriage in the wake of non-Jewish FSU immigration. As a conversion official in the Ministry of Education explained to me, " [The national mission] is primarily 'our problem'; it applies to us all." Or as Eyal, a senior staff member at Mali, told me: "The State of Israel has a problem. My son and your son face a problem. I can't prevent my son from marrying his university colleague who is named Orit but could easily be a non-Jewish Sveta. That's scary. This is the Jewish state. Don't get mixed up here. No one should be confused by [the idea that Israel should be] 'a state for all its citizens,' or anything like that."

Eyal is a religious Zionist Jew. He knows I am a secular Jew but unhesitatingly assumes that I, like him, also conceptualize my son's potential romantic involvement with a non-Jew in terms of a "problem." On its face, his assumption makes sense. A recent survey (Itim 2015) shows the extent to which Jewish society in Israel—including secular Jews—cling to the principle of endogamy.[22] The survey illustrates the fact that endogamy is not only a halakhic principle in the service of the rabbinic establishment but also part and parcel of a broader Israeli ethos that seeks to preserve the boundaries of both the family and the imagined community (cited in Weiss 2001:55).[23]

During my fieldwork I occasionally heard conversion agents express their fear that the value of endogamy is growing increasingly weak among secular Jews, a sociological process resulting in the fragmentation of the Jewish-Israeli nation. "In a few decades," writes a rabbinic judge in the conversion court, "a huge chasm may eventually come to separate those utterly secular Jews who don't care about marrying non-Jewish olim (or their non-Jewish offspring), from religious and traditional Jews who refuse to marry such Israelis. Thus, the Jewish people is liable to split into two peoples that themselves do not intermarry" (Bass 2007:29).[24]

Similarly, while advocating for a more robust and comprehensively inclusive conversion policy during a parliament committee meeting, Yedidia Stern (vice president of the Israel Democracy Institute) brought up the fear of eventually having "two states for three nations" (Knesset 2013). "It is only a matter of time," he warned "before the grandson or granddaughter of any of us one day falls in love with Noam, with Tomer or with any other Israeli who won't be Jewish. If this is true, and my claim here is, indeed, based on research that 75% of Jews in Israel see assimilation in Israel as both a national and personal tragedy, then the Knesset must take care of that problem" (ibid.).

Given the central role of endogamy in Israeli society, the fears of intermarriage are neither foreign nor new in Israel's political discourse. Usually, these fears crop up in regard to potential romantic involvement between Jewish Israelis and their ultimate other—the Palestinians.[25] As mentioned earlier in the chapter, fears about intermarriage between Jewish-Israelis and non-Jewish volunteers in the kibbutzim clearly catalyzed Rabbi Shlomo Goren's first initiatives of the proconversion policy in the 1970s. In the context of mass non-Jewish FSU immigration, those fears reached unprecedented scope.[26]

Generally speaking, public discourse about non-Jewish FSU immigration revolves around the tropes of "danger," "risk," "threat," and "security." Tellingly, idioms of risk and danger also appear in the tense institutional relations between the Israeli state and the Feres Mura community. As Don Seeman (2010:187) documents, these immigrants are perceived as "risky populations" not only for public health (having historically been suspected by the medical system of having HIV) but also for Jewish genealogical purity.

"Nowadays," Rabbi Levin, a court representative, explained to me, "when each Jew is exposed to—I don't know if the correct word is danger—but yes, exposed to the possibility that the woman who might be the mother of his children is not Jewish, and that he might not even be aware of the matter, certainly not ahead of time, I think it is important to help people [non-Jewish olim] connect to the Jewish people, to whatever extent possible." The danger Rabbi Levin speaks of is internal. Unlike the Jewish-Palestinian conflict, which often generates a sense of an ultimate other, in this case the threat is internal—posed by the "other within" (Bauman 1991, 1992).

In the emergency discourses about state conversion, the danger implied by non-Jewish FSU immigration is often quantified. These discourses' point of departure is numerical: three hundred thousand non-Jewish immigrants currently in Israel. Although it is only an estimate, one that tends to fluctuate, this number has been widely adopted. In public and bureaucratic discourses, it represents a monstrous icon, one that epitomizes the essence of the national problem. Augmenting this number's ominous associations are demographic forecasts of the immigration, birth-, and conversion rates of citizens from FSU backgrounds, including the number of non-Jews arriving in Israel annually, the number of non-Jewish infants born each year to non-Jewish women, and the number of non-Jewish enlistees in the IDF each year. In an interview I conducted with Avigdor Leviatan, head of the conversion division in the Immigrant Absorption Ministry, he expressed this sense of existential danger by drawing on numerical data: "Statistically, there are more non-Jewish children born here every year than the number of people who convert. So, in fact, we have accomplished nothing. If our goal was to reduce the 300,000 non-Jews who have immigrated to Israel in the past twelve years [1995–2007] to the smallest number possible, we have failed. In other words, the numbers we are dealing with remained the same, and may have even grown a little because the number of children born is greater than the number of converts."

If the number three hundred thousand does not seem sufficiently monstrous as a statistical icon, inflationary demographic forecasts evoke scenarios of total chaos. "We did not learn how to deal with the conversion issue wisely," said former MK David Rotem, of the Russian-speaking immigrants' party Yisrael Beytenu, during one Knesset committee meeting. "Today we have 300,000 non-Jews, but a generation from now we will have 800,000, and in 40 years, 2.5 million non-Jews!" (Knesset 2007).

It is not surprising that a pessimistic demographic outlook like this features so prominently in the alarmist discourses surrounding conversion. Counting Jews is a common political practice in the modern and contemporary Jewish world. In many post-Holocaust Jewish contexts, demography has become a code word for existential anxieties regarding assimilation and the position of Jews as a minority group (Kravel-Tovi and Moore 2016).[27] In the Israeli context, demographic awareness touches on core issues of Jewish sovereignty and the Zionist project writ large. What has been called the "demographic demon" or the "demographic problem" enjoys nearly sacred status in multiple Israeli spheres. The importance assigned to demography is connected to collective sensibilities among Jews regarding their long history of persecution and political insecurity, primarily in Europe and the Middle East. These existential fears—the deep sense of being "few against many" (A. Cohen 2006:93–94)—feed some of the most profound political sensibilities in contemporary Israel.

As a result, demographic awareness is closely tied in Zionist discourses to the "Arab problem" (Zureik 2008) and to a key tenet of Zionist ideology, according to which the maintenance of a Jewish majority is a basic condition for the existence of a Jewish nation-state. The assumption is that without a significant majority of Jews, it will be difficult for Israel to justify the Zionist vision of Jewish hegemony in political, cultural, and economic Israeli life. Several fundamental policy issues, including the Palestinian state, immigration, birthrates, and the environment, entail national demographic considerations.[28] Furthermore, national demography is perceived as a security issue (Stypinska 2007) and therefore any discussion of it involves militaristic and quasi-sacred idioms. For example, high Palestinian birthrates within Israel and in the occupied territories are considered a threat, while reversing low Jewish birthrates and reducing the emigration of Jews from Israel are framed as causes worth struggling for. Non-Jewish FSU immigration joins the long list of demographic threats and positions conversion policy as another battle in the existential struggle over the future of the Israeli State.

In the case of conversion, the drama of demographic numbers extends to the words and narratives that frame these numbers and provide them with their existential weight. This sense of drama underwrote the rhetorical line of questioning posed to me in an interview I conducted with Rabbi Saul Farber—the director of the non-profit Itim, a civic organization dedicated to helping Jews and non-Jews alike cope with Israel's rabbinic bureaucracy: "What will happen to the state if it doesn't perform conversion? What will happen to it?" Similarly, Rabbi Moshe Klein, former deputy director of the Conversion Administration, described a parallel, existential demographic concern during a parliamentary committee meeting (Knesset 2007): "If we don't answer some essential questions about conversion in Israel now, we can close up shop, sing *Hatikva* [lit. "the Hope"; the national anthem], and ask ourselves in a few generations where we went wrong." In an interview with me he said: "The story of conversion is the story of Israel's future. It is as clear and simple as that. I anticipate large-scale intermarriage here and now; it is going to be a total disaster."

Rabbi Klein's words exemplify the extent to which the temporal language of emergency construes the present as a crucial historical moment demanding firm and quick action before non-Jewish demography decides Israel's fate. To the extent that *now* is the time to act, *later* simply becomes *too late*. As Danny, a conversion teacher at Mali told me: "From my point of view, conversion is the most pressing need we have now. It is a national project—no question about it. I see it as a national project because if we don't solve it, if we act like ultra-Orthodox Jews who sit and do nothing, then, in my opinion, very soon the situation here will become similar to what happened to the American-Jewish community."

The engagement with such a demanding present entails an acute awareness of the passing, if not the waste, of time—an awareness that is translated into a call to work immediately in the here and now. This call construes non-Jewish FSU immigration as a time bomb and conversion as a race against time. "If, at the very beginning of the [FSU] immigration waves, we had known how to effectively confront the problem," Rabbi Or, a senior rabbinic judge in a conversion court explained to me during an interview, "we would be much calmer now, knowing that we already dealt with the substantial part of the problem. But we didn't: we didn't do enough; so much time has been wasted. It's a shame because there is so much work to be done." Like this rabbinic judge, Yair Tsaban, a secular, leftist politician and former minister of Immigrant Absorption, highlights the theme of lost time, explicitly invoking the idiom of mourning. As he told his audience during a public conference on conversion I attended in 2008: "If I were a religious person, I would rend my garments and "sit *shiva*" because there is no chance in the world of converting a significant proportion of the 280,000 [referring to the non-Jewish immigrants who did not identify as Christian]. Natural reproduction amounts to 4000 births every year, and the volume of Druckman's [state-sponsored] conversions is 1,200 per year [referring to FSU immigrants seeking conversion]."[29]

With these grave temporal and numerical images in mind, politicians, state functionaries, policy makers, rabbis, and other advocates for state conversion attempt to moderate, if not utterly prevent, apocalyptic scenarios. Theirs is a national mission.

The Biopolitics of Belonging

Because the national problem of non-Jewish FSU immigration relates to the composition, size, and boundaries of populations that constitute Israeli society, I propose that it is a biopolitical problem. As noted in the introduction, my discussion of biopolitics is grounded primarily in the work of Michel Foucault, who describes the concept as definitive of the state's involvement in population management. Foucault ([1976] 1978, [1978] 2006) argues that since the eighteenth century, power began to be exercised in relation to biological dimensions of life (e.g., sex and health) that bear on broad population trends. In Foucault's writing, the biological and political dimensions intersect when life processes, or the biological existence of individuals, cumulatively affect the body politic.[30] The state develops scientific and administrative fields of knowledge that map the life processes of the population; statistics, demography, epidemiology, economy, and related fields put into practice technologies that intervene in these processes. The population, as a result, becomes both an object of knowledge and the means of intervention.

Biopolitics is central to my analysis of the national mission of conversion. The concept reinforces the fact that Israel's conversion policy is grounded in concerns about the future of the Jewish-Israeli population. It also highlights why state conversion intervenes in the lives of a very particular subset of Israeli citizens. Understood in these terms, conversion in Israel becomes intelligible as a process whose aggregate implications have motivated the state to intervene in it in the first place. At stake for Israel in its national mission are the life processes of non-Jewish citizens from FSU backgrounds, whose full national belonging the state desires. By theorizing conversion through the lens of biopolitics, we learn that national belonging (like the biological variables Foucault and his followers wrote about) represents a political but also biologically related variable in which Israel seeks to intervene. Hence, I propose that we think about the inclusive politics of belonging that organize Jewish conversion in Israel with recourse to a concept that more precisely captures the state's engagement with its population—what I call the *biopolitics of belonging*.

Foucault used the concept of biopolitics to underscore how the state manages individuals who are, simultaneously, legal subjects and biological creatures (Lemke 2011). Hence, the framework of the biopolitics of belonging allows us to show how legal parameters (in this case, of Israeli citizenship) and biological parameters (relating to the reproductive life processes of individual converts) intersect in order to explain why the Israeli state has transformed conversion into a national mission.

To illustrate the biopolitics of belonging implicit in conversion, let us examine the "attainable conversion" (*giyyur bar hasaga*) campaign jointly launched in 2014 by the Ministry of Religious Service and the Prime Minister's Office. Under the slogan "Today, more than ever—attainable conversion," the state appealed to non-Jewish FSU immigrants (over the radio, on Facebook, and on YouTube) and promised them conversion would be an achievable goal with a more considerate and lenient process. On government websites associated with the campaign, the exclusive appeal to citizens (and not, for example, to migrant workers, tourists, temporary residents, etc.) helped define its audience. Punning meaningfully on the slogan "attainable housing" (*diyyur bar hasaga*), popularly associated in Israel with the social protest movement of the summer of 2011, the government implied that Israelis should understand conversion, just like housing, as a public service that the state benevolently offers its citizens.[31]

That this campaign targeted Russian-speaking Israeli citizens was neither new nor in any way disguised. In fact, this was not the first Immigrant Absorption Ministry campaign presented in the Russian language and concentrated within Russian-speaking populated areas. Ten years earlier a ministry campaign, characterized by its slogan "Conversion—it's not what you think," had delivered similar proconversion messages in both Hebrew and Russian.

No less conspicuous than its Russian target was the "attainable conversion" campaign's unmistakably gendered nature. Although it made no explicit reference to gender, women were clearly the campaign's primary target.[32] Most campaign posters featured young women. The audio clips featured women, clearly Israeli citizens, describing in unaccented Hebrew their surprisingly positive conversion experiences. These women addressed other women (evidenced by their use of Hebrew pronouns and gender-inflected verb forms) and invited them to contact the Conversion Department.

The theme of national belonging typified the campaign narrative. The women it foregrounded were clearly troubled by their, and their future children's, problematic belonging. The conversion advertised offered them a tangible opportunity for full and secure belonging, stamped with the authority of the state. One campaign image displayed the face of a young woman set in the middle of a nearly completed puzzle, with only a few scattered pieces missing. The scattered pieces, set off to the side, bore captions expressing questions and doubts that, presumably, troubled the protagonist of the campaign: "How will my child integrate into society?" "Will everyone recognize me as Jewish?" "What will the family I create look like?" "What identity should I provide my child?" "Is our marriage recognized by the rabbinate?" "Will I be able to have a Jewish wedding?" In a poster displaying the face of another young woman, these questions were answered and the puzzle was completed. "I too am Jewish, no question!" read the caption, transposed onto the completed puzzle. Another version of these posters articulated the ultimate justification for conversion: "For belonging and for the sake of continuity." Underneath the young woman's image in the second poster, one found contact information: "Phone the call center [of the Conversion Department] and ask to speak to Shira."

During the radio campaign young women talked about familiar life scenarios that include dating, marriage, raising a family, and conversion: "I thought I was Jewish; we met a year ago and he asked me about conversion;

Figure 1.4 A poster from the "attainable conversion" campaign. Ministry of Religious Service and the Prime Minister's Office, 2014.

Figure 1.5 "I too am Jewish, no question!" Ministry of Religious Service and the Prime Minister's Office, 2014.

I mulled it over, decided to convert, and was surprised. We're marrying in a month. I've come full circle." And in another example: "I always felt Jewish, but when my eldest son was born, I felt I owed it to him to convert. I had fears, [but] I found a conversion track designed for people with full time jobs. I began the conversion process for the sake of my child, and completed it for my own sake. I've come full circle."

The campaign's call for conversion was explicitly addressed to those women whose non-Jewish (and potentially Jewish) status would impact the genealogical purity and demographic makeup of future generations. Grounded in the perception that motherhood is a national mission (Berkovitch 1997), the proconversion policy prioritizes women as objects whose potential conversion holds special significance. The conversion policy thus does not count women and men equally. As Rabbi David Bass argues:

> Apparently, the relative number of converts is actually very small. But here we should take note of something that is often overlooked: a great majority of converts (except those from Ethiopia) are young women, most of whom are single, approximately between the ages of 17–25. A quick calculation reveals *that about one out of three young, non-Jewish women from an FSU immigrant background comes to our courts to convert at some point during the three years prior to her marriage*. The Jewishness of the next generation is determined by the mother, of course, and not by the father; therefore, the conversion of young women is what will determine the future of the state. No one should underestimate the *conversion of about a third of the reproductive potential* of the non-Jewish immigrant population. This is quite an accomplishment.
>
> (Bass 2007:32)

Rabbi Israel Rosen, a senior colleague of Rabbi Bass in the rabbinic conversion court, also writes in gendered terms about the national mission of conversion. For him, proconversion policy can and should eradicate the "danger" embodied in non-Jewish women by channeling them into conversion, which will provide productive resources for the nation. In direct, if not overly blunt, language Rabbi Rosen speaks of non-Jewish women as land mines that must be swept away: "In Israel, every conversion is like a mine swept away; the foreign women will marry and have children, loyal citizens of Israel. It is a commandment to clear away such mines" (Rosen 2010:214). When a woman is no longer a threat, her Jewish reproductive potential actually makes her useful. As Rabbi Rosen declared during one parliamentary committee meeting: "For the national mission, I propose that we recruit the female converts. We should do this because of fertility issues. It is obvious to everybody that our main motivation is fertility" (Knesset 2010).

The conversion of women carries special urgency in the biopolitical scheme of belonging. It is in relation to women that the time—biopolitical time—calls for conversion. At this nexus between the political and the biological, the temporal scheme of emergency is fully realized: the hourglass of political demography overlaps with the biological clock, and together they index the importance of converting fertile women and adolescents before the national problem intensifies. While the biological clock begins to tick as women become less fertile (Amir 2005), what I call the *biopolitical clock* of conversion begins to tick much earlier, before and during women's reproductive years. The biopolitical clock is, essentially, a political clock that takes into account biologically related processes of a particular cohort. Above all, it takes into account the life courses of non-Jewish female citizens from an FSU background: those who are either born or grow up in Israel, become sexually active, build families, and produce the next generation. The following quote, taken from an interview with Eyal, an academic coordinator at Mali, illustrates the nature of the biopolitical clock: "The ultimate goal of the process, as I see it, is to convert the critical mass of the non-Jews who determine the future of the next generation. . . . There are young women here who surely will have kids. . . . It is they we need to look after; in essence, the moment we take care of this issue, Mali will have no more role to play."

Clearly, in addition to gender, age represents another important biological factor that conversion policy makers take into account. In particular, the biopolitical clock reveals to us the extent to which Israel's state proconversion policy rests upon an age-related logic, one in which the variable of age determines the possibility of reproducing the nation as Jewish. Indeed, most FSU immigrants and Israeli-born citizens with FSU backgrounds who seek conversion are young—thirty or younger. Seventy-five percent of young Israelis with FSU backgrounds seek conversion; among Israeli-born conversion seekers, the proportion of young people is even higher—98 percent (Fisher 2015:27).

Informed by this age-related logic, the Conversion Administration has made a number of attempts in recent years to establish conversion programs in boarding schools and high schools known to have a large percentage of FSU students. In addition, over the last few years more advocates for conversion (especially liberal Zionist rabbis) have called on the state to develop conversion tracks for minors (that is, boys and girls before their Bar and Bat Mitzvah, at ages thirteen and twelve, respectively)—for example, in the framework of summer day camps run by the Ministry of Education.[33] The focus on minors is informed by the lenient halakhic requirements pertaining to them. According to halakha minors have yet to develop satisfactory judgement and are hence not required to accept the commandments as a condition for their conversion. In the context of the national mission the call to convert children constitutes not only an ingenious halakhic detour around the most complex barrier to conversion; it also simultaneously facilitates the conversion of those whose future life courses will significantly impact the composition, size, and character of the Israeli population.[34]

The proconversion policy is a new addition to the older and more established domains of Zionist biopolitics: aliyah and pronatalism. Israel's aliyah policy has played a key role in shaping the life of Jewish-Israeli society as an immigrant-settler society (Kimmerling 2004) that relies on Jewish newcomers to maintain ownership over the land (Yonah 2005; Yuval-Davis 1996).[35] The pro-aliyah policy is foundational to Israel's self-perception as a "national home for the Jewish people" (Lustick 2011). Israel's pronatalist policy is organized by a similar (though generally less explicit) Zionist logic. Pronatalism in Israel is rooted in a religious perception of the Jewish family's centrality, in religious definitions of Jewish kinship, in security-oriented calculations about the need for soldiers to defend the country, and, more generally, in the demographic consciousness that has historically been an inherent aspect of Zionism and of the Jewish state (Berkovitch 1997; Kahn 2000; King 2002; Portugese 1998:34; Schiff 1981).

The biopolitical dynamics of Israel's conversion policy highlight how, since the mid-1990s, the state has consolidated conversion into a third component of its Zionist population policy. As Susan Kahn (2000) suggests, this component had always existed as a hypothetical, and comparatively marginal, tool of Jewish Zionist policy. "Jewish citizens of the Jewish state," Kahn writes, "come from only three places: from immigration, from conversion and from Jewish mothers. Since immigration is unpredictable and conversion hotly contested, Israeli Jewish women are left as the primary agents through which the nation can be reproduced as Jewish" (ibid.:4).

I make the case that in the context of mass immigration from the FSU, Israel instrumentalized what had previously been a hypothetical means of population regulation into a more concrete and elaborated policy route. While Kahn traces the role of the Ministry of Health's regulations on medically assisted reproduction in "making Jews for the Jewish State" (ibid.:76), this chapter exposes an identical policy logic in the field of state conversion.

As Many as Possible

During an intersession break of the conversion court, Rabbi Naftali, a rabbinic judge, shared an anecdote with his two colleagues, Rabbi Levy and Rabbi Yosef: "Usually, people invite me to speak about conversion. Several weeks ago, I was invited to speak about fertility. At first, I had no idea what to talk about. But later I thought to myself, 'oh well, what's the difference really? In both cases we are devoted to making as many Jews as possible.'" All three judges burst into laughter; I laughed too.

In this private, backstage moment, the judges laughed because Rabbi Naftali's anecdote clearly exposed the reproductive logic of the conversion policy. The humor lay in the phrase "as many as possible"—an expression with which the rabbis seemed familiar. They likely heard the phrase at any number of staff or government meetings. As Arik, a senior employee at Mali told me in an interview: "every governmental meeting will repeat this phrase: 'to convert as many people as possible.'" Or they might have heard it at the meeting of the Committee for Immigration, Absorption and Diaspora Affairs in 2005 (Knesset 2005b), where Ofir Pines, a Labor (*Ha'avodah*; lit. "the Labor") MK and the minister of the interior, declared: "It is a national interest to convert as many as possible. . . . [Conversion] serves the collective desire of all—religious and secular, Orthodox and non-Orthodox—to preserve and strengthen the Jewish majority in the State of Israel. . . . Ultimately, the rationale of this state is to be a Jewish and democratic state, and it is our most legitimate right to try and preserve Jewish hegemony and the Jewish majority in this state."

These pervasive numerical discourses regarding conversion did not escape the critical attention of Haredi communities. For example, in *Yated Ne'eman*, a daily newspaper identified with a number of ultra-Orthodox communities, columnist Jonathan Rosenblum equated the state's attempt to convert "as many as possible" with cutting corners in rabbinic procedures. He wrote: "The very idea of setting numerical goals for conversion, as Sharon did, and as his successor Ehud Olmert has indicated he will continue to do, represents an inherent contradiction to *geirus* [giyyur]. Each full-hearted commitment by a non-Jew to attach him or herself to the Jewish people and to accept upon him or herself the yoke of mitzvos [commandments] represents an amazing exercise of individual free will. Free will, by its very nature, cannot be subjected to numerical quotas or some bureaucrat's time table" (Rosenblum 2006; italics mine).

Because converting as many as possible defines the aims of Israel's pro-conversion policy, most conversion agents I met during my fieldwork understood this policy as a resounding failure, a grave shame. Indeed, over the past decade the public, bureaucratic, and academic engagements with state conversion have focused intensely on the troubling gap between the policy's numerical goals and its results: How can one explain these poor results? How can one account for the fact that only a small fraction—some 23,000 people (1996–2013), comprising only 7 percent of the non-Jewish FSU immigrant population—have converted, and around half of those who began the process (some 50,000) dropped out (Fisher 2015:26)? Even if we focus on those cohorts understood as highly predisposed toward conversion (i.e., women, youth, and those with some Jewish background), as opposed to the entire non-Jewish FSU population, this percentage remains low.

Israel has devoted a great deal of effort and many institutional resources to determine the root of the problem. Are non-Jewish immigrants simply uninterested in conversion? Perhaps these poor outcomes are the result of the Conversion Administration's inefficiency or maybe the unrealistic demands of the rabbinate (M. Finkelstein 2013:6–8). If non-Jewish immigrants are simply uninterested, is this due to the sociological conversion that provides them a sufficient sense of belonging, thus rendering conversion unnecessary (see also Yakobson 2010), or is it due to the immigrants' deep aversion to both religion and state intervention in their private lives?[36]

The sensitivity about the low conversion numbers has also helped sour the relationships between various conversion institutions. Each institution has tracked its own numbers, and each one's agents have constantly blamed others for the poor results—a dynamic that has left most conversion agents angry, frustrated, and burnt out. Disputable as the numbers might be, they clearly remain well below expectations, and the vast amounts of money invested in the project only deepens the sense of failure (Ilan 2007). Various committees and state agents have sought to address the low enrollment numbers. The Halfon Committee, for example, an interministerial committee convened in 2006 with the purpose of discussing ways to increase the number of non-Jewish immigrant conversions, formulated practical recommendations, which for the most part were not implemented (see A. Finkelstein 2013:10–14; Knesset Research and Information Center 2008). And a few years later Israel's state comptroller carefully investigated the reasons behind "the low numbers of conversion" and provided his own critical report (Ettinger 2013).

In order to produce results, conversion officials developed a number of programmatic endeavors. The frenetic organizational changes I mentioned briefly in the beginning of the chapter, as well as the "attainable conversion" campaign I described later on, are prime examples of these endeavors. In addition, the state removed bureaucratic barriers thought to impede FSU immigrants from considering conversion. For example, state officials decided that every citizen and permanent resident could initiate the conversion process simply by joining one of the institutions certified by the Conversion Administration.

The selective nature of these endeavors to make conversion more appealing is sharpened when juxtaposed with the steps the government has taken to exclude certain legal categories of people from the conversion process. Temporary residents and tourists, for example, encounter a much more restrictive and obstructionist conversion bureaucracy. In fact, their conversion requires the authorization of a special committee—the Committee for Exceptional Cases of Conversion, which is notorious for its inefficient service and lack of transparency. This committee is composed of representatives of both secular institutions (the Ministry of Interior and the legal department of the Prime Minister's Office) and religious authorities (especially of the Chief Rabbinate). Some religious officials familiar with the work of this committee described to me an organizational culture, led by secular bureaucrats, of suspicion directed at temporary residents and tourists seeking conversion.[37] The committee members believe that applicants will often exploit conversion in order to receive citizenship, including the economic and civilian benefits for which new olim are eligible. Not surprisingly, the work of the committee reinforces a highly stratifying logic, establishing the greatest barriers to citizens from the third world or developing countries. As one of the court representatives told me, half-jokingly: "The worst is to be Romanian. You definitely don't want to be a Romanian if you're applying for conversion." The Shin Bet security agency acts as an additional gatekeeper, intervening in the conversion processes of those deemed to present security concerns or of those from "sensitive populations," including the rare cases of Palestinian citizens of Israel who seek conversion. Clearly, the state prefers to convert as few Arabs as possible.

In contrast, in order to further encourage the conversion of as many non-Jewish citizens as possible, the state has removed financial barriers, fully subsidizing the conversion process. Prior to the 1970s, before the state regulated the preparation process for conversion, the financial burden fell on conversion candidates, who had to hire their own private tutors. But since the end of the 1990s conversion candidates have enrolled in state-funded conversion prep courses (involving five hundred hours of study, including excursions and Sabbath weekends in hostels). For many years Mali required minimal tuition payments, but over the past two years costs have been completely subsidized.[38] Fees for the Ministry of Education's course are also small, as they are for the classes offered by non-profit organizations authorized by the state to prepare converts. As a senior official in the Immigrant Absorption Ministry told me during an interview in 2007: "We made a decision to fund everything. On average, the State of Israel covers the costs of NIS 4000–5000 per student, and the student pays nothing."[39] For a time, the state even substantially subsidized conversion preparation for citizens who requested private tutoring (e.g., celebrities who did not want to expose their non-Jewish identities and people with learning disabilities). In a state whose public education system suffers from constant budgetary limitations, from the state school system through the higher education system, the fully subsidized nature of conversion preparation is remarkable.

In addition, in 2005 the state cancelled the fee converts had previously paid to the rabbinic conversion courts. The state has thus distinguished conversion from many other administrative services for which Israeli citizens are required to pay, from the issuing of ID cards, passports, and driver's licenses, to the management of changes in personal status such as marriage and divorce. In the case of FSU immigrants, who might still be dealing with the challenges that come with immigration, this package of economic incentives should not be underestimated.[40]

The institutional effort to produce results is further augmented by marketing campaigns like the one mentioned earlier. The Jewish Agency and various aliyah agencies sometimes approach immigration candidates in their countries of origin, before they leave for Israel. The army also reaches out to non-Jewish soldiers (sometimes even before they are enlisted), offering them the opportunity to participate in the IDF conversion track. "I market the program," Eyal, coordinator of class recruitment at Mali, told me. "Yes, and I'm not ashamed to say it. I do it very aggressively. For example, we get into immigrants' Hebrew language schools and talk about our program. We go to concerts and hand out booklets. We distribute pamphlets in mailboxes in areas known to be populated by Russian immigrants."

Rabbi Rosen articulated a similar marketing strategy: "The campaign needs to be marketed not only in the Russian-speaking media, to which the Russian youth are indifferent, but also in Hebrew. The Jewish neighbor or employer will be our missionary, and I'm not ashamed to use such crass language given these emergency times. The heart of the campaign should be: 'come one and all! You can convert in Israel! You are loved and wanted here!'" (Rosen 2006:37).

Political bodies, civic associations, rabbis, and policy researchers associated with liberal Zionist religious groups have long claimed that these institutional initiatives are insufficient. Their central argument is that those in charge of these initiatives have already forfeited their national mission: that the state only feebly embraces and hesitantly enacts this duty, that politicians make faint declarations instead of boldly appealing to the immigrant public, and that the chief rabbis have not really mustered the courage to push back against the halakhic stringencies that restrict the fulfillment of the national mission.

In line with this critique, several religious civic bodies have attempted in various ways to reform the Conversion Administration. In doing so, they have hoped to loosen both bureaucratic and halakhic barriers to conversion, thereby encouraging non-Jewish FSU immigrants to undergo the process. This was the impetus behind the Conversion Law—a parliamentary initiative to demonopolize the special conversion courts' authority over conversion by including municipal rabbis who would be allowed to establish local conversion courts (operating alongside the extant conversion courts).[41]

Equally concerned about the low numbers of converts, Itim and the Israel Democracy Institute jointly proposed to secure conversion through primary legislation and to authorize senior rabbis who would work with the rabbinate to conduct conversion (Stern, Farber, and Caplan 2014). Similar numerical concerns were reflected in the 2014 establishment of the Conversion Order (Tzav Giyyur)—a coalition of organizations, rabbis, and religious activists united under the shared conviction that "the scope of halakhic conversion in Israel can and must be broadened in a way that is inclusive and accepting" (Tzav Giyyur Facebook page 2014). Tzav Giyyur seeks to "shake off the Israeli public's indifference" to the failure of conversion policy (ibid.). Its call for public mobilization is reflected in its name, which plays on the expression *tzav giyyus* (the Israeli military's call-up order), thereby construing conversion policy as a collective, national responsibility. In the same spirit, the Hiddush (a Hebrew acronym for "Freedom, Religion, and Equality") association called on the public, on the eve of the Shavuoth holiday,[42] to write personal letters to Prime Minister Benjamin Netanyahu, asking him to pressure the rabbinate to open up the gates of Judaism.[43] Probably the most dramatic of all initiatives was the establishment, in summer 2015, of a network of alternative, privatized rabbinic conversion courts operating outside the framework of the Chief Rabbinate. Under the name Halakhic Conversion (*Giyyur Kahalakha*), a double entendre in Hebrew meaning both "according to halakha" and "proper conversion," this court began conducting conversion, primarily of pre-Bar-Mitzvah-aged children and non-Jewish FSU immigrants. All of these initiatives have been backed by people and agencies that oppose the extant state conversion policy precisely because they embrace the idea of the national mission. They believe that, in its current form, conversion policy subverts its own goal of converting as many as possible.

The trope of "as many as possible," I would contend, generates what we might understand as a nationally informed missionary spirit. This spirit differs from the well-documented missionary characteristic of Christian or new religious movements. Shaped by specific Jewish and Israeli sensibilities, the missionary spirit of Israel's conversion policy is implicit, subtle, and discreet. It is derived from national concerns about the nature and boundaries of the Jewish-Israeli collective rather than investment in the religious subjectivity of newcomers.

As mentioned earlier, Rabbi Rosen implicitly sensed the crassness of the word *missionary*. Indeed, the term sounds awkward in the Jewish-Israeli context. Yet its absence from the conversation discourse conspicuously marks its presence. Conversion agents may mention the term and discuss it, but they do so apologetically and in a self-deprecating manner. Their discomfort is palpable. As Dr. Rabbi Shaul Farber from Itim conveyed to me: "At the first session of the forum for conversion in the Prime Minister's office, I asked the following question: 'do we or don't we want to be missionaries?' I've still not received an answer to this question." I asked him what he thinks the right answer is, and he told me: "I believe people want to missionize, but they refuse to admit it."

This sensibility stems from the confluence of two cultural and historical dynamics. The first is the fear of, or at least ambivalence toward, religious missionizing—sentiments structured deep in Jewish self-conceptions (M. Cohen 1982; Polish 1982).[44] The second is a concern over the issue of cultural missionizing to immigrants by the Israeli state—specifically, the fear of falling back into the paternalism that shaped the early years of Israel's immigrant absorption enterprise. With these sensibilities in mind, it is not hard to understand why conversion agents attempt to avoid connotations of missionizing. One sees this avoidance, for example, in the concerns of Colette Avital, a former MK who, in her capacity as the head of the Committee for Immigration, Absorption and Diaspora Affairs, acknowledged that "the problem, and we discussed it more than once in this committee, is the fear of being perceived as missionaries" (Knesset 2005a). It is also not hard to understand why conversion agents favor subcontracting with nonreligious mediators (such as the Ministry of Immigrant Absorption) in order to disseminate conversion programs. As Rabbi Rosen explained to me, "Spreading conversion must not be the job of the Rabbinate, since the halakha forcefully objects to missionary tendencies. However, there is no problem with public organizations that tell those living in Israel: 'Come and convert.'"

The Social Production of Care

"You are loved and wanted here!"

—Israel Rosen

In his influential book *The Social Production of Indifference*, Michael Herzfeld (1993) addresses the manifestation of indifference in state institutions. The indifference that interests him is not comprehensive or total. On the contrary—it is inherently selective. Its boundaries are determined in accordance with the boundaries of the imagined community, mirroring exactly those points where national, bureaucratic taxonomies demarcate "self" from "other." Unlike the compassion expressed to those produced as self, the indifference to the plight of those produced as others fosters tyrannical national taxonomies that function brutally against those who are misplaced. As he writes: "It [bureaucracy] is a resistance to the dangerous powers that rise from categorical ambiguities. This is where we begin to discover the conceptual link between insiders who are not quite 'of us,' the usual victims of bureaucracy, and outsiders who have to be treated as though they might become 'of us' and who must therefore be made victims—if this is not too strong a word—of oppressive hospitality" (Herzfeld 1993:67).

Non-Jewish FSU immigrants are both insiders who are "not quite 'of us'" and outsiders who "have to be treated as though they might become 'of us.'" The biopolitical dynamics of belonging targeted at them can be understood, in Herzfeld's terms, as an extreme, overenthusiastic, missionizing, and even oppressive form of hospitality. Some claim that this aggressive hospitality begins in the FSU, where the aliyah agencies work tirelessly to encourage the immigration of those eligible under the Law of Return (Avineri 2007); it then continues in Israel, as the state invites non-Jewish FSU immigrants to convert instead of allowing them to remain as they are (see Zhensker 2014).

What secular liberal Jews in Israel characterize as an offensive effort to force immigrants into the religional fold, conversion agents perceive as a morally justified mission undertaken on behalf and for the benefit of those immigrants. Indifference hardly characterizes the emotions underlying their sense of mission. Furthermore, the state mobilizes this missionizing discourse to combat public Israeli indifference. The goal in employing this moral discourse is the social production of compassion, commitment, and care regarding the national problem and toward non-Jewish olim themselves. "You are loved and wanted here!" wrote Rabbi Rosen in a religious Zionist, right-wing journal, thus distilling—both descriptively and prescriptively—the emotional and moral core of the conversion project.

Why does Rabbi Rosen "love" non-Jewish FSU immigrants? Why are these immigrants worthy of his (or more broadly, of the state's and society's) love? The answers to these questions relate to the moral economy that inspires conversion's biopolitics of belonging. This moral economy conceptualizes non-Jewish FSU immigrants not only as subjects of return and

Jewish solidarity but also as worthy Israeli citizens who are morally entitled to Jewish belonging and recognition in and by the Israeli state. Israel, meanwhile, is given the opportunity to construe itself as a good, generous, grateful, and ultimately moral Jewish state.

I heard the specific articulations of this moral economy from many rabbis and conversion agents throughout my fieldwork. To begin with, so this logic goes, non-Jewish immigrants deserve a lenient and friendly conversion process, facilitated and subsidized by the state, because they are related through kinship ties to the Jewish people. As mentioned earlier, many of them have Jewish ancestors, and some of them are even considered "the seed of Israel" (*zera Yisrael*)—a halakhic category describing the offspring of Jewish fathers and grandfathers, which various halakhic arbiters have interpreted as permitting more flexibility with respect to conversion requirements. This halakhic concept reinforces the importance of return in Jewish and Israeli morality: the idea that Jews have an unlimited burden of responsibility for all the dispersed and lost parts of the family. This burden falls on the nation and, therefore, on the state that strives to effectively represent it in political terms.

In addition, these non-Jewish immigrants deserve the state's efforts because they suffered as Jews in the Soviet Union. In this sense, their conversion draws on a shared history of suffering and is therefore construed as a required moral act of Jewish solidarity. If anti-Semitism, communism, and the Soviet terror took little note of halakhic boundaries, so the argument goes, why should the Jewish state enforce them now? To the extent that these immigrants sought refuge from a political regime that coerced them into assimilation, intermarriage, and identity loss, they are not considered responsible for, or guilty of, their predicament. Hence, they should be treated as "modern conversos [*anusim*]" (Lavie forthcoming), and the Jewish state should redress the injustices of the Soviet state. "This is our national responsibility, our society's responsibility," according to Nehemia Citroen, the director of Mali. "We are responsible for these people. It's not their fault that they are not Jewish. It's not because they chose to abandon the faith but because of what happened in the communist countries during those years."

Many of the conversion agents I met employed kinship metaphors to describe the sense of responsibility that drives them. In giving voice to this genealogical imagination, they reflect the existential anxiety and forms of solidarity that so characterize the post-Holocaust Jewish experience. They also reflect the idea that kinship, as Don Seeman argues, "is broad and flexible enough to encompass multiple phenomenologies of belonging that include but may not be limited to genealogical continuity, shared ritual commitment and the sense of shared history or destiny that modern Jews frequently invoke" (Seeman 2013:62). For example, my interlocutors often spoke about "our brothers and sisters" or "our own flesh and blood." In the face of historical circumstances that arbitrarily determined who would remain a halakhic Jew and who would not, the conversion agents appealed to both the essentialist logic of biological relatedness and the historical, or mythical, story of the extended family. As Rabbi Iram, a senior staff member at Mali, explained to me: "What guides me are the words of Rabbi Druckman when he became the head of the Conversion Administration. He said, 'you need to think as if the convert is your cousin, your nephew, your brother. What would you do then?—That is exactly what you will do for the convert.'"

From the perspective of these conversion agents, kinship metaphors help frame conversion as an internal Jewish affair. It represents for them a project of return or a constitutive moment of the "ingathering of the exiles," as opposed to an outwardly directed missionary endeavor. As Benny Ish-Shalom, the chairperson of Mali, explained to me in an interview: "I do not see it as missionizing because I do not view these people as outsiders. They are not gentiles, as I see it. They are our brothers and sisters. Something happened during the course of Jewish history . . . intermarriage happens not only in Russia. . . . How do I know that I myself am not a descendant of conversos or of the Khazars?"

Apart from their Jewish ancestry or history, non-Jewish immigrants are often given credit for the fact that they have chosen to link their fates to that of the Jewish people in its homeland. They are presented as active and productive Israeli citizens (i.e., in social, economic, and national domains) who fulfill their civic obligations. The state's moral obligation to welcome the conversion of such immigrants is predicated to a large extent on ethnonational and republican notions of citizenship that require the state to give back to citizens who give themselves to it (Peled and Shafir 2005). Conversion, in this sense, represents a moral expectation based on mutual exchange between the state and its citizens.

Let us take for example Michael Kaplinsky, an Israeli citizen featured in a campaign by the Tzav Giyyur coalition mentioned earlier. While we never learn what Michael looks like, we know quite a bit about him from the advertising campaign: "Michael Kaplinsky, 24 years old from Netanya, son of a Jewish father. Born in Russia and made aliyah to Israel in 1998, served in the Israeli Navy, currently studies computer science at Ben Gurion University in the Negev. Michael wants to marry 22 year old Na'ama. Michael and Na'ama are unable to register for Jewish marriage with the Chief Rabbinate." This poster, titled "Michael, there's a place for you," shows the seat reserved for Michael at synagogue, in a row with other empty seats reserved for well-known public and political figures—all "kosher," religious Zionist Jews. Michael, the ad implies, is "one of us," and it would thus be both absurd and unjust for the state's rabbinic institutions to refuse to recognize him as Jewish. Michael seems to have done everything right, fulfilling all the middle-class Jewish-Israeli cultural scripts, both religious and secular: he served in the army, trained in a profession that will contribute to the Israeli economy, and wants to start a family with a woman who is clearly an Israeli Jew. The implied logic is that he deserves a lenient and friendly conversion, state services that ensure him full belonging—that reserve a place for him.

Because the routine moral system of exchange that binds Jewish-Israeli citizens to the Israeli state depends heavily on the highly masculine domain of military service, the Tzar Giyyur conversion campaign includes male figures like Michael. Alongside the young Russian women, Israel's "present and future mothers" featured in the "attainable conversion" campaign, Michael, the ex-soldier, represents another type of potential convert. Indeed, public discourses about conversion frequently highlight the figure of the soldier, especially the combat soldier (whether alive or dead). The heated debate over the burial of non-Jewish immigrant soldiers (that is, whether these soldiers can be given a halakhic burial within a Jewish military cemetery) is evidence of what the Israeli public conceptualizes as an imbalanced relationship between the state and its citizens—an intolerable gap between inclusion and exclusion, giving and receiving (see Yehoshua 2016).[45] In an address given during a Knesset committee meeting (Knesset 2007), MK Sophia Landver of the FSU immigrants' Yisrael Beytenu party reveals how the economy of sacrifice helps constitute the moral economy of conversion policy. The blessed memory of deceased soldiers, their love for the Israeli

Figure 1.6 "Michael, there's a place for you." Tzav Giyyur, 2014.

state, and the conversion policy they deserved but never had—all blend together in an address that resembles both a political speech and religious lamentation:

> During the war [the Second Lebanon War] I, together with the chair of Yisrael Beytenu and our other party members, visited almost every bereaved family. I must note that the soldiers who died during this war never complained about fighting, nor did it bother them that they had yet to complete the conversion process. They fought for the sake of Israel. Pavel Slutzker, a young man whose mother is not Jewish and whose father is, was killed in the war. The war also took the life of Piotr Ahutzky from Lod, whose mother is also not Jewish. Andrey Blodner of Rishon Le-Zion was killed, Yevgeny Tzimtiev was killed, and also killed was Dinis Lapidus of Haifa, whose mother Svetlana is not Jewish.

> When I entered her home, as the family was sitting shiva, I could not help but to weep with the family. They live in a small room. The boy had already undergone conversion, and before he fell in battle, he wrote a letter which ended up being his farewell address. He wrote that he had indeed undergone conversion even though throughout his entire life he had always felt that he was no less Jewish than his Jewish-born father. In his letter, he described how, both before and after conversion, he always felt that he was the same person who loves the state. He is glad he arrived in Israel, and that he immigrated to Israel because he loved the state. He wrote that he feels like every trail and road in this country belongs to him, and he feels like he belongs to the state. It is intolerable that these people fight for the State of Israel and afterwards must go through conversion under impossible conditions.
>
> (Knesset 2007)

In the framework of Israel's economy of sacrifice (Weiss 2014), Israelis demonstrate civic virtue when they enlist in the army and thereby give themselves over to the state, sometimes at the cost of their lives. It is difficult to imagine a higher form of civic belonging—a more precious gift to the state (Yuval-Davis 2007). In this context, the equation between citizens as soldiers and citizens as converts, and between giving to the state and the state giving back, resounds strongly. Conversion becomes a moral debt of the state (Kravel-Tovi 2014).

* * *

Like many policy agendas, Israel's national mission serves as a powerful political instrument (Wedel et al. 2005:37). Even though Israel has not yet accomplished its mission, the symbolic potency of this political instrument is extremely important. In both distilling and reconfiguring the nature of the relations between subjects, populations, and the state, it exposes fundamental principles of Jewish life in Israel. Driven by Zionist ideologies, the mission instrumentalizes the role of individuals in the ongoing, precarious production of Israel as a Jewish state. As will become clear in the following chapters, this instrumentalization enmeshes both conversion candidates and the state in tense but also highly creative entanglements.

The national mission is rooted in the efforts of state agents and institutions to take moral and national responsibility—for the sake of the collective, the future of the Zionist state, and the fate of its deserving citizens. In order to better understand this layered institutionalized effort, the next chapter focuses on those religious Zionist citizens and civil servants who take up the duty of speaking and acting in the name of religious Zionism, conversion, and ultimately the Israeli state.

TWO

State Workers

THE GREAT MAJORITY of conversion agents I met throughout my fieldwork identified as religious Zionists. Their dominance was reflected in the sociological makeup of government ministries and institutions in charge of conversion, as well as among the grassroots: volunteer rabbis and public figures, nonprofit associations, and the host families and communities that help candidates throughout the conversion process. To be sure, because Israel's conversion policy is Zionist at its core, secular Zionists often endorse it and even participate in it (from former prime minister Ariel Sharon to the few secular teachers employed by Mali). On the far margins of conversion institutions one can even find a handful of ultra-Orthodox Jews (e.g., rabbinic judges in the conversion court). For the most part, though, state-run conversion is strongly identified with religious Zionism.[1] In this chapter I tell the story of the national mission by focusing on its agents' religious Zionist identity.

Of course, the religious Zionist public, like other publics in Israeli society, is not homogenous. Religious Zionists speak in different ways about the state, halakha, religion, nationalism, and conversion. And I certainly do not mean to imply that the religious Zionist public uniformly embraces the calls of religious Zionist leaders to place conversion at the center of the movement's political agenda. Nor do I ignore the fact that ultra-Orthodox parties, and not the religious Zionist ones, have often gained control over key positions throughout the rabbinic bureaucracy.[2] Yet the work force that has established, driven, and maintained state conversion as a national mission for over two decades comes from the diverse ranks of this public.[3] That is, whatever the nuances of their individual political and religious orientations, conversion agents have worked for the national mission as a result of their religious Zionist commitments.

By calling attention to the religious Zionist identities of conversion agents, I aim to unpack the otherwise intangible concept of *state conversion agents* and to understand how and why members of this particular ideological group take upon themselves the work of embodying the morals and ambitions of the Jewish state. This approach coincides with the call, expressed in the anthropological literature on the state, policy, and government, to avoid restricting research to the abstract analysis of the state and to try, instead, to understand the cultural profile and political location of the actual people who embody it (Fassin 2013; Herzfeld 2005; I. Feldman 2008; Reeves 2014; Wedel et al. 2005).

I argue that by taking responsibility for state conversion and imbuing it with the sacralizing meaning of a national mission, rabbinic, educational, and political elites within religious Zionism rework their movement's distinct character. In light of volatile political circumstances that have disrupted the relationships between religious Zionist and state institutions, these elites use conversion as a means to remind their public of their commitments to the state and their defining ethos of giving to the state. Conversion becomes an organized opportunity for the movement to shore up that ethos. By placing the national mission of conversion on their movement's public agenda, these elites offer their public a constructive starting point for engaging with the burning question "Who are we?"

When religious Zionist rabbis, educators, and politicians describe conversion as a national mission, they in fact urge their community to dedicate itself to this mission. When they attempt to socially produce care for and commitment to the problems of non-Jewish immigrants, they appeal to the religious Zionist public's morality in an effort to mobilize it. And when they fail to fully achieve their goals, they reconsider the movement's future path. The question of who they are—what drives, defines, and differentiates religious Zionists as a community—continually emerges and reemerges throughout debates over state conversion.

By foregrounding this question in the context of public discussion of state conversion, these elites encourage members of the religious Zionist public to resume their ideological role as what Thomas Bernhard (cited in Bourdieu 1998:35) called "state persons," by which he meant "henchmen of the State" (ibid.).[4] As religious Zionists, conversion agents are part of a movement that attempts to fashion such subjects. But while Bernhard refers to people tainted by their subjugation to state institutions, I wish to emphasize the constructive, generative formation of religious Zionists as state persons. These persons are shaped by their ideological and moral commitments to the Jewish people, as well as the ideas of return and solidarity that underwrite Israel as a Jewish state. Thus, the institutional field of conversion is a site where the Israeli state allows not only non-Jewish FSU immigrants to work out the terms of their belonging to the state; it offers this opportunity also to religious Zionists—allowing them to reclaim their role as state persons.

The Hebrew term for "civil servant" foregrounds work (*avodah*, as in *ovdei medina*; "public workers" or "state workers"). The interrelated meanings of service and work suggest the entanglement of religion and nationalism for religious Zionists and the high value they place on working for the state, serving it, and even worshipping it. In religious and liturgical contexts, *avodah* means "service" in the sense of "ritual." For example, avodah is the name of the temple ritual and of a section in the Yom Kippur service, and the actual act of prayer is called "service of the heart" (*avodah shebalev*). In colloquial Hebrew, "service" is an important term within the Zionist lexicon regarding the relationship between state and citizens—referring mainly to the centrality of military service. By titling this chapter "State Workers," I wish to emphasize the substantial communal and individual effort that religious Zionists invest in conversion as a means of "doing good" (I. Feldman 2008:70)—in this case on behalf of the Israeli state, the Jewish people, and religious Zionism itself. Whether understood narrowly (salaried work) or more broadly (the investment of effort), the concept of work helps us understand how the institutional field of state conversion has become a religious Zionist workplace in both concrete and metaphorical terms. In that capacity, conversion provides an important arena for the religious Zionist community to do its own identity work—to serve the state while also working through some of the issues that define its symbiotic relationship with the state.

Following sociologist Philip Abrams ([1977] 2006), one can say that in order to define itself religious Zionism utilizes both the "state-system" (a system of governmental structures and institutional practices that endow the state with form) and the "state-idea" (the symbolic objectification of the state). These two aspects are intimately linked: by working within the state-system of conversion, religious Zionists work for the idea of a Jewish state.

In what follows, I trace the religious Zionist moral economy of conversion through an analysis of two ethnographic accounts: one of a crisis in my relationship with a rabbinic judge that I faced during fieldwork, and the other of a public conference on conversion. In doing so, I also analyze religious Zionist discourses of national responsibility and situate these discourses within the broader political and historical contexts that have shaped the religious Zionist relationship with the state. Of particular importance for me in this context are the political struggles over the future of the occupied territories and the competition of religious Zionists with the ultra-Orthodox for control over state rabbinic institutions, including control over conversion. I conclude the chapter by analyzing the "Druckman affair," an attempt by ultra-Orthodox rabbis to overturn longstanding conversions authorized by Zionist rabbis, including Rabbi Haim Druckman, then the head of the Conversion Administration.

Crisis of Representation

I liked Rabbi Cohen from the start. Candidates often called him "the nice judge." I could see what they meant. He really was nice: perceptive, attentive, always encouraging candidates after each correct answer, and never interrupting them midsentence (unlike so many of his colleagues). He was nice to me as well. His curiosity and open-mindedness made possible free-flowing conversations that I could by no means take for granted. Such conversations filled pages in my field notes and filled me with delight. During the fall and winter of 2005, a few months after the Gaza disengagement, I relished the opportunity to engage with a religious Zionist rabbi. Through our conversations, I could tell myself a story about a dialogue between the political left and right. For his part, he was acquainted with the academic world and—through me—had the opportunity to play up that part of his biography. "I am what the journalist Yair Sheleg would call 'The New Religious Zionist Jew'" (see Sheleg 2000), he once professed to me, using a term reflective of bourgeois religious Zionists' efforts to integrate into Israeli secular society. Our dialogue was complex, even tense at times. But most of the time, we managed to keep it going. In retrospect, I know that our conversation, like the entire research field of state conversion, was mediated by winks—half-smiles, things left unsaid, and exchanges loaded with multiple meanings.

My first day of fieldwork at the rabbinic court was exhausting. Memories of sentence fragments that had circulated the room during eight full hours of court hearings overloaded my brain. My hand throbbed from note taking. Luckily for me, I had come with a stiff-backed notebook. I wrote the last few pages of notes over a late lunch in a café just below the rabbinic court. In these pages I briefly described my first conversation with Rabbi Cohen at the end of the day. During our chat Rabbi Cohen confessed, half-smilingly, that when he first met me earlier that day, he thought Rabbi Yosef Shalom Elyashiv (a powerful ultra-Orthodox leader and halakhic arbiter) had sent me to spy on him in anticipation of the regional rabbinic court appointments committee's upcoming deliberations. He had recently applied to work there. Now though, he had concluded I was "alright." "For some reason, I trust you," he said. I half-smiled to myself as I wrote down his words. But as he spoke candidly with me about his work as a rabbinic judge, I lost sight of the fact that these smiles were never full ones. After all, he seemed so unguarded as he discussed the blinding invasiveness and the addictive sense of power that came with his job or the dynamics of teamwork on a panel and the petty politics surrounding the appointment of rabbinic judges. He also opened up about his gnawing fears that the conversion project would not solve Israel's dire demographic situation.

By and by, I forgot Rabbi Cohen's initial suspicions that marked the beginnings of our dialogue. During the months that followed, his suspicion would occasionally resurface, but it never influenced how much I valued his input. I felt grateful for my good fortune as an ethnographer, and I fell captive to the sense that we were engaged in an open conversation. Rabbi Cohen answered my questions between court sessions, voluntarily provided me with articles he had written on conversion, and informed me about public events that seemed relevant to my topic. He asked for my impressions of the conversion court's conduct and listened attentively when I shared my thoughts. I once joked, half-smilingly, that he was my best informant. I managed to set aside the fact that he once compared our relationship of confidentiality to that of a police officer and an informer. I also ignored, perhaps willfully, his panicked reaction when I asked to record his interview, and his quick rejoinder when I attempted to persuade him by explaining that a nonrecorded interview would be less precise and reliable: "Excellent, that's best." I was empathetic to his heightened alertness. It seemed like a reasonable response in light of the minefield in which he conducted his professional life. We eventually held the interview on a wintry Friday morning in February 2006, in the lobby of a hotel of his choosing, far from the rabbinic courthouse. I left my recording devise in my handbag.

A relationship of half-smiles conducted in a minefield, though, is a volatile one. In spring 2006 I participated in an academic conference at Ben-Gurion University of the Negev. During my talk I presented an ethnographic excerpt from the rabbinic conversion court, based on a discussion in which Rabbi Cohen had played a central part. Motivated by Rabbi Cohen's attraction to academic thinking, the dialogical climate of contemporary anthropology, and the relationship of mutual trust I thought we had created, I decided on my own accord to send him my conference paper. I considered him an excellent reader and a reflexive and critical insider, and I was curious to hear his views about my work. The following morning, when I opened my inbox and found an e-mail from him with a revised version of my paper attached, I realized I had made a serious mistake.

> *Basad* [an Aramaic acronym for "with the help of heaven"], 8 Nissan 5766
>
> April 6, '06
> Hi Michal,
> What you wrote is very interesting. Please find your paper attached with my corrections in the body of the text, marked with "track changes." I am sure you will not be offended by my remarks; after all, that is precisely why you sent me what you wrote. I have corrected the citations attributed to me in the body of the text. For lack of time, I have done only this, which I thought was very necessary; I hardly touched anything else, not even your interpretations of my words and what you concluded from them. Mostly, I have filled in parts of what I said to the convert's spouse (which were missing surely because of the speed with which you had jotted them down). Please do not pass on the text to anyone before making these corrections—this is important!

> As mentioned, apart from correcting the actual quotes, I didn't touch anything. It is certainly your prerogative to interpret the facts, including my own statements, and draw the conclusions you see fit, even when what you write conflicts with my own interpretations of my words. But I would like to say, in any case, for the record, that I do not always agree. If it is truly important for you, I will do my best to review your entire research project and comment on other matters. I would be glad to do so, especially in regards to those sections in which I am mentioned, like the part based on the interview with me. Naturally, errors may occur in an oral interview and I would like all things said in my name to be accurate. In any event, the text is very interesting, and I am sure you will advance in academia and go far.[5]

When I finished reading Rabbi Cohen's corrections, I realized that he had not intended his final sentence as a compliment. I looked closely at the red, track-changed sentences where he lengthened, shortened, deleted, and added statements from the rabbinic court discussion. The corrections I saw in the ethnographic text made me nervous. I tried to buy time. I knew that I could not accept Rabbi Cohen's revisions to my ethnography—for better or worse, it was my text. I drafted him an e-mail, which I never ended up sending, in which I tried to provide a nuanced explanation of my refusal. I wrote about the nature of field notes and anthropological representation, which, partial as they might be, still must be empirically grounded. I delicately rejected Rabbi Cohen's implicit assumption that he—from a remove of four months, and after thousands of words exchanged with scores of candidates—could more accurately represent the discussion that I had documented, within the limits of my ability, in real time. "We are not co-authoring a text," I ended.

I shared the story of my clash with Rabbi Cohen with colleagues and friends. They urged me to express empathy for his concerns and do what I could to avoid outright confrontation. Fieldwork, they reminded me, is an ambiguous gray area that always involves competing interests, the ongoing presentation of selves, and complex connections between strangers. I listened to them but knew that Rabbi Cohen and I no longer inhabited the gray zone that had thus far enabled our relationship.

During our phone conversation the next day, the words we exchanged were harsh and angry, even insulting. Rabbi Cohen demanded the right to censor quotes I attributed to him. I demanded he take responsibility for having spoken with me. He claimed ownership over an objective truth that had taken place "out there" in the conversion court and accused me of maintaining an a priori bias that had consciously led me to be selective while documenting court discussions. In response I claimed ownership over the ethnographic text and insisted that I had undertaken research in good faith and with integrity. He argued that the text in question, if published, would impede his professional advancement, because it could be interpreted by ultra-Orthodox readers as illustrating that he had knowingly authorized conversions of insincere converts. For my part, I offered textual solutions to camouflage his identity, but I insisted on my autonomy in the production of the ethnographic text.

When our conversation reached an impasse, Rabbi Cohen turned to a nationalist, statist rhetoric. He spoke in the sacred voice of "the state." His authoritative tone echoed, in my mind, his positions of power: as a rabbinic judge accustomed to wielding power (even if politely and gently), as a member of the religious Zionist elite, and as a gatekeeper of my research. I recognized in his words the price anthropologists can pay when they conduct research in nexuses of power. At the time, I took offense to his comments; but in and of themselves, they interested me little. The nationalist rhetoric he embraced contained a more illustrative insight. That is, despite its belligerence, it also revealed a profound ethnographic truth about Rabbi Cohen's role as a state person: he saw himself as an embodiment of the national mission.

In his distress Rabbi Cohen attempted to recruit me for the national mission of conversion. He appealed to my heart. He addressed me as an Israeli Jew, as someone he had seen shed a tear during more than one conversion ceremony. He asked me to consider Israel's well-being at what he described as "the nation's decisive moment." He even charged me with endangering the entire conversion project and sacrificing the State of Israel on the altar of my academic career. By employing this grand rhetoric, he helped confirm the analytical productivity of my earlier, somewhat intuitive choice to ethnographically explore the state via those who claim the moral right to speak and act in its name. His reaction augmented what I had already begun to comprehend about the double bind that characterizes the work of conversion agents. While Rabbi Cohen could not see it through the phone, when he spoke about my ethnographic work in terms of the nation's destiny, I broke out in a half-smile.

Rabbi Cohen spoke to me as a state person. He possessed this identity in two senses: institutionally, he worked on behalf of the state, and ideologically, he invested himself in goals he believed benefit the Jewish state. Like many other members of the religious Zionist elite, he understood himself as shouldering the weighty responsibility of the national mission.

In our conflict, he tested me to see whether I would shoulder the national mission as well. He discovered I would not. Unlike Rabbi Cohen, I am neither interested nor able (as an ethnographer or an Israeli citizen) to speak in the name of the converting state. My ethnographic encounter with Rabbi Cohen reveals the relationship that he, as a religious Zionist, has had with two significant others: secular Jews and ultra-Orthodox Jews. As a secular person, I betrayed his trust in the partnership that he envisioned between religious Zionists, who carry out the conversion project, and secular Zionists, who support it. He understood my ethnographic representation as a suggestion that religious Zionists mishandled conversion—a representation that could supply ultra-Orthodox readers with the ammunition needed to undermine it. In the vignette with Rabbi Cohen, Rabbi Elyashiv (who was still alive then) embodied ultra-Orthodox Judaism's critical stance against state conversion. He also signified the ascendant political power of ultra-Orthodox Judaism, whose representatives have gradually displaced religious Zionists from state rabbinic institutions since the end of the 1970s. Some of the political complications I describe in this chapter, as well as some of the ethnographic entanglements I relate in the ones that follow, emerge from the fraught relations between religious Zionists and the ultra-Orthodox. The former have not managed to dismiss the gaze of the latter.

I could have used the account of my relationship with Rabbi Cohen in the context of a broader methodological discussion about ethnographic work. This section's subheading, "Crisis of Representation," refers to both the literal crisis that emerged in my fieldwork and the dilemmas of ethnographic representation in general. By gesturing toward these dilemmas, I aim to wink at an academic audience familiar with the recent history of anthropology. But my encounter with Rabbi Cohen is relevant to more than just methodological discussions. In fact, it serves as an informative ethnographic point of departure for this chapter. In particular, it fleshes out the story I wish to tell about the agents of the Israeli state's conversion policy and their ideological predispositions to become state persons.

Religious Zionists and the State

Among the significant factors that distinguish religious Zionism from ultra-Orthodoxy are the two groups' divergent attitudes toward both the Zionist project and the State of Israel. Religious Zionism—as a political movement, an idea, and some would even say, an emotional decision (Sheleg 2004a)—came into being in Europe in 1902 with the establishment of the Hamizrachi (lit. "the Eastern") faction in the Zionist Federation. Hamizrachi's leaders, including Rabbi Isaac Jacob Reines, were bona fide Orthodox Jews. However, they distinguished themselves from other Orthodox Jews by their willingness to participate in the political Zionist project. Non-Zionist Orthodox rabbis attacked Hamizrachi rabbis for operating within a secular organization led by apostates and sinners and for lacking the patience to wait for the messiah. Hamizrachi activists, for their part, justified their position in both pragmatic and spiritual terms: they argued that joining the Zionist movement could push against the trend of Jewish secularization and that they sought to precipitate a spiritual revolution among the Jewish people.

Some proponents recognized the practical value of Jewish political revival—especially as a safety measure against anti-Semitism. Some viewed settling the land as a religious commandment. Others believed that the hand of God, which moves the wheels of history, also pushed forward the Zionist national redemption (Schwartz 2009). By choosing to collaborate with secular Jews, the Hamizrachi movement consecrated the value of national unity and positioned itself as a necessary bridge between non-Zionist religious Jews and secular Zionists. During its early stages of political formation, religious Zionism developed the two sets of features that have defined its agenda to this day. The first is its simultaneous, conflictual commitment to nationalism, modernity, and halakha, and the second is its triadic commitment to the land of Israel (*eretz Israel*), the people of Israel (*Am Israel*), and the Torah of Israel (A. Cohen 1998).

The sanctification of national unity and cooperation with the Zionist project remained central to religious Zionism, even as the movement developed offshoots that distanced themselves from the original politics of the Hamizrachi faction. These core Zionist commitments were evident, for example, in the 1921 establishment of the Chief Rabbinate as a supreme unifying rabbinic institution for all Jews in the land of Israel (Palestine)—a move instigated by Rabbi Abraham Isaac HaCohen Kook, a prime religious Zionist leader. They were reflected as well in the 1922 establishment of Hapoel Hamizrachi (lit. "the Eastern Worker") movement—a religious Zionist labor movement that adopted the socialist values of secular Zionism within a religious framework. The fact that from the state's establishment in 1948, religious Zionist parties represented integral parts of all Labor Party–led governments also reflected such national commitments.

During the first two decades of statehood, Mafdal (a Hebrew acronym for the "National Religious Party") garnered marginal government roles and functioned chiefly as gatekeepers of religious issues. Generally speaking, classic religious Zionist politics were pragmatic and compromising. Instead of advancing an independent agenda, the political leadership of religious Zionism constructed itself as a partner within the nation-building project. They aimed at encouraging their members' civic participation in the Israeli national project as it was defined by the politically moderate and secular elites of the state.

Unlike ultra-Orthodox groups, religious Zionists actively participate in Israeli civil religion (memorial days, Independence Day, and other national symbols and holidays), they enlist in the army, and they live alongside secular Israelis in mixed neighborhoods.[6] Even the aesthetic code adopted by religious Zionist men (knitted skullcaps [*kippot*; plural of *kippah*] and thin or no beards) sets them apart from ultra-Orthodox men (often identified by black cloth skullcaps and hats, thick beards, black suits, and white shirts) and, in this sense, is closer in style to the aesthetic code of secular Jewish-Israeli men.

What has nourished the religious Zionist partnership with secular Zionists has been the movement's favorable theological approach to the Jewish nation and the State of Israel. Religious Zionists understand Am Israel as a unified spiritual entity that both demands and permits political collaboration for the sake of collective goals. To be sure, religious Zionist attitudes toward the state have never been monolithic or static, and the ideal of Israel as a Jewish state has always encompassed a variety of meanings.[7] Nevertheless, the mainstream of religious Zionism has always maintained a position that accords religious meanings to the Jewish state. This position has underwritten a variety of messianic interpretations, according to which the state realizes redemptive biblical prophecies (e.g., "the blooming of the desert," "the ingathering of exiles," and "the return to Zion") and constitutes a necessary evolutionary stage on the road to redemption (Ravitzky 1996). The prayer for the well-being (*shlom*; lit. "the peace") of the state—a prayer recited every Sabbath and holiday in religious Zionist synagogues—includes a liturgical expression of this outlook, referring to the state as "the first flowering of our redemption." Messianic rituals and discourses have long been symbolic hallmarks of religious Zionism. But this messianic outlook does not negate the fact that in practice religious Zionists contend with what they perceive as a compromised Jewish statehood: a state that does not conduct itself according to a messianic blueprint, does not subordinate itself to the rules of Jewish law, and is home to many Jewish citizens who are not religious.

Over time, the religious Zionist movement grew restless with its minor role as a supporting actor in the secular Zionist enterprise—as a "subcontractor" for religious affairs. It gradually repositioned itself as a political path maker. Starting in the late 1950s, it began to cultivate a more ambitious political model. Religious Zionist political parties and their grassroots bases have presented the movement's leaders as morally superior alternatives to the secular Zionist elite (who allegedly had abandoned their ideals in favor of bourgeois hedonism). Religious Zionists expressed aspirations for leadership in various policy domains, including security and foreign relations.[8] The transition in Mafdal from an older generation to a new one—and the 1967 war whose results (chiefly the conquest of the West Bank and East Jerusalem) religious Zionists interpreted as part of a messianic script—provided the movement's leadership with the opportunity to take the reins.

Under the aegis of the religious and nationalistic radicalism that had been burgeoning during the 1960s and 1970s in religious Zionist yeshivas, certain segments of the movement broke to the right of the political spectrum. Driven by their hawkish agenda, these segments redirected the classic prestate Zionist imperative of settling the land to the West Bank. This was accompanied by a radicalization on the religious spectrum as well. Religious Zionist communities have begun to imitate moral, behavioral, and aesthetic norms associated with the ultra-Orthodox world, developing what is now recognized as ultra-Orthodox nationalism (*harediut le'umit*, or the acronym *Hardaliyut*).[9] Within the school of thought connected with the prominent Merkaz ha-Rav (lit. "the Rabbi's Center") yeshiva, nationalism came to be understood as a religious commandment, and the State of Israel came to be seen as an instrument for the realization of the messianic vision of settling greater Israel. Alongside the political and religious radicalization that has redefined the agenda of religious Zionism, broad swaths of the religious Zionist public have remained, ideologically and practically, within the 1967 borders; they continued to develop a moderate version of modern Orthodoxy. These more liberal approaches have sought to integrate halakhic Judaism with lifestyles, fields of knowledge, and moral frameworks typical of the liberal, bourgeois Western world.[10]

Some religious Zionists settled in the West Bank as part of a messianic religious program. Some moved there in the name of classic Zionist values. Some were drawn by the attractive housing opportunities that the government offered Israelis settling in the occupied territories. The motivations of individual settlers aside, with the movement's commitment to the settlement enterprise, religious Zionism positioned itself at the vanguard of Zionist action—as a group willing to work hard and mobilize itself for the sake of ideals, while sacrificing security and convenience for the sake of the state.

Yet ironically, what made religious Zionism so central to political life in Israel also tested its public's loyalty to the state. Those tests often took the form of dramatic public confrontations. Such confrontations include the religious Zionist resistance to the evacuation of the Sinai in 1982 and the movement's struggle against the Oslo Accords in the 1990s—including the 1995 assassination of Prime Minister Yitzhak Rabin by a member of the religious Zionist public. Such a test was also seen in the religious Zionist campaign against the 2005 implementation of the Gaza disengagement. Each of these moments forced religious Zionists to confront heavily charged and volatile questions concerning their movement's self-definition: What are the boundaries of struggle against state institutions and representatives, and what are the terms of obedience to rabbis? Where does one draw the line between the regime and the sacrosanct entity that is the Jewish state?[11] The fault lines that revealed themselves over time vis-à-vis the state and Israeli society also represented internal fault lines that have divided groups within the religious Zionist movement. As we shall see, these fault lines frequently emerge when religious Zionists engage with conversion, provoking the question "Who are we?"

Let's Talk About Us

As I approached the yeshiva of the religious Kibbutz Ein Tzurim in southern Israel, I noticed the empty parking lot—a sight that belied the tumult I would experience a few moments later. The few people making their way to the yeshiva building were all men, young and old, wearing knitted skullcaps. Their religious appearance varied. Some were bearded, others were clean-shaven; some tucked in their *tzizit* (the four-cornered garment worn under one's clothes), others left them hanging outside their trousers; some sported smaller skullcaps while others preferred larger. As I watched them, I tried to guess their place within the geographical, religious, and intellectual spectrum that makes up religious Zionism: whether they arrived from the West Bank or from a bourgeois metropolitan center; whether they were modern Orthodox or ultra-Orthodox nationalists.

This overly simplistic guessing game was brought to a halt as I passed through the wooden door leading from the external courtyard to the yeshiva's study hall. There, I looked out into an overwhelming yet methodical chaos. The place teemed with activity. Teenagers came in and out of the room, studied in groups, or simply stood around talking as they waited for the afternoon prayer service to begin. Only the women's section of the synagogue remained quiet; it was virtually empty and I easily found a seat. Glancing through the curtain separating the women's and men's sections, I saw the colorful mosaic of skullcaps swaying during the prayer session. Like the women beside me, I was grateful to the young man who drew open the curtain when the service ended, opening a sightline into the center of the synagogue. The conference "Conversion—an Unsolvable Dilemma?" began. The quotations I provide here are based on field notes I took throughout the session.

The panel chair opened the conference by introducing its first speaker, Dr. Asher Cohen, a political scientist from Bar Ilan University. "It is important for us to be attentive to what is going on outside of the realm of halakhic discussion," the chair explained, "so we invited Dr. Asher Cohen. Only by understanding the reality emerging from research data can we make progress in discussing halakha." Clean-shaven and sporting a moderately sized, knitted skullcap, Dr. Cohen emerged from the audience and headed to the podium. He stood out among the other panel speakers, all of whom wore beards, large skullcaps, and suits. Dr. Cohen presented the central arguments of his book *Non-Jewish Jews*, a study dealing with the paradoxical reality of non-Jewish FSU olim. He concluded his lecture with the following words: "This [conversion] is a problem for religious Zionism. My son is eight years old, and in fifteen years he will march at the head of a unit of soldiers, so I hope at least. Tomer Sofer [a non-Jewish Israeli second-generation immigrant from the Soviet Union, about whom Dr. Cohen had spoken earlier] will be his signalman and will walk behind him. I fear the moment that my son comes to me and asks 'what do you mean Tomer isn't Jewish?' 'Tomer, who might save my life on the battlefield, Tomer who has no accent.'" Someone called out from the audience: "Never mind that. Your son will come home and introduce you to his non-Jewish girlfriend." Dr. Cohen answered:

> That's something I don't even want to think about. In any case, he will ask me "Is this the halakha you have? And don't you have any solution for this kind of problem?" I am concerned about the decline of halakha's authority among the religious Zionist public. It is already happening in a number of ways. But in this context it will be a catastrophe. The problem is no longer just on the horizon—it is already here. Someone has to "Zionize" halakha. I am not talking about changing or breaching halakha; all I am saying is that there is a range of possibilities within halakha: there are majority versus minority opinions, there are different approaches. If someone wants to solve the problem, he can and should do it. The boundaries of the collective are important and a Jewish majority is important. When I approach halakha with this kind of thinking in mind, I choose what is feasible within its framework, and not what the ultra-Orthodox determine. Again, I am referring only to what exists within the boundaries of the halakha.

Rabbi Meir Lichtenstein, the head of the yeshiva, spoke next. He turned to Dr. Cohen smilingly: "You passed the buck to me. Let's see what I can do with it." He turned to the audience:

> When Maimonides wrote about conversion, he was interested in the conjugal matters within the Jewish community. Likewise, this is an increasingly important issue in the State of Israel, and it can be considered from two perspectives—in regard to those who might marry our sons [looking at Dr. Cohen], and in regard to the large population who cannot marry in Israel

> within the rabbinate. Both issues are troubling. There are voices within the ultra-Orthodox community, and even on the more stringent margins of religious Zionism, which say: "We will look out for ourselves and see to it that our children do not marry non-Jews. It isn't a problem within our own public but of the general Jewish public in Israel." The question is whether we have eyes only for our own public or for the general Jewish public in Israel. The rationale behind this entire conference is the conviction that we are responsible for all publics in Israel and that we should not look out only for ourselves. The role of religious Zionism is to look after all Jews. We now face a huge paradox, and both the political system and the rabbinic establishment are responsible for it. The reality of mass immigration to the country does not mesh with the traditional concepts of conversion. The concepts of Judaism in contemporary Israeli society are different from those of halakhic Judaism, and there is confusion between Jewishness and Israeli-ness—all these elements together create a catastrophe.

In the time that was left for his presentation, Rabbi Lichtenstein offered a number of subversive and rather revolutionary ideas about the need for a lenient approach to conversion, for a reorganization of the dependency on ultra-Orthodox rabbinic authorities, and even for civil marriage.

A short and agitated break ensued. The conversation that began during the conference spilled out into the hallway and around the refreshment table. When it came time to resume the conference, things had hardly calmed down. Rabbi Yoel Bin-Nun spoke first. He proposed his mass conversion ritual (as I described in the prologue) and continued:

> I once offered a political deal—you, the state, will close the grandchild clause [in the Law of Return] as a de-facto arrangement. Stop trying to bring complete gentiles to Israel. We, religious Zionists, will take care of those who are already here. But no one wanted to hear about this political deal. [The murmurs in the audience grew louder]. I sound angry to you and rightly so, because I feel we have wasted many years. Those who think it won't effect the religious Zionist community are wrong. It will harm our community too. If we don't reach out to every citizen and family affiliated with the religious Zionist public, and if we don't open our homes to converts and help lead them to conversion, we may lose the battle for the Jewish character of the State of Israel. Redemption will find its path no matter what, but it will be much harder.

Rabbi Mordechai Bar-Eli, then a rabbinic judge at the conversion court (who passed away in 2011) spoke next. He rejected Rabbi Bin-Nun's idea for a mass conversion ritual but added some words of support for the army's conversion project:

> If converts only pay lip service to accepting the commandments, and they are not truly willing to accept them, then we have not solved the problem. We will do what we can. Redemption will be brought by the Holy-One-Blessed[-Be]-He. In any event, a large number of the non-Jews have already passed the marrying age, so they are less important for conversion: their impact on the state and on the next generation is not so great. The younger generation is the primary challenge, and that is why it is tremendously important for us to convert them during their army service. Today, conversion must first of all target soldiers and especially female soldiers, and be pursued in the army.

The audience was in an uproar; many interrupted the Rabbi's speech: "So, now you're not even bothered about the conscription of girls into the army"; "Where is your sense of modesty?" "What has become of us?" One of the women sitting next to me said to her friend, "What does conscription have to do with conversion?" Her friend answered: "What do you want? When people talk, everything is on the table." Rabbi Bar-Eli responded to the audience with a smile: "So now you are all attacking me about the conscription of girls." Rabbi Bar-Eli managed to continue his speech despite the uproar. He expressed his support for Rabbi Bin-Nun's call for "our public" to dedicate itself to the national mission of conversion: "I wish to join Rabbi Yoel's call and say to you that this is a national mission. Everyone sitting in this hall who can help and host converts will contribute enormously to the character of the state. Help converts out at the synagogue."

During the question and answer session one of the people who had earlier interrupted Rabbi Bar-Eli asked permission to speak. He was barely able to contain his rage:

> I am amazed at Rabbi Bar-Eli who spoke about female soldiers in the army; this is precisely the heart of what happens to us, to religious Zionists; this is exactly what I am talking about. This is a distortion of concepts. When it is convenient for you, girls will go to the army so that they will undergo conversion, instead

of dipping themselves in the sea [glances at Rabbi Bin-Nun]. When it is inconvenient, female soldiers are even referred to as prostitutes, and you do everything in your power to prevent girls from doing their military service. Do you really think that this is the correct path for religious Zionism? Don't make me laugh.

A barrage of claims and catcalls from the audience, on a variety of topics, continued throughout the remainder of the session. But the speakers never managed to produce a satisfactory response. Nor was there a sense that any of the topics had been exhausted. Looking at the clock, the chair of the session apologetically noted the time, wrapped up the discussion, and summoned all participants to gather for the evening prayer. Routine, it seemed, helped calm the stormy debate.

This conference was similar to many other public events on conversion I attended during my fieldwork. The backgrounds of the speakers, the tone of debates, and the identities of the audiences were all alike. An event of this kind took place every few months, sometimes in response to a ruling by the High Court of Justice, to discuss a documentary film on conversion, in honor of the Festival of Shavuoth, or for no specific reason at all. These public events were grassroots in nature. As local initiatives organized by academic and cultural institutions, they reflected domains of activity often associated with civil society. And while these events were not organized by state institutions or representatives, the state had a distinct presence in them. As Yael Navaro-Yashin (2002) writes about civic associations in Turkey, the public sphere is not devoid of the state's traces. On the contrary, the tremendous impact that the state has on people's lives is to no small degree produced due to activities that take place in the spaces of civil society.

The kinds of public spaces in which conversion discourses unfold are undoubtedly religious Zionist in nature, in particular religious Zionist yeshivas and nonprofit organizations. Furthermore, the discussions of conversion that take place in them are all informed by religious Zionist perspectives. "The travelling band did another show together," said Eyal, a senior coordinator at Mali, describing an evening panel that I had missed. The list of speakers often comprised the usual suspects, its slots filled in with the names of religious Zionist figures. These panels always included a representative of the conversion rabbinic court, a representative of the conversion ulpans, a representative from academia, and either an MK or a representative of one of the government ministries that deal with conversion. Only seldom did members of non-Orthodox Jewish denominations participate; those with secular or ultra-Orthodox profiles almost never came.

These events were, naturally, open to the public, unlike other sites of my fieldwork, and I did not need anyone's permission to attend. I simply showed up. Yet these events' cultural and political boundaries created a sense that they were closed—reserved solely for the religious Zionist public. They were marked by the same sociological diversity that characterizes—and ruptures—the religious Zionist community internally. It is not surprising that within such a religious Zionist space, the movement itself often became the topic of discussion. The partial documentation of the conference in this section encapsulates such discussions' central themes. To unpack those themes, I move now to a more thorough analysis of the event.

It Is Our Problem

Literary scholar Yael Shenker writes that the possessive pronoun *our* "continuously appears in religious Zionist discourse in a number of variations" (Shenker 2004:284); for example, in discussions about "our artists" or "our writers." Her claim is that the term *our* deliberately obscures the heterogeneity of the religious Zionist community and ostensibly produces a "homogeneous public that signifies itself in reference to an 'other' whose identity is also clear" (ibid.). Likewise, the term features extensively in the religious Zionist discourse of conversion: our problem, our public, our responsibility, our state, and our rabbis. In this context, as in the other contexts about which Shenker writes, *our* functions not only as a discursive anchor that helps the leaders of the community create a sense of togetherness; it is also intended to harness the kinds of images that religious Zionists use to mobilize their community on behalf of the national mission—to make them feel as though it is their problem and their mission.

The national mission of conversion is construed as "our mission" because the national problem is construed as "our problem"—it enters our homes and it affects our children. The underlying assumption here is that religious Zionists are not immune to the threatening implications of non-Jewish FSU immigration. Because large segments of the religious Zionist public are so deeply integrated into the secular Jewish majority (see A. Cohen and Susser 2003:118; Klein 2004:202; Sheleg 2000, 2006:10), the possibility of social and romantic ties with non-Jews is just a question of time and luck.[12] I frequently heard conversion agents presenting "our problem" as the high, but reasonable, social price that religious Zionism pays for its ideological choice to integrate itself into Israeli society. Some even argued in interviews with me that religious Zionists suffer the most from the national problem because secular Israelis ostensibly don't care. I was told that secular Jews "are indifferent toward their Jewish identity," and that the ultra-Orthodox are protected since "they live in a religious ghetto anyhow." The conclusion is clear: conversion is "our battle."[13]

It Is Our Responsibility

Even if the religious Zionist public is not yet significantly affected by the national problem, the message of some of its leaders is that the problem is "custom made" for them. Despite—or perhaps because of—the fact that the national problem concerns the general Jewish-Israeli public these leaders argue that the religious Zionist community cannot exempt itself from this mission.

In his book on Christian citizenship, Kevin Lewis O'Neill (2010) elaborates the idea of *weight* to describe how Christians in Guatemala City feel about their responsibility to produce a better future for the country—to save Guatemala from itself. O'Neill chooses the bodily metaphor of "shouldering the weight" to describe how this responsibility feels as though "something is pressing down on someone" (5). The word "someone" is not arbitrary. At the center of the political drama that O'Neill describes, we find individuals who are interpellated. *Interpellation*, as Louis Althusser used the term, refers to the means through which a dominant ideology mobilizes individuals and subjects them to its social force. In being hailed—"Hey, you there"—the individual is turned into a subject precisely by recognizing that the call was addressed to him or her. To the extent that O'Neill's interlocutors are hailed as Christians—that is, called to invest in rigorous religious work for Guatemala—they become political subjects. In Guatemala Christian interpellation mobilizes individuals to work on the formation of their religious personhood for the future of Guatemala.

The metaphor of weight also pertains to my analysis of religious Zionists as political subjects and state persons. It explains the sense of mission that informs religious Zionists' participation in the state conversion project and helps illustrate how they commit themselves to work on behalf of the Israeli state. However, in the political drama about Jewish conversion in Israel, we find more than just individuals working on their moral selves; here we find an ideological community working on its moral, collective self. Of course, in actuality individuals respond (or do not respond) to the interpellative hailing of leaders and rabbis. Ultimately, individuals shoulder the weight of the national mission. Some enter the field of Jewish education to teach in conversion schools, others volunteer their families to host conversion candidates, and some, like many of those I met at the conference at Ein Tzurim, make time to attend conferences on conversion. But the "you" addressed by the elites of the religious Zionist community is chiefly a collective one. If in the case of Christian citizenship in Guatemala, "I [not we] am supporting the weight for us" (6), then in the case of Jewish religious Zionist citizenship in Israel, we (not I) support the weight for us all.

What then do religious Zionists talk about when they discuss the morality of religious Zionism? Mostly they talk about national responsibility, as they did repeatedly during my fieldwork. Juxtaposing themselves with (Ashkenazi) ultra-Orthodox groups, supposedly characterized by a sectorial and separatist ethos, religious Zionists described religious Zionism as a unique movement characterized by a broad, pannational outlook (see Ariel 2004; Elon 2004; Kahan 2005; Rosnak 2006; Tur-Paz 2005). For example, Benny Ish-Shalom, the chairperson of Mali, explained to me why, as he understands it, religious Zionists must shoulder the weight of the national mission of conversion: "In my mind, religious Zionism is not a movement or a political party, but an approach or a way of looking at things. Religious Zionism is the custodian of a certain Jewish tradition. It is committed to the continuity of Jewish life, the Jewish people and the State of Israel as the grounds upon which Judaism—in as complete a form as possible—may be sustained. This understanding required me to take on the responsibility for the entirety of the Jewish people and not only one sector of it. This is also how I perceive the conversion question."

The voices interpellating religious Zionist communities into the pannational responsibility of conversion echo across various venues: on social media, in religious Zionist print media, on the study pages for the weekly

Torah portion distributed each Sabbath in synagogues, and on government websites. For example, the following appeal was published in 2011 by Rabbi Haim Druckman, one of religious Zionism's most senior rabbis, in his capacity as the head of the state Conversion Administration: "This role can be fulfilled best by the mass volunteerism of host families who serve as the gateway for converts to join the Jewish people. . . . This [volunteering for conversion] is a prime front, relating to the roots of the Jewish people's existence. It does not require going out or changing one's life patterns, but rather inviting the convert into our own homes, drawing him close, encouraging him, strengthening him, accompanying him—as part of the great vocation of religious Zionism to deal with the Jewish character of the state of Israel" (Druckman 2011).

The centrality of responsibility in these discourses can be understood in light of the fact that in religious Zionist circles the question posed by Rabbi Lichtenstein, "Do we have eyes only for our own public or for the public in general," is answered in multiple ways. Specifically, the ideological discussions of national responsibility take place in the conversion field in relation to two intense, ongoing discussions among religious Zionists. The first focuses on the limits of resistance to the state's political, territorial policy. The second is concerned with the responsibility of the state's rabbinic authority (i.e., the Chief Rabbinate and the rabbinical courts). Both discussions foreground questions about the relationship of religious Zionists with the state and the value of statism, colloquially known in Hebrew as *mamlakhtiut*. The first discussion deals with the question of compliance to state institutions, and the second with the assumed pannational (rather than sectorial) responsibility of religious Zionists.

Orange Time

During my fieldwork the religious Zionist movement was in the midst of a historic low point in its relationship with the state. In response to the formulation of the disengagement plan intended to effect Israel's withdrawal from the Gaza Strip and selected settlements in the northern West Bank, the religious Zionist public initiated a trenchant civil protest that was far-reaching in both form and scope. Founded on religious, security, and moral arguments, the protest movement took the form of an impassioned yet nonviolent public campaign. It included mass marches, billboards, demonstrations of support for the evacuees of the Gaza Strip, prayer convocations, and a deployment of symbols of solidarity, mourning, and victimhood. Most notable among these symbols were the orange ribbons tied to car antennas, clothing, and accessories. But as the withdrawal date approached (August 2005), the campaign's numerically negligible but publicly prominent militant fringes increasingly incorporated anti-mamlakhti discourses and outright violence. In particular, some religious Zionist leaders called on religious soldiers to refuse orders to evacuate Jewish settlers (and some soldiers did indeed refuse). Some settlers used violence against military and police personnel. Fake explosive devices were planted in public spaces, right-wing activists carried out terrorist attacks against Palestinians, and a few performed self-immolations. The television channels that provided nonstop coverage of the evacuation of the Gaza Strip brought into every Israeli household dramatic images that highlighted a deep rift between the evacuees and the state.

On one side of this rift, the state's incompetent bureaucratic handling of the evacuees exacerbated their feelings that the state had disengaged from them and had in fact betrayed them. Moreover, many religious Zionists perceived the evacuation of the Gaza Strip as an early and alarming political harbinger of the state's willingness to disengage from the settler enterprise as a whole. In settler circles, some refrained from reciting the prayer for the well-being of the state or at least ceased to pray for the well-being of the state's leaders. On the other side of the rift, religious Zionists' violent distancing from the values of statism suggested to many Israelis that the former had in fact disengaged from the state. The silent majority of religious Zionists—that is, the new urban middle class residing within Israel's recognized borders—together with most settlers continued to express democratic and statist sentiments and confined itself to symbolic participation in the protests (Leon 2010b). However, the movement's more radical fringes painted the public image of religious Zionism in an orange confrontational hue. The series of incidents in February 2006 known as the Amona events only deepened that rift: as the state made clear its intention to destroy illegal residences in the Amona outpost in the Samarian hills, violent confrontations broke out between the police and settlers.

The rift also deepened internal disputes within religious Zionism. The religious Zionist public, which was already grappling with its own internal heterogeneity, was now forced to confront the boundaries of resistance to the disengagement. Some rabbis criticized others who had called for conscientious objection and insisted that the entire movement maintain a mamlakhti stance: to uphold the obligation to obey state laws even if its politicians pursued disastrous political strategies that might leave its citizens heartbroken.

The conversion agents that I met during my fieldwork were indeed heartbroken. Many of them lived beyond the Green Line, and practically all of them were part of social and family networks that took part in the civil protests against the disengagement plan. In truth, the word "disengagement" was seldom used in their everyday speech; other words like "expulsion" or "uprooting" were used instead. I had not originally planned to address the political stances of the conversion agents. But it proved impossible to avoid the orange shade of the state conversion field. There were "orange moments" in the conversations between conversion agents (typically in the form of black humor) and during meetings with candidates. Such a moment occurred, for example, when a rabbinic judge told his colleagues on the bench, and the candidate whose case they were deliberating, about the violent demonstration in which he had participated the day before to protest the evacuation of Amona. Another orange moment occurred when Rabbi David, a court representative, a man whose briefcase was decorated with many orange ribbons, interviewed Nicole, a candidate, and Ronen, her partner and an officer in the border police who arrived at the interview in uniform. When I met the couple before their meeting, the officer explained to me that he chose to appear in uniform "to impress the court representative." But he soon discovered this choice had the opposite effect. During the interview the representative devoted a great deal of time to the couple's religious lifestyle, and when the man admitted that because of his tight operational schedule he did not always get around to praying three times a day (as required of Jewish males), the representative sarcastically replied: "Of course. You have a holy mission—to expel Jews from their homes." Ronen did not respond, and Rabbi David quickly returned to his original line of questioning.

These moments illustrate empirically what Timothy Mitchell articulates in theoretical terms: that the boundary between the state and society is elusive and mutable (Mitchell 1991). But they also illustrate how the conversion field represents a site through which religious Zionists seek to maintain their partnership with the state. On the day after his violent confrontation with police forces, the rabbinic judge stepped back into his role within the state's conversion institutions. And the court representative could momentarily express his "orange voice" as a brokenhearted citizen facing a police officer and then just as easily switch back to his official, institutional voice.

During the conference at the Ein Tzurim yeshiva, the panelists did not create any explicit orange moments. Nor did they bring up the trauma of the disengagement. But the soul-searching sparked by the disengagement informed how they hailed their audience—interpellating them as a public that must demonstrate responsibility for the nation.[14] Fully aware of the central place of the land of Israel in the ideology of the radical right wing, many within the conversion field, including those heard at the Ein Tzurim yeshiva, called for the movement to return to its ideological commitment to the state, to the Jewish collective, and to the heart of the religious Zionist consensus.

It is not uncommon for liberal Zionist rabbis, educators, and academics to voice frustration and criticism of the religious Zionist community's failure to act sufficiently on behalf of the national mission of conversion. Many leaders worry that the overall commitment of the community to conversion is too little, too late, and that the majority of religious Zionists remain indifferent, silent, and passive in the face of the conversion issue. Key religious Zionist figures lament the fact that the settlement project has almost entirely taken over the agenda of religious Zionism and that this issue dwarfs any other social, spiritual, or moral issue that could and should be at the center of the community's concerns.

In this vein, some liberal religious Zionists criticize rabbis associated with the settlement enterprise for the fact that, while they speak clearly and consistently about political and territorial issues, they remain resoundingly silent about many others. Such rabbis are accused of failing to point out the wrongs of capitalism, class inequality, and the corrupting power of the occupation and even of failing to properly address the issue of conversion (A. Cohen 2004a; Fisher 2015; Villa and Hess forthcoming). Some critics have argued that religious Zionist rabbis have failed to create a lenient halakhic framework capable of supporting conversion from a Zionist perspective (Fisher 2015) and that they have not done enough to sway religious Zionist public opinion.[15] Some religious Zionist rabbis, these public figures charge, betrayed the conversion agenda twice over: once when they single-mindedly focused on hawkish politics related to the West Bank, and again when they surrendered to the authority of ultra-Orthodox rabbis, mounting their opposition to the national mission through half-hearted and timid halakhic politics. In both cases, the rabbis' conduct resulted in abdicating the religious Zionist vocation. The interpellative call "Hey, you there," sounded in the conversion field, is meant to rouse the religious Zionist public to action—to remind it of its core commitments and demand greater responsibility from its rabbis. As Rabbi Moshe Klein, the deputy chief of the Conversion Administration, said to me in an interview: "My public must press the 'refresh' button; my public certainly needs a 'refresh.'"

Irresponsible Rabbinate

The discussion of religious Zionist responsibility for conversion should also be understood in the context of the religious Zionist leaders' preoccupation with what they understand as the lack of mamlakhti responsibility shown by the Chief Rabbinate in a range of socioreligious domains, including conversion. With regard to conversion specifically, rabbis and other prominent figures in the liberal branches of religious Zionism demand that the Chief Rabbinate boldly adopt a more realistic and lenient halakhic policy (Fisher 2015). Only a responsible and Zionist halakhic approach, these individuals maintain, can preserve the central role of the rabbinate, rehabilitate the standing of Jewish law among the younger generation of religious Zionists, and secure the status of Orthodoxy in the face of religious alternatives.

The notion of pannational responsibility is central to the institutional and public struggles within the field of conversion. This is the idiom through which Mali, alongside other liberal religious Zionist organizations, campaigned against the rabbinic conversion court (most of whose rabbis are identified with the more stringent *Hardali* [ultra-Orthodox nationalist] branches of religious Zionism). In 2007 Mali ratcheted up its campaign by refusing to refer its students to the court. Senior employees at Mali went so far as to promote the idea of creating alternative, independent rabbinic conversion courts outside the framework of the Chief Rabbinate. These ideas came to fruition in June 2015, when it was decided to create a mobile

Orthodox court that would make itself available, through the Jewish Agency, to Jewish communities in the diaspora (Ettinger and Maltz 2015).

A few months later, in the same revolutionary spirit, senior liberal religious Zionist rabbis established a network of private conversion courts under the name Halakhic Conversion. The initiative, presented by the media as a "rebellion of the dissident rabbis" (Nachshoni 2015a, b), was a response to the cancellation of the conversion reform by Netanyahu's fourth government. This reform, as described in chapter 1, was meant to grant municipal rabbis the authority to conduct conversions of Israeli citizens. As expected, the subversive establishment of alternative courts provoked furious and derisory responses from the ultra-Orthodox press, as well as harsh responses from preeminent religious Zionist rabbis who found it difficult to accept any challenge to the rabbinate's authority (Ettinger 2015a; Nachshoni 2015b).

The rabbis involved in the Halakhic Conversion initiative framed their strategy in terms of moral responsibility for both the FSU immigrants and the Jewish people as a whole. In their view, the existing Conversion Administration failed to sufficiently demonstrate this responsibility. The rabbis hoped that their initiative would create public pressure and force the rabbinate to recognize these private conversions (Nachshoni 2015a). It is ironic that the rabbis who rebelled against the Chief Rabbinate came from the public most identified with the historical attempt to preserve the sanctity of this very institution. Furthermore, those affiliated with the religious sector that worked to nationalize conversion (see chapter 1), led efforts to privatize this institutional field, encouraging its separation from the religious services provided by the state.

These developments illustrate a broader push by liberal elements in the religious Zionist public against the rabbinic establishment. This push is demonstrated in the initiatives of the Tzohar rabbis (*tzohar*; lit. "window"; an umbrella organization of Orthodox Zionist rabbis who seek to bridge gaps between secular and religious Jews). Tzohar rabbis offer, for example, alternative, more liberal-oriented Orthodox marriage rites for secular Jews and aim to decentralize the governance of Jewish dietary laws. Equally important, this push is manifested in the efforts of feminist religious organizations to oppose the rabbinic court's abuse of women's rights.[16] These initiatives, like those in the conversion field, privatize de facto religious services by making them independent from state institutions. Such initiatives have accompanied the "silent revolt" taking place among growing Israeli publics who seek to disconnect themselves from the religious services provided by state institutions (S. Friedman 2015).

The multiple struggles over the Chief Rabbinate's halakhic policies are unsurprising given the power dynamics at play between religious Zionist and ultra-Orthodox authorities. These dynamics revolve around control—of resources, authority, salaried positions, and appointments. They are as much struggles over political power as they are principled, ideological struggles over the relationship between halakha, Zionism, and the state (Edrei 2010). Religious Zionist rabbinic and academic elites are keen to advance what they call "Zionist halakhic rulings,"[17] which enable halakha to provide an answer to problems relating to the entire Jewish public and to sovereign life in a Jewish state. [18] Ultra-Orthodox rabbis oppose what they consider to be the subordination of halakha to such extraneous considerations.[19]

In an interview with me Professor Ish-Shalom, an active leader in struggles against the rabbinate's policies, clearly articulates how the fight to liberalize conversion represents a crucial test for both a mamlakhti halakhic ruling and the character of religious Zionism itself: "It is a struggle over the kind of responsibility we bear. Are we part of the Jewish people or are we a sect? This is a much broader question than that of conversion. The question of conversion is a microcosm. It is the litmus test of this broader issue. On the issue of conversion, like other issues, the Chief Rabbinate has consistently proved its irrelevance to modern Jewish existence and for the State of Israel; conversion is just a manifestation of this."

About Our Religiosity

During one of the more heated moments at the Ein Tzurim conference, a number of men in the audience castigated Rabbi Bar-Eli for expressing support for the army's conversion project. In fact, at the heart of the rabbi's claims was a biopolitical Zionist logic, as was evident in his highlighting the acute urgency of converting young women during their army service. But the audience's religious Zionist commitments filtered his comments. He spoke of women's conversion, but he sounded as though he was talking about women's conscription. Religious Zionists maintain a consensus about the conscription of religious men, which they understand as an expression of their partnership with the state and Jewish society in Israel. In contrast, the conscription of religious women sparks controversy and debate—about gender equality, sexual permissiveness (supposedly enabled by military service), and the normative limits of societal integration.[20] Critics in the audience took issue with Rabbi Bar-Eli because they perceived him to be legitimizing contested issues like women's conscription for the sake of conversion. The angry responses to his suggestion illustrate how the debate over conversion contains another debate, one that is focused on the religious trajectory of religious Zionism itself.

Religious Zionism encompasses a wide range of religious orientations, stretching to include "almost ultra-Orthodox to almost Conservative Jews, and everything in between" (Gvaryahu 2005). Tamar Hermann and others (2014) have shown how thin the category of *religious Zionist* is, including, as it does, all those who self-identify as such by virtue of their ethnocentric, nationalistic Jewish orientations. Such thinness naturally sparks concerns over the viability of continuing as a single, unified religious movement (see Bin-Nun 2004; A. Cohen 2004a; Gvaryahu 2005; Stollman 2005; Zivan and Bartov 2005). Many discuss the death of religious Zionism and the birth of multiple religious Zionisms. In academic and journalistic writing, the schism is often articulated as Hardaliyut versus modern Orthodoxy (see Ben-Meir 2005) or as the "faith/Torah stream" versus "the silent bourgeois majority" (Sheleg 2000). Scholars divide religious Zionists into three (Mozes 2009) or even eight (in Hoberman 2011) subgroups.

As noted earlier, those on the right, however labeled, are identified with the elite yeshiva Merkaz ha-Rav in Jerusalem and with the settlement enterprise (Aran 2013; Don-Yihya 2005). The Hardali ideal person is chiefly characterized by his or her embrace of a messianic and nationalist politics, an acceptance of the ultra-Orthodox aesthetic code, puritanism with respect to modesty and gender, utter obedience to rabbinic authorities, a Torah-study and yeshiva-oriented lifestyle, an ideological rejection of Western and secular knowledge, and geographical separatism (Pfeffer 2007; Sheleg 2000). In contrast, modern Orthodoxy is identified with Anglo-American Orthodoxy, the religious kibbutz movement, religious academics, Tzohar rabbis, and religious feminist organizations. This ideal model includes a range of sociological and religious processes: bourgeoisification and incorporation into the new middle class, a turn toward integration within Jewish-Israel society, relatively flexible attitudes toward male-female interaction, and variation in voting patterns. Some, for example, vote for nonreligious parties (Leon 2010b; Sheleg 2000).[21]

The religious Zionist voices that dominate the public discussions about conversion both represent and challenge the dichotomy I have described. Some of the speakers and institutions identify unequivocally, in regard to all issues, with one of the two poles. Other rabbinic and public figures identified with the Hardali trend unanimously support modern Orthodoxy when it comes to conversion. In this sense, the field of conversion allows religious Zionists, if only temporarily, to overcome internal tensions and imagine themselves as a unified community.

The debates about the religious requirements of conversion overlap with those about religiosity within the religious Zionist community. Interestingly, while most of the debates about the latter take place within religious Zionist forums (e.g., in community media) and are concerned with intragroup topics, like the impact of feminism on religious Zionist synagogues, in the case of conversion the debates project these internal struggles outward onto state institutions. Since religious Zionists are employed by the state system of conversion (Abrams [1977] 2006), the tension between conservative and liberal religiosity crosses over from religious civil society to the state. For example, when rabbinic conversion judges refused to recognize the right of a famous feminist Orthodox synagogue to host conversion candidates and write letters of recommendation for them, they did so as Hardalim who oppose the tenets of liberal Orthodoxy (e.g., Ettinger 2015b). When Mali campaigned against the stringent modesty requirements that the rabbinic conversion court imposes on candidates, it also took up the liberal religious Zionist position against the Hardali positions. And when Mali challenged the conversion court's preoccupation with modesty of candidates, stressing instead, for example, Jewish morals, its staff ended up arguing against this trend in their own communities as well.

Our Conversions, Our Rabbis

In June 2008 Israeli newspapers exposed an incident in which the ultra-Orthodox-controlled Great Rabbinical Court (the court of appeals for all rabbinic courts) had retroactively annulled all the conversion certificates signed after 1999 by Rabbi Haim Druckman. A few days later, supporters held a mass rally for Rabbi Druckman at a religious Zionist yeshiva in southern Israel. Senior religious Zionist rabbis, together with huge crowds, convened there to protest what they understood as an insult, not just to Rabbi

Druckman and religious Zionist rabbis, but also to the Torah itself. Simultaneously, in front of the Great Rabbinical Court building in Jerusalem, organizers demonstrated in support of both converts and the national mission of conversion. Religious Zionist rabbis and conversion advocates attended this event as well. A few days after the two protests, a petition signed by dozens of Tzohar rabbis supporting Rabbi Druckman appeared in both the general and religious Zionist newspapers. The petition stressed the biblical commandment to love the convert, called for support of the Conversion Administration, expressed support for rabbinic judges and teachers, and called on religious families to host conversion candidates (Nachshoni 2015a).

The issue that had led to the Great Rabbinical Court's precedential ruling was the case of an Israeli citizen who had undergone conversion fifteen years earlier in Rabbi Druckman's conversion court. After filing for divorce at the regional rabbinical court (staffed by ultra-Orthodox rabbis), her conversion was annulled retroactively by one of the rabbinic judges on the panel. The rabbinic judge, who had interrogated the woman about her religious observance, ruled that her level of observance was inadequate and that her conversion was therefore invalid. By implication, the ruling invalidated both her marriage and her children's Jewish identities. The woman appealed to the Great Rabbinical Court, which not only upheld the lower court's ruling but also appended another general ruling that sweepingly undermined Rabbi Druckman's halakhic authority to convert.

Although these rulings lacked legal validity, and were subsequently banned by Rabbi Shlomo Amar (then chief rabbi of Israel and president of the Great Rabbinical Court), it was difficult to ignore their far-reaching political implications. They represented nothing less than an outright campaign by ultra-Orthodox rabbis against the authority of Orthodox Zionist rabbis to perform halakhic conversions. Even more paradoxically, the campaign pitted one state institution against another. Converts paid the highest price for this paradox. They discovered, sometimes years after their conversions, that their state-authorized conversion certificates would not necessarily be recognized by the (ultra-Orthodox) marriage registrar in the state's regional councils. These kinds of personal stories made their way into the press and social media, and in the process only stoked the flames of what became known notoriously as "the Druckman affair."

The Druckman affair led to parliamentary discussions and legal proceedings. The Knesset discussed the rabbinic ruling at an emergency meeting of its Constitution, Law, and Justice Committee, and the High Court of Justice was petitioned to appeal it.[22] In these discussions religious Zionist parliamentarians, journalists, organizations, and activists spoke out strongly. They regarded the ruling as an additional chapter in the history of bad blood between the ultra-Orthodox and religious Zionist communities. The discursive terms that structured these discussions were those of national responsibility versus separatism, a concern for the entirety of the Jewish people versus self-preservation, religious Zionism versus ultra-Orthodoxy. By framing the Druckman affair through these binary sets of values, religious Zionists again cultivated their self-understanding and public image as state persons.

* * *

The Druckman affair dominated the religious Zionist agenda for a brief time, but its aftershocks reverberated for much longer. Its effects were felt with regard to several issues, including controversy over Rabbi Druckman's retirement, the status of the female convert whose case initially incited the Druckman affair, and the legal and halakhic feasibility of annulling state conversions. Two years later a new controversy erupted about the status of army conversions, again pitting ultra-Orthodox and religious Zionist leaders against each other. The latter spoke of national and moral responsibility, while the former chastised the army's winking conversions. Every once in a while, religious Zionist leaders would instigate public discussion about conversion, expressing support for a more lenient and inclusive conversion policy and interpellating their public as state persons.

In the chapters that follow I focus on the everyday engagements that unfold within the institutional encounters between conversion agents—those who have taken up the religious Zionist appeal to shoulder the weight of the national mission—and those seeking conversion. These are encounters between those who embody the national mission and those who embody the national problem.

PART 2

The Conversion Performance

THREE

Legible Signs

IT WAS ALREADY 5:45 pm, but the squat two-story building looked empty. I rechecked the address I had written on a folded piece of paper. Yes, this was the place. Eyal, a senior Mali administrator, had called me that morning, much to my relief. Finally, after several delays, Mali had opened a new conversion class in the Tel Aviv area. "If you want to do this research you told me about, you are welcome," he had said, "Yesterday I met the students. Today at 6:00 pm, they will have the first session with a teacher. I can update Dvir, the teacher, that you are coming."

I entered hesitantly, taking a seat on a staircase leading up to a long, windowless corridor. Somewhat run-down, set in a vibrant downtown area, the building was not really empty. It hosted the offices of well-established religious Zionist organizations. Several men wearing skullcaps, apparently ending their workday, began making their way out. But still no one came. A few more minutes passed and I finally heard footsteps approaching.

Fair skinned, in trousers and a bright short-sleeved blouse, a tall young woman sauntered in, chatting on her cell phone. We exchanged a polite nod. She continued her conversation, speaking a fine Hebrew with a mild Russian accent. Shortly after, another young woman joined us, amiably meeting our eyes. Next, a young dark-skinned man, bare headed, came in.

In native Hebrew he asked if we were certain this location was where the conversion ulpan would take place. I asked if perhaps we had gotten the time wrong. Another new arrival, a woman in her forties, worried whether the session would be held at all considering how few of us had arrived. The first woman, now off her cell phone, confidently replied, "Yes. Yesterday was exactly the same. I was here for the first meeting with the senior administrator of the conversion program and most people only came right as it started, or even showed up late." Smiling, she added, "You know how it is with Israelis."

At 6:00 pm we were indeed sitting in class. About fifteen students listened attentively to Dvir, a young Israeli sporting a knitted skullcap. Welcoming us to Mali's "class number 254," Dvir introduced himself as one of the two teachers for the class, mentioning it would likely grow in size over the coming weeks (and the class did grow to about thirty students at its height, though some students also left during the course). Then the students gave brief self-accounts. Trying to memorize their names, I learned, unsurprisingly, that all but two (the lone man and the older woman) were FSU immigrants. Most were the daughters, granddaughters, or partners of Jewish men. Two men were spouses of converts. The class included college students, a nurse, a high-tech worker, a kindergarten teacher, and technicians of various kinds. They had all been living in Israel for at least a few years.

I also took the opportunity to introduce myself. I said a few words about being a native Israeli, a secular Jew, and an anthropologist interested in conversion. I asked and reassuringly received the students' permission to join the conversion ulpan. I promised their identities would remain anonymous. However, the students seemed much more concerned about what Dvir had to say about the course syllabus and requirements than what I had to say about confidentiality and research ethics. In the remaining two hours Dvir surveyed the course's primary topics and began to teach, fittingly commencing with customs associated with the upcoming Jewish New Year.

Conversion is essentially a learning process. In the broadest sense, it is a process through which people acquire knowledge and skills that allow them to join a religious world. Departing from previous understandings of conversion as a religious epiphany (James [1902] 1985) or a psychologically motivated quest (Levine 1984; Ullman 1989), recent anthropological literature has engaged with the training, apprenticeship, and rehearsal techniques involved in the formation of new religious selves. Saba Mahmood (2001) has examined how Muslim women in Cairo undergo religious awakenings by acquiring bodily and ritual skills of devotion. Susan Harding (2001) has argued that Americans become Evangelical believers through appropriation of a bible-based language. And in a similar American Christian context, Tanya Luhrmann (2004, 2012) has demonstrated how metakinetic techniques teach believers to develop an intimate relationship with God.

In this chapter I, too, focus on conversion as a learning process. Because the successful culmination of Jewish conversion depends on the recognition of rabbinic authorities, it is not surprising that candidates must learn how to manage appearances before these gatekeepers. In particular, I argue that in addition to its stated pedagogic objective—that is, to introduce converts to Orthodox Jewish life—the conversion ulpan provides candidates with dramaturgical discipline and skills so that they may pass as credible converts. Candidates learn that Jewish conversion not only encompasses a religious change but also an intelligible performance of that change. The dramaturgical learning process equips converts to leave impressions on various conversion agents about the religious lifestyle they are required to embrace—to communicate specific legible signs of their conversion.

To be sure, the dramaturgical principles organizing conversion as a learning process do not vitiate other pedagogic principles and content. Similar to Jewish converts in other contexts, conversion candidates in Israel are introduced to Jewish history, philosophy, theology, and practical know-how for leading a Jewish way of life.[1] In accordance with the framework of Orthodox conversion, candidates learn to follow Jewish law and practice—celebrate Jewish holidays, pray, recite blessings over meals, keep the Sabbath, observe kosher dietary laws, and, finally, practice the rules of conjugal purity. From the outset, Orthodox Judaism dictates an orthopractic approach to Jewish life, privileging practical commandments over faith or spiritual religious experiences. Hence, Orthodox conversion emphasizes "doing" over "being," requiring candidates to demonstrate a willingness to practically observe religious tenets (see Egorova 2015).

However, in the framework of the national mission, preparation for conversion is not confined to teaching candidates how to engage in Orthodox religious conduct. Rather, this pedagogic process focuses on molding religious personas, on teaching candidates how to demonstrate appropriate behaviors in strategic arenas—how to "be seen doing" (D. Taylor 1997:119). Ultimately, students in conversion classes not only practice accepting the yoke of commandments; they are also disciplined in how to convey an impression of this acceptance.

Central as this dramaturgical preparation is, its significance is neither explicit nor direct. It involves winking relations: interactions constituted by nuanced transactions, subtle gestures, and mixed messages. Such interactions accord conversion preparation an additional, if unspoken, layer of shared understandings about what is actually going on. Dramaturgical messages are conveyed through winking relations because teachers cannot permit themselves to openly transmit them. These relations are grounded in the fundamental paradoxes that shape and constrain the national mission.

Two aspects of these winking relations engage me here. The first aspect refers to the educational framework of the conversion process. In the classroom, teachers promote the idea that the conversion ulpan initiates a formative stage of religious learning, internalization, and growth, ultimately leading to a deep and lifelong transformation centered on accepting God's commandments. Although ulpan teachers are skeptical about the feasibility of their students' experiencing such a foundational religious transformation, they often relate to them as if indeed they will undergo this kind of change. Moreover, because the teachers are more dedicated to the national mission than to their students' potential religious transformations, they invest a great deal of class time and resources in training students for the bureaucratic encounters they will face at the conversion court. Hence, teachers' pedagogic strategies focus primarily on cultivating appropriate conversion performances, as it is precisely such performances that enable rabbinic judges to authorize conversion and, in so doing, carry out the national mission.

For their part, conversion students understand that their teachers implicitly advance an educational agenda incongruent with the one explicitly proclaimed. They understand that their teachers, who often invoke the trope of internalization, actually teach them how, when, and where to externalize religious practice. In the process, they also become aware of their teachers' ideological priorities.

The second aspect of winking relations explored here relates to teachers' double messages regarding sincerity. While they often employ dramaturgical language to condemn students' potential lies or "acts," teachers cooperate in dramaturgical interactions focused on constructing converts' outward personas. And while these interactions blur clear distinctions between falsehood and truth, the dramaturgical language that teachers employ projects the existence of such a distinction. Finally, whereas teachers often preach in support of what they call "true performance," they themselves sometimes turn a blind eye to suspicious signs in their students and reconcile themselves to half-truths. Caught up in these contorted interactions, conversion candidates see through the tacit dramaturgical collaborations and begin to doubt their teachers' pedagogic sincerity.

Conflicting Missions

Avner joined in teaching the ten-month-long conversion course around six months into it, after Rabbi Yossi, one of the two original teachers, abruptly left to serve as an emissary in a Jewish community outside Israel. The students loved Rabbi Yossi and were sad he was leaving them. They worried that the new teacher would not animate the class with lively stories as Rabbi Yossi had. But shortly after his arrival, Avner—gregarious, convivial, and beardless (hence looking less stringently religious)—quickly managed to reach them. The original division of labor with the other teacher, Dvir, placed Avner in charge of the "fun stuff," as he called bible study, the Jewish calendar, Jewish history, Jewish ethics, and Zionism. Similarly candid and informal, Dvir was nevertheless in charge of teaching the "dry stuff": kosher dietary laws, blessings, prayer liturgy, Sabbath rules, and other halakhic practices (according to Jewish law and tradition). Dvir jokingly offered his own definition of this demarcation: "I'm the 'bad teacher.' Avner is the 'good teacher.'"

I also found Avner a very good and dedicated teacher. Twice a week, after a demanding day of work teaching Jewish history and philosophy to teenage boys at a religious Zionist yeshiva, he would arrive punctually at the three-hour-long conversion class. Despite the distance he travelled and the modest compensation he received, Avner always arrived prepared, keen, knowledgeable, and patient.

A few months after the course ended, I met Avner for an interview one early afternoon at his modest but pleasant home in a midsized town near Jerusalem. Standing by his big front window, he pointed out the yeshiva where he taught and the neighborhoods where most of its students lived. Our conversation confirmed my impression of him throughout the course, about how delighted he was to teach, in general, and particularly for conversion. In hearing Avner's enthusiasm, I recalled one of Mali's senior administrators explaining to me he had managed to survive working for conversion for so long because he had "caught the conversion bug, an untreatable contagious disease." Avner was a young and relatively new conversion teacher, but he already spoke as if he had caught the same disease. He told me he was still struggling with how and in what contexts to convey his true intentions to the students:

> My main motive is to be part of the solution of the big problem, no doubt. And yet, it's hard for me, as it is for anyone on the liberal side of conversion, to renounce any hope that conversion will, after all, produce Jews who do observe something. For me, the concept of observing the commandments is not an empty one. I do aspire to influence my students so that after converting they will want to keep kosher and keep the Sabbath, on some level at least. I haven't even worked out myself what level of observance I expect. But I am realistic. My guess is that most of my students do not observe a religious lifestyle.

When I asked him if such an assumption troubled him, he gave a telling answer, worth relating at length:

> Yes and no. It's on my mind, as a teacher, as someone who wants to transmit a way of life. But it doesn't trouble me in terms of the larger picture. In terms of the larger picture, I want to pass them—"convert, convert, convert them." I agree with all those who claim that the non-Jewish olim are sparks of the Jewish people, who must be reunited with the Jewish people. The big issue concerns the sparks that went missing in the world, and the social, national issue that is on the table here.
>
> I consider myself a soldier in this mission. From the religious point of view, yes, my desire is that if they convert, it should truly be for the sake of keeping the commandments, but that goal is less urgent for me. I'm not all worked up about the fact that I helped people convert and yet they don't observe. I'm not worked up about it because my big motive is still there. But if I hear that nothing [is observed], not Shabbat, not kashrut, not modesty, nothing, nada, as if to say "I've already played my role, I got my signature and that's it," then it might hurt because it means I was unable to make an impact. I didn't help them internalize anything.
>
> If I hear that a student of mine, as the expression goes, *ochel shratzim* [is a dedicated sinner; literally "eats bugs"; in practice, anyone who eats shrimp, lobster,

> and other nonkosher meat], that is, she simply went back to her former life after immersing in the mikveh, then I consider it a shame. But if it's merely a matter of her not fully observing the Sabbath or not fully keeping kosher, that won't surprise me. That is not where my ambition lies.

Avner's words resonate with the accounts of several other conversion teachers I interviewed, expressing the ideological, and hence pedagogic, priorities they set in light of their commitment to the national mission. Take, for example, how Rabbi Yitzhak, a senior conversion teacher in southern Israel, justified his negotiated objectives:

> The reality is one that cannot be ignored. Otherwise it will balloon. I understand this and make an effort. It may be true that they [candidates] don't perform commandments, and there are some slips, but what should you do? Leave them [non-Jewish immigrants] by the wayside?
>
> The idea is not to despair. Even if only one good convert comes out of a class we teach, we've performed our job. There are one thousand reasons to go ahead with conversion even if you know that in reality they won't be exactly like you wanted. You fix other things—intermarriage, assimilation, a split family, you know the whole story. The situation must be mended, so at least let them be Jews, then at least the next generation will be born Jewish.

Or take the words of Mali teacher Danny, who managed to resolve his adherence to the national mission by employing a nonreductionist approach to teaching:

> I told you before that I regard this as a national project. But a national project can't just be done with no accountability. If I had undertaken it as a national project alone, I would have only been required to show results. Conversions are necessary, right? Lots of people need to be converted, because we have 300,000 of these people, so, "come on, let's do it wholesale: pass on your knowledge to them, have them take a test. If they know their stuff, tell the court they're prepared, they're knowledgeable." So what have I achieved by this?
>
> If that's how it had been for me, then my attackers who say "you are passing people you know won't keep commandments" are right. If that were the case, I'd have to drop conversion immediately. But I do not work like that. Some converts keep something at least. Despite all this criticism, I still say that when you

> weigh the two things side by side, I prefer not to sit on the sidelines but rather to take the chance that a few of my converts, maybe even most of my converts, will not fulfill my expectations in keeping Torah and the commandments after they convert. What is the alternative? To sit back, let them assimilate and Jews will just marry them? This will lead to assimilation, and soon enough you won't know who your children will be allowed to marry.[2]

Both Danny and Rabbi Yitzhak admitted to me they do not tend to disclose in class their ideological and pedagogic positions. Likewise, I never heard Avner unveiling in class his position as a soldier of the national mission. Paraphrasing his words, I did not hear him communicate to his students his "true intentions." Moreover, the notion of the national problem was barely mentioned in the classroom. Aside from throwaway remarks about the efforts invested by the state to welcome the conversion of non-Jewish immigrants (usually in response to students' gripes about the rigorous religious requirements), the nationalist core drive of conversion policy seemed to be a nonissue. The teachers never mentioned the iconic number of three hundred thousand non-Jewish olim in a classroom of nearly thirty of them. They also never touched upon mixed marriages and non-Jewish births—precisely the concerns that raise the specter of national emergency and that brought Avner, Dvir, and Rabbi Yossi on board the conversion project—even though most conversion students were young women associated with, if not fully embodying, such looming scenarios. In a certain sense, the national mission was the elephant in the room.

The teachers instead focused on their students' conversion process, as if how they treated it in practice were unconnected to how they regarded bigger questions about conversion policy. They simply encouraged, taught, disciplined, supported, and guided students on matters related to adopting Jewish practice, often foregrounding the ideal of conversion as a true religious change in one's life.

Rabbi Yossi, Avner, and Dvir depicted religious acts as the hallmark of the conversion course. But this rhetoric, dissociated from the context of the national mission, did not always convince students. Over corridor chats during breaks, as well as in interviews, it became clear to me that some of them did not give much credence to these messages. They even suspected the teachers were not themselves convinced when invoking this framing and overlooking the national mission. Miri, easy going and seemingly accepting in class, surprised me by astutely commenting on the national mission of conversion: "My take on conversion is that it tries to increase the Jewish population. Look, the program is subsidized by the state. Nothing is free, you know. The institute clearly has a goal, for Israel to have more Jews. I once took a 'society and politics' class in college. It was in sociology and I can tell you that conversion is an artificial method used by the state to make more Jews. Muslim families are big, and you cannot force Jews to reproduce or to immigrate, so you look for other methods. You convert people."

Sveta, Miri's close classmate, shared with me similar understandings, particularly regarding the teachers' stakes in conversion. She also related how her and Miri's perceptive ideas circulated among a good number of students. Several of them lived in the same neighborhood and used to either walk or ride the bus together back home, taking the opportunity to exchange impressions: "We talked a lot about this between us, the girls, during the course, you know, what the teachers think of us, how they look at us. I'll tell you something. We totally agreed that no, they don't think [we are turning to religious life]. I think they see precisely that we are not. They say to themselves: 'We'll do what we know to do. We'll teach them everything they need to know in order to pass. And we'll have more Jews in Israel. If one of them also becomes religious, so much the better. Great.'"

Viki, who was part of this group, similarly described the silent admission she spotted in her teachers. "I am pretty sure they understand that not everyone is going to observe. I don't think they're seeing everything through rose-colored glasses. I think they know there is a problem, and people want to solve it, and this is some kind of silent compromise. I don't believe they are unaware of what is going on, otherwise half of the state of Israel would have already become *hozrim bitshuva* [newly religious or returnees to the fold, also known as *ba'alei teshuva*]. They must know. They have their own reasons why they keep [teaching for conversion]."

Miri, Sveta, and Viki were not privy to the backstage conversations their teachers had about them, yet their insights were quite accurate. As an ethnographer exposed to several backstage areas—pedagogic seminars organized by Mali, conversion conferences, and informal chats with teachers—I could attest to teachers' realistic forecasts regarding students' religious futures. They fully knew that by and large conversion students were not in the process of becoming religious Jews.

My most interesting backstage discussions took place at pedagogic seminars Mali organized for its teachers every couple of months. In attending several such seminars, I realized the extent to which they provide teachers crucial opportunities for sharing dilemmas and airing some of the tensions defining their work. In this context, Avner, Dvir, Rabbi Yossi, and other teachers spoke candidly about their disillusionment as educators who desire, but generally fail, to profoundly influence their students. Many teachers articulated reconcilement with more modest pedagogic goals. "I'll be pleased if they become traditional"; "I will be satisfied if they stop hating religious people"; and "I wish they would come to appreciate the Sabbath" were among the realistic aims I overheard.

Teachers also reflected, somewhat painfully, upon their unrealized, impractical, and idealistic hopes for conversion instruction. Many of them explicitly associated their willingness to renounce a certain degree of instructional agency with maintaining their ideological and moral commitment to the national mission. It was a price they were willing to pay.

For example, in these seminars teachers often discussed compliance with the conversion court's orthopractic demands, noting how doing so runs counter to their own understanding of both conversion and Orthodox religiosity. Avner was a dominant participant in such discussions. Like some of his interlocutors, he felt it was more important for his students to embrace Jewish social values than adhere to what he perceived as sociologically constructed interpretations of Orthodox religiosity. He cared more about their religiously informed morality (such as giving to charity and volunteering for social causes) than the lengths of their skirts or shirtsleeves. But he joined in his colleagues' strategic decision to conform in class to the conversion court's demands, a decision he viewed as benefitting both the national mission and his students who wished to undergo a successful conversion.

Likewise, as a senior employee of Mali explained to me, "You have no choice. You bow down to this Moloch [an ancient deity mentioned in the Bible, used today to denote making a costly sacrifice]. . . . What should you do? Can you convert them on your own?" Dedicated to the national mission yet bound by the rabbinic court's authority, conversion teachers and Mali were ultimately bound in a structural and political straitjacket.

Relatedly, although Mali encouraged teachers to hold high aims for their students and never relinquish the hope of inspiring a deep, even lifelong transformation in their lives, it also encouraged them to teach for conversion as a calculated preparation for court hearings. Even though Mali provides teachers with materials conducive to meaningful experiential learning, so that, as the curriculum supervisor told teachers, "conversion will be more than just an item [students] 'tick off' by 'jumping through hoops,'" the institute was still obliged to "produce results" (see chapter 1). Therefore, Mali staffers urged teachers to push for maximum successful conversion rates and to keep them updated with class statistics so that, as one said to me, "We won't later be accused of not converting enough." Thus, in addition to providing pedagogic training about "experiential" and "fun" learning, Mali also distributed glossaries of terms that teachers were to "have their students memorize prior to the court hearing."[3] It stressed the importance of candidates learning about those religious practices of concern to judges even if such actions had little practical value in Israel (e.g., koshering meat even though nonkosher meat is hard to come by in Israel). Success in conversion court under these constraints was a goal in its own right.

Rite of Passing

In order to help conversion candidates make it in the rabbinic court, teachers shaped the conversion process as a performance revolving around religious observance. Above all, that performance centered on the presentation of a subject who has undergone a significant religious rite of passage in becoming an observant Jew. In contrast to the Evangelical conversion Susan Harding describes as an "inner rite of passage" (2000:38), this Jewish rite of passage is remarkably external—visible, intelligible, and assessable by various audiences—evoking the sense of a "rite of passing."

Passing includes a wide range of practices through which individuals perform their identities and are classified by others. These processes generally involve crossing (or even transgressing) social boundaries. This concept initially arose to describe the strategic practices of individuals striving to conceal disparaged or marginalized aspects of their identities (see Ginsberg 1996; Norton 1997). However, the notion of passing has since been extended to encompass practices of positioning in an increasingly broad variety of contexts (Kidd 2004; Rueda and Mehan 1986). In all cases, it is through interactional encoding and decoding of legible signs (R. Maltz 1998) that individuals convey information about themselves and claim recognition of who they are, wish they were, or pretend to be.

Similar to the Goffmanian notion of interaction as performance, passing refers to a set of intelligible practices associated with interactive management and communication of information about one's identity.[4] Like performance, passing addresses an array of possibilities, ranging from an unwitting practice to a highly calculated deed. It can be integrated into routine processes of self-identification or deployed pragmatically, used to present "the true self" or involve deception. Thus practices of passing, like those of performance, generally provoke anxiety about insincerity and impersonation.

Drawning on such understandings of passing, a rite of passing refers to the fact that conversion candidates in Israel are expected and actually trained to communicate through their conduct, style of clothing, and bodily and verbal language how to pass as genuine Orthodox practitioners. In other words, they learn to incorporate legible signs of having undergone a meaningful religious change. For one, they learn to convey information about themselves, but they also learn what kinds of information they should convey.

I observed conversion teachers coaching students on how to develop certain aspects of their role as conversion candidates—how to embody and manifest the right persona and in the right locations in order to appear convincing. During the final months of the program, conversion training consisted of simulation—students role-playing the court procedure. Given this extensive dramaturgical discipline, it is clear why most candidates entered the rabbinic courtroom ready to perform, well-prepared to take up their roles.

Front Stages and Audiences

Like Avner, Dvir was young and a new and inexperienced conversion teacher. He learned about the conversion ulpan and its teaching opportunities by chance from a friend, a fellow religious Zionist who knew some converts and advocated for the national mission. A few weeks later, lacking a professional or activist background in Jewish education, yet seeking ways to generate income while unemployed from his usual work as a medical technician, Dvir began teaching in the class where I conducted fieldwork.

In our ongoing informal conversations, he several times admitted feeling awkward about presenting conversion's requirements in class. It took him over a month to introduce the requirement that students cultivate a connection with both a synagogue and a host family. Sitting in their usual places in neat straight rows, the students were aroused and anxious. A discussion ensued.

DVIR: Everyone will have a host family, hopefully a religious one, a family that you can learn from, that will accompany you. This is required with the purpose that following your conversion, you will have some sort of support. You know, you are thrown into a mostly secular world and the point in conversion is to continue to observe Torah and commandments. The court won't approve someone who doesn't have a host family. It's helpful if the family writes a nice recommendation letter, and it is even better if families show up in court to persuade the judges that the convert is indeed serious and intends to observe commandments.

YULIA, *a vocal and dominant student in class, raised her hand*: Do we have to visit them every Friday night?

DVIR, *laughing*: It isn't mandatory, but the more the better. They should be on your side. You will figure out yourselves what that means. The synagogue also should get to know you.

YELENA: What does it mean "the synagogue should get to know us"?

DVIR: They should make your acquaintance—the *gabbai* [sexton, a person who assists in running the synagogue services], the community. Walk up, tell them you are undergoing conversion.

YULIA: But women aren't obligated to go to the synagogue.

DVIR: True, but since you want to undergo conversion, the judges expect you to be super-Jews.

OLGA: But the gabbai is a man, so how will he see that I'm there?

As men and women do not mix in the synagogue, this question catalyzed a sequence of ironic suggestions: "Send over a paper plane from the women's section"; "Ask him to stamp your ticket"; "Wave hello from above"; "Use your regular whistle"; "Text him." The class laughed. Dvir joined in the laughter but then tried to return to the message at hand: "Again, each of you should figure out on her own what it means for the synagogue to get to know you." The first part of the class ended. While most students went out on break, several remained. Circling Dvir, they attempted to attain clarification.

ORA: Can we go to a Reform synagogue? They have good vibes.

DVIR, *smiling and responding gently*: Our orientation is Orthodox and that is what the court prefers. We are less about vibes and more about commandments.

ORA: How will I find a synagogue?

DVIR: You step outdoors, turn right and left, open your eyes. Typically, you will recognize the building.

LYDIA: And how do you begin? I can't just go alone. How would I know how to pray?

DVIR: We will teach you here and, in addition, you should find someone there who can guide you.

LYDIA: I don't know about that. Should I disturb someone in the middle of her prayers?

TANYA, *amused by the scenario*: Yes, in between all the swaying back and forth and side to side.

The gathered group burst out laughing.

YULIA, *uncharacteristically quiet until now, turned to Dvir, concerned*: I also have a question. Is it possible to have a host family that is traditional rather than a real religious one? It's just a family I've been with for years. They really adopted me, and I have been spending so much time with them.

DVIR, *laughing*: What do you mean by "traditional"? What is their Sabbath like?

YULIA: They do everything, *Kiddush* [benediction over the Sabbath], they light candles. Sometimes they go to the synagogue.

DVIR: So what is the problem? From what you are telling me, they are religious, not traditional.

YULIA, *hesitatingly*: They don't actually observe everything.

DVIR: What is the issue? Do they drive on the Sabbath?

YULIA: Yes.

DVIR, *laughing*: So a religious family is preferable. That's what the court prefers. But make sure you don't join them on their car trips on the Sabbath.

YULIA: I can do that, but I really want them to be my host family.

DVIR: Wait; is it your boyfriend's family?

YULIA, *pausing, replied shyly*: Yes.

DVIR: Do you intend to marry?

YULIA: You could say so.

DVIR: Will they write a letter for you?

YULIA: That's another problem. They don't know I'm not Jewish. It is only my boyfriend who knows. They must not find out.

DVIR: So you want them to be your host family without them knowing about it?

YULIA, *suddenly aware of her request's oddity, laughing*: Yes.

DVIR: That seems a bit too complicated, and you can't get by without a letter. If a wedding is in the air, then I need to see the guy, to make his acquaintance. Let him come to the classes here so that I can get a sense of him.

YULIA: Look, it is serious. Why does he need to come? He is a born and bred kosher Jew. He knows a lot. Why does he need to come?

DVIR: Because if he is part of you, part of your life, we need to get to know him.

LYDIA, *who had stood aside listening, interrupted*: What do you actually expect from us? To become like all those returnees to the fold or just be traditional?

DVIR, *smiling*: What do you mean by returnees?

LYDIA: You know—all included, [observing] everything.

DVIR: Look, we will learn about conversion in an orderly manner, but in principle, yes, observance of commandments is a central tenet that the court is strict about. Yes, you are expected to keep Sabbath and keep kosher. The court will want to see that you observe, and the family has to testify that they saw you observe. Yes, they [conversion judges] expect it.

Lydia made a grimace and looked upset. Seeing how late it had become, Dvir signaled that break was about to be over.

As this vignette demonstrates, Dvir was the one to introduce the language of visibility and impression management in class, portraying the synagogue and host families not only as meaningful socializing arenas but also as front stages for the rite of passing. In so doing, he did not distinguish between the requirements of embracing Orthodox routines and displaying these practices in public. He did not separate the demand placed on candidates to authentically interact with religious communities from his disclosure that these communities play potentially significant roles as audiences and advocates in court.

Similar messages about conversion as a rite of passing recurred throughout the conversion ulpan. The three teachers straightforwardly stressed that conversion is an ongoing process of being viewed by multiple gazes involving intensive impression management. The hierarchy of gazes—who looks at whom—was experienced by conversion candidates as a type of state mechanism of surveillance and discipline. Furthermore, the burden of proof placed on them—the requirement that they make themselves seen—weighed heavily and even bred resentment.

Nevertheless, we should be careful not to solely understand the field of gazes involved in conversion performance through a unidirectional framework of power relations. The conversion teachers' field of gazes is hardly a panopticon.[5] Instead, teachers continually conveyed visibility as a vital strategy that conversion candidates could and must employ wisely. Visibility was within students' power to manage.

In conversion's performance spaces, observers are not unseen, and conversion candidates are granted a significant degree of agency in managing their visibility in front stages: the conversion ulpan, the synagogue, the host religious family, and of course, bureaucratic encounters in the conversion court. Sometimes students joked that the conversion court employed spies, but they sincerely worried about running into a front-stage viewer on the street. Even so, they knew they were not being incessantly watched. For the most part, they had advance knowledge as to where they might meet a disciplinary gaze and had opportunities to use this gaze for their own best interest.

Dvir placed the obligation of being seen on the conversion candidates themselves. They had to actively situate themselves in others' fields of vision and make themselves known. How were they meant to do so, and how frequently? Dvir urged each student to understand on her own what this meant. Because Orthodox synagogues maintain gender divisions, with women usually seated in upper galleries overlooking the men, the obligation to be seen by the synagogue gabbai was collectively ridiculed, underscoring its artificiality and expediency.

Yosefa, an experienced teacher at a Ministry of Education conversion ulpan whom I met in the conversion court, told me in an interview how she had devised a way for female students to make themselves visible to the gabbai. More interesting than the solution itself was the way Yosefa spoke about her responsibility to guarantee students' visibility.

> I have to guide them how to make their entry. I had a student or two. They were together. They went to the synagogue, went in and went out. Eventually they needed to get a letter from the rabbi that he had seen them at the synagogue. He said, "I never saw them." They had seen him, but he hadn't seen them. And he didn't want to give them the [recommendation] letter. Now, after such an incident [I decided I will have] no such thing. I told them: "You go up to the rabbi,

> speak to him, and every Friday, every Sabbath you wait for him to come out and you say to him 'Shabbat Shalom.' Then he sees you. Otherwise how will he see you?" Do you understand? I have to become involved in all these things.

Under this strategically oriented framework, various mediators of the conversion process were considered suitable for the additional role of audience, composing a stable of future recommenders. A Reform synagogue was regarded as ineligible for this inventory, as were families incompatible with the court process (such as merely traditional families or ones unable to write a letter of recommendation).

Not surprisingly, the classroom itself became, if informally, a critical front stage in the rite of passing. During the conversion ulpan Avner, Dvir, and Rabbi Yossi often positioned themselves as audiences and as future recommenders for the students' performances. They made repeated remarks such as "our endorsement carries a lot of weight," and "of course we will vouch for you." Because teachers were indeed such an important audience of their rite of passing, students expended substantial effort in managing both their conduct and appearance in class.

Early in the course, nearly all the students had arrived wearing trousers or low-necked tops. Only two months into it, they began appearing in below-the-knee skirts and closed-necked shirts. The first to set this standard was Sylvia. Being the oldest (in her forties, while the others were in their twenties or thirties) and one of two candidates without an FSU background, as well as one of two married students, Sylvia already stood out as unique. It was fascinating to see how in the third or fourth session, Sylvia's new appearance in a long dress with sleeves below the elbow ignited frenzied debates during breaks, eventually compelling her classmates to adjust their appearance accordingly. They worried that her performance would outdo theirs. Gradually adhering to a similar religious dress code, which would remain generally consistent throughout the process, students comported themselves by strategically passing as good-enough candidates, broadcasting personas whose legible signs their teachers had taught them. For some, this alteration also served to hide what would be considered legible signs of their secular bodies; namely, tattoos on their arms and legs.[6]

Coaching and Rehearsals

The conversion rite of passing was in part written on the body, or more accurately, on converts' clothing. The demand to "dress appropriately"—for women at the very least to wear below-the-knee skirts and fully cover their arms and for men, whether conversion candidates or Jewish partners of female candidates, to wear a skullcap—was usually tacit or implicit, appearing like a recommendation. Concerned about scaring away candidates, teachers often chose (sometimes in consultation with Mali staffers) to present the demand incrementally and delicately. To the students, however, the message was loud and clear. As Sveta told me with a smile and implicit wink the first time she wore a skirt to class: "They didn't say it was mandatory; they hinted it would be to our advantage. Really hinted, I mean."

The demand to incorporate religious visibility in the conversion process was perceived by many candidates as a stark violation of their privacy. Most of them passed as Jews in multiple social milieus and did not publicly disclose the fact they were converting. The demand to visibly embrace an Orthodox dress code, obviously at odds with their previous tastes in fashion, imposed upon them a choice between two discomfiting social possibilities—to be exposed as converts-in-process who had previously misled their social circles or to be misconstrued as newly religious. When I complimented Rona, somewhat jokingly, that in her new long skirt she looked like someone newly religious, she laughed and said this was both a compliment and an insult. During breaks the female students gave each other tips about strategies of visibility and concealment—where they could change clothes on the way to class, what type of shoes could go both with the trousers they wore to work and the skirts they changed into, and where to find shops for "cool religious women."

Prior to students' meeting with Rabbi David, a court representative, the teachers devoted a considerable amount of time coaching them on how to dress modestly. Talking to women about adhering to a modest dress code, the teachers' embarrassment as religious men—which I had overheard them sharing with each other—was not palpable. "Do you see what fashion mavens these teachers are?" Lydia said in jest to Sveta and me after several classes in which Dvir scrutinized the concept of modest dress at high resolution: "They aren't fashion mavens," Sveta replied, "they're court mavens."

Both aspects were of course intertwined. The teachers were initiating candidates to insider social knowledge about female modesty, including the difference between fully or partially concealing the hair, between a tight or loosely fitting skirt, and a below-the-knee versus a maxiskirt. They prepared them for the kinds of judgments the court would apply to their look from head to toe, from their makeup to their shoes, advising them to seriously consider not only the dictates of halakha but also the strict religious communities in which the judges were embedded.

Rabbi Yossi told Sylvia that some religious married women choose not to cover their hair and that he personally finds this position acceptable. Yet he hastily advised her to wear a hair covering to court, because "this is what the judges are used to in their communities." Avner said that in the Anglo-Saxon community in which he and his family live, women, including his own wife, wear sandals in the summer, but in the court "this is undesirable. . . . Wear a closed shoe." Dvir directed students to apply makeup gingerly. A female teacher from another class told me she specifically asked students not to use black nail polish: "It really bothers the judges." A teacher at a stricter conversion institute, where men and women are taught separately, explained how he began to teach male students how to correctly sport a skullcap:

> There is *mari'it 'ayin* [lit "appearance"; the matter of impression]. A student of mine came wearing an extremely small skullcap to a meeting with the court representative, and explained to me he didn't want to fake appearances. I said to him that [court representatives] have their own perspective and for them it's a sign that maybe you don't always wear a kippah. He is shooting himself in the foot, undermining himself by wearing a small skullcap and giving them a reason to assume his conversion isn't genuine. What can you do? That's conversion. It's not just about being okay, but also about looking okay. Conversion means to be genuine but not to forget about impressions, you need an internal engine and then show it on the outside.

Correct visibility in court focused not only on candidates' clothing but extended also to their artifacts. They were expected to arrive at court appointments equipped with a prayer book (*siddur*) or a booklet with the grace over meals (*birkon*). It was also expected these items would correctly appear as well-used objects. In Dvir's words, students' prayer books "should already look worn." Avner suggested they insert post-it tabs to mark the sequence of the prayers: "This will help you remember if you happen to forget when in court, and you have no idea how much it will impress the judges."

Dramaturgical training for court hearings included significant rhetorical work. Following Mali advice to "prepare converts for court as if it were a job interview," Dvir repeatedly guided students how to talk confidently and properly to court agents. When asked about their observance of commandments, he instructed candidates to avoid saying *mishtadlim* ("trying"): "'Mishtadlim' doesn't sound good. It sounds like 'sometimes yes, sometimes no.' Not good. Delete. Also 'to the best of my ability'—that's not good." Rabbi Yossi frequently urged students "to reply promptly" and "convey self-confidence." "I tailor my students to the particular style of each judge. I'm not ashamed of this," said Mali senior instructor Rabbi Haim Iram during a pedagogic seminar: "How would you like your steak? That's how I prepare [students]. I am not being dishonest. If I think the person deserves to be converted, then why not provide guidance? Help them formulate their answers. But no one should get the idea we are trying to manipulate something here."

On another occasion he told his fellow teachers: "It's very important to prepare converts to provide correct and complete responses. For example, when asked, 'Do you keep kosher at home?' [rather than just say] 'Yes,' teach them to respond in detail, to expand: 'Yes, I have two sinks at home, I've separated the dishes,' and so on. They need self-confidence and this can be practiced."

Mali encouraged teachers to coach their students, but they equally expected them to attend to their own impression management in court, to build a solid reputation that would allow rabbinic judges to rely on their word. At teaching seminars Mali staffers advised teachers to learn in advance about each judge, as well as to project credibility, never whitewash facts, never lie, and, for Russian-speaking teachers, to faithfully translate the answers of Russian-speaking conversion candidates so that, as Mali's director general Nehemiah Citroen warned, "the judges won't think we are pulling wool over their eyes."[7]

The dramaturgical imagination impelling conversion performance was particularly manifest in the last few weeks of the course, when preparation for court hearings took the explicit form of role-playing, with candidates acting out court scenarios. As teachers intensified such training, they constructed simulations and encouraged students to take part from the points of view of both judges and candidates. To illustrate, I wish to narrate one such rehearsal.

As if anyone needed reminding, Dvir opened the class by mentioning the big day awaiting students tomorrow—the second round of appointments with Rabbi David, the conversion court's representative. The class proceeded like an emergency drill. Dvir began to go over the list of required concepts with the class and suggested the students enact a simulation of the court hearing, similar to what they had done two weeks prior. They objected: "No, we want to study for tomorrow"; "Ugh, not again." Dvir suggested a compromise: "We'll go over the concepts during the simulation. It's great and a very effective tool."

Ronen, Nicole's Jewish-Israeli partner, raised his hand, volunteering to act as judge. Dvir rejected his candidacy: "You already were a judge before." Ronen responded, "You don't replace a good judge. Besides, judges are state employees. They have tenure." Dvir laughed, and since no one else had volunteered, he invited Ronen to the front of the class. Nicole cheered him on.

Next to the blackboard Ronen and Dvir set up three chairs facing a single chair with a table interposed. Olga complained, "Don't overdo it." Dvir insisted, "Let's go all the way, do it right, so that the simulation is as real as possible." The stage was set and Dvir tried to cast the roles of a candidate and two additional judges. The students volunteered each other, trying to avoid the stage.

After a few failed attempts, Dvir recruited three performers. Yael jaunted up to the front of the class proclaiming, "Come on, let's convert!" Eyal, the only male conversion candidate in the class, and Ina were also selected. Ronen, Eyal, and Ina (with jokes fired about her playing a man) took their seats as judges. A list of terms had been placed before them on the table. Yael faced them, visibly embarrassed. Dvir entreated, "Treat this like a dress rehearsal."

The actors entered their assigned roles, just as their classmates had two weeks prior. A young native Israeli, Yael joined the conversion class in its second month upon traumatically discovering she was not halakhically recognized as Jewish (due to her American mother's Conservative, not Orthodox, conversion). Eyal immigrated as a boy from Ethiopia in the 1984

Operation Moses but for uncertain reasons was not recognized as Jewish by the rabbinate. Ronen came from what he described as a "traditionalist home" and wanted to marry Nicole in an Orthodox wedding. He had participated in the course from day one, attending whenever he was not on duty as a border police officer. An immigrant from Russia in her early twenties, Ina was usually quiet in class. The judges conferenced among themselves. From the back of the class someone shouted, "Speak up!"

DVIR, *explaining jokingly*: They're just going over the convert's file. They want to get to know her. There isn't always time to have a look before the convert enters.

YAEL: Enough, they already know me.

DVIR: Earlier, it was the court representative who met you, now it's the judges who want to get to know you.

JUDGE INA: Tell us what commandments you keep.

YAEL, *laughing*: The moment I wake up, I recite Modeh Ani [a prayer of thanks upon awakening in the morning] in order to become conscious that God is by my side.

JUDGE EYAL: How do you recite it?

Yael recited the prayer by heart. Standing to the side wearing a pleasant smile, Dvir provided running commentary: "They were impressed that you recited it by heart. The real judges will also be impressed." Judge Ronen cautioned: "Don't show up with cram notes." The class laughed. Yael continued to talk about her daily routine, describing the rite of hand washing before meals in detail, and how after using the bathroom she recites Asher Yatzar (the blessing uttered after defecation).

YAEL, *turning to Dvir*: Do you do this with a *natla* [a ritual hand-washing cup]?

Dvir nodded.

YAEL: How many times, three?

DVIR: Not three. Once is okay.

ANNA, *interjecting*: The book says three times.

DVIR: Take my word for it. You don't need to.

JUDGE RONEN: Why are you observing the commandments?

DVIR: Wow, excellent questions!

YAEL: Because I believe that the commandments, the ones I understand and the ones I don't understand, all have a meaning. And also because I want to connect to Judaism. So the external expression protects my thoughts and keeps me close to God.

JUDGE RONEN: Do you believe in God?

YAEL: Yes.

JUDGE INA: If you perform certain commandments, does this make you more of a Jew?

YAEL, *thinking for a moment*: Because I am choosing this path, and desire to be closer to Judaism and observance, so yes, it interests me. It has become part of me. I believe that, over time, one feels the connection more and more.

DVIR: To whom do you feel the connection?

JUDGE INA, *offering the expected answer*: To the creator of the world.

ANNA, *from the audience*: Don't be afraid to say it out loud.

The simulation of the court hearing carried on eclectically, with the three judges interjecting questions as they leafed through the glossary of terms on the table. The court discussion roamed from one topic to another: the recital of blessings, the Hebrew calendar, the creation of the world, the Friday night evening prayer service, and so forth. True to form, they did not ask Yael about possible national or social motivations that drove her toward conversion, highlighting only questions relating to Jewish religion. When the hearing was over, the judges pronounced that Yael had been approved for conversion. The class applauded. Dvir looked satisfied.

At Mali simulation was advocated as a fun pedagogy for practice and preparation. But it was more than fun. Its effectiveness lay in engaging conversion students in a playful dynamic dramatizing the very processes of gatekeeping and boundary crossing animating their lived experience. In the course of the simulation just described, conversion students performed their candidacy and took the role of rabbinic judges, candidates' ultimate audience. The theatrical framework of their roles was structured from the outset, as were the general courtroom rules and list of relevant themes. But the direction the plot would take could not be fully controlled. Rather, Dvir invited his students into an improvised role-play with no predetermined outcomes. Placing his students in front of a favorable audience and in a position of power and confidence, Dvir enabled them to practice inhabiting the scene that would critically determine their conversion. As a setting that included a clear "as if" element, it exemplified the interactive, performative space in which candidates would present themselves.

Sincere Performance

After writing up an analysis of my fieldwork at Mali, I sent the draft to Nehemiah Citroen, in keeping with our prior understanding. A few weeks later he invited me to his office, wanting to talk. Based on my fieldwork crisis at the rabbinic court (see chapter 2), I anticipated another crisis, so this time I asked a senior university mentor to join me. Nehemiah and Rabbi Iram received us just as warmly as they always had during my visits to them, but they did not spare their criticism. As I expected, they were concerned about the dramaturgical analysis I proposed. They listened as I tried to explain Goffman, how I do not view performance as a lie, that I do not equate role-playing with cynical conniving, and that dramaturgical training is by no means an induction into make-believe but, rather, an invitation to project a certain front inscribed with the proper legible signs. Needless to say, translating Goffmanian sociology into colloquial Hebrew in such a complex and sensitive field was not an easy task. Nehemiah and Rabbi Iram justly insisted that anyone who read my work would unavoidably apply conventional meanings to the dramaturgical lexicon, with its connotations of lying, imposture, and wink-wink conversions.

Indeed, I often encountered these conventional meanings in my fieldwork. In conversion classes, in corridor talk, at pedagogic seminars, and during interviews, both students and teachers routinely employed such notions as "actor," "audience," "act," "role-play," and "performance" to indicate faking and inauthentic, wink-wink conversion. For example, teachers would wonder whether their students "only looked real" and were "putting on an act." In class they would condemn lies, playacting, and performances using these terms interchangeably to mean the same thing. On their end, candidates were concerned that they could be suspected as "actresses." Thus dramaturgical language served as an interpretive framework for both sides to engage with troubling anxieties about conversion's sincerity.

In *Sincerity and Authenticity* literary critic Lionel Trilling (1972) traces the development of sincerity as a moral imperative in social life in Western culture before it gave precedence to the rising notion of authenticity.[8] *Sincerity* first entered the English language from Latin during the sixteenth century, initially in relation to the genuineness of material objects and foodstuffs considered of value—such as "sincere" gems or wine—and only later in relation to people considered trustworthy and real (Magill 2012:28–29). Trilling argues that the weakening of social, communal structures bred anxieties about the possibility that persons might present themselves as different from who they really are. He shows how sincerity became inseparable from abiding by the social role of the moral person: "Society requires of us that we present ourselves as being sincere, and the most efficacious way of satisfying this demand is to see to it that we really are sincere, that we actually are what we want our community to know we are. In short, we play the role of being ourselves, we sincerely act the part of the sincere person, with the result that a judgment may be passed upon our sincerity that it is not authentic" (Trilling 1972:10–11).

Like Trilling, Goffman recognizes sincerity as a fundamental condition for the success of social situations. As I mentioned in the introduction, Goffman undermines the dichotomy between true and fraudulent performance but still recognizes the supreme value attributed to sincerity in the mundane dramas of social interaction. Performances become felicitous only when audiences assume they are sincerely played.

In certain historical and institutional formations, the value of sincerity as a moral expectation intensifies, creating a particular alertness (see Kidd 2004). Religious conversion is often such a formation. Frequently rooted in political constellations associated with worldly rewards on the one hand and with purist religious ideologies on the other, conversion readily generates suspicion about its potentially cynical abuse. Scholars of conversion document enhanced ritual and discursive attention to sincerity (Spyer 1996; Keane 2002, 2007). When this attention is accompanied by an improbable demand for purity of heart, as in the case of the "return to Judaism" program of Feres Mura in Israel, the endeavor collapses "under its own weight of doubt, suspicion, and unmet expectations" (Seeman 2010:188). Seeman describes how the hermeneutics of suspicion extends to the teachers responsible for keeping the program running: "Almost inevitably, religious educators who had been sold on the discourse of pure hearts were disappointed to discover a more complex reality in which immigrants willed many things, including some that were incompatible with the religious messages they were being taught. . . . Some became disillusioned and convinced that their students' failure to conform fully to expectations constituted a kind of dishonesty, or even a personal affront" (ibid.:187).

That conversion agents might themselves be driven by multiple motivations, including political and practical considerations that can sully religious intention and action, only intensifies these anxieties. For example, under the aegis of the missionary Christian encounter, an encounter wherein missionaries have capitalized on mass conversion in occasionally doubtful circumstances, Peter Van der Veer (2006) writes the following about the politics of sincerity: "Sincerity has to be performed in a context, in which one of the missionaries' greatest anxieties is that of the 'backsliding' of so-called 'rice-Christians,' many of whom were converted as part of mass conversions during famines and epidemics. The missionaries' quest for sincerity is constrained by the fact that it is ultimately the number of converts that counts for the funding missionary society back home, and that many converts are made during famines and epidemics" (ibid.:11–12).

If we expand the concept of religious conversion to include conversion to civil and national religion, we can further augment our comparative perspective. A compelling case in point is the conversion to a communist Soviet identity—"the new religion of the soul" (Kharkhordin 1999:48–49)—which placed the sincerity of political converts at the center of collective rites and spectacles. The concern that people would wish to become communist party card holders in order to gain a slice of the governmental pie raised misgivings about the sincerity of those who sought entry (Halfin 2006:7–28). The value of sincerity was unquestionable. Communist party authorities, and later the Soviet state, violently and piously demarcated dichotomies distinguishing sincere revolutionaries from opportunistic impostors. Such theatrical metaphors as "masks" and "staging" were used in public trials set up for this purpose (Fitzpatrick 2005:13).

Undoubtedly, similar bifurcating discourses mark conversion in Israel, denoting two seemingly exclusive poles—sincere converts versus opportunistic impostors. As discussed in chapter 1, the assumption that people would opportunistically seek conversion for the sole purpose of acquiring Israeli citizenship generated bureaucratic arrangements to significantly limit the ability of migrant workers, tourists, and other foreigners to undergo conversion. It is interesting to see how, notwithstanding the legal obstacles to what state bureaucrats would consider crude opportunism, conversion discourses retain their binary nature. "Insincere conversion" remains in play to describe citizens who appear to not truly accept the commitment to keep commandments in the Orthodox fashion.

How do conversion teachers pedagogically address their lingering doubts that students may be insincere, perhaps displaying an empty and deceitful religious performance? In interviews some of the teachers described employing a tense pedagogy of suspicion: "We must admit that we don't have x-rays for examining souls," said Danny, a Mali teacher, "but I examine how they [students] pray. You can tell within three minutes, even less, within thirty seconds, whether a person is [really] praying or just saying that he is praying." Rabbi Shlomo, also a Mali teacher, recounted a comparable strategy: "Let me tell you, the simulations I conduct towards the end of the course reveal to me many things I did not find out during these ten months, and the two Sabbaths we spend together are also a tremendous test. . . . I see things there that can't be seen in everyday reality. You can't keep up an act for twenty-four hours."

In the class where I conducted my fieldwork, the approach to sincerity and insincerity was no less bipolar and rigid, but it was transmuted into gentler pedagogic strategies. The three classroom teachers did all they could in class—counselled, beseeched, preached—to try to circumvent a potential "sincerity problem" in the conversion court. They did not expressly discuss what might constitute a sincerity problem, but they did occasionally provide their students with tangible examples that elucidated their concern.

Such was Rabbi Yossi's account to the class of a sincerity problem that had come to light when a court panel discovered that a candidate had driven in a car on the Sabbath during the conversion period. Her entire process had been tarnished by this revelation, even though she had observed other Sabbath commandments and her conversion was of great personal significance to her. One time, Dvir spoke in class of a candidate who had not disclosed in court her romantic relations with a Jewish-Israeli man. He presented the sincerity problem this convert had created, implying by his omission that her religious observance had thereby become largely irrelevant.

Throughout the conversion course Dvir repeatedly warned the students against the danger of lying; it did not pay to lie; a lie was easily discovered. Taking a different pedagogic approach, Avner adopted the voice of Jewish morality, stressing that sincerity was an inherently Jewish choice. During the final session of the course, just before taking leave of his students, he told them: "I see myself as a teacher for life and not only as a guide to the conversion court. With my previous class, I continued to be there for my students [postconversion] because of my conviction that what we do here is life-changing. My own life has changed as a result of supporting converts. I think that someone who doesn't want to change must say so in the courtroom. It is neither right nor proper to come to court to put on an act."

A few students responded to his words, gently suggesting what I heard them say more explicitly later on in interviews. In their view it was not right to think about their conversion in mutually exclusive terms of sincerity versus insincerity. They were put off by lies just as much as he was. Conversion was not just an act to them, because the process endowed them with power, knowledge, meaning, and belonging, albeit perhaps not fully in line with the conversion court's parameters for complete acceptance of commandments. I felt amazed, even moved, by this sudden open dialogue, just before the course's completion, when students seemed most on edge about their impending hearings. I sat bewildered, admiring those students who dared speak so frankly in this arena critical to their impression management. I knew, though, that Avner would not betray their trust in him. Leaving the classroom for the last time, I could not avoid thinking that it was one of the most sincere exchanges I had heard in class.

Compromised Truths

Early in the conversion ulpan Rabbi Yossi and I discovered we live in the same town, a few blocks from each other, and so we often shared rides to class. Our roughly thirty-minute drives to and from class, as well as our trips to Mali's pedagogic seminars, were valuable opportunities for me to engage in informal conversation with him. One day, on the way to a seminar held in a community center north of Tel Aviv, Dvir also joined us. During the drive Dvir related to Rabbi Yossi what had been happening with Kati. One of the class's best students, Kati actively participated, almost never missed a class, and often raised practical religious questions that indicated she was, as Rabbi Yossi described to me, "an extremely serious and promising convert." Dvir reported:

> Two weeks ago Kati approached me during break, telling me that she has a boyfriend. I explained to her that he must accompany her to class so we can form an impression of him. She argued for a bit, telling me that he is traditional. She told me his name. You wouldn't believe who he is, Rami Ganot [my pseudonym for a famous PR professional]. Last week he showed up, this Rami Ganot, sat for three hours and didn't say a word. Then he spoke. Boy, did he speak.
>
> There is no way to best him. He is so quick and he has a counter-argument for everything. We argued about whether he should attend the classes and I was unable to persuade him. Finally he told me, "So she'll say that we broke up." Yesterday she came and told me they had broken up. I really don't know what to do now. Ignore it? Speak with her? Believe her? I don't think I believe her.

Rabbi Yossi sat beside me listening attentively; he had no insight to offer but suggested Dvir speak with Rabbi Iram at the seminar. Dvir indeed approached Rabbi Iram during a break. He briefly recounted the story, and Rabbi Iram advised him not to do anything at the moment: "At the very most, write it down later in a separate letter to the court." Around a week later Kati shared with me privately that she had a boyfriend but did not reveal his name. I did not tell her what I knew from Dvir, nor did I remind her that I had witnessed Dvir and Rami's interaction in the classroom.

A few months passed and I heard nothing new about Kati and her boyfriend. The first round of meetings between Rabbi David, the court representative, and the conversion students was to take place. In a small room in the rabbinic court sat Rabbi David, Dvir, Kati, and I. Kati was appropriately and elegantly attired. Over her buttoned-up blouse she wore a golden chain with a Star of David pendant—a common legible sign of Jewish allegiance among Jewish Israelis. Rabbi David read aloud the biographic statement in Kati's conversion file and whistled with appreciation. He was not used to converts writing such refined Hebrew.

Kati's letter was indeed impressive. Literate, polished, and concise, albeit complex, it was no doubt written by someone with a way with words. Rabbi David attempted to follow Kati's many peregrinations and transitions from one status to the next. She had immigrated from the FSU to one of Israel's poor development towns, studied at a boarding school, moved to the Tel Aviv metropolis, and changed her profession. Her narrative told of a life battling poverty and marginality, culminating in a new path and sense of gratitude. However, Rabbi David still had questions.

RABBI DAVID: Who is the host family?

KATI: The Ganot family.

RABBI DAVID: How did you find them?

KATI: Once, when I was still working for the Israeli television, Rami Ganot came to be interviewed and we met. We went out for about a week but then broke up. You should know, he is a great man. He helped me a lot. His entire family is religious or even ultra-Orthodox.

RABBI DAVID: His name is familiar.

After a few more words from Kati about Rami Ganot, Rabbi David blurted out a nationalist, orange response (see chapter 2): "Wait, didn't he support the evacuation, the expulsion [referring to the disengagement from Gaza]?"

KATI, *trying to justify*: He had all sorts of reasons.

RABBI DAVID: Okay, let's switch subjects. Why do you want to convert?

KATI: I belong here. This is my place. It's also an internal thing. My fate has changed so much and I believe that someone is supporting me from above and I want to give thanks to that force. It isn't just by random that I ended up in Israel.

RABBI DAVID: Who changed your fate?

KATI: I did, but through him.

RABBI DAVID: Should everyone convert?

KATI: Everyone should make his own decision.

RABBI DAVID: What, anyone who was badly off and now is better off should convert?

KATI: We weren't badly off there. We came to be in Israel.

RABBI DAVID: Most olim don't convert and aren't religious.

KATI: I am. This reflects my decision to be at one with the Torah and commandments.

The conversation moved to focus on the synagogue that Kati regularly attended. Although a second meeting was yet to take place, pleased with Kati's conduct, Rabbi David allowed himself to already challenge her, asking about the blessings and prayers, issues he generally reserved for second meetings. Kati's accurate replies seemed to impress him all the more.

RABBI DAVID: Okay, Ms. Kati, it looks like you are all set, from all angles, the synagogue, the host family, everything.

KATI, *smiling*: When I do something, I do it seriously.

RABBI DAVID: Okay, we'll see later on how you continue to move forward.

Rabbi David signaled to Kati to leave the room. Leafing through the documentation in Kati's file, he turned to me: "What do you think, Michal? You're a woman, you understand women's psychology." Committed to the converts' confidentiality and even a bit offended by Rabbi David's chauvinism, I evaded responding. He turned to Dvir:

RABBI DAVID: Something here is too sweet. On the surface, everything is fine, but I felt something. I made a note of it. It reminds me of another case where I wrote down to myself, "something here is too perfect" and really, two weeks ago, I got a phone call from the host family [in that case] telling me that they are retracting their letter of recommendation. They found out she was a pathological liar. They saw her in the street in immodest dress. Immodest is an understatement. They discovered a web of lies. And here, something about her motives.

DVIR, *interrupting*: What? You mean the guy?

RABBI DAVID: Yes, that too.

DVIR: Well, maybe, I don't know. Look, she excels in class.

RABBI DAVID: I don't know. I'm noting down, "Something here is too perfect."

Later in the day, when Rabbi David left the room during a break, I said to Dvir, more concluding than asking, "So, you chose not to tell." Dvir instantly understood I was referring to the inconsistencies between Kati's story to Rabbi David and his own, more complete knowledge, which he had chosen to conceal. He said, "Yes, it was a real dilemma, but that was my decision."

A few days later I met Kati in class. She pulled me aside and told me how insulted she was when Dvir called her, telling her that Rabbi David suspects she is being dishonest and that Rami Ganot is still her boyfriend. She asked me whether I had heard something when I was in the room. I was embarrassed and unprepared for the question, so I lied. I said that I had just left the room after the meeting with her and therefore had not heard anything. "Well, I will stand up for my version," she asserted.

Dvir also updated me, telling me that he had called Kati because he wanted to give her some shock therapy: "If she is going ahead with her version of things, then let her go for it, but I wanted to give her pause to rethink." I was not present at the second meeting between Kati and Rabbi David, but it clearly went well. Kati underwent conversion with the first round of conversions in the class. A few months later a local newspaper's gossip section featured a picture of her wedding to Rami Ganot. Some three years later I saw on her Facebook page photos of her new family. In a few of the photos I noticed that Kati was still wearing the Star of David pendant.

Did Kati lie during her conversion performance? The answer is probably both yes and no. Did Dvir lie in his performance as a conversion teacher? Also probably yes and no. Do these questions help us understand the complexity of the lived experience, relationships, and messages making up the situation I have been describing? Again, yes and no. Yes, because the dual answer to these questions illuminates how the dichotomy between sincerity and insincerity breaks down under the impossible circumstances in which the national mission unfolds. No, because the attempt to understand Dvir's nontrivial decision to unequivocally support Kati's rite of passing is, in my opinion, a much more interesting endeavor. Dvir did not believe Kati's official story but chose to collaborate (some would say connive) with her and—unbeknownst to her—rescue her "too perfect," "too sweet" to be true conversion performance.

When challenging Kati, Dvir did so privately, backstage. During "on-camera" discussions with Rabbi David, Dvir played an undercover member of her team. He could not reveal to her what he had done on her behalf because he, too, had to save face as a teacher and he also hoped to educate her. For someone who idealized the notion of a sincere performance, Dvir both compromised his principles and took a risk. Rabbi David might have suspected that Dvir too had a sincerity problem, potentially marring their working relationship and Dvir's ability to advocate for converts. "Yes, it was a difficult dilemma, but that's what I decided," he had said laconically, telling me all and nothing.

At Mali's pedagogic seminars Dvir met with other teachers who, like him, were often troubled by dilemmas of advocacy. How can a teacher recommend students who do not inspire trust to court representatives and rabbinic judges? Should secrets and known lies be exposed to the court, preserving sincerity in front of the court but violating relations of trust between teachers and students? How can teachers maintain personal, professional, and religious integrity without dooming certain candidates? These dilemmas were connected to the teachers' position as "mediators" (Goffman 1959) between the conversion court and students and between sites that constitute the back- and front stages—those where candidates learn about the court and those where the court learns about candidates.

Most of the murky cases teachers brought up during seminars revolved around harboring suspicions about students' romantic involvements.[9] In response, Mali senior staff would emphasize the ideal of sincerity, stressing the institute's political combat against the conversion court, particularly its complicity with shameful wink-wink arrangements. Over and over, they reiterated the position Mali chairperson Benny Ish-Shalom expressed to me in an interview: "We are adamant that a lie cannot be a gateway into Judaism. But, implicitly, this is exactly what the court tells them: 'Lie to us. We will turn a blind eye and pass you with a wink. If it looks ok, you've satisfied us.' That's not how we educate at Mali."

At the same time, Mali did not translate the high value it placed on sincerity into any firm guidance. Teachers were left to decide these matters alone, based on their own moral compasses, receiving only vague and even conflicting advice: "Wait, don't do anything now, and intervene maybe later"; "Look at your students supportively. Act like parents who know that their son is not perfect, but still do everything for him"; "Confront your student in private, not in court. If she lied to you, it is personally insulting. It is between you and her, not between her and the court"; "Turn a blind eye."

Not surprisingly, teachers responded with a diverse array of pedagogic approaches. Recall how Avner spoke very persuasively in class about the importance of sincere conversion. However, in an interview he admitted to me: "On a personal level, I pretty much ignore that type of thing." Danny, also a Mali teacher, recalled a scandalous case he had once handled, one that led him to weigh the lies he is willing to accept in support of the national mission. He concluded: "Some people lie to me in this project, right, so what am I to do? I will carry on with my truth, because I believe that the ultimate truth, the general truth, the national truth calls me to go for it." And Eyal, a senior administrator at Mali, interpreted converts' lies as an encouraging sign of their genuine wish to undergo conversion. Essentially construing and empathizing with lying as a "pragmatic mode of sociality" (cited in Davis 2010:130),[10] Eyal told me: "For some people it might be really-really important to play the game. I don't see this as a bad thing. It is morally objectionable that they are doing this, but let's look at the positive side. You see how much effort people make to go through with conversion."

The gap between the moral ideal of sincerity and teachers' actual willingness to tolerate "playacting" did not escape converts' notice. Needless to say, conversion students could not allow themselves to confront their teachers on this subject, but during retrospective interviews I had with them after their conversions had been finalized, many spoke realistically, at times angrily, about the double standard of sincerity. Sveta reflected:

> Let's say that they made a compromise, because I don't know what they saw or didn't see about me. I don't know to what extent they even deeply probed into how sincere I was, how much they really did. Between us, I don't think it was such a matter of principle. They talked a lot about it, but I'm not sure how much was really behind it. I think there is one thing extremely important [in Judaism]: appearance. That is very, very important. And in a sense they applied this principle to us during the conversion process as well. Because if you come to class in a skirt and behave well and ask all sorts of questions, it looks as though you are ok. So it's not about how true it is, as long as there is the appearance of your being ok.

Vera noted scornfully how teachers purposely ignored the fact that students were sure to have partners. Their deliberate indifference lent them very little credibility in her eyes: "Let's take Rabbi Yossi or Dvir. What? Don't they understand? They're sitting in front of a group of thirty girls and only two have boyfriends? You're kidding me. We're not talking about 18-year-olds. We're talking about 24, 25-year-olds. . . . No way. They knew. They knew it all along. They just decided not to know. Good for them!"

Yona expressed greater sympathy: "They talked to us a great deal about sincerity. You heard them. But I felt as though they knew that not everything can be utterly sincere from start to finish. I got the feeling that it is ok for them to not know everything about us. It was convenient for them to turn a blind eye. They had their own reasons."

As these excerpts reveal, it was no secret that conversion teachers had to work from a position of compromised truth. Whether regarding them empathetically or critically, converts insightfully voiced understandings of how, like themselves, their teachers must enact their own religious and moral performances.

* * *

The winking relations demonstrated throughout this chapter tell a story of precarious, nuanced, and tense collaboration. Far from a harmonious or smooth partnership, these relations create pedagogic compromises, moral dilemmas, and lingering, sometimes unresolvable, doubts on both sides. All of these mechanisms and experiences continue to unfold in the institutional arenas further mediating the conversion performance—the conversion court and the ritual bath, the sites of focus in the coming chapter.

Primarily at the conversion court, the drama of sincerity takes a particularly tense shape in encounters between conversion candidates and the rabbinic gatekeepers. In meetings with court representatives and before rabbinic panels, candidates' conversion performances become the object of trial-like scrutiny. Even if well-rehearsed and well-dressed, candidates enter these encounters trembling from fear and excitement, knowing they must convince their most significant audience that they are sincerely ready and deserve to be included in the Jewish fold. Their task is formidable. In addition, rabbinic judges' charge to assess and approve these presentations also carries its own demands. Both sides shoulder the burden of constructing believable performances

FOUR

Dramaturgical Entanglements

> Rabbinic judges want to pass [converts] because it is a mission. But they also want to look at themselves at the mirror and love what they see there.
>
> —Rabbi Sirkis, a senior official at the rabbinic conversion court

RABBINIC JUDGES GENERALLY have from thirty to sixty minutes to decide if the person appearing before them is a worthy and trustworthy candidate for Jewish conversion. Most likely they have never met her before, but they need to quickly decide if they can authorize her conversion. In order to make this decision, they must attain sufficient knowledge of the candidate's practices, habits, and motivations they find intrinsic to the conversion process. Has she genuinely embraced the Orthodox lifestyle? What drives her toward this change? Is her commitment strong enough that she will continue pursuing religious practice after completing conversion?

In light of the thin encounter permitted by the court arrangement, court agents' reliance on legible dramaturgical signs takes on immeasurable significance, stemming from the extent to which rabbis can only grant conversion by relying upon believable demonstrated manifestations of religious change. Bureaucratic uncertainty took shape in the vast institutional processes revamping the state's conversion apparatus in the 1990s (see chapter 1). These macrolevel processes resulted in the fragmenting of the conversion procedure into relatively brief and distanced bureaucratic encounters between candidates and conversion court agents. Today these encounters take place in administrative settings, usually at local branch buildings of the rabbinate or at government office buildings. With their bureaucratic climates, such settings differ remarkably from synagogues, yeshivas, and classrooms, as well as the homes of rabbinic judges, where conversions had frequently taken place prior to the policy changes.

While bureaucratic conditions pertain to conversion court hearings for candidates from all backgrounds, they weigh all the more heavily in cases of high relevance to the national mission. When conversion rabbis encounter members of the target population of the national mission—mostly those young female citizens they are especially eager to include in the nation—their dependence on intelligible signs of credible conversion becomes amplified. For in these cases, judges are especially pushed to prove their rabbinic credentials to themselves, to the Israeli public, and most importantly, to powerful ultra-Orthodox rabbinic authorities. By so doing, they aim to prove that the conversion process they govern is valid and that the national mission is fulfilled within a sound, legitimate, halakhically kosher policy.

This chapter focuses on the bureaucratic arena of the conversion court and on the conversion performances, or rites of passing, that unfold there—how working from a position of bureaucratic uncertainty, court agents employ strategies conveying both suspicion and trust. Court agents meticulously interrogate conversion candidates' performances and exhibitions of legible signs, as well as those "audience members" charged with testifying to their consistency—conversion teachers, synagogue rabbis, and religious host families.

Even when held graciously, these exchanges are invariably harsh. Conversion is defined as a juridical practice (*ma'aseh beit din*) and is enacted in court. Whereas in the Talmudic period, when the juridical form of conversion emerged, "the potential convert [was] not grilled at any length about his motives, and apparently [needed to] reveal only an attitude of modesty and contrition for the ceremony to proceed" (S. Cohen 1999:203), the conversion procedures that I was exposed to in my fieldwork were intrusive in nature. Most of the courtrooms are spacious rooms, with rabbinic judges sitting behind raised benches, unavoidably peering down at candidates, although one courtroom did have the judges' bench placed on equal height and not that far from the candidates' desk. Another courtroom had a gallery area for spectators. In any case, the hard wooden benches, black leather armchairs for judges, Israeli flag standing firm to one side, and menorah emblazoned on the front wall as a symbol of the state clearly conveyed a judicial setting.

Yet court exchanges tended to have a softer and more collaborative dimension than their physical setting indicated. In particular, rabbinic judges displayed a certain leap of faith by tacitly assisting in dramatizing the very conversion performances they had to assess, helping to cultivate those particular dramatizations they believed they could trust. One rabbinic judge admitted to me that most cases "are in a gray area," leaving him and his colleagues often undecided even after thoroughly interrogating candidates and witnesses. This hesitance renders the mechanisms of trust building particularly formative. Both strategies of suspicion and trust are precariously collaborative, a defining feature that becomes all the more apparent in those rare cases where candidates (or their spouses) fail to do their share in sustaining the tense bureaucratic encounters, thereby triggering their breakdown.

Cynical approaches to the court procedure cannot do justice to the morally loaded and profoundly engaged attempts by conversion judges to both influence and believe the candidates they encounter. Court agents work in good faith and take pains not to betray what they believe is the core of Jewish laws of conversion. Whereas these judges have been accused of approving deceptive wink-wink conversions (see Brandes 2008), the two-edged strategy I analyze here reveals a considerably more convoluted microsociological dynamic. The idea of wink-wink conversion implies inviting candidates to lie, whereas rabbinic judges actually invite candidates to present legible signs that they can trust but also interrogate from a place of suspicion. It is precisely by relying on both trust and suspicion that rabbinic judges rework their professional integrity, developing confidence in their ability to approve sincere-enough conversions under less than ideal conditions. I make the case that judges' dual strategy entangles all participants in elaborate dramaturgical transactions grounded in self-presentation and impression management. These transactions permit not only court agents but, sometimes, also candidates and teachers to construe the procedure as producing genuine-enough converts.

Uncertainty, Suspicion, and Trust

During my fieldwork more than a few court agents expressed painful awareness of their imperfect ability to become acquainted with conversion candidates. "Tell me, how can I know if someone is ready for conversion in one hour?" said Judge Rabbi Shemi. Rabbi Zvi, another judge, confided, "I never met this person before. I've only read about her in a file, so there's no way I can know for sure who she really is." Rabbi Peres, a senior representative of the chief rabbi on matters of conversion, employed a somewhat Foucauldian technology trope to question the prospect of successfully evaluating a candidate's genuineness: "How could Rabbi Cohen know this convert? How could he know if she is really sincere? What do you think, that he has some kind of mind-reading technology?"

Clearly lacking such technology and working under bureaucratic conditions creating distance and uncertainty, court agents often developed attitudes of suspicion and trust. Both strategies were commonly enacted toward the same candidate, by the same judicial panel, even by the same judge. These strategies were by no means mutually exclusive. Though contradictory in nature, suspicion and trust share a common tenet. Both dispositions constitute assumptions or conjectures about others' conduct and equally stem from an inability to fully know that conduct or foresee its future. In other words, suspicion and trust are modes of knowing; they are means for bridging gaps in contexts of incomplete knowledge.

Talal Asad writes: "All judicial and policing systems of the modern state presuppose organized suspicion, [and they] incorporate margins of uncertainty" (Asad 2004:285). Several compelling ethnographies of suspicion, all of which focus on encounters between state professionals and "insufficiently known" individuals, trace this institutional connection between uncertainties and suspicion (see also Sztompka 1999:67). For example, working in terrains of Greek psychiatry, Elizabeth Davis identifies the clinic as a space of knowledge production wherein fragile psychiatric truths are generated. She describes how "the problem of 'the unknown,' rooted in the unreliability of speech" (Davis 2010:138), creates deeply entrenched suspicions toward patients. Among migrant workers in contemporary Russia, Madeleine Reeves examines the uncertainty surrounding their being authentically documented, whereby "suspicion itself becomes the dominant mode of governing uncertainty" (Reeves 2013:512). Examining political asylum courts in France, Carolina Kobelinsky (2015) demonstrates how suspicion toward asylum requests plays a central role in the ways adjudication procedures unfold. In this legal context, where truth is defined in legal terms and regarded as something that can and should be verified, and yet a dearth of empirical evidence for determining truth exists, judges and other asylum court representatives resort to suspicion as a compensating strategy.

Likewise, suspicion was a common point of departure for the conversion judges and court representatives I met during my fieldwork. Suspicion constituted a working tool, a predisposition that from the outset led them to consider the possibility that candidates might lie or pretend. Suspicion was a highly routinized and normalized strategy court agents learned to increasingly employ as they grew professionally. As I will show later in this chapter, candidates' court performances were hardly ever taken at face value. Suspicion had an intensely felt presence, evident in the court's most frequently occurring question, a question judges and representatives directed at each other, conversion teachers, host families, and even me: "Do you believe her?"

Naturally, court agents held and enacted suspicion to differing degrees, each drawing upon his own interpersonal skills and style of communication. Furthermore, agents deemed it necessary to exhibit varying levels of suspicion with different candidates, as some provided more substantial reasons for suspicion than others. Cultural stereotypes and sentiments toward the national mission additionally played a role in mediating degrees and forms of distrust directed at particular candidates.

Judge Rabbi Zehavi linked the context of the national mission to the question of suspicion, calling upon his colleagues to display "a distinctively low level of suspicion" toward candidates from an FSU background as something "needed now," particularly if they claimed Jewish ancestry. Another judge told me during a break between hearings why suspicion is not conducive to the national mission: "Look, we are trapped. I agree with you that not everyone whose conversion I govern truly underwent a transformation." As if to explain his sense of being "trapped," demonstrating once again the extent to which court rabbis tend to overlook lenient, Zionist halakhic approaches available in rabbinic literature, he paused for a second and then asked me rhetorically: "But do you have a better way to convert 270,000 [FSU] non-Jews?"

Somewhat contrary to these voices, several other judges expressed distinctively heightened levels of suspicion toward FSU candidates, describing them as the least trustworthy. "The South Americans never lie," one judge told me, quickly juxtaposing them with "the Russians [who] always lie." A court representative concurred: "Of course the Russians lie. What do you expect of people who lived for so long under a regime that constantly forced them to lie, particularly as Jews!?" A court representative explained to me why Russian-speaking candidates' distrust toward state officials lead him to reciprocally feel distrust toward them: "We have a great problem of trust with the Russians, not because they necessary lie, but because they come from a political culture wherein for 70 or 100 years they learned that any regime representative, no matter who he is, is their enemy, is against them. They constantly think to themselves, 'What should I say to this person to please him?' I might meet someone who truly keeps commandments, but he would fail on credibility issues with me because of such Russian attitudes of mistrust."

As predominant as suspicion was in the work of most court agents, they understood their labor as resting in no small measure upon trust as well. "Our default is to trust people, not suspect [them]" (Rosen 2010:212), Rabbi Israel Rosen, a senior rabbinic judge, writes in an article responding to accusations of having approved wink-wink conversions. He continues: "We give a basic trust in each soul that did well in the conversion ulpan and reaches out her arm to be accepted into the Jewish nation out of acceptance of the commandments. We reach out to her in our hand and heart, and we rely on the teachers who tutored this soul, as well as on the host family that accompanied her, and of course on a direct and skilled hour of acquaintance" (ibid.:211).

Even though Rabbi Rosen frames these techniques in idealist terms of trust, I see them as representing merely the opposite of the logic of suspicion described by other court agents. I met a number of agents who related to trust in ways similar to Rabbi Rosen. For example, Judge Rabbi Mizrahi reacted somewhat angrily when I asked him about examining candidates through a mode of suspicion: "No way would I work through suspicion. [If I did so] what is the point for me in this job? Where is the joy of conversion?"

Other court agents spoke about trust as a provisional mode they employ until candidates prove they deserve otherwise. Rabbi Levin told me:

> In my basic approach I certainly do not seek lies, God forbid! If I sought them, it would be unfair. I don't see it like that, and I don't have the mental capacity to work like that. I extend a huge credit. I trust [candidates] but this trust is not limitless. They must prove [to] me they warrant my credit, my trust. "You tell me you have a host family? No problem. I believe you. But next time when I see you, I expect that when I ask some questions about festive Sabbath dinners, you would know what to tell me." If they lie to me, I'll probably discover it but I'm not constantly troubled by this possibility.

"The possession of full knowledge," writes Georg Simmel, "does away with the need of trusting, while complete absence of knowledge makes trust evidently impossible" (Simmel 1906:449). As a strategy of investment in the potentiality of the future, trust is a mixture of knowing and not knowing, of evidence and expectation—a precarious attempt to rely on limited knowledge.[1] As Simmel teaches us, mass urban societies depend on trust in the most mundane and practical engagements, simply because individuals cannot possibly examine all the information they consume and have no choice but to accept what they are told in good faith.

The machinery of "good faith" requires individuals to develop a tenuous, depersonalized trust toward inadequately known systems, institutions, and people (Govier 1997:6). These tenuous formations of trust unavoidably entail risky decisions and vulnerability.

Focusing on such depersonalized and vulnerable relations, James Henslin (1968) offers a Goffmanian analysis of how cab drivers develop trust toward passengers, emphasizing some social actors' (passengers') dramaturgical self-definitions and other social actors' (cab drivers') willingness, or lack thereof, to interact with them upon this basis. I do not follow Henslin's strict dramaturgical approach and I do not view court agents as social actors in a narrow sense. Rather, in my attempt to understand their strategies of trust, I take into account the richer moral and political layers of their labor—how they are situated in the national mission as committed citizens and state persons. I also take into account their positions as leading rabbis and gatekeepers who need to constantly defend their labor and save face professionally in response to vast public and religious critique.

Thus court agents are situated in a concurrently powerful and vulnerable position.

It is clearly counterintuitive to view court agents as vulnerable. Undeniably, the young women dependent upon their discretion are from the outset far more vulnerably positioned. However, in order to understand court agents' simultaneous reliance on competing modes of suspicion and trust, we need to understand their position as both powerful and vulnerable. They demand, but also depend upon, successful conversion performances. They might firmly scrutinize these performances yet have no choice but to trust that they are not merely encountering empty shells.

Can We Trust You?

A version of the rhetorical question "Can we trust you?" was invariably directed by court agents at candidates and their spouses. The positive, reassuring answer given by all—none ever said no—was never simply accepted but instead constituted a point of departure for a rather painstaking assessment of the candidates' religious conduct and sincerity. An elaborate exercise in truth seeking, this assessment was essential for agents to decide whether to believe candidate performances.

The agents' understandings of suspicion and trust closely coincide with their legally oriented understandings of truth. As in juridical processes undertaken in civil legal systems in most industrialized states (Barnes 1994:35–42), for conversion court rabbis, truth holds a pragmatic rather than an absolute meaning. It rests on tangible and verifiable data, on evidence out there in the world (see also Good 2011; Kobelinsky 2015). Judge Rabbi Levi expounded in an interview: "Sometimes, to explain the conversion process to converts, I paraphrase the saying about justice: 'It should not only be done, but should manifestly be seen to be done.' Conversion too must not only be done but must also be seen to be done."

The common juridical demand for truth telling, "Tell the truth, the whole truth, and nothing but the truth," often articulated in jest during conversion hearings, ritualistically affirmed the value of truth as grounded in the working premise that candidates commonly, or at least potentially, lie.

With a nod to Rabbi Peres's cynical comment on "mind-reading technology," I maintain that the conversion court's labor actually rests on a "performance technology." This technology positions court agents not merely as an audience to converts' exhibition of correct legible signs but also as performers of bureaucratic expertise who know how to tell an authentic sign from a fraudulent one.

At the beginning of each court proceeding I observed, a rabbinic judge usually read aloud the candidate's conversion story as provided within the conversion portfolio. In chapter 5, I will discuss the scripted nature of these stories, but here I wish to note how conversion stories served as a means to assess candidates' sincerity. The pace of the narrative and its aesthetics, poetics, flow, and intonation all needed to cohere within the prevalent legalist-religious framework. Court rabbis frequently compared candidates' written stories to their spoken ones, looking for gaps, inconsistencies, and contradictions. They carefully attended to vocabulary, to a storyteller's tone, and to body language when observing a speaker. Did the language seem too rich, vernacular, or elegant for new immigrants? Did the personal letter appear artificial, as though written by someone else? Did the candidate speak too quickly or avoid eye contact, indicating that she might have simply memorized her narrative?[2]

In addition, court agents carefully inspected the personal appearance and dress style of candidates. Because rabbis knew candidates could strategically manipulate their attire for impression management, they expressed concern as to whether candidates' appearance while in court was typical or only tactical. In closed case discussions, judges raised the question of whether a candidate's partner's skullcap "sits well on his head," essentially asking if it appeared familiarly worn or awkward and therefore phony. Did female candidates' modest outfits appear "natural" to a religious community or, as a judge observed about a candidate, "She doesn't really know how religious women dress."

Beyond the religious norms of personal appearance, candidates were clearly also required to demonstrate practical knowledge of daily religious routines.[3] Judge Rabbi Nachum explained to me the logic of this assessment: "Blessings, prayers, and other practical issues are good indicators for us because they are measurable and detectable." Thus court agents invariably asked candidates to recite blessings and prayers and listened for their authenticity, judging whether they occupied an integral part of the candidates' lives or were memorized solely for the hearing. Regarding daily routines, judges asked candidates a grueling series of questions concerning, among other things, what blessings they said when they woke up, at what times they prayed, and what they liked to eat for breakfast, lunch, or dinner—assessing observance of kosher dietary laws, knowledge of what blessings are appropriate for which foods, when and with whom the candidates socialized, and how they tended to dress. Some court agents shared with me the ways experience had helped them develop and professionalize their methods for acquiring relevant information. The following brief excerpt demonstrates commonly used mechanisms for such investigations. It comes from an exchange between Rabbi David, a court representative, and Sveta, a student in Avner and Dvir's class.

RABBI DAVID: Do you do Kiddush [lit. "Sanctification"] and Havdalah [lit. "Separation"]?

SVETA: Yes, and I also light candles and go to synagogue.

RABBI DAVID: When did you light candles this past Shabbat?

SVETA: 7:20 p.m.

RABBI DAVID: When does Shabbat end?

SVETA: 8:15 p.m.

RABBI DAVID: How did you know this?

SVETA: I checked it on the internet.

RABBI DAVID: Tell me how you do Havdalah.

SVETA: I hold and light the Havdalah candle, fill a glass of wine, and let it overflow a bit.

RABBI DAVID: How long does it take you?

SVETA: Five minutes and then I say the Havdalah blessing.

RABBI DAVID: Before or after the meal?

SVETA: After.

The order of these questions was not arbitrary. By beginning with yes, no, and brief response questions about religious practices, followed by questions that sought descriptions of those practices in detail, Rabbi David skillfully worked to determine whether Sveta was sincere about having direct, experiential knowledge of Jewish ritual conduct, to determine whether she deserved his trust.

Such suspicion-filled dynamics did not always serve court agents in constructing a supportive ambience in court hearings and providing converts with pathways for their life-changing journeys. However, these dynamics were much in line with the conversion court's fundamental charge to gather salient information about candidates. The court's administrative head, Rabbi Eliahu Maimon, told me, his voice tinged with frustration, "Sometimes it bothers me, but there is no other way for the judges to get to know a person. You cannot do it without intrusive questions.... The question is how to find the right balance so that I am both being pleasant and getting the information I need to have about [a candidate's] ways of life."

With the exception of Rabbi Maimon, I got the general impression that rabbinic judges were not disturbed by the court's intrusive, suspicion-laden working tools. Identifying with the national mission and asserting their power as gatekeepers, the judges viewed their suspicion-laden modes of communication as an integral and justified part of their work routines. One judge found no relevance in my question about the court's intrusiveness, whereas another quickly answered: "Of course I am intrusive. She might invade the People of Israel in unkosher ways, so I'm on guard!" A third rabbinic judge admitted he sometimes feels uncomfortable with the necessity of suspicion, but added: "There is no other way to authorize conversions. Because conversion is such a prime Israeli national interest, my penetration [into candidates' lives] is vindicated."

After a few publicly disclosed, seemingly rare occasions in which rabbis obtained information about candidates through inappropriate means, discussions of the moral and legal ramifications of intrusive conversion procedures have arisen both within and without the conversion court system. One such case involved a rabbinic judge searching the call log of a candidate's cell phone and finding phone calls made on the Sabbath. He subsequently concluded the candidate was insincere and rejected her application (Nachshoni 2010). In another case, a judge searched the casing of a candidate's state identification card and found a prescription for birth control pills, which implied sexual immodesty. Her application was also rejected. The public and bureaucratic attention given to these exceptional cases highlights the common institutional mechanisms of suspicion that have generally proceeded unhindered.

Jewish Sincerity

Rabbinic judges used the notion of truth interchangeably with that of sincerity. In asking whether a candidate was "a true person" or "speaks the truth," they were essentially asking about her sincerity. Sincerity was presented as a hallmark of the entire conversion process. As we can infer from scholarly accounts of Jewish law, this rabbinic focus on sincerity is grounded in a long history of halakhic debates over the acceptance of the commandments. The notion of sincerity is an integral, and much discussed, component of these rabbinic debates. Shaye Cohen argues that during the second century AD, conversion to Judaism became not only a public affair but also a judicial act wherein the rabbis sought to verify the candidates' sincerity (S. Cohen 1999:223). As Sagi and Zohar (2007) teach us, rabbinic literature on conversion has since circled around debates over the requirement for converts to sincerely commit themselves to a life of Torah study and observance. The nature, importance, and assessment of converts' sincerity are all contested.

In my fieldwork the motto of sincerity encompassed the court agents' own institutional credentials. Rabbinic judges and court representatives presented their professional and religious selves by insisting on converts' sincerity. However, in line with the inclinations I identify in chapter 3, conversion candidates did not always trust judges' commitment to sincerity. A few said as much in postconversion interviews. According to Sveta: "If it really mattered to the rabbi who interviewed me, if it was really important for him to see if I plan to be religious, he wouldn't have been so careless and superficial with me. He wouldn't have asked such standard questions. But I think his goal, their goal, is to pass us, not to really look at us." Ania expressed her view as follows: "The rabbinic judge is a state worker, and the goal of the state is, you know. In point of fact, they understand they help in converting people who are not going to be religious. Even if I don't turn out to be strong enough [in religion], at least on my ID card I'll be Jewish. There will be one more Jew. This is how I see it."

The ways rabbinic judges judicially assessed the sincerity of candidates' performances teaches us about the ways sincerity is construed as coherence between words and deeds. Thus the formation of what I see as "Jewish sincerity" differs from the modern, primarily Protestant notion of sincerity, which can be essentially described as coherence between words and inner states. Lionel Trilling (1972) defines sincerity as a direct relationship between words and preexisting inner states. Following Trilling, Webb Keane (2002, 2007) theorizes the ways the metadiscursive concept of sincerity is embedded in Protestant and modern semiotic ideology—the set of assumptions modern people have about language. To the extent that the modern subject is defined as an autonomous interiority, words and other material constructs are assumed to only reflect and mediate the subject's interiority. Therefore, sincere speech makes the interior state transparent: "Sincere speech adds and subtracts nothing in words that was not already there in thought" (Keane 2007:210).

Sincerity is interactive in nature. In various Christian contexts, anthropologists of conversion document how converts interact with their new communities as sincere speakers of the language of faith (see Harding 2000, Keane 2002). Peter van der Veer also points to this interaction: "Sincerity of conversion is not only an interior state, but is located precisely in a performative act of communicating to others that one's sincerity is anchored in an interior state of self-questioning and self-accounting" (van der Veer 2006:11).

However, as Jewish Orthodoxy emphasizes religious, sometimes public, practice rather than an interior state of belief, we would hinder our understanding of sincerity or sincere speech about Jewish conversion if we only considered the relationship between words and inner states. In a religious setting evoking normative mottos such as "hearts follow deeds" (*acharei hama'asim imashchu halevavot*) and "We will do and obey" (*Na'ase venishma*), a setting clearly not premised on the semiotic production of inner truth (see Carr 2013), we are obliged to recognize the role of words in relation to deeds.

Indeed, in the conversion court words did not primarily reference inner states, such as beliefs, emotions, thoughts, or intentions; these inner states were not important in themselves. Rather, words exchanged in the rabbinic court were mostly linked to real deeds and actualized commitments in the world: "I light the candles"; "I listened to *Kol Nidrei* [lit. "All Vows"] on the eve of *Yom Kippur*"; "I am strict about eating only kosher food." Judges regarded these claims as sincere only so far as candidates provided additional and facile articulation of their respective deeds: the blessing over the candles and the exact time set for lighting them (which changes weekly); the opening of the Kol Nidrei prayer or knowledge of its ritual significance; practical rules for keeping kosher in one's own kitchen (such as how to separate dairy and meat foods in the refrigerator or how to manage with only one sink).

Rabbinic judges extended converts' words the greatest currency when those words were supported by demonstrated performances. When they were unsupported, judges reprimanded candidates about creating a sincerity problem for the court. Candidates passed when they demonstrated sufficient coherence between their life setting and religious conduct and their declaration of intentions and commitments. In these cases, they earned judges' trust and positive appraisal: "We are impressed with your sincerity"; "We have no doubt you are sincere."[4] Conversion performances were trials of sincerity.

To be sure, judges did not completely disregard the relationship between candidates' words and inner states. To some degree, they expected to learn about the intentions and emotions fueling converts' personal recounting of their paths toward conversion. Judges also asked some questions about Jewish tenets of faith and took candidates' affective declarations of oaths as evidence of true religious commitments. Furthermore, I did at times hear judges suspiciously speculating about some candidates' "real intentions," concerning whether they expressed what they "really felt" and "really intended to commit to." Nevertheless, because of the court's orthopractic orientation, candidates' internal, subjective states of intent and commitment were generally understood as measurable constructs evidenced in the empirical link between words and deeds.

For my interlocutors at the conversion court, this marginal significance attributed to inner truths was grounded in, and justified by, a significant principle in Jewish law—"Things of the heart are not things" (*Dvarim shebalev einam dvarim*), meaning that unspoken intentions cannot constitute valid grounds for legal decisions. Conversion judges often raised this principle in their closed discussions, generally when disagreeing about a particular candidate's merit. In so doing, they reminded each other that according to Jewish law, their debate must not focus on inferred intentions but follow clear, observable evidence. In the context of wide rabbinic and public discussions of conversion, senior judge Rabbi Israel Rosen names this principle as validating the conversion court's working methods, including basing decisions on in-the-moment observations. Referring to this "halakhic safety net" he writes:

> Halakhically-wise, we lean to some extent on the opinion that in conversion, as in property, marriage, and divorce laws, "Things of the heart are not things."

> Here is not the place to detail about which Jewish legal scholars do or do not hold this view. . . . One can find converts with integrity who, within time, have become more religious, and hence have started to have retrospective doubts about the level of sincerity they had had when they were authorized as Jews. Now, after two or three years, they want to re-convert with full conscience. It is inconceivable to think of opening a new track of "upgrading" conversion! No, it is not our way. . . .
>
> We judge each convert favorably, relying on the fact that we don't have before us any concrete counter-evidence, and, of course, no explicit expression on the part of the convert that conveys doubts about some of the commandments.
>
> (Rosen 2010:212)

The implied logic in Rabbi Rosen's words—converts should be presumed credible and sincere at the time of the conversion procedure—allows him to fully accept court performances. The emphasis on what converts demonstrate at the time of the giyyur procedure is prevalent in rabbinic discussions of conversion in modern times (see Sagi and Zohar 2007). In the course of my fieldwork I encountered this logic several times. For example, Rabbi Levin, the court representative, explained to me why he was not troubled by reported evidence of low levels of religious observance among approved converts: "I'm not alarmed by the fact that converts do not observe commandments after conversion. Life is dynamic and unexpected. Various streams pull them after conversion. They meet a secular boyfriend. They get confused. They become tempted and observing becomes impossible. We have to remember that we examine them at a very sterile, static moment, and I can only check whether at that moment they keep [commandments] or not."

Multisited Performance

> We really don't know as much about converts as people think we do. This is why the convert must show us the right signs and present the right figure, and I am extra cautious not to take it even further and say "the image" of "a real convert." Even the convert's friends have to think she is observant.
>
> —Judge Rabbi Bar

Despite thorough interrogation of conversion performances, rabbinic judges remained aware of the uncertainty of their assessments of candidates' sincerity and hence their susceptibility to empty and deceptive performances. Thus they expanded their field of vision to outside the court to compensate for their blind spots. In so doing, they constructed court hearings and the entire conversion process as multisited performances—spectacles of legible signs delivered by arrays of meaningful witnesses, including conversion teachers, synagogue sextons, host families, and the court's own representatives. At the court individuals positioned in all of these categories served as witnesses to the reliability of conversion performances, whether in writing, over the telephone, or in person. Synagogue sextons (*gabbaim*) tended to send letters of recommendation, whereas adopting families often sent representatives (usually host mothers who, expectedly, were more active than host fathers in guiding female converts) for court appearances.

In their testimonies, witnesses generally focused on those legible signs of religious conduct that candidates broadcast on their way to the conversion court. The language witnesses used to describe these signs was both empirical and impressional, referring not only to what candidates had been observed doing (lighting candles, reciting blessings over food, dressing appropriately, and the like) but also to general impressions they had made along the way.

To one candidate's benefit, her host mother noted her integrity: "She seems like a strong person with great willpower." Another host mother applauded her candidate's progress: "I saw her totally immersing in religious life. I can tell she did it with true intention." A third candidate was not as fortunate when her host mother told the court: "I evaluate her as an easily tempted woman." Yet another host mother described her candidate as "amazing": "She goes to the synagogue even more than I do. I admit, I get tired sometimes, but unlike me, she is very strict and consistent." This positive feedback elicited a pleased response from a judge: "Wonderful, the most important thing is that you saw her do all that and you know her as someone who observes the commandments."

In one case, a synagogue gabbai wrote in a letter read aloud in court: "I can attest to seeing her in synagogue during services a number of times, even in the winter on rainy nights." In another case, a teacher told the court: "[The convert] was doing well in class, but to tell you the truth, I was never really 100 percent convinced that her conversion went beyond that." At best, such testimonies converged to support a coherent conversion performance, whether or not they absolutely agreed with each other. In the rare cases in which clear discrepancies arose among these voices, or between them and the candidate's words, judges faced what they regarded as a sincerity problem requiring them to reevaluate the performance, sometimes by holding additional hearings.

By designating various players first as audiences and then as witnesses in the conversion rite of passing, rabbinic judges expanded their simultaneous strategies of suspicion and trust. Witnesses permitted rabbinic judges to assess whether particular candidates deserved their trust or must be treated with suspicion. Piotr Sztompka writes how trust develops easily when grounded in long-term interpersonal relations allowing a consistent flow of information and a high level of social visibility. When lacking thick textures of acquaintance, people must rely on secondary information from witnesses, experts, and others deemed trustworthy (Sztompka 1999:72).

Precisely this logic informed conversion rabbis in interviewing witnesses who had the chance to get to know a candidate throughout her process, who could attest as to whether they had developed trust in her performance. Put differently, in order to make determinations about candidates they hardly knew, rabbinic judges had to rely upon information from trustworthy observers. Anthony Good notes, "Truth is a statement made by a credible witness" (Good 2011:98). Judge Rabbi Dahan illustrated this logic well when he said to me: "Whatever the convert tries to sell us won't pass. We have 'people on the ground' who tell us how she's really doing. Their impressions are invaluable to us." Similarly, Judge Rabbi Tzadok explained: "Because I can't get to know the person in an hour, whether it's because the convert is too excited or simply dishonest, we must have people who report to us."

Court representatives were invariably regarded as dependable witnesses. Professionals, insiders to the court system, and presumably free from hidden biases, they provided judges with information they could readily embrace. All others testifying in court were fellow citizens and religious Jews, not specialized experts or practiced witnesses. Their authority derived simply from their role as spectators of the conversion performance at junctures deemed critical to the conversion process. Some witnesses carried more weight than others. Witnesses with established or demonstrable credibility, whether personal, religious, or professional, generally gained the court's trust easily, whereas witnesses who raised questions—due to inappropriate external appearance or untrusted religious affiliation—were taken with a grain of salt.

In court hearings I observed how conversion teachers enjoyed varying levels of trust and authority, primarily based on their histories at the court. While highly esteemed teachers' recommendations were welcomed with great respect, those from less-regarded teachers were accepted only hesitantly. For example, one judge explained to me why he was relatively easy on the candidate in a case I observed: "I am confident every time we work with Rabbi Moshe (the candidate's teacher). I know I can always trust his judgment. So after he gave us such positive feedback, I didn't need much." When new teachers appeared before the court, judges were cautious in relying upon their words. In one such case, judges hesitantly listened to the teacher's descriptions. Later when discussing his students' applications, they largely disregarded what he had said, even though he was still present in court and heard their deliberations, and instead relied more heavily on the testimony of the court's representative.

With regard to host families and synagogue gabbaim, judges tended to trust the testimony of those with whom they had already developed some personal or professional acquaintance, as evident from the words of one judge who, upon hearing the name of a gabbai authoring a recommendation letter, was quick to endorse it: "I personally have known this gabbai for a long time. I totally trust him, and suggest we take at face value everything he tells us about her." In another case, a pleased judge informed his colleagues that the host mother about to enter the court was his sister-in-law, advising them to "take her words seriously [because] she is a serious religious person." However, by and large, judges did not have any prior history with witnesses.

In trying to find ground for trusting unknown host families, judges often searched for cues about their religiosity and character, to the degree of occasionally interviewing them about their own lives. In one phone call with a host mother, a judge learned with marked concern that she was undergoing divorce, noting the "negative personal example" she might provide for her "adopted" convert. In another case, after an intensive phone call with a teenage girl in a host family, a judge cynically remarked, "I think the host family needs a host family." Judges were not particularly selective about the kind of religiosity host families needed to present so long as it fell within the wide realm of Orthodoxy. Even so, it was clear that host families, who conformed to those stringent and particular patterns of religiosity characterizing court agents, were given greater credence. From the outset, those families deemed merely traditional—that is, not religious enough—were not admitted.

I never observed a case in which candidates outright erred in selecting an acceptable host family, but I did observe cases in which candidates worked at presenting the trustworthiness of their host families by highlighting their appropriate religiosity. For example, in response to a judge's query, one candidate explained: "[The mother of my host family] is really-really religious. She always prays and studies Torah. Her husband studies in the evenings as well. And they have five kids!" The judges nodded approvingly. I also observed cases wherein religious women appearing in court in the capacity of host mothers made clear efforts to pass as good-enough, meaning religious-enough, witnesses.

The involvement of host families in the court procedure was significant in two senses. First, these fellow citizens (most of whom, unsurprisingly, were associated with religious Zionist communities) helped rabbinic judges to evaluate the viability of candidates' future religious conduct. Recall how judges were largely concerned with assessing candidates' levels of religious conduct in the here and now. Yet they also wanted to assess whether the candidates' current social settings would support them in maintaining religious conduct in the future. Since most candidates came from secular surroundings, host families served as possible hooks into religious communities, carrying the promise and potentiality of long-term religiosity. Very often, judges urged host families to continue relations with "their" converts so that, as one judge put it, they "won't fall back into secular habits."

When judges gleaned enthusiastic cooperation from families, they treated them as full partners, expressing deep gratitude for "helping [us] fulfill the national mission." They spoke to me of how calm these families enabled them to be, "knowing that converts would be in good families' good hands." It was clear that in such cases judges felt more secure, more confident in having authorized the conversions.

Secondly, host families lent public credibility to the national mission. They functioned as audiences, not only of candidates' multisited performances, but also of court hearings where judges performed meticulous evaluations of converts' sincerity. These families witnessed the ways conversion is a detailed, scrupulous procedure, too serious and too careful to be reductively associated with the public stereotype of a wink-wink conversion. In providing the court with legible signs of legitimate conversion, these families verified the procedure, rendering it more solid, more legitimate, and more robust.

The multisited performance described here depended upon subtle teamwork between rabbis, candidates, and witnesses. Such collaboration was necessary for both managing the flow of information between the parties and treating the conversion process as a serious enough rite of passage. This collaborative dynamic's centrality became most apparent in those instances when it broke down.

Breaking Down

In those rare cases (five out of the seventy-one hearings I observed) when candidates or their spouses disturbed the court's familiar dramaturgical routine, hearings broke down. These cases' particulars reveal much about the mechanisms regularly sustaining court encounters. On these occasions, rabbinic judges were bereft of valid information about candidates and were clearly embarrassed and frustrated, having been left alone in what usually worked as a collaborative endeavor. Partnerless, judges' general dependence upon legible signs and cooperative performances became all the more evident, highlighting the dramaturgical entanglements that regularly underlie court encounters. In what follows, I focus on excerpts taken from two of these unsustained conversion performances.

You Tie Our Hands

Chairing the conversion panel, Judge Rabbi Berko thumbed through the portfolio, trying to extract the salient details in Tanya's application. "Well, she is a [candidate] the court has met in the past," he informed his colleagues, then read aloud the documented recommendation of the panel that reviewed the case six months prior:

> We talked with the couple (married in a civil marriage). They were not ready for conversion. We revealed contradictions between the husband and his wife, so we asked them to further their advancement. It first seemed to us like they started a transformation, started to internalize a new way, but the facts we exposed didn't match this impression. We decided to let her undergo the "acceptance of the commandments" ritual, out of consideration of her illness (diabetes) and as an attempt to encourage them, but we postponed immersion [in the ritual bath] and conditioned our approval upon a fourth hearing.[5]

The three judges eyed each other with raised eyebrows, clearly expressing pessimism. They had good reason. After all, nearly all conversions are approved in one or two hearings, after which candidates are sent to immerse in the ritual bath. Only in this case did I observe a fourth hearing.

Rabbi Berko turned to Malka, the couple's teacher, asking for her opinion. She responded, "What can I say? They are okay, just okay. They do have a host family, though. It is a good thing. Look, this is the most we can get from them." The couple, Tanya and Sergei, was then invited to enter the courtroom.

I had already seen them earlier in the hallway and noted to myself how nervous they seemed; they paced back and forth, smoking, talking to each other quietly in Russian. They both seemed in their thirties. He was tall and muscular; she was petite and remarkably elegant in her skirt suit and high boots. Their command of Hebrew was good enough to allow a conversation with no need of translation.

It took Rabbi Berko only about five minutes to form an impression of them and their engagement in highly sporadic and selective religious practice, mostly consisting of occasional synagogue attendance and Sabbath observance. What most disturbed him was discovering that they had not fully attended synagogue services on Yom Kippur.

> RABBI BERKO, *raising his voice*: On Yom Kippur! What did you do on Yom Kippur? Where were you?
>
> TANYA: Here and there, and at home, resting, sleeping.
>
> RABBI BERKO: How come? Why didn't you go to the synagogue?

The questions hung in the air, meeting a regnant silence. Sergei and Tanya sat stiffly, appearing depleted and resigned. Malka shook her head disappointedly. Clearly trying to save the discussion, Rabbi Berko moved on to Simchat Torah [lit. "Joy of the Torah"], the holiday of rejoicing with the Torah, asking about the couple's observance then. Malka immediately jumped from her chair, declaring, "They celebrated. I have pictures! I saw them celebrating at the very end of Simchat Torah." She showed the judges the pictures, but they appeared unsatisfied. They continued to ask questions about the couple's celebration of the entire week of Sukkot (taking place immediately before Simchat Torah). Their questions were once again met with an embarrassing silence, yet the hearing went on. Rabbi Berko: "Explain to us, how do you decide when to go to the synagogue? After all, it is a place you attend for your own soul, not for Malka or for us. So how is it that on one Sabbath your soul urges you to go to synagogue but on the next Sabbath it does not?" Tanya and Sergei sat with their heads and eyes lowered, not looking at Rabbi Berko or even at each other, silently accepting his rebuke.

RABBI BERKO, *losing patience*: You don't respond. Tell me, how do you feel?

SERGEI, *searching for the right words*: I feel that, that . . .

RABBI BERKO: You want to say that you feel it is deeper than . . .

TANYA, *interrupting*: Yes, yes, he has been putting on tefillin for four months now!

RABBI BERKO: But Yom Kippur! Jews in Moscow risked themselves to go to synagogue, and you? You sit here in Israel, worthless, wanting your wife to be converted, but you hamper the conversion process every time anew.

TANYA: We think this time is different . . .

RABBI MENI, *crying out*: How different? Explain to us, what stops you from going further, stronger, deeper?

SERGEI *and* TANYA, *clearly looking nervous, speaking at once*: It is difficult. We are like returnees. It is hard at the age of 30 to change your life all at once!

RABBI MENI: Why do you say all at once? It has been since 2001. Four years! We all want and try hard to help you. But you, you don't move even one step further!

RABBI ISRAELI: Isn't it important to you?

SERGEI: It is extremely important, otherwise I would have given up by now. I want a Jewish *huppah*. I want to bring a child into a Jewish family.

RABBI MENI: You must understand. It is our responsibility to make sure that you progress nicely. We are emissaries of the People of Israel.

SERGEI: But we did advance!

RABBI MENI: Do you wear a skullcap all the time?

SERGEI: No.

RABBI BERKO: I just wonder when you will stop desecrating the Sabbath, when you will fully observe the Sabbath.

Tanya and Sergei stayed silent.

RABBI MENI: Is my question clear?

TANIA: Yes, but it is hard to give a specific date. See, we don't drive on the Sabbath.

RABBI MENI: Did you stop watching TV on the Sabbath? Have you gotten used to avoiding using electricity on the Sabbath?

SERGEI, *admitting*: Sometimes we forget.

The three rabbis, as well as Malka, Sergei, and Tanya, all looked despondent, without avenues for ameliorating the situation. After a long silence, Rabbi Meni asked Tanya and Sergei to leave the courtroom.

A man who appeared to be ultra-Orthodox, roughly in his forties, entered the courtroom. He introduced himself as Pinkas, the father in the couple's host family, a coworker of Sergei, and a returnee. The judges were visibly happy to converse with him, seeking his impression of Sergei and Tanya. They wondered aloud why Sergei was not as enthusiastic as Pinkas about religious life, beseeching him: "Help us. They are four years in the system. Each time we give them assignments. Usually most people are in our system a year, and if our impression is positive—we cannot tell what happens with them later on—but if in the court they make [a] good impression, we let them in. But here, tell us, can we trust Sergei that he will go to synagogue? They already announced the acceptance of the commandments and they still desecrate rules! Does Sergei go [to synagogue] only for us or has he really decided to make a change?"

To the judges' chagrin, Pinkas did not have much information to offer and was soon asked to leave the courtroom. Malka then asked permission to reenter the conversation: "Tanya was excellent at first. Sergei told me in our last session, 'Believe me, you will be pleased with us. We'll reach a point that you will tell me I'm doing good.' I told him, 'But we need this point to be here and now.'"

The judges did not know how to proceed. "I have never dealt with such a case," admitted one of them. His colleague shared his astonishment: "What are we asking? Only not to desecrate the Sabbath. That's all." Finally, after some debate, they decided to let the couple name the time frame they needed to further their observance to the point of fully observing the Sabbath. Sergei and Tanya were invited back into the courtroom.

RABBI BERKO *to Sergei*: Pinkas loves you and wants you to be like him. What do you say Sergei? Maybe if you decide to wear a skullcap all the time, you will also later decide not to desecrate the Sabbath?

SERGEI: I hope we'll reach this point sometime.

RABBI BERKO: You tie our hands. We want to help and you make it impossible. I have an offer. You tell us how much more time you need and we'll give it to you. Look, we are not detectives or investigators. We go only with your words, but we need to work according to religious law. There is no other way.

Tanya and Sergei sat silently.

RABBI BERKO: What do you want?

SERGEI, *sounding about ready to burst into tears*: I want a huppah.

RABBI BERKO: Tell yourself, "I will keep the Sabbath for three months and then we'll have a huppah." What is more on the table than this offer? What is your problem?

Tania and Sergei remained silent.

RABBI BERKO, *starting to lose his temper, shouting*: Give me a date. Give me something!

Still receiving no response, the judges finally gave up. They discussed the matter quietly and informed Tanya and Sergei that they expected to see them for the fifth time in three months' time. Agreeing in weak voices, their faces impassive, Tanya and Serge left the room. Rabbi Berko cried out to them: "Be strong, guys! Please, Sergei, do you promise me to be strong?"

Once again, the three judges looked at each other and at Malka, all raising eyebrows in bewilderment. They agreed that Sergei was "an especially hard nut to crack." Malka apologized for providing no solutions, and they moved on to discussing the next case awaiting them. At the lunch break a few hours later, Rabbi Berko stood beside me and sighed audibly. Grabbing the opportunity for a quick chat, I asked, "Tough day?" He spoke frankly: "So-so. Some days are harder, but today the first case was certainly odd. They are already years in the system. If they had wanted to, they could have played the game, had said to themselves, 'We'll go to synagogue for three months, do whatever it takes, come to the court and impress with our knowledge.' But no, they don't do it. They continue with conversion and yet they are also very quiet. We did whatever we could to help them here and in previous cases. But no, they don't let us help them. I don't get it."

In my field notes I titled this court hearing "The Stuck Couple." I observed them stuck in an exceptionally long procedure, stuck between their wish for a Jewish huppah and their "resistant souls," which only sporadically led them to the synagogue, and, finally, stuck between judges who manifestly tried to help them and their own silences.

Similar to silences in other social contexts, the couple's silences were burdensome and uncomfortable for all concerned. In this context, silence was a fruitless option because it directly countered the interactive nature of the court's dramaturgical guidance, undermining the formative, active role assigned to candidates in generating impressions.

With their silences, Tanya and Sergei left the judges puzzled and stymied, divested of their basic courtroom tools. To be sure, the three rabbis did not suspect Tanya and Sergei of insincerity. To the extent they had a sincerity problem, it came from being excessively sincere—disclosing too much of the truth—about their markedly insufficient religious conduct. Yet Tania and Sergei did constitute a pedagogic challenge and even a riddle the judges strove to comprehend, essentially asking themselves: Why, given their open desire for conversion, don't they simply do what it takes to convert? How come they don't take advantage of the clear and generous offers put on the table? Why do they tie the court's hands? Working in the name of the national mission, and feeling empathy for the couple's wish to get married halakhically, the judges could not simply reject Tania and Sergei. The degree of labor they invested in an attempt to maintain this couple's prospects was unique, and yet it illustrated a broader inclination of the conversion court: to never completely close the door to candidates. Throughout my fieldwork I did not observe or hear about any case in which converts were outright denied the option of conversion.

In my lunchtime chat with Rabbi Berko, he explicitly articulated his working assumption that most candidates and their spouses project themselves as willing to do whatever it takes to complete conversion. Sergei and Tanya strayed from this dramaturgical scheme. Interestingly, although the judges viewed the case as hopeless, they did not dissuade the couple from continuing to pursue conversion but instead once again offered deals and concrete routes for them to achieve their goal.

I Want to Help You but I Can't

Orly entered the courtroom. With her confident body language, firm voice, and direct gaze at the rabbis, she captured my attention. Curiously, she told her story in reverse. Pointing to her sixth-months-pregnant belly, she lead the judges back to the moment she discovered that she could not marry her boyfriend Motti through the rabbinate. Her mother had passed away in the FSU when she was young, and although Orly had been raised in Israel in a Jewish family and knew her mother was Jewish, she could not at that time trace official documents or locate a grave to confirm her mother's Jewish identity. The rabbinate therefore decided that Orly needed to undergo a speedy conversion process (*giyyur michamat hasafek;* lit. "conversion to eliminate doubt"), which meant she needed to partially join a conversion class (which she did for several sessions) and appear before the court prior to ritual bath immersion.

Orly elaborated how in the course of this hastened conversion process, she began to observe the Sabbath, recite blessings over the foods she ate, pray daily, and dress modestly. Her conversion performance continued soundly, and the rabbis seemed very pleased with both her sincerity and level of religious conduct. However, when they asked her about Motti, she indicated he was less inclined to embrace a religious way of life. Orly was asked out and Motti invited in.

Motti was "not very presentable," as one of the judges said mildly afterwards. His face unshaven, legs exposed in ripped jeans, Motti clunked in noisily in wooden clogs and sat down. From the outset, his Mizrachi, working-class appearance further disadvantaged him in the largely Ashkenazi-controlled rabbinic court. Somewhat theatrically, the judges used flattering and lofty words to commend Orly and her impressive willpower.

MOTTI, *nodding in agreement*: Yes, she has been an influence on me.

RABBI USHPIZ: One second, she needs to influence you? How come?[6]

MOTTI: I'm secular. I'm a big boy, already forty. Because of Orly's conversion, I started to lay tefillin sometimes. But I'm not religious, and I won't lie to you. I don't intend to become religious.

RABBI USHPIZ: What bothers me is that Orly shares her life with you. Will you keep family purity laws?

MOTTI: Yes.

RABBI TZUR: Great. I'm writing it down in Orly's file. Please wait outside.

Although the encounter with Motti was extremely brief and seemed to go smoothly, the rabbis proceeded to discuss Orly's case at length and arrived at the decision to reject her application. Throughout their discussion, Rabbi Ushpiz set the tone, arguing to his colleagues that there was significant cause for concern. Orly and Motti did not have a religious host family and had hardly attended conversion classes. Most importantly, the conversion file cited Motti declaring his religious adherence as only temporary. Rabbi Tzur suggested that they call in Motti and see if he might express regret at having made this statement, but the other two rabbis thought it is pointless. "Despite all good intentions, it won't work," summarized Rabbi Ushpiz.

When Orly and Motti reentered the courtroom, Orly was smiling. Yet within a few minutes, she was in tears. Rabbi Ushpiz straightforwardly explained the situation. Motti sat stunned. Rabbi Ushpiz continued in a long monologue, concluding with: "If Orly converts, your home and the family you raise must be religious." Motti responded crisply "That will never happen. We will return to being secular." Orly glared at him severely.

RABBI USHPIZ: I will not argue with you. That's fine. That is what I imagined to myself and that is why we cannot accept Orly for conversion.

MOTTI: But it is her conversion, not mine! I am a Jew. And what would have happened if she had come here without a partner? And if one day she would like to become secular again?

RABBI USHPIZ: She cannot. She is supposed to promise here, and it cannot be an empty promise.

MOTTI: But this is exactly what you force her to do.

RABBI USHPIZ: On the contrary. I respect your choice, hence I think conversion is not feasible. I don't want her to lie. Observance is the basis of conversion.

The debate appeared as if it could have raged forever in repetitive circles, but the court representative came in and urged the judges to hurry up (having four more cases still scheduled for the day). Rabbi Blau offered to wrap things up with Motti and Orly in another room, while his colleagues began on the next case. The three entered a small side office with me as a captivated observer. The conversation went as follows:

RABBI BLAU: It is not ok that only now you are hearing a full explanation about what is required of you.

MOTTI *agitated, raising his voice and interrupting*: I have many friends who became religious. I don't know if and whether it will ever happen to me. But not this way, not forcibly. Of course you expect me to wear a skullcap. This is the system.

RABI BLAU: Not the system, halakha.

MOTTI: So you are telling me that because of me, Orly cannot undergo conversion?

RABBI BLAU: Not because of you, because of her, because she is choosing to live with a non-religious spouse.

MOTTI: So, practically, you coerce us.

RABBI BLAU: Not me, halakha.

MOTTI, *shouting*: But you are the representative of halakha. You shove it down my throat (his hands gripping his throat, demonstrating his feeling strangled).

RABBI BLAU, *speaking in a patient and emphatic voice*: I can be angry with you but it won't help. I'm subjected to halakha just like you.

MOTTI: So I should have come here a liar? Come with a skullcap and say amen and promise to observe everything? How should I have felt about this? (banging on the table and further raising his voice) "Ah, I tricked you." I would have turned out a liar but I don't want to. I am a truthful man. I came from a religious home, but I chose to be a secular Jew.

RABBI BLAU: Everything you say is true. But I cannot help you. I want to help you, but can't.

MOTTI: What do you want from me? Do you want me to come here with a mask?

RABBI BLAU: It is not a mask.

MOTTI: It is [a mask] because I'm not a religious person. Will you write in the file it is because of me that you didn't convert her?

RABBI BLAU: Of course. We must explain the reason for our refusal. It must all be documented.

MOTTI: Enough, this is a useless conversation. (Turning to Orly) Next time go without me, tell them we broke up.

ORLY, *appearing embarrassed, ignored Motti and turned to Rabbi Blau*: See, there is an improvement. He calls himself secular although he does observe things.

MOTTI, *interrupting her heatedly*: The fact that I go to synagogue does not mean I'm religious. It's not my place! [*Turning to Rabbi Blau*] What else do you want from me? I say blessings over food, put on tefillin every morning . . .

RABBI BLAU, *smiling*: I'm beginning to think you are not as secular as you are saying you are. We demand that you wear a skullcap, keep the Sabbath and holidays, keep kosher. With such a strong wife, it will be easier.

MOTTI, *appearing momentarily tempted to consider such a scenario*: Yes, you are right. She has already influenced me.

RABBI BLAU: So, look, there is a chance. Get to the basics of all this . . .

MOTTI, *interrupting*: We just keep going in circles. I could have come out from here with a wish to respect the process she's going through, but now I will say [bleep]. [*Whining*] I so wanted us to have a Jewish wedding.

RABBI BLAU, *looking at his watch*: So what do you say? I'll give you a list of themes to study?

MOTTI: But I know all this. I graduated from a religious school, but I'm telling you, I'm secular.

RABBI BLAU: Begin the process, wear a skullcap, keep kosher, do something, begin somewhere.

MOTTI, *commanding*: I want Orly to immerse [in the ritual bath] before the baby is born.

RABBI BLAU: No, I first need to see you wearing a skullcap.

MOTTI, *in a serious voice*: When?

RABBI BLAU: Let's say in a few months.

MOTTI, *cynically*: So how about next week? I'll come with a mask and that's it?

RABBI BLAU, *losing patience*: Do you want a list of subjects or not?

MOTTI: Yes, no, ugh. [*grumbling*] I don't want to get married [in a civil marriage ceremony] in Cyprus.

Rabbi Levin, the court representative, entered, indicating to Rabbi Blau he must end the meeting. A month later Rabbi Blau told me that Orly had called him to personally thank him for his patience and sensitivity and to update him about their meeting's influence on Motti, who was now willing to observe whatever was needed.

Orly's quickened conversion resembled common circumstances that lead many other young Israeli women from an FSU background to seek conversion—romantic relationships with Jewish-Israeli men. Yet Orly's advanced pregnancy and belated discovery of her non-Jewish status generated a palpable time pressure and radicalized these circumstances. Other times during my fieldwork when evidently pregnant women appeared before the conversion court, judges seemed to understand the cases' urgency, tended to be somewhat gentler with the candidates, and moved things along rapidly. But in Orly's case, the judges' intransigence showed how something had clearly gone wrong. While Rabbi Ushpiz generally tended toward stringency and high demands, it was Motti's performance that actually thwarted the hearing. Rabbi Blau expressed to the couple how he "wanted to help but couldn't."

From the moment Motti entered the court, he broke basic rules sustaining its interaction. His absence from conversion ulpan sessions contributed to his dramaturgical ignorance. To begin with, Motti's attire was thoughtless and ill mannered, conveying misunderstanding of the court's formality or even a lack of respect. More importantly, Motti was exceptionally, inappropriately (to the court) candid, lacking any filters to refine his speech. Sometimes he even spoke to Orly with untoward familiarity—"Go without me. Tell them we broke up"—crossing boundaries between front stage and backstage.

From the outset, Motti declared himself a secular Jewish Israeli. To be sure, "secular" was anomalous to the court's normative conversion performances. "Secular" Jews did not appear in court, or to be precise, spouses and certainly candidates never presented themselves as secular before the court. When rabbinic judges asked spouses about their self-identities and social classification as Jews, they typically received answers positioning the speakers as traditionally inclined Jews. I heard: "I'm traditional"; "I come from a traditional background"; "I'm trying to get closer to religious life"; "I'm open to taking up more commandments"; and "I had distanced myself for a few years from religious life but now I'm falling in love with it again."

While Motti may have observed religious commandments as rigorously as some other candidate partners, he persistently and proudly called himself secular. He spoke as a "big boy," who knew a thing or two in life, who had made a deliberate choice that cannot be undone. In speaking boldly and candidly, Motti handicapped the judges, initiating an inextricable standoff. Tapping into the politicized Israeli discourse pitting secular against religious Jews, Motti invited a direct confrontation with the judges. Instead of fostering common ground with the court rabbis—after all, they cared deeply about Jewish marriages—he undermined any potential ratification of Orly's conversion performance. Only after Orly informed Rabbi Blau that Motti was willing to play the endorsed spousal role would the judges reconsider the case. Only by recommencing the conversion performance, and correctly this time, could the conversion procedure resume.

Affective Passwords

There is one subtle collaborative form that hardly ever fails—ritual dramatization. By composing and staging affect-laden rituals that formalize acceptance of the commandments, rabbinic judges provide climactic moments whose profound effects on candidates offer additional evidence of their sincerity. In this sense, court agents not only fastidiously evaluate performances whose framework they helped establish, as I argue earlier, but also participate in producing them. In so doing, they partake in creating the very impressions that candidates made on them. Requiring candidates to convince them, rabbinic judges also help create the legible signs needed to convince them. These dramatized moments of testimony help judges foster trust in conversion as a genuinely significant rite of passage. They additionally serve as a means for advancing public trust in conversion.

The acceptance of the commandments ritual is generally performed during the concluding stages of court hearings, as a final ratifying act before converts are sent on to the culminating immersion ritual. Whether the ritual is used to indicate final approval of the conversion application or serve as an intermediate means for encouraging or further testing candidates, rabbinic judges told me that they often approach this moment with lingering doubts. For these judges, the acceptance of the commandments ritual is a moment of grace, order, and reassurance concluding a process marked by uncertainty, doubt, and suspicion.

Such moments create the possibility of what Adam Seligman calls a "space of a shared 'could be'" (Seligman 2010:12)—a meaningful "as if" experience not only for converts but also for their audiences and orchestrators. Regarding the effects of Dutch naturalization ceremonies on the cynical civil servants who organize and perform them, Oskar Verkaaik writes: "The local bureaucrats remake the ritual, but the ritual also transforms them . . . thanks to a form that does not allow irony or ridicule to continue" (Verkaaik 2010:70, 78). In a French bureaucratic context, Carolina Kobelinsky (2015) shows how the success of political asylum applicants depends in part on applicants' ability to elicit emotional responses from asylum court judges: "Emotions reinforce the distinction between those who are regarded as real refugees and those who are believed to exploit the system, as the affective reactions of the judges become an indicator of the sincerity of the applicants" (Kobelinsky 2015:85).

Returning to the conversion ritual, the power of what Theodore Jennings (1982) describes as "ritual knowledge" in the creation of trust rests upon two attestations. First, candidates repeated verbatim a declaration stated by a rabbinic judge. Then they were asked to recite the daily and definitive Jewish prayer, "Hear O Israel." One such ritual proceeded as follows:

> RABBI: Repeat after me, I take it upon myself . . .
> CANDIDATE: I take it upon myself . . .
> RABBI: To keep all the commandments . . .
> CANDIDATE: To keep all the commandments . . .
> RABBI: To which women are obligated . . .
> CANDIDATE: To which women are obligated . . .
> RABBI: And I believe in one God which is not flesh.
> CANDIDATE: And I believe in one God which is not flesh.
> RABBI: Congratulations. We are delighted to welcome you into the Jewish nation. Now you can say Hear O Israel.
> CANDIDATE, *often out loud*: Hear O Israel, the Lord is our God, the Lord is One. Blessed be the Name of His glorious kingdom for ever and ever.

Some candidates then continued the prayer quietly by heart or reading from their prayer books.

Like other components of the conversion rite of passing, this two-stage avowal is interactive and theatrical. In the first stage, candidates affirm their acceptance of religious observance, as if orally signing a contract of conversion. The details, as well as the exact phrasing, of this contract are predetermined; candidates' own spontaneous words would not suffice for symbolizing their joining the Jewish nation. Rather, the gatekeepers representing the judicial and bureaucratic power of both the Jewish state and Jewish law furnish legitimate and legitimizing utterances. This formality sanctifies the ritual, demarcating and elevating it from the more mundane, trial-like exchanges that had unfolded prior to it.

In the next stage, candidates recite a central, even iconic, Jewish prayer, this time not as a display of religious proficiency but as a performative password to full Jewish belonging. Prosaic as this prayer is, it also dramatically connotes intense moments in the lives of Jews and the Jewish experience writ large. Hear O Israel—known to be the final words recited by Jews entering Nazi death chambers—is historically associated with horrifying moments of private and collective uncertainty and mortality and has provided Jews with a powerful prayer for expressing utmost fear and hope (cited in El-Or 2006:150).[7]

As expected, this well-structured ritual is both highly effective and affective. Nearly all of the candidates whose conversion procedures I observed appeared overtly excited and sentimental in this moment. Many were in tears, sometimes to such an extent as to almost hinder the ritual's completion. Spouses, friends, teachers, and host families were habitually invited back into the courtroom to attend the ritual and also appeared quite moved. Even judges themselves at times seemed touched, albeit to a lesser degree. A few of them told me that when they had begun their work at the conversion court, they would become highly emotional and even shed tears during the ritual. Some also expressed regret for their current mellowed sentiments. I related to their experience, having my own sensibilities attenuated by the ritual's routinization. Whereas at my first hearings I felt emotions grip my throat anew each time, over time the ritual gradually lost its poignancy.

Judges often intensified the affect-laden ambience by constructing this conversion ritual as marking a substantial, dramatic departure from candidates' previous non-Jewish identities. For example, they invited candidates to regard the hearing date as a "second birthday," evoking the metaphor of a delivery room and asking candidates about their selection of a new Hebrew name to mark their transformation. In those cases where candidates wanted to simply keep their old Hebrew or "foreign" names, judges urged them to at least add a name to signal their rebirth.

There was an "as if" element in this theatrical construction. Judges did not often personally favor such a radical biographical model (see chapter 5), yet their efforts to support that model were not mere empty performances. Rather, these performances drew on the religious imagination; in particular, the Talmudic dictum associating giyyur with birth (Sagi and Zohar 2007:271). In addition, by orchestrating these performances, the judges aimed to mark the conversion ritual as a memorable and binding moment, with the hope that it would enhance converts' religious conduct in the future. Rabbi Cohen described to me his approach: "I'm not usually a big fan of rituals but, in conversion, it is much nicer that we turn it into a ritual. . . . I think the candidates like this kind of talking, about being born again and having a new birthday. Halakhically speaking, it is not precise because we don't really forgive the person for former sins and she's not really a new person. But in the framework of greeting the convert with *Mazal tov* [lit. "good luck"; "congratulations"] it is a nice thing to say."

The affective dimension of the conversion ritual is both well orchestrated and eagerly embraced as a sign of sincerity. Similar to conversion rituals in other contexts, the fact that this ritual is conducted in front of meaningful audiences augments its public authority.[8] Thus Rabbi Bar told me he did not want "to develop immunity or become indifferent to the conversion ritual." Indeed, judges seemed pleased to see host families' emotions and even my own, our reactions supplying important evidence of the sincerity of the process. Building on the gripping power of the conversion ritual, judges sometimes outwardly publicized it as a dependable indication of their trustworthy work. The following extracts from articles written by conversion court judges appear in periodicals for religious audiences. They demonstrate public framings of reliable conversion:

> "I invite Rabbi Brandes [who had criticized wink-wink conversions; see Brandes 2008] to join us at the court and experience the acceptance of the commandments ritual, which is the pinnacle of a long process of learning and practice of Jewish life. Many converts shed tears on this occasion, and these are not artificial tears or an expression of delight following a successful deceptive trick. We

> are convinced that the great many of those standing before us are sincere at the time of the ritual, and do not stage a show or an impersonation. (Rosen 2010:211)
>
> We accepted her wholeheartedly; she said the customary wording of acceptance and "Hear O Israel" in great excitement. The heart of the hosting mother was filled with blessing. After the candidate and the host mother went outside the courtroom, we were free to look at our guests sitting in the corner. For us it was one hearing among many, but not for our Haredi guests—their eyes red and wet, their voices quivering, soulful. It was evident they understood now that the newspapers' representation does not reflect the court reality. In thrilled hearts they bid goodbye to us with "well done." It is a common phenomenon to see the tears and crying of converts when they accept the commandments and say "Hear O Israel."
>
> (Bass 2008:41)

Similarly, both teachers and converts shared with me their understanding of this conversion ritual as distilled evidence of sincerity. Regardless of whether converts would indeed fulfill their promise to observe commandments, their affect-laden experience in the court produced legible signs of sincere conversion. Interestingly, in their accounts of the ritual moment, my interlocutors largely, if implicitly, presented sincerity as a correlation between words and inner states as opposed to words and deeds.

Yosefa, a teacher in an Education Ministry ulpan, told me: "In that moment, when she is there at the rabbinic court, she fully commits herself, and she means it from the depths of her heart. I'm sure of it. Look at her, look! She is undoubtedly going through something. Later, you know, things change." Except for one convert, who spoke scornfully about the acceptance of the commandments ritual, comparing it to empty communist oath taking, the converts I interviewed cherished their ritual. They framed it as a wholehearted promise and stood behind their words even if admitting they had never before actually considered becoming religious Jews. I listened puzzled to Sveta when, a moment after recounting her highly selective adherence to religious practice, she expressed faith in her own words of promise and prayer: "I didn't lie to them one bit. It is true that [the rabbinic judges] have a different understanding than I do of what it means to observe commandments. Ok, so what? Each of us has his own answer. When I promised, when I confirmed my wish to become Jewish and when I said

'Hear O Israel,' I meant it all." Similarly, when I asked Lena if she felt discomfort during the ritual, knowing that she did not plan to live religiously, she said she was not at all troubled by it: "I had no problem whatsoever. After all, I know what the commandments are. . . . You convince them and you convince yourself and it is all fine. It is a matter of nuances what kind of Jew you eventually become. I was whole in my mind and my words."

These accounts demonstrate the effective and formative role played by ritual knowledge in sustaining conversion performances. As an interactive mechanism of trust building, it allows its various audiences and performers to frame conversion as a sincere and trustworthy act. This interactive labor arrives at its culmination in the ritual bath.

You Are a Jew Now

On their way out of the courtroom, candidates authorized to immerse in the ritual bath would generally hear the judges congratulating them with a warm "Mazal tov!" These festive words also titled the formal missive sent to those finally destined to immerse in the ritual bath, framing their upcoming mikveh experience as unforgettable. Converts were advised to mark the special day by inviting family and friends to join the occasion, to toast them and take pictures.

However, in my days observing at the mikveh, I hardly ever saw such markers of celebration. To begin with, the ramshackle building hosting the ritual bath chambers, set in a poor urban neighborhood in Tel Aviv, did not readily lend itself to such recognition. On the humid summer days of my observations, the long wait in the stifling reception room was far from pleasant. Over my repeated visits I grew to appreciate the plastic flowers set in a cheap vase atop a stained tablecloth and the raucous but useless ceiling fan gyrating above. Xeroxed proverbs that nobody ever read hung taped to the walls. Most converts came alone or with a friend or spouse. I was not surprised to see them rush out once the ritual was completed and papers signed.

The mikveh attendants themselves—three male attendants and one female attendant—did not live up to the vivid framing suggested by the formal missive sent to converts. They always seemed short on time, overloaded, understaffed, and running behind schedule. Two days a week they began their work early, first supervising the conversion of about a dozen young children—usually non-Jewish children adopted by Jewish Israelis. Then they handled the conversion of approximately twenty-five adults, most of them women, which had to take place before sunset.

After finishing her morning shift in the conversion ritual bath, Manuela, the female attendant, had to travel to another ritual bath, where she supervised the immersion of Jewish women in ritual cleansings for sexual purity, which must always take place after sunset. Two of the male attendants took afternoon shifts in the adjacent ritual bath designated for Jewish men.

Relentlessly rushing in and out of the four mikveh chambers, taking care that they remain clean, and handling conversion procedures (accepting converts before immersion and filling out forms afterward), the mikveh attendants were continually occupied. Given this taxing routine, their profound engagement with immersion as a dramatic and affect-laden ritual was remarkable. They made notable efforts, dedicating precious time and energy to constructing moving ceremonial acts.

In doing so, mikveh attendants hunted for legible signs of religious sincerity and seemed eager to treat affective verbal and bodily components of immersion as just such signs. They took pride and genuine delight in the ritual, employing religiously discursive means to augment the understanding they shared with converts that a moving ritual indexes a meaningful, transformative conversion. Manuela was particularly expressive in constructing the immersion as a rebirth and spiritual uplifting—a moment of heavenly mercy when converts open a new chapter in their lives and pray for God's blessing.

Interestingly, these efforts to build trust in the ritual's signification did not preclude suspicion. The mikveh attendants sometimes wondered about the sincerity of the converts they met and, relatedly, about the worthiness of the conversion procedure they had undergone in court. "I have my own suspicions," admitted one attendant. Another one told me, "I cannot avoid wondering whether I am participating in a dishonest conversion." Mikveh attendants do not hold any authority to question the conversion petition. Lacking any halakhic or bureaucratic prerogative, they simply govern the ritual's conduct to validate it halakhically. Thus I never witnessed attendants pursue interrogative exchanges with converts or openly express suspicions.

In interviewing Rabbi Ron, the Conversion Administration's official in charge of conversion ritual immersions, I learned that he instructs his mikveh attendants to refrain from such interrogations since they are "not productive. They lead you nowhere. . . . Ultimately, they will embarrass themselves. Anyway, they can do nothing about what they discover in the mikveh. The decision has been already made." One mikveh attendant confessed to me: "I try to repress these questions, these suspicions I have." Another one said: "I sometimes prefer to know as little as possible. It might only frustrate me." In what follows, I describe one case of a successful—that is, moving—ritual immersion. In doing so, I aim to emphasize its dramaturgical work, which contributes to cultivating trust in the state's conversion process.

Katya was in the water when the three male attendants and I entered the mikveh chamber. Katya had already immersed naked in Manuela's presence, but by then Manuela had dressed her in the pastel-flowered gown worn by all female converts for the ritual. Long and of dense cloth, it fully covered her body, but it also floated up stubbornly, causing Katya evident discomfort. Blinking vigorously and knocking water from her ears, she tried to engage with the male mikveh attendants as they asked some preliminary questions and then administered the prescribed ritual. Manuela and I stood to the side.

RABBI AMRAM: Do you want to be a Jew?

KATYA: Yes.

RABBI AMRAM: Are you happy to be a Jew?

KATYA: Yes.

RABBI AMRAM: Are you married?

KATYA: No, I'm divorced.

RABBI AMRAM: What commandments does a married woman need to observe?

KATYA: Family purity.

RABBI AMRAM: OK. Listen. I will say the words of acceptance of the commandments and you will repeat everything after me. Then you will fully immerse and then say the blessing of immersion. Then you'll immerse once again. It is only after the first immersion that you become a Jew, so we let you bless over the immersion and immerse again as a Jew. Clear?

Katya nodded.

RABBI AMRAM: I take upon myself to keep . . .

KATYA, *her voice quivering*: I take upon myself to keep . . .

RABBI AMRAM: the Torah and the commandments that the people of Israel received on Mount Sinai . . .

Addled by the long sentence in formal Hebrew, Katya finally made it through.

RABBI AMRAM: and all the sanctified customs of the people of Israel.

KATYA: and all the sanctified customs of the people of Israel.

RABBI AMRAM: And I take upon myself to keep the Sabbath and kosher laws.

KATYA: And I take upon myself to keep the Sabbath and kosher laws.

RABBI AMRAM: And when I get married, with God's help . . .

KATYA: And when I get married, with God's help . . .

RABBI AMRAM: I will keep family purity.

KATYA: I will keep family purity.

RABBI: And I believe only in one God.

KATYA, *crying*: And I believe only in one God.

Manuela looked over at Katya warmly, while the three men avoided doing so, seeming to guard against impure thoughts. Later, one of them explained to me that they tried to be righteous and have good thoughts in these moments of conversion and to remember it is a mitzvah and not only a routine. Katya then fully immersed in the water. When her head emerged, she invoked: "Blessed are You, My Lord, Ruler of the Universe, Who has sanctified us with the commandments and commanded us concerning immersion." Crying, she immersed once again, now for a longer time, sinking down, bending her body into a fetal position.

Rabbi Amram looked at Manuela and me pleased, saying: "She is a Breslov [a branch of Hasidim, known for its religious zest]—doing everything with enthusiasm." Manuela nodded. Katya's head emerged for a second time. Rabbi Amran asked her to place her left hand on her belly (to distinguish her upper from her lower body, between those organs associated with wisdom and those with corporeal functions) and her right hand over her eyes, and to recite "Hear O Israel." She did as told. Upon conclusion, Manuela congratulated her: "Mazal tov, mazal tov. You are a Jew now." The three male attendants echoed perfunctorily "mazal tov," and then I added my own embarrassed greetings.

The male attendants then asked Katya for her new Hebrew name. She appeared to have been anticipating this moment and joyfully declared: "Ma'ayan" (lit. "wellspring").[9] "Great. I'm writing down Ma'ayan, the daughter of Abraham and Sarah,"[10] said Rabbi Amram and added, "Now, because you got so emotional, you can say 'Who Has Given Us Life' [Shehecheyanu; a common Jewish prayer marking special occasions and expressing gratitude]."

Katya-Ma'ayan did so, and the three male attendants left the mikveh chamber. She climbed out of the bath, wet and smiling, to receive from Manuela warm kisses on each cheek.

About forty minutes later, as the mikveh was quieting down after a busy day, I sat with Rabbi Amram in the reception room. He explained to me that only when he feels a true, genuine delight on the part of converts does he suggest that they recite Shehecheyanu: "It is not a must to say it. If I feel someone is not overtly happy, I do not suggest it so that I won't implicate her in a wasted blessing." Sitting there, we saw Ma'ayan preparing to leave the building. She had likely taken a shower and blow-dried her hair. After finalizing her papers with another attendant, she greeted us on her way out. We said hello back. After she stepped outside the building, Amram asked me, "Who was she?" I reminded him, "That was Katya, now Ma'ayan. You just handled her immersion." Rabbi Amram: "Oh, that's her. I didn't recognize her. They look so different when their hair is wet and when it is dry. It's really hard to recognize them."

Katia's immersion ritual proved compelling for all participants and audience members. Its strength lay precisely in its ability to align her and the mikveh attendants in a shared "affective economy" (Ahmed 2004), producing, circulating, and building upon sentimentality. The communicative, interactive, and legible nature of this sentimentality was vital for the ritual's success. In cases I observed where converts were reticent, mikveh attendants were unsure as to how to pursue and construe the ritual. For example, when a convert was unresponsive to the attendants' queries as to whether she was happy to be there, they persistently repeated the question despite being baffled and embarrassed. After a few long silent minutes, the convert responded evidently annoyed: "I heard you. I was in my own world. Is that not legitimate? Do you want me to tell you how I feel? Yes, I'm happy!" On the other hand, when converts visibly expressed delight—one convert recited "Hear O Israel" with a special melody; another said she felt like she was in heaven—the mikveh attendants clapped, cheered, and shed tears. The ritual worked.

During Katya's typically brief ritual, Rabbi Amram and the other mikveh attendants deciphered her affective performance. Although conversion ritual immersions occur as a somewhat impersonal, factory-like process, the attendants felt as if they could peer into Katya's soul and detect what conversion meant for her. They needed to determine whether it was fitting that she recite Shehecheyanu. Tellingly, despite his insight into her soul, less than one hour later Rabbi Amram did not even recognize her.

* * *

The authorization of conversion is a dramaturgical achievement, one not to be taken for granted given the uncertainties and tensions underlining the national mission. The fact that the court situation hardly ever breaks down is rooted in the preparatory labor initiated in the conversion ulpan and in the well-orchestrated religious performances enacted collaboratively, if precariously, in the court. The projection of credible-enough, sincere-enough conversions is a win-win achievement, allowing both court agents and conversion candidates to advance their interdependent goals. Yet this achievement also rests upon additional supporting performers and audiences—some of whom are present in court and others who are physically absent but critically present in the political dynamics constituting and surrounding the conversion policy. Precarious as they are, conversion performances cannot fully efface the scathing critique directed at the conversion policy. However, they do make the actual interactions between converts and court agents manageable. As Rabbi Sirkis suggested in the epigraph opening this chapter, the daily routines at the court allow participants to look at themselves at the mirror and love, or at least accept, what they see.

In the next chapter I focus on a critical piece of this precarious dramaturgical achievement—the collaborative scripting of convincing conversion stories. Through these mechanisms, candidates learn to tell gatekeepers plausible stories about who they are and who they wish to become. These stories fill conversion performances not only with words but also with meaning and sense.

FIVE

Biographical Scripts

Tell Us About Yourself

YELENA DIDN'T WAIT for Dvir's permission to speak. Interrupting him forcefully, as she often did when teachers discussed the requirements for conversion with the class, she cried out in frustration, "So what should I tell them? What do they even want to know about me?" Dvir, the conversion teacher, who had grown impatient with such interruptions, looked at Yelena, holding up his hand to stop her barrage of questions. A few minutes earlier he had begun the lesson with news that in two weeks Rabbi David, the court representative, would begin his first round of meetings with students. Now was the time to start preparing. In most conversion classes, he explained, the first round of interviews takes place much earlier, roughly two months into the course. But for some reason, in their class it had been delayed. He continued: "Here we are, already five months into the course, so now we really have to focus on the interviews." In order to prepare for this meeting, he told his students, they needed to write an autobiographical letter. "This isn't a standard CV, like a job resume. It's more like a kind of story—where you came from, when you made aliyah, how you got into this conversion thing, stuff like that—so that they [the court agents] can start to get to know you. If you have someone Jewish in your family, you should add that, it's extremely important."

He stopped and looked at me, partly asking, partly stating: "Maybe Michal can tell us a little about it; I believe she's familiar with the procedure, at least more than I am. You know I'm a relatively new teacher."

I was embarrassed to take on this role, one I had not asked for. But I shared what I knew. I told the class that the letter was usually a brief text, only one or two pages long, which the court representatives generally read before or during their initial meetings with candidates. The letter, I explained, is submitted as part of the conversion file initiation procedure, filed alongside the formal conversion application and read aloud at the court. I added that during my fieldwork I had seen how impressed rabbinic judges had been by the converts' accounts of their Jewish educational experiences during their childhood and teenage years. My description apparently made Tanya, another conversion student, nervous: "This is really hard for me," she blurted out. "What should I say to [the court representative]? What should I write? I think I'll just explain everything to him out loud." Helena, who sat behind Tanya, responded critically: "Do you want to convert or not?"; "I want to" Tanya replied, "But I never had a Jewish education and I don't remember anything Jewish that happened to me." Turning to me, she asked, "Do I also have to write why I wanted to convert?"

About a year later, I interviewed Yelena in her rented apartment, in a suburb of Tel Aviv near the college from which she was about to graduate. When I asked her to tell me her conversion story, she laughed. At first, I thought her laughter was a sign of relief, a reflection of our shared memory of that classroom situation, when she was remarkably more vulnerable than she was now. Instead, she explained that "this is exactly what they [conversion agents] asked me to do so many times during the conversion process—to tell my story." "So you are an expert," I said ironically, "Yes," she replied, "I've had quite a bit of practice."

Indeed, throughout the conversion process Yelena and her classmates had many opportunities to "practice" their stories—stories that largely referred not only to the conversion process but to their biographies more generally. In this chapter I focus on these opportunities and argue for their interactive, scripted nature. I trace how scripting works as an institutional mechanism in the production of a reasonable conversion performance. The collaborative labor invested in this mechanism is another facet of the dramaturgical winking relations that unfold between conversion candidates and agents. Through nuanced processes—materialized in subtle gestures, feedback, and narrative cues provided by teachers and court agents—conversion candidates learn how to tell an adequate story.

After their initial alarm in response to Dvir's announcement about the upcoming meetings, the conversion students collected themselves and began working on their letters. When I accompanied them to their meetings with Rabbi David two weeks later, all of them had something to submit. Two of the students had consulted with me during the writing process, and I was made privy to the contents of the others' letters when Rabbi David read them aloud. Interestingly, the teachers provided little additional instruction about how to craft letters. But as I will show later in this chapter, the classroom discussions about conversion implicitly divulged hints to the students about how they might script their stories.

More formative than these periodic class discussions were the two encounters candidates had with Rabbi David. These encounters allowed them to rehearse their scripts and receive feedback about their narrative. During these meetings, Rabbi David monitored, in real time, what he often defined as "the process" they were going through. The meetings involved painstaking assessments, not only of the candidates' levels of religious observance, but also of the ways they narratively framed their religious journeys: What was their biographical background? How did they explain their motivation to convert? Did the religious transformation they described possess an internal logic? Since they were considered to be "in the process," they were still permitted to experiment and make mistakes, the assumption being that they would improve their self-understanding and personal narrative the next time. Indeed, I could track the ascent of the converts' "learning curves" from their first to second meetings with Rabbi David. A story that started hesitantly and tentatively but received positive feedback became a more confident one, while a negatively evaluated narrative was considerably amended later.

Not yet proficient performers, candidates brought drafts of their presentations to these encounters (especially the initial one). During these meetings they edited and sharpened their conversion narratives—reorganized, filtered, and rewrote them into more coherent and "passable" schemes. The relational and dialogic nature of these scripting processes was especially compelling in light of the trial-like context in which they were established; whereas it is reasonable to expect attorneys to structure their clients' accounts to better align them with court rhetoric (see Good 2011:101), it was surprising that court agents, responsible for evaluating the presentation of the candidates' selves, in fact collaboratively rewrote their narratives.

Through these collaborative scripting processes, candidates gained a better understanding and a degree of confidence about what might be the right story for them to tell. One might wonder why they did not know from the outset what the right story to tell really was—what were they confused about? I argue that the context of the national mission is critical for understanding this ethnographic question. To begin with, because the conversion candidates I met during my fieldwork were already, in most ways, insiders to Jewish-Israeli society, it was often unclear to them how to describe their conversion *into* the Jewish fold. Unlike other contexts in which religious conversion entails a clear-cut change and adoption of a newly encountered culture, for non-Jewish FSU immigrants, and even more so for those who immigrated early in their childhood, conversion involved a more formal adherence to a familiar national culture they already regarded as their own. Under these conditions, conversion candidates struggled with how, or indeed whether, to portray conversion as a life-changing process.

Furthermore, as subjects of a nationally informed policy, conversion candidates were unsure how to narrate the religious changes expected of them. In particular, they struggled to describe their adherence to Orthodox observance in a way that was neither instrumentalized nor overly exaggerated. Too pompous a description, they knew, might arouse suspicion, while too pragmatic a story might make their conversion appear forced and devoid of religious sincerity.

To further complicate these matters, as Israeli citizens, these conversion candidates were familiar with Jewish cultural scripts of return to Orthodoxy (*hazara bitshuva*) or "religious intensification" (*hitchazkut*) available for nonobservant Jews. Thus, they often expressed uncertainty about whether the conversion court representatives expected them to embrace such scripts, and if so, how these scripts should feature in their stories. These confusions were augmented for the few candidates in class whose Jewish-Israeli partners joined them during the conversion process. Because the conversion court agents also expected these partners to offer a convincing-enough story of religious return or intensification, candidates pondered the difference between the role assigned to them as converts and the religious role assigned to their partners. As a conversion teacher I met in court explained to me about the confusion converts often experience about these questions: "In the eyes of halakha, conversion makes a gentile into a Jew; but from an Israeli perspective, conversion takes a secular Jew, and makes her religious."

Conversion, Narrative, and Change

> To study conversion is to study stories.
>
> —Scot McKnight, *Turning to Jesus: The Sociology of Conversion in the Gospels*

> When we ask a person why they converted to a particular religious community, we are not surprised to receive a narrative in response, and, indeed, a narrative often serves as a satisfying form of explanation. It is a natural progression for religious conversion to lead to conversion narrative.
>
> —Bruce Hindmarsh, "Religious Conversion as Narrative and Autobiography"

The link that Scot McKnight and Bruce Hindmarsh draw between conversion and narrative is implicitly rooted in another connection scholars of conversion often make between conversion and change. The logic is simple: conversion seems to naturally progress toward narrative, calling for new chapters in one's biography, precisely because it marks a fundamental shift, a new direction one takes in life. Such a shift supposedly lends itself well to reflexive narratives. Indeed, the ethnographic problem that engages me in this chapter lies exactly at the intersection of narrative and change—that is, in the requirement placed on conversion candidates to write, tell, and, ultimately, perform a story of change.

The idea of change is central to a range of analytical and disciplinary engagements with the topic of religious conversion. From the radical language of "transformation," "departure," and "rupture" to the softer frameworks of "reorganization" and "passage," a conception of change underlies the variety of ways scholars write about conversion. In fact, if the "notoriously slippery concept" (Chua 2012:511) of religious conversion is sustainable at all (see also Stromberg 2014), it is due only to a dependence on the notion of change that is assumed to organize conversion's varied manifestations. In many ways, the notion of change has determined the terms and questions around which scholarly discussions of religious conversion have evolved: Is it a "paradigmatic change" (Jones 1978), a "change of heart"

(Heirich 1977), a "change of identity" (Hefner 1993), or a "transformation in the personal relationship with the supernatural" (Lohmann 2003)? Are people really and sincerely changing or only partially and superficially so?

Conversion narratives are rhetorical, reflexive mechanisms through which converts provide accounts to themselves and to various audiences of the changes they have made. Such accounts are assumed not only to reference but also to constitute the sense of change that underscores the personal experiences of conversion (Harding 2000; Stromberg 1993). Often, such an account is called for by the congregation or polity one seeks to join and thus functions as a public rite of passage. Such ritualized modes of conversion storytelling implicate narrators and listeners in extensive processes of socialization, gatekeeping, and the corroboration of communal identity. To the extent that such accounts are always culturally formatted and historically situated, they have much to tell us about the broader religious and linguistic relations in which these personal experiences are embedded.

Conversion to (and within) Christianity, with its overriding metanarrative of redemption, has provided a particularly rich set of contexts in which scholars have demonstrated how conversion is culturally constructed through narratives of change. As Joel Robbins writes: "Most forms of Christianity provide their adherents some forms of disjunctive narrative by virtue of plotting conversion as a decisive break with a past self" (Robbins 2003 cited in Gooren 2014:101).[1] Equally suggestive, conversion to communism, with its own metanarrative of salvation, has been theorized as a domain that is highly conducive to narratives of transformation. For example, Igal Halfin's (2006, 2011a) account of 1920s Bolshevik political culture examines how autobiographies of Soviet citizens were regimented to conform to a binary and linear logic of political conversion. Publicly performed and scrutinized, "red autobiographies" were constructed to move from darkness to light, thereby delineating the old, yet-to-be-saved self and a new, true revolutionary one—a self worth including in the community of the elected.

Conversion narratives do not necessarily have to follow a radical, binary logic of transformation from an old to a new self. In fact, the broader and more significant argument for my purpose is how institutional and religious ideologies shape and ultimately script the stories individuals must tell about the changes they undergo.[2] For example, Lynn Davidman argues that secular Jewish women who return to Orthodoxy learn to narrate their conversion as a continuous and growing attraction to the values of Orthodox Judaism, rather than as an abrupt change in their biography (Davidman 1991:84). By listening to stories of veteran converts, newly Orthodox women learn to emphasize, in their own stories, the feelings of disenchantment they had long held about the liberal, modern promises of the secular world and the fascination they had always had with an observant Jewish life. Tellingly, when Davidman listens to those who converted out of Orthodox communities, she discovers they have no parallel ready-made accounts and that they remain "scriptless" (Davidman 2015; Davidman and Grail 2007).

Building on this body of work, I want to emphasize the collaboratively constructed nature of the narratives that Israeli conversion candidates learn to tell conversion agents. This argument, to be sure, does not equate scripting with deception, or pragmatic self-presentation with empty storytelling. It does refer, though, to deliberate and collaborative editing—that is, the interactive erasing, aligning, and highlighting of certain autobiographical details.

In blurring the boundaries between a "true" and "untrue" conversion story, I take a similar theoretical approach to Sheila Fitzpatrick (2005) and Igal Halfin (2011a) in their accounts of conversion stories in the context of communism—a context to which I have already drawn parallels in chapter 3. Both historians take biographical constructions to be less of a deceptive, exploitative manipulation and more of a reasonable strategy of self-presentation and self-invention. Drawing on Goffman's work, Fitzpatrick (2005:12–13, 91) and Halfin (2011a:10) destabilize the boundary between sincere and insincere communist narratives—the very boundary that Soviet political culture was so anxious to preserve. Both scholars show how biography was masterfully transformed into a public performance, one used effectively by a regime that sought to discern true communists from impersonators. Logically, these public performances became a domain through which candidates for membership in the party could learn how to incorporate permissible narrative schemes as they reconfigured their stories—and selves—accordingly.

You Are the Letter

During one of the final sessions of the conversion ulpan, the class hosted Nehemiah Citroen, the director-general of Mali. The students had not previously met him and were flattered by his visit. After informing the students that he had come to help relieve the anxiety they might be feeling before their court hearings, he spent a few minutes introducing himself. We learned much from his introduction about his personal life: he lived in Jerusalem, had immigrated to Israel from the United States thirty-two years ago, had been happily married for thirty-four years to the same woman, and was the father of four children and a proud grandfather of ten. He ended by joking that "after 30 years, life in Israel gets easier." He then turned to the class and asked, "Tell me, why did I do this? Why is it that the first thing I did was present myself to you in this way? Can anyone guess? Besides the fact that I like to talk . . . ?" Anna, one of the most avid participants in class discussions, was quick to respond: "So that we can get to know you."

NEHEMIAH: Exactly, I wanted to let you know that you are about to meet people who want to get to know you.

ANNA: Should I just tell them who I am?

NEHEMIAH: Yes. You will meet with three people, who happen to be rabbinic judges, who want to know who you are. My purpose in meeting with you today is to show you that a great deal of what happens at the court is under your control. First of all, you're not coming to court as guilty people; rather, each of you is coming with "pockets" full of merits. You have to show them what you're carrying in your pockets! Tell me, did you make aliyah to Israel?

STUDENTS: Yes

NEHEMIAH: That is already a great merit. Did you study in class twice a week?

STUDENTS: Yes

NEHEMIAH: That's already a great merit. Was it easy?

STUDENTS: No

NEHEMIAH: That's already a great merit. Do you want to complete the conversion process?

STUDENTS: Yes

NEHEMIAH: That's also a great merit. Look, imagine I go into the courtroom. I sit down and exchange "Good mornings" with the judges. They then ask me, "Why did you come here?" And I ask myself, "What, don't they know why I'm here? What, are they dummies? Are they pulling my leg?" You need to understand their terminology. This is a deliberately open question. They ask it to learn who you are. They want to know why you're here: Here in class, here at

> the conversion court, here in Israel. They want to hear where you came from and where you're going. And in response to their questions—"Why are you here?", "Why do you wish to convert?"—you already have many merits to your credit. Remember, there is no correct answer. Every person has their own correct answer, and it is unlike anyone else's. What you present in court is terribly important, and you determine what that will be. Each person is a world unto herself, and this is what needs to be presented. The judges ask: "Why do you want to convert?" and she responds, "Because I want to be Jewish." Come on. What kind of impression does that make? Answer in detail, speak your truth, your story, and don't just wait passively for the next question. Practice for this. Choose a classmate and, together, rehearse the answer to this question: "Why do you want to convert." Practice telling your story.

During his short visit, Nehemiah conveyed a central message, one that reemerged repeatedly throughout the conversion course: that the rite of passing depended to a large extent on narrative performance. Nehemiah emphasized to the conversion students that they should not be passively content with what they had already written and submitted as their autobiographical letter. Rather, they should understand their written narrative as an introductory account requiring a more elaborated performance in court. Candidates were to actively prepare for this performance.

When Nehemiah spoke, I recalled a candidate I had once met at the conversion court, who, in response to the judges' query about whether she had a letter ready, said: "I am myself the letter." This, in effect, was what Nehemiah articulated to the class: "You are the letter." Undoubtedly, their written letter was important in and of itself, and the narrative performance could not be disconnected from it. For example, it was not unusual for the court representatives and the judges to assess the reliability of the letter and to check whether the persona appearing before them was the same protagonist portrayed in writing. But Nehemiah underscored that candidates could and should own their narrative performance—they must know how to tell, in their own voice, where they were coming from and where they were going.

No one in class seemed surprised by Nehemiah's message. It surely did not surprise Avner, the teacher, who heard this message repeatedly during Mali's pedagogic seminars. As discussed in chapter 3, at these seminars he and his colleagues received instructions about how to equip their students with the mental and rhetorical tools to confidently face the rabbinic judges. As one senior Mali staffer told the teachers: "Take the question: 'Why do you want to convert?' An incredibly frustrating question for converts; for the millionth time! It's written down five times in the convert's file so why does the court ask? Explain to your students that it is not because the judges don't know the answer, but because it's a conversation starter. [The judges] want to chat? No problem, let's talk up a storm. Let's talk until they're tired of listening. Talk, pile it on, practice narrating long, life-stories in class. Have them lead 'a roots tour' of their lives. It all builds the convert's confidence."

The conversion students were also unsurprised by Nehemiah's message. To the extent that they had heard it throughout the course, they already knew how critical their story would be to the success of the entire process. During the first month of the course, for example, Rabbi Yossi devoted a great deal of time in his class to interviewing his students. He repeatedly asked them to tell their life story, beginning with their lives outside of Israel, and ending with their immigration to Israel and adjustment to life in the country. "Tell me about yourself, don't be embarrassed, I want to get to know you," he often told them. In these intake interviews with students, Rabbi Yossi highlighted the biographical points they should emphasize. He advised them: "Stress the fact that your father is Jewish"; "Say that you went to a Jewish Agency day camp"; "Mention your job in the army; that will impress them." When, during the first few months, a number of students expressed their initial feelings of embarrassment about going to synagogue on Friday nights, the teacher encouraged them to cope with their feelings by "opening up" to their fellow worshipers and "talking about themselves and their lives." In another case, I heard Dvir advise a student, one who had approached him about her awkward initial interactions with her host family, to share her story with them: "You will see, when they get to know your story, the ice will break, and the conversion process will flow much more easily." The students knew, then, that their conversion needed to be rendered into a narrative.

Scripting Conversion

In *Scripting Addiction: The Politics of Therapeutic Talk and American Sobriety*, Summerson Carr (2010) reveals how much depends on stories in the institutional setting of mainstream American addiction treatment. On the path to sobriety, a path governed by multiple administrative and clinical gazes, drug users learn to script their apparent recovery (if not conversion) from chemical abuse and poorly managed lives. Carr's account is informed by semiotic, rather than dramaturgical, perspectives. However, her evocative analysis of the establishment of terms by which clients are encouraged to talk about themselves, as well as her focus on institutional, interactive entanglements between narrators and audiences, resonate powerfully with the narrative performances of converts to Judaism in Israel.

As Nehemiah explained in class, much depended on the stories conversion candidates told to court agents in the course of presenting their selves. What did these stories have to convey? To begin with, they had to portray conversion as a formative moment in their biographies, a process of becoming something new. Court representatives perceived conversion to be, ideally, a major change in one's life course, one's responsibilities and even one's essence; and they expected to hear narratives grounded in such understandings. "They become Jewish! Do you know what that means?" a rabbinic judge once told me, when I asked about the peculiar situation of conversion candidates who already feel Jewish. He continued, "Conversion touches the very core of who a person is. The fact that many of the people I see [in court] already identify as Jews is not the point. In our eyes, conversion should still be a tremendous thing in one's life."

The task of telling a story of becoming something new turned out to be tricky for the conversion candidates I met. On the one hand, the three teachers occasionally encouraged them to stress their Jewish roots and upbringing, thereby portraying conversion as a natural evolution in the lives of those who already feel and live as Jews. On one occasion, when the class joked about Jewish food, and Helena recalled with a tinge of nostalgia how she loved her Jewish grandma's special chicken soup, Avner responded, "You can mention it when you meet Rabbi David." The class laughed, but Avner was quick to emphasize: "I'm serious. I truly think it would help the rabbis sympathize with your situation. It shows them how authentic you are, and how natural being Jewish is to you." On another occasion, Dvir referred to Yulia's memories of a Zionist youth group she attended before her immigration to Israel, indicating to her in passing that she "should bring it up" in her upcoming interview with Rabbi David.

Yet candidates could not simply speak as Jews and tell a story of conversion as a static process—as an event devoid of any aspect of becoming something new. Such a possibility might indicate that conversion was a superficial, strategic move, conducted only for the sake of bureaucratic and social benefits. Narratives had to revolve in some way around the idea of conversion as a deeply transformative change in identity, rather than a purely legal change in one's status.

In light of this double message regarding continuation and change, it is no wonder that conversion students often expressed confusion about how much change they should stress in their stories. In the rare cases when candidates emphasized to Rabbi David that they "already are Jewish," they opened themselves up to critique in ways that sometimes led the conversion situation to break down. The following example reveals how a conversion candidate's failure to adhere to the narrative framework of becoming something new can disrupt the conversion procedure.

RABBI DAVID: Why do you want to convert?

RONI: For me, it is not really a conversion, it is more . . . as far as I am concerned, I'm Jewish.

RABBI DAVID: But you are not.

RONI: My father is Jewish. For me, conversion is more of a formal thing, to follow the rules of the Rabbinate.

RABBI DAVID, *in a protesting voice*: Of the Rabbinate?

RONI, *moving uncomfortably in her chair, searching for the right words*: Of tradition.

RABBI DAVID, *crying out*: Of tradition?

RONI: Well . . . of religion.

RABBI DAVID: You need to understand. It comes from the Bible. It is not something made up by rabbis with short or long beards. These rules come from God.

RONI: I know they come from God, but the rabbis continued God.

RABBI DAVID, *seeming at this stage desperate and impatient, trying a new strategy*: So why do you want to convert if you are already a Jew?

RONI, *appearing to think the matter over, delaying her response*: For me, my identity is not complete until it's written on my ID card that I am a Jew.

RABBI DAVID, *concluding teasingly*: So, basically, you're just after the registration.

RONI, *seeming exhausted and confused*: Not only that. Judaism makes me a better person. It gives you moral rules to live by. It fits me.

RABBI DAVID, *glancing at his cell phone and realizing how late it has become*: Keep working and think things over.

The fact that in her self-representation, Roni did not narrate a story of becoming something new caught the attention of Rabbi David. Not only did Roni deny the authority of God, the rabbis, and Jewish tradition to determine her identity (a claim that I usually heard only in personal and confidential conversations I had with conversion candidates); she also breached the basic conversion scheme of becoming something new. Relating to the bureaucratic procedure in reductionist terms, she left little room for conversion to function as something that makes a difference in her biography. Once she realized her mistake, she turned to the seemingly safe anchor of conversion as a pathway to a religiously informed moral life.

A few days later, when I caught up with Roni, she told me how troubled she was after the meeting. Having seen Rabbi David's reaction, and after comparing her experience with that of her classmates, she explained that she knew better now what to say to Rabbi David next time: "It is so twisted. Conversion is so important for me precisely because being Jewish is so important to me. But somehow he got me talking as though I don't care about conversion. I didn't know how to redirect the course of the conversation, and I just kept making mistakes."

Indeed, Roni's next meeting with Rabbi David went significantly better. After a sarcastic remark, Rabbi David quizzed Roni on her knowledge of biblical stories and her level of observance. Then he asked her: "So what has changed for you?" Roni responded: "My daily life. I pray in the morning." Rabbi David interrupted Roni, asking her to demonstrate her familiarity with the morning prayer by reciting an excerpt from it. But Roni, who failed in doing so, explained: "I'm just so very nervous."

RABBI DAVID: Why are you so nervous?

RONI: I'm anxious because it [conversion] is important to me.

RABBI DAVID: Why is it important?

RONI: Listen, it's important. I put so much effort into this and I want it.

RABBI DAVID, *continuing to push the issue*: Why?

RONI: I've always wanted it, since I made aliyah. It was obvious to me that one day I'd go for it. And now, when it's really part of me, when I'm totally immersed in the process, it's even more important. It gets to me, unlike before.

In order to narrate conversion as a transformation, non-Jewish immigrants needed to articulate that their current, ambiguous position as incomplete citizens bothers them. In general, they were expected to describe their journey from categorical incongruity and an awkward experience of partial belonging to categorical clarity and a sense of wholeness as proper Jews. Such a story needed, therefore, to depart from an admitted problem and to ascend toward repair. Tellingly, this narrative script did not inform or frame the biographical performances of non-FSU conversion candidates (particularly immigrants from Ethiopia and noncitizens) whose appearance before the court I occasionally observed during my fieldwork.

The biographical letters candidates wrote tended to describe the pains of incomplete belonging: their Jewish upbringing, their experiences of family immigration (often described in Zionist terms), the efforts they exercised toward social assimilation, and the longing for full belonging. The responses of conversion candidates to the common question "Why do you want to convert?"—a question raised both in court and in the preliminary meetings with a court representative—also exemplified this narrative of repair. The following two excerpts clearly demonstrate this narrative line of corrective conversion. The first excerpt is taken from a court hearing with a candidate I had not previously met. The second comes from a meeting between Rabbi David and Rina, a conversion student from the Mali class.

RABBI SASSON, *a rabbinic judge*: Why do you want to convert?

YE'ELA: The truth? When we arrived in Israel, I was told about the process, but I didn't get why I needed it. I felt just like everyone else. I didn't understand its importance.

RABBI SASSON: The problem was that you felt Jewish but weren't Jewish. Now you understand and accept the truth.

YE'ELA: Right

RABBI SASSON: So this is the problem we need to fix.

RABBI DAVID: Why do you want to convert?

RINA: Because I made aliyah. I thought I was Jewish. I always highlighted my Jewish identity everywhere I went. When I made aliyah, I realized that something wasn't quite right—that I'm not really Jewish. I graduated from elementary and high schools here, I feel part of this place, and I'm planning to stay here for the rest of my life. This is my place. I will never emigrate from here.

RABBI DAVID: Why? Do you think everyone who comes here must convert?

RINA: No, only those who want to. We have [Jewish] tradition in the family, but it's not enough. I don't have family who can pass on all this knowledge to me.

RABBI DAVID: Why is it important for you?

RINA: Because otherwise I won't feel complete here. It bothers me that I'm not Jewish, and there's no better way for me to learn all this than to study it from the real source of Judaism. I feel like conversion lets me come full circle [with my Jewish identity.]

Imbued with national meanings of completion rather than with religious meanings of transformation or awakening, conversion narratives described a process of coming full circle with the issue of partial national belonging. Within this scheme, religiosity in itself was construed not as a motivating factor for conversion but rather as an indispensable component necessary for full inclusion within the national fold. As one of the rabbinic judges once told me, "I cannot demand that converts come with gleaming eyes. I can only demand that they observe religious practices."

Occasionally, teachers addressed the tense relations between candidates' national motivations for conversion and the religious path they must follow in order to reach their goal. In those instances, teachers both validated the script of national correction and realistically acknowledged the nonvoluntary nature of the religious change involved. In so doing, they provided formative narrative cues and helped confirm a certain script. Take for example the following exchange that unfolded in class between the conversion teacher Avner and one of his students, Victoria. In a class devoted to the subject of religious laws dealing with conversion, Avner allowed himself a critique of how the rabbinate treats converts as "second-class citizens." Victoria had not yet reached the stage of formal authorization as a convert, but she could not agree more. While she usually shied away from class discussions, on the few occasions she decided to participate, she did so firmly and confidently. As if she had been waiting for an opportunity to voice her own frustrations, she interrupted Avner:

VICTORIA: What I find most disturbing is how the Rabbinate creates difficulties for those who, like me, are part of the Jewish nation. My father is Jewish and yet, [the rabbis] are tough on me. Why? I'm part of the Jewish people, I belong!

AVNER: What do you mean? Part of my own worldview is that people like you, with Jewish sparks, should be reunited with the Jewish flame. But what can we do? The halakha constrains us. We cannot simply regard you as Jewish just because you feel Jewish. This is why you must undergo a process. There's no way around it. People study seven years in order to be physicians, so what's the problem with asking you to study only ten months? It's a totally reasonable requirement.

VICTORIA: But the rabbis are not welcoming. Dvir saw how suspiciously Rabbi David questioned me. You can ask him yourself, he'll tell you.

AVNER, *laughing*: Rabbi David's role is to be suspicious. So what? Seriously! I'll be honest with you, I have so many criticisms of the rabbinic court, but one thing I'm sure about is how delighted the rabbinic judges are to accept candidates. What do you want them to tell you? —to exempt you from observing commandments at all? That they will accept you as you are? They understand your situation but, please, be realistic. You cannot just come to court, tell them you want to join the Jewish people, and assume they can simply approve you. It doesn't work like that. Belonging is a privilege, and all of you need to take upon yourselves some religious commitments to prove your readiness.

VICTORIA: Give me one example where rabbinic judges eased the conversion requirements.

AVNER: I have many examples from students in my previous classes. Instead of acting petty, I saw how rabbinic judges went to great lengths to accept converts. Even if conversion is mainly a national thing, the fact that the court maintains halakhic standards for conversion is totally fine. [*Gesturing as though stamping a pile of papers*] The rabbinic court is not merely a stamp factory![3]

Much of what Avner said was right. The rabbinic court agents could not simply settle for conversion stories driven solely by motivations of national belonging. Although such stories made complete sense to them, reverberating, as they did, with the ideology of the national mission, they could not disregard the religious component. In other words, even if conversion agents could not demand that converts come with "gleaming eyes," they nevertheless could not abide conversion stories that blatantly portrayed religious change as instrumental or inconsequential.

Conversion stories needed to include more than that: an account of a more motivated, more profound, more voluntary wish for some kind of religious change. How much more, and how to describe that religious change, constituted practical dilemmas that preoccupied conversion candidates. Their exposure to Jewish scripts of religious strengthening or return—circulated widely in various Jewish-Israeli public culture venues—intensified their dilemmas. Because candidates associated religious strengthening with spiritual seeking and transformative life passages, usually in the course of becoming ultra-Orthodox Jews, they pondered whether they should incorporate such narrative threads in their conversion performance. A few candidates did indeed point out, in their encounters with Rabbi David, their efforts to search for new meaning; for example, through experimentation with Kabbalah or with Chabad Hasidism.

As the following excerpts reveal, the encounters with court representatives helped candidates strike the right chord and find the appropriate words to describe the religious change they were supposed to experience throughout their conversion process:

RABBI LEVIN: Why do you want to convert?

SVETA: Because I want to live in Israel.

RABBI LEVIN: So what? It is not "a must." What are you lacking?

SVETA: I want. I want to be a standard Jew. Why do you ask why? It is obvious why.

RABBI LEVIN: So, practically, you just want to be like everybody else, that's all.

Displeased, he and the conversion teacher looked at Sveta.

SVETA: No, not only because of that. I also want to keep Shabbat, Mitzvoth.

RABBI LEVIN, *smiling*: Oh, OK, so next time begin with this.

SVETA, *apologizing*: I'm just very tense.

Or take the following exchange:

RABBI DAVID: Why did you wait till today?

LANA: I always wanted to [convert] but it didn't work out before.

RABBI DAVID: Why did you want to convert?

LANA: I live in this country, my father is Jewish, I have the Jewish spark and I want to be a kosher Jew. I want to belong to the Jewish nation.

RABBI DAVID: How do you feel about this process? Are you happy with it?

LANA: Yes, very much so.

RABBI DAVID: Why?

LANA: This stuff really interests me. In Russia, I participated in a Jewish youth program. We studied Jewish holidays and so, when I arrived here, I got into it even more. My friends are Jewish.

RABBI DAVID: With so many Israelis around you who celebrate the holidays but don't care about fully observing the commandments, like all those "traditional" Jews, you know, how do you see yourself in the future? Do you see yourself continuing with what you have studied during the conversion course?

LANA: I will do both.

RABBI DAVID: Do you mean that you will keep the commandments?

LANA: Yes. I feel it's the right thing to do. I believe in Hashem [God].

RABBI DAVID: Does Hashem want all gentiles to be Jewish?

LANA: No, but those who are from the seed of Israel need to.

RABBI DAVID, *sounds alarmed*: Are they obliged to convert?

LANA: No, but . . . [*searching for the right words*].

RABBI DAVID: It is you who feels you must. OK, tell me, is it difficult or easy to be Jewish?

LANA: Very difficult

RABBI DAVID: So why are you doing it? Objectively, not subjectively, you don't have to. I have to because I have no choice, but you have a choice, so why?

LANA: The commandments really interest me.

RABBI DAVID: "Interests" is not a good word.

LANA: Oh, I love it, I love the commandments.

RABBI DAVID: How can you love something that is so difficult?

LANA, *looking stressed*: I don't know, I just love it. I also love Jewish history.

RABBI DAVID: OK, I wanted to delve deeper with you but I won't confuse you further.

It would be simplistic to say that Rabbis David and Levin explicitly put words in Lana's and Sveta's mouths, strategically directing the course of their stories. It would be equally reductionist to think they helped shape these narratives in order to add two more young women to the national stock. Such interpretations would definitely miss the more nuanced, implicit collaborations that unfold between court agents and candidates in the context of the national mission. Such interpretations would also ignore the rabbis' own understanding of the situation. For example, Rabbi David's perspective revealed more of an intuitive, even impulsive, reaction to what he considered to be shallow accounts of conversion. As he once told Avner during a break between meetings, "I just sometimes get so annoyed by what I hear and I respond, you saw me [laughing]." Similarly, Rabbi Levin once told me over lunch how he sometimes teases his interviewees, not, God forbid, to upset or throw them off, but to educate them; that is, to help them more thoughtfully choose their words to describe the profoundness of conversion. When I shared with him my observation that court agents, including himself, seemed to substantiate and mold a certain story line, he answered proudly: "Of course! I'm an educator here, not merely a bureaucrat. When I meet converts, I help them understand the tremendous process they go through. So much is going on for them in these meetings, and, yes, I'm happy I can help them find their way and words."

In order to better explain, then, the collaborative mechanisms of scripting at play here, I call attention to two key factors that shape these bureaucratic encounters. The first is, simply, the three-fold structure of the conversion procedure—that is, the two preliminary meetings and then the court hearing. This structure provides candidates with at least two occasions to rehearse the role of a conversion candidate in front of a significant audience. The fact that court representatives read the personal narrative in the application letter aloud, ask questions that call for reflexive accounts, and react orally and gesturally to biographical details, necessarily allows candidates the opportunity to interactively sharpen their narrative skills. In this sense, even "disastrous encounters" (as I described earlier in the case of Roni) become productive in due course, providing candidates with a better understanding of what their narrative performance should sound like.

The second factor is that pressure from Mali on the rabbinic conversion court affects the court representatives, essentially pushing them not to hinder the candidates' path to the conversion court. During my fieldwork, Mali repeatedly sought to undermine the court representatives' authority to determine whether candidates would be granted a hearing in the conversion court. Rabbi Levin once told me he felt as if Mali "was breathing down [his] neck," pushing him to speed along or smooth the process even if he held reservations about the suitability of particular candidates. Communicating to candidates what constitutes a legitimate story and suggesting alternative narrative lines when stories seem inadequate ultimately foster more acceptable conversion candidates for the rabbinic court.

The conversion narrative, practiced and sharpened during the preliminary meetings with a court representative, culminates in the rabbinic conversion court. There, based on another round of collaborative scripting, this time with the court judges, the story takes its final shape. Once this meeting ends, converts are no longer asked to repeat their story. In the ritual bath, as I showed in chapter 4, the mikveh attendants speak briefly with converts, focusing primarily on the halakhic procedure and confirming that converts are sure about their decision to become Jewish.

The ways in which rabbinic judges react to different conversion narratives by candidates from diverse backgrounds (including candidates who were not on the agenda of the national mission) has much to tell us about the narrative conventions that develop in light of the national mission. In what follows, I map two models that stood out throughout my fieldwork. The first model, emphasizing radical religious and spiritual transformation, serves here as a contrast to the more typical narrative model of national belonging; by virtue of its exceptionalism, this model demonstrates the extent to which the Israeli state's conversion policy is inherently a political project of national inclusion rather than a religious mission.

Reborn

"Look at Israel-Rafael," said Rabbi Haim, a Mali teacher I knew from the pedagogic workshops. He pointed at the quiet man sitting near us; "for him, conversion is really [a transformation] from death to life." Israel-Rafael nodded smilingly in agreement. Rabbi Haim continued, recounting to me and another acquaintance he had just met the "miracles and wonders" of his student's fate. Prior to making aliyah to Israel, Israel-Rafael lead what Rabbi Haim referred to as a "lawless life" in France with his non-Jewish wife. His own father was Jewish, and therefore he was eligible to immigrate to Israel under the Law of Return. After a horrible motorbike accident that left him in coma for three months, he dramatically regained consciousness, and, appreciative of his fortune, ultimately started to pursue Jewish conversion.

A few minutes after Rabbi Haim concluded his account of Israel-Rafael's background, Rabbi Dotan (a court representative) invited Rabbi Haim and me into the courtroom, where two rabbinic judges already sat waiting (the third would arrive a few minutes later). Rabbi Meiri, the rabbinic panel's chair, read aloud Israel-Rafael's biographical details (age, country of origin, place of residence in Israel, profession, and so forth) and then the personal narrative from his conversion file. The letter roughly repeated the plot Rabbi Haim had earlier described to us in the waiting room. Rabbi Padan, Rabbi Meiri's colleague, listened with an amazed look and whistled with enthusiasm. After a short exchange with Rabbi Haim and Rabbi Dotan, during which the rabbinic judges learned about the good impression Israel-Rafael had made on both, and the reasonable impression made by Rachel, Israel-Rafael's partner, they invited Israel-Rafael in. His Hebrew was weak, so they let him speak French with Rabbi Haim translating between Hebrew and French as well as between the first and third person.

RABBI MEIRI: I see that you already applied for conversion back in Paris. What did you do there to advance your application?

RABBI HAIM, *translating for Israel-Rafael*: I was in contact with a rabbi. I attended a Sephardic synagogue each day and I took classes.

RABBI MEIRI: Why do you want to be Jewish?

RABBI HAIM: I always wanted to. Unfortunately, I had a terrible accident in east France. I was in a coma for a long time. I saw many things during the comma.

RABBI MEIRI, *sounding entertained*: What did you see?

RABBI HAIM: He saw angels.

The judges smiled at each other.

RABBI MEIRI: Did they talk with you, these angels?

RABBI HAIM: Yes, they had a conversation with Israel, a chat, like friends. He also talked with deceased people.

RABBI MEIRI, *smiling, as though trying to suppress his laughter*: And did you actually meet God?

RABBI HAIM: No, but the rabbi at the synagogue in France told him that he did hear God's voice. He was given the choice—to step up or go back down.

The three judges looked amused.

RABBI PADEN: So what did you choose?

RABBI HAIM: To stay down. I saw a huge light and a tunnel and then I was told: "that's it." A gate was opened for me and I went down. I had a wife and a child, so I chose to remain with them, to go down.

RABBI PADAN: Why didn't you see God when you were in heaven?

RABBI HAIM: He did not want to turn around.

RABBI MEIRI, *seeming confused, asks Rabbi Padan*: Just one second, let me make sure I understand—who did not want to turn around, Israel-Rafael or God?

RABBI PADAN, *in an assuring voice*: Israel-Rafael didn't want to, not God. [*Looking back at Israel-Rafael*] Why? Why didn't you want to see God?

RABBI HAIM: I was afraid. I'm not allowed to see God.

RABBI PADAN, *nodding*: Right, you probably didn't get permission to see God. Now tell me, do you ever see God here, on earth?

RABBI HAIM: Everywhere

RABBI MEIRI: You really saw him for real? Did you really see him?

RABBI HAIM: I saw him only by the miracles he has been doing for us here. I know he is here.

RABBI MEIRI: So why don't we see him? If he is here, shouldn't we see him?

RABBI HAIM, *laughing at Israel-Rafael's response and turning to Rabbi Meiri*: Israel-Rafael asks if you've ever seen God.

RABBI MEIRI, *smiling*: No, I haven't.

RABBI HAIM: So Israel-Rafael is just like you, a human being, and God is heavenly.

RABBI PADAN: Tell me, Israel-Rafael, do angels have wings?

RABBI HAIM: Huge, unbelievably tremendous wings.

RABBI MEIRI: Do you sometimes talk with God?

RABBI HAIM: Yes. When I'm talking with God, I'm crying.

RABBI MEIRI: Do you know that when a person undergoes conversion, he makes a decision to observe the commandments?

RABBI HAIM: Of course. All Jews must observe the commandments.

RABBI MEIRI: Do you [observe them]?

RABBI HAIM: Yes, my father is Jewish.

RABBI PADAN: Who is your dad? Where is he from?

RABBI HAIM: His name is Yehoshua. Unfortunately, he doesn't live religiously.

RABBI MEIRI, *appearing anxious to wrap up the discussion and move forward*: OK, Israel-Rafael. So, now, would you tell us how you live religiously?

During the next ten minutes, the court panel questioned Israel-Rafael about his religious practice—in the kitchen, the sukkah, and even in the toilet and bedroom. They seemed satisfied with what they heard. He had been living as a fine, fully observant Jew. The rabbis asked him to leave the room and send in Rachel, his partner. Rachel, also an immigrant from France, albeit Jewish, had a better command of Hebrew than Israel-Rafael, so the conversation proceeded in Hebrew.

RABBI PADAN: Ok Rachel. We just talked with Israel-Rafael. He told us he wants to observe everything he can. Everything. So, our basic question is whether you see yourself as a partner in this way of life. He can't do it all by himself. What do you say?

RACHEL: Fine with me.

RABBI PADAN: How have you learned to observe the commandments? Do you study on your own?

RACHEL: Yes. I also have someone who tutors me a bit in halakha. Don't forget, I was enrolled in a Jewish school in France.

RABBI PADAN: A real religious school?

RACHEL: Yes, sort of.

RABBI PADAN: And have you been observant since then?

RACHEL: I've had ups and downs, but, in principle, yes, I'm observant. Thanks to Israel-Rafael I'm even more observant.

After a lengthy assessment of Rachel's religious practice, the rabbinic judges asked her to leave the courtroom. In the discussion that followed, they agreed that Israel-Rafael was "more serious" than Rachel. However, no one pushed to condition the authorization of Israel-Rafael's conversion on further religious commitment from Rachel. They called in the couple, informing them that Israel-Rafael's conversion had been approved. Israel-Rafael reacted emotionally, alternating between crying and laughing. After exchanging warm congratulations with him, the rabbis turned to Rachel and asked her to schedule a date in the near future for their wedding. That way, the judges explained, they won't have to live in (sexual) sin. Rachel, though, was uncompromising. Unintimidated, she sat up straight and bravely confronted the three rabbis. To my amazement, she insisted on her dream of a big wedding party. "We don't have much money, we need to save more before we get married," she explained to them. Rachel worked, as the judges knew, as one of only a few cleaners in Israel-Rafael's small janitorial services company. The couple had little money to spare. "No," she concluded, "we can't have a wedding soon."

RABBI PADAN: Ok, let's leave that issue for now. What about modesty? Will you keep it?

RACHEL: I will try to.

RABBI PADAN: What do you mean you "will try to"?

RACHEL: I want to do things from my heart. I won't go against my feelings only to please you. If my heart opens slowly, so be it. It will determine my pace. I don't want to progress quickly in my religious observance, burn myself out and fall down [to revert to a secular lifestyle].

RABBI MEIRI: Let's be clear: You're not doing anything for us! Everything you do is for God alone. You're right that sometimes in life we do things slowly. But every once in a while there are special circumstances; conversion is such a case.

RACHEL: Right, but you want me to go up rather than fall down, right? This is how kids grow up—slowly, step by step. I already went up [religiously] quickly and then I fell down. I don't want that to happen again. I won't do things only so that people will look at me and think I'm religious.

RABBI MEIRI: But Israel-Rafael is already a completely righteous person [*tsaddik*], he's completely observant.

RACHEL: Right, but I'm not him. I'm a different person. I cannot live observantly [*lehiot b'torah*; lit. "being in the Torah"] only because of him. I want to be observant because of me.

RABBI MAOZ, *who had remained quiet until now*: Think about it: People who see you in the street and don't know you, will judge you by your appearance. It's unfair but this is how it works. So please make sure to be observant so that it won't seem like conversion is empty, meaningless.

RABBI MEIRI: I don't get it: A fully covered back? Covered legs? Is this too demanding a request?

RACHEL, *quietly*: No, that's Ok.

RABBI MEIRI: So you promise to observe it?

RACHEL: Ok.

Ten minutes later, after the couple had left the courtroom, Rabbi Maoz was still busy recording a summary of the hearing and the court's final decision. When he finished, he turned to me with a smile: "What a case we arranged for you, ah?—a case for anthropologists!"

As an anthropologist, I found this remark funny but unsurprising. It was clearly grounded in the popular conception of anthropology as a discipline focused on "other," colorful, if not eccentric, forms of human life. Rabbi Maoz's remark was interesting precisely because it suggested that he (and his colleagues) understood Israel-Rafael in those terms: as colorful, other, and eccentric. Iconizing, in their view, low-class religiosity associated with Mizrachi Israelis, Israel-Rafael appeared foreign to these rabbinic judges, who embodied the Ashkenazi religiosity of Israeli elites (recall also Motti, whose appearance before the court I described in chapter 4). But there was something more profound here beyond patronizing gazes: a deep ambivalence about conversion narratives that seemed too dramatic, unusual, and religiously motivated. On the one hand, the rabbis trusted Israel-Rafael's conversion performance and were pleased with how enthusiastically he observed the commandments. On the other hand, they did not know what to do with his unique life story and unusual spiritual account. Waking up from a coma—epitomizing the religious metaphor of being born again—Israel-Rafael was simply too colorful, other, and eccentric for the court rabbis.

In other exceptional cases in which candidates shared narratives anchored in dreams, visions, and other transformative religious experiences, court judges were equally ambivalent. Even when candidates related less dramatic and more normative religious experiences (e.g., a search for meaning, an exposure to theological doctrine, or an encounter with charismatic role models), the conversion court reacted with ambivalence. Such reactions were especially evident in response to those who had neither a Jewish background nor a Jewish partner.[4] Judges were reserved, for example, when Ruana from Brazil told them how her soul led her to a synagogue in Rio de Janeiro and how immediately she felt enchanted and "at home." One judge asked in response, "What do you mean that your soul led you to synagogue? And why did you 'immediately feel at home' there?" One of his colleagues continued cynically: "I don't always feel at home in synagogue; tell me the secret so I'll know." Rabbi Shlomo, another rabbinic judge, expressed similar reservations to me about a candidate from Ukraine. This convert had explained to the court how she had fallen in love with the tradition of the Jewish family she worked for, and consequently decided to leave Ukraine and undergo conversion: "I don't get it. They come to us from nowhere, what do they want from us? What is their 'thing' in life? What are they trying to find here?" Similarly, Rabbi Ziv told me that Maria, a former Catholic from Spain who was writing her PhD in theology, "is impressive, no doubt. But I just don't get it. Where did her connection to Jewish religion come from?"[5]

Interestingly, the rabbinic court also displayed ambivalence toward Israeli citizens who overly emphasized motivations of religious return in their conversion narratives. These feelings of ambivalence were augmented when, as often was the case, these citizens came from the FSU and had atheist backgrounds. On the one hand, court rabbis took pleasure in seeing what they interpreted as clear-cut cases of religious sincerity and appropriate observance. They enthusiastically shared with candidates and each other their dreams for the candidates' religious futures, often pointing out how wonderful it was for them, as rabbis and educators, to witness such significant religious transformations. They even used the language of return in their conversations with candidates, asking them, for example, if they felt like "returnees."

On the other hand, court agents were suspicious of overly religious stories and expressed concern, even aversion, about cultural scripts of religious return. Interpreting the process of return as too radical a religious change, one associated with a turn to ultra-Orthodox life, rabbinic judges worried about converts who seemed headed in that direction.[6] "It is too extreme," Rabbi Sharon, a rabbinic judge, explained to me. "Some of them [the converts] push it to the limit," another told me. A third judge, talking about a specific convert, noted: "It's funny. I think she wouldn't have eaten at my house because it wouldn't have been kosher enough for her." When I shared with Rabbi Sharon my sense that he was ambivalent about religious return, he nodded, saying: "I really don't like it. But if this is what it takes for me to be able to convert them, ok, so be it." Furthermore, several rabbinic judges I spoke with expressed antagonism about what they described as crude, charismatic rabbis (most of them newly religious themselves) who proselytize to secular Jewish-Israelis (see El-Or 2006; Goodman 2004; Leon 2010a). When rabbinic judges discussed such rabbis, they routinely distanced themselves and their own work in court from them.[7]

To the judges, Rachel, Israel-Rafael's Jewish partner, did not seem like someone undergoing religious return, someone in the process of becoming an ultra-Orthodox Jew. Rather, she described a slow strengthening of religious observance in several domains of her life, a gradual process of working toward becoming more observant than before. She even argued with the court rabbis about the level of observance and the pace of progress she was willing to undertake. Paraphrasing *Reserved Seats: Gender and Ethnicity in Religious Places*, Tamar El-Or's (2006) ethnographic work on the "industry" of religious intensification among Mizrachi Israeli women, I would say that Rachel reserved a future seat for herself in a potential Orthodox Jewish life. Like many of El-Or's interlocutors, Rachel was not in a hurry to take on all religious obligations. And thus, the court rabbis worried about her pace. Unlike the charismatic rabbis who work for the cause of religious intensification El-Or describes, the rabbinic judges I met in the conversion court did not care about the religiosity of individuals (candidates and spouses) in and of itself. Aiming elsewhere, they sought to harness the religious efforts of individuals as a means to authorize and enable the national mission. Once they decided to convert Israel-Rafael, they insisted that Rachel immediately commit herself to observing what they considered fundamental and visible signs of religiosity (i.e., sexual abstinence until marriage and conventional modest dress). This is why they attributed great significance to whether she looked religious and urged her to marry soon; they were in a hurry.

Making Peace with the Burden of Conversion

The rabbinic judges asked Yuli to leave the room so they could discuss her case in private. Rabbi Shmueli sighed, looked at me and said: "Do you see this Yuli? She is just like most cases we hear. This is the kind of material we deal with these days." "This Yuli" had a typical profile: she was a young, female Israeli citizen who immigrated from the FSU as a small child. Her biographical narrative was also typical. She shared stories about her immigration to Israel and described her wish for full belonging within the Jewish state. Religious motivations did not feature prominently in her conversion story but were instead encapsulated within the narrative of corrective conversion. That narrative made clear that Yuli understood the inseparability of national and religious components of Jewish identity. Her story was well received. During the hearing, in response to her immigration account, one of the rabbis cited the famous passage from the Book of Ruth (1:16): "Your people shall be my people, and your God my God." In referencing this passage, one widely used in Israeli public discourses about conversion, he expressed compassion for the vulnerable status of new immigrants (like Ruth) and the importance he attributed to national motivations for conversion.

Despite their empathy for Yuli, though, the rabbis found her religious observance a bit wanting. She seemed sincere, but her irregular attendance at the synagogue caught their attention. After a lengthy debate among themselves, and another dramatic exchange with Yuli, the judges decided to conduct a quick ritual oath—mainly as a strategy of encouragement (see chapter 4)—but to condition their final authorization upon her subsequent religious progress.

Generally, the rabbinic judges wanted candidates to embrace an understanding of conversion as a package deal, one that involved a certain religious burden. They hoped conversion candidates would even come to enjoy this burden. The judges were particularly pleased when candidates conveyed a linear narrative of progression from treating the religious burden of conversion as irrelevant and compulsory to embracing it warmly and enthusiastically. For example, they commended a convert who told them: "At the beginning of the conversion ulpan I went to synagogue only because I had to, but now I do it for myself, because I love it." They responded enthusiastically when another convert told them: "At first, I didn't think I would enjoy all this so much, but I really do. It really grabbed a hold of me." Similarly, a third candidate once told the panel: "I love being Jewish, I wholeheartedly love the holidays and the joys of being together. When I first discovered that I'm not Jewish, I was angry. But now, I'm happy. I think that God wanted me to study and learn more, and I think I never would have done it if I hadn't had to convert. Everything in life has a reason."

The currency of such narratives increased when converts repeated them at the second or third hearings, which were held in cases when the court rejected their application in the first hearing. I observed several cases in which candidates or spouses thanked the court for initially rejecting them, thereby forcing them to demand more from themselves. One spouse confessed: "I was really angry at you the first time, because I didn't understand why you were being so stubborn and tough on us. But now I see. You really wanted our best. Now I can appreciate why you needed to push us in this direction." In my interview with Rabbi Maimon, then the head of the Conversion Court, he took pride in these cases, emphasizing his vision of the conversion court as a pedagogic arena (see also chapter 4). Rabbi Nave, a rabbinic judge, once admitted to me that each time he rejects a conversion application, thereby inviting the candidate to another hearing, he worries that he or she might give up conversion entirely. "It's a delicate dance, what we do here," he explained to me.

Final Words

On my way to interview converts, usually a few months after I had last seen them in the Mali conversion ulpan, I used to play a guessing game about what they would look like and the kinds of stories they would tell me. Not only did I fare poorly in these games, but more importantly, I often found little clear-cut compatibility between how a convert dressed and the narrative she told me about her experience. In coffeehouses, apartments, and public gardens I listened to ten converts whose stories were rich and layered, weaving complex narrative threads in gripping, often unexpected ways.

Because I wanted to enable free-flowing conversations, I opened the interviews by asking the converts to tell me their stories. These stories included a great many biographical details that were new to me. The dynamic of talking in jeans that I described in the introduction, the relatively negligible political stakes of talking to me (as opposed to talking with conversion agents), and the retrospective nature of our conversations—all these factors combined to inspire exchanges that were less defensive in content and tone than those converts had held with conversion agents.

Yet the frame of these stories did not surprise me. Generally, the converts repeated the conversion stories they had initially drafted in their biographical letters and sharpened through their encounters with court representatives. In fact, the general contours of these stories even resembled the official state narratives of conversion, illustrated, for example, in the "I am also Jewish, no question" campaign (see chapter 1); these were stories of people seeking to repair their damaged membership in both the Jewish nation and Jewish state.

No doubt, the differences between converts' stories were remarkable. Some spoke angrily about conversion, others were more accepting. Two converts spoke about an exhausting experience of long-term deception, while most interviewees emphasized the connections between their presented self and their understanding of their "real" self. Some blamed the Israeli state for abandoning them to the whims of the rabbinate; others spoke with more understanding about the state's political commitment to Orthodox conversion. Some stressed the similarities between the story they told me and the one they presented at court; others highlighted the differences. Beyond these and other important variations, a common feature shined through in their narratives: these converts told me their conversion stories as Israelis demanding a place in, and recognition by, their own state. They spoke as citizens who felt a connection to the place and society in which they had built their lives, who had not been satisfied with the common routes of "sociological conversion," and who, as a result, sought out a more secure, state-authorized mode of belonging. They hoped their formal validation as Jews would provide them and their future children with official recognition—a status that was not merely instrumentally useful.

As expected, I did not hear stories of spiritual transformation. The converts I met were not motivated by religious insights or a search for life-changing meaning. Not one of them would have voluntarily adopted (even temporarily) a religious lifestyle had this not been a precondition for conversion; not one of them would have chosen conversion unless she felt it was right, even necessary, for herself and her family, social status, and bureaucratic standing. Conversion did not transform their lives entirely, nor did it cause them to view themselves differently. But its deep meanings became increasingly, and sometimes surprisingly, clearer to them throughout the process.

For them, conversion was far from an empty wink-wink performance. Several of them enjoyed the conversion process and appreciated the opportunity to practice traditional or religious rituals. They waited for the moment they could practice these rituals selectively and on their own terms. Some talked about how, after their conversion, they grew more vigilant about eating kosher food, while others mentioned occasional visits to synagogues or lighting candles on the eve of the Sabbath. Equally important to them was how conversion made them conversant with many issues of Jewish history and culture about which they had previously felt ignorant. Some prided themselves on having become more knowledgeable in these areas than most secular Jewish Israelis. Such experiences were not outcomes required or evaluated by the conversion court, but they were dear and real to converts.

Before I move to the epilogue, the final analytical word about my study's theoretical implications, I want converts to have the final word about the experience of conversion in Israel.

Ana, twenty-eight years old when she completed the conversion process, immigrated to Israel in her early twenties with her Jewish spouse. Though she had no Jewish background, after she and her husband divorced and he emigrated back to Russia, she decided to undergo conversion. Four years after the completion of her conversion, she e-mailed me with news about her upcoming marriage, this time to a Jewish-Israeli man. In her interview she expressed, more than once, her wish to put down roots in Israel: "I already felt at home in Israel, but, still, I didn't have a family here and I wanted Israel to be my family. You need to belong to something, to open your heart. I don't want to feel like I'm just a guest in Israel. Many people ask me, still, if I'm Jewish, and even though they pretend that they don't care, they do care—they ask about it, so they care."

Sveta, in her mid-twenties, was raised Jewish by her father. However, when she immigrated to Israel, she learned for the first time that the rabbinate wouldn't recognize her as a Jew. During our interview I was amazed at how collected she seemed as she described what sounded like a potentially traumatic, outrageous revelation. Calmly, she told me how conversion allowed her to lay claim to a place in which she already felt at home:

> Suddenly I had this thunder, this shock; suddenly I was told that I'm not Jewish. Think about yourself. Imagine that, in the middle of your life, as if from nowhere, somebody tells you that you're not Michal anymore. So, do you tell yourself: "I won't be Michal anymore?" No way! [you tell yourself that] you'll do whatever it takes to be Michal, right? This is how I felt and that is what I did. I said, "Ok, if this is what it takes, so be it. I don't want any problems when I get married, to have to travel to Cyprus or something like that. No way. I'm an Israeli and I want to get married in my place, in my country, with my friends, and my parents. No overseas civil marriage. Here. This is my place.

Yulia, also in her mid-twenties, made aliyah to Israel with great enthusiasm. Raised Jewish by her father, she felt a deep sense of belonging in Israel. Ironically, precisely because she already felt Jewish and identified with

Jewish worldviews, she was receptive to ideologies of endogamy. Describing to me her understanding of Jewish-Israeli men, including her boyfriend, she explained: "Practically speaking, the fact that you are Jewish must be officially documented. As much as he might love you, it's still very important to him and his parents that you're Jewish. He wants his kids to be Jewish. Most people think like that. So even if you already feel Jewish, your feelings aren't enough for others. You don't need to be angry at those other people. It's just taken for granted here. This is how Israelis are and this is a Jewish state. They want their families to be Jewish. It makes sense."

And, finally, Moran, the young woman whose story I opened the book with: in her interview Moran told me about the harsh family circumstances that, beginning at a young age, forced her family to emigrate several times. She arrived in Israel at age eleven and was "very determined," as she put it, "to finally belong." As she explained:

> I suffered a lot here in school. I was "The Russian" girl in my class. It's weird thinking back on it, actually; this was already during the big immigration waves, so I wonder why there weren't more Russians in my school. Anyway, it was so bad for me. People were violent with me. I was just different from all the other girls in school, and even though I spoke decent Hebrew, I still had an accent, and I paid for it big time. Oh boy, did I pay for it. I graduated from high school, and like every other Israeli, I went into the army. In actuality, it was here, in Israel, that I really became myself. All my friends are [Jewish] Israelis, and even if some of them are Russians, they are the type of Russians who are already Israelis. All my friends know that I'm not Jewish; it doesn't bother anyone.
>
> But—and this is the crucial point—I've been dating someone for the last five years. He doesn't care about conversion. He loves me as I am. Right now, it's not an issue. But when does it become an issue?—When we talk about getting married and having kids. You see, they need to be Jewish. When I thought about what I went through as a child, being such an undefined person, I knew they would be better off as Jews. Our society is so racial, you know. It is the kind of feeling you get when people make faces at you. For example, when you go to the bank teller, and she is religious, and she looks at your ID [and realizes that, with no Hebrew date, its owner is not Jewish]. So my boyfriend really wants our future kids to be Jewish. If that makes their life here easier, then I'm willing to do it for them.

Toward the end of the interview I asked Moran if she and her boyfriend had told his parents about her conversion. Like most converts I met, Moran had kept her non-Jewish identity a secret. She paused for a moment: "I meant to tell them, but then we thought about it again. You know, I'm already a Jew now anyway. So what's the point?"

Epilogue

Winking Like a State

WHENEVER I BROWSE the Internet, a certain ad invariably pops up, inviting me to consider undergoing a pleasant and friendly conversion to Judaism. Disruptive as the ad sometimes is, I never remove it. I like how it maintains my attention to conversion and arouses memories of incidents I experienced and people I met during my fieldwork. I am particularly reminded of Yulia, who shortly before her second meeting with Rabbi David, the court representative, whispered to me nervously but playfully how lucky I am to already be recognized as Jewish. I also smile in recollection of a conversation I had with Judge Rabbi Shilon, who, in a telling Freudian slip, referred to secular Jews like myself as "gentiles." Embarrassed, he quickly corrected his mistake, yet I, unable to resist the temptation, joked that perhaps I should indeed pursue conversion and finally become "a real Jew." Relatedly, the ad also evokes a couple of perplexing dreams I had during fieldwork, in which court rabbis notified me that I am not really Jewish according to halakha. I do not remember these dreams in great detail, but I do recall there was no other way than to comply and convert. I had to present and remake myself under the gazes of the conversion court.

Clearly, the pop-up invitation to convert regularly appears on my screen because of my frequent searches related to conversion. As I close it, I cannot help but wonder how rarely it appears on other Israeli citizens' browsers—how few people make the same searches. Only a minority of those identified as potential converts ever seek conversion options and even fewer actually pursue conversion. Statistically, the state project described in the pages of this book could be considered a resounding failure. However, as I have argued throughout, for those few Israeli citizens who do seek to convert and for those rabbis seeking to convert as many citizens as possible, the actual realization of conversion is a creative, remarkable achievement.

In this book I have unpacked the unspoken dramaturgical mechanisms underlying this achievement, demonstrating its concerted, if counterintuitive, dynamics and convoluted nature. I have ethnographically depicted the kinds of conversion performances that unfold between agents and candidates in the context of the national mission and demonstrated the ways these performances implicate both sides in defining situations and selves. By telling the story of both those who wink at state agents and those who wink on behalf of the state, I have revealed the unavoidable maneuvering and subtle dance required of those engaging with conversion under the framework of the national mission.

This book offers ethnographic perspectives on religious conversion employed as a tool of a Zionist policy. I argue that by examining the lived enactments of this grand political endeavor, we can access the Israeli state's complex engagement in dramaturgical relations, in this case driven by the aim to mediate inclusive, even missionary, Zionist aspirations while contending with stringent rabbinic gatekeeping procedures. These relations help both sides of the conversion interaction pursue their interdependent national goals. Rather than emphasizing the state's obvious power to govern the religiosity of its citizens, I highlight the precarious collaborative labor invested in the making of both the Israeli state and its Jewish converts.

By tracing the pedagogic, bureaucratic, and ritual routines of this "coproduction," I reveal the extent to which, rather than merely an objectified political trait, Israel's Jewishness is an array of mediated socio-institutional transactions, comprising a delicate work in progress. I also argue that in accounting for such transactions, we should evade cynical, simplistic approaches that denounce wink-wink conversion as a kind of organized trick and instead embrace a more complicated understanding of these unfolding, dialogic winking relations. Working hard to preserve Israel as Jewish or to establish themselves as Jewish in Israel, my interlocutors on both sides of the conversion encounter taught me a great deal about the profound stakes involved in this collaborative and invariably political endeavor. They also helped me develop the idea that the winking relations undergirding Jewish conversion have much to tell us about the sentiments, investments, and mechanisms feeding both Israel's struggles as a Jewish nation-state and the struggles with which it burdens its national subjects. Winking relations contribute to theorizing the lived experience and mundane bureaucratic routines of both collective and individual Jewish identity in Israel.

This book can be read as an ethnographic account of Jewish Israel. For justified reasons, most ethnographies examining Israel as a Jewish and Zionist state focus on the Israeli-Palestinian conflict. The political violence spurred by this conflict has much to reveal about core aspects of Israeli-Jewish political culture. Ethnographies of various Jewish, non-Jewish, and unendorsed Jewish groups in Israel also furnish crucial vistas of the varied experiences of citizenship in Israel. A third and equally rich line of scholarship addresses the legal, religious, and ideological features marking Israel as a Jewish state, primarily in relation to its designation as a liberal democracy. My analysis of conversion adds to each of these discussions by showing how the paradoxes involved in the conflation between Jewish ethnonational and religious identity, as well as between state and religious institutions, affect real people who construct subjectivities within the state's institutional framework. To be sure, recognizing winking relations does not solve or harmonize these inherent paradoxes, but it does identify the existence of flexible spaces for maneuvering between and within them and for enabling their continuity.

My analysis of winking is deeply grounded in the social and historical context of conversion in Israel. But this conceptual framework's relevance transcends the conversion context. Here I want to weave together the book's theoretical strands about winking and discuss its workings within the Jewish state and state institutions more generally.

To attain a broader understanding of the Jewish-Israeli context, I suggest considering the role of winking relations within Jewish law, which also enters the often tension-filled encounters between state Orthodox institutions and a predominantly secular Jewish population. Since these institutions govern various personal and public matters pertaining to the life of Jews in Israel, they unavoidably create intricate off-the-record, "as if" arrangements as well as shared unspoken dramaturgical performances that allow religious bureaucracies and secular citizens to manage the gaps marking their engagements.

Extrapolating beyond the context of religion-governed institutions, I also want to interrogate the weight assigned by scholars of the state to seeing; I do this to foreground the analytical utility of the metaphor of winking as an additional framework for understanding relations between institutions and individuals. Together with the extensive literature devoted to how the state exercises its power by seeing its citizens over a range of domains, I want to call attention to the nuanced modes of communication and alliances involved in the making of both state power and state subjects. In other words, I suggest that we take seriously what the interactive gestures taking place within socio-institutional state spheres can tell us about states' routine enactments.

Winking Relations, Halakhic Loopholes, and Unspoken Arrangements

In a recent sketch on *The Jews Are Coming*, a controversial satire on Israeli public television, the association between winking and Jewish religious practice receives a clear performative expression. Broadcast a few weeks before Passover 2016, the sketch mocks the customary practice where observant Jews "sell" their *chametz* (bread and other leavened foods banned on Passover) to non-Jews, in keeping with the halakhic rule prohibiting Jews from eating and even possessing such foods during the holiday. The sketch features two medieval European Jews engaging in an economic exchange just before Passover. The merchant, failing to sell Jewish ritual artifacts to the client, suggests that his shop will handle the selling of the client's chametz.[1] In marketing his service, he says: "How can the gentleman be sure that he cleaned [his] home completely from all the chametz? After all, ants always carry crumbs of chametz into the house, thereby unkoshering it for the holiday." The client appears to ponder this line of thought for the first time, and the merchant takes the opportunity to further clarify: "It is a very simple procedure. All we have to do is to 'sell' the chametz to a gentile [winking and gesturing quotation marks]. I go and 'sell' [winking again] your chametz to the gentile, so that you can get rid of all your chametz. It becomes not yours anymore."

The following day, the merchant's lackey brings the client to the shop. The merchant informs him that the neighborhood gentile offered too low a price for his chametz. "I think we can get a better deal," he argues. The client seems confused by the merchant's profiteering approach: "Let's just sell it to him and that's it. What's the matter? We only do all this 'as if' we sell. It is not for real." The merchant raises his eyes heavenward, as if to make sure God is listening, and exclaims with marked exaggeration: "What are you talking about? No way do we sell chametz in only an 'as if' fashion." He turns to the client and in a whisper spells out the details of the collusion: "If we want the guy up there to believe our story, we must be very trustworthy. We have to bargain on the price, issue invoices and receipts. This is not a three-year old toddler we are talking about—it is [bleeping] God!" The client seems to get the point. He agrees to any arrangement that will conclude the perplexing matter. The merchant, invigorated, looks at him squarely and winks, loudly annunciating each word: "Okay, no problem. We will get you the best price for your chametz."

In the sketch's final scene, the client stands alarmed next to a man presented to him as a gentile willing to buy his chametz, but who is in fact seeking to launder money. The client squirms at the suggestion, but the merchant shames him by saying, "What, it is okay to lie to God but not to the income tax service?" Confused and depleted, the client resigns to signing a contract with the gentile. "It is a done deal," the pleased merchant loudly asserts twice, his announcement inviting two policemen into the shop, who wink at him, excuse his parking ticket, and then quickly arrest both the Jew and gentile. As the two are escorted out, the Jewish merchant roars at the bewildered client: "That is the punishment you get for lying to God!"[2]

The sketch's humor relies upon a predominant cynical secular perception of religious practices as ludicrous at best, shameful at worst, and invariably rife with winking. To the extent that Jewish law sanctions Jews to play childish make-believe games with God, so the logic goes, it emboldens a more elaborate cultural logic of winking and lying. After all, Jews do not genuinely sell their chametz, yet God is regarded as fully accepting of their ritual "as if" exchange. Such practices result in wink-wink observance and cunning tricks in daily life.

Religious actions that secular Jews regard as deceitful or at least as preposterous winks are recognized by observant Jews as normative halakhic loopholes (*ha'arama*)—necessary arrangements created by rabbinic authorities to ease the observance of demanding laws, ameliorate tension-filled issues, or avoid problems hindering observance of more foundational laws. Under this interpretive framework, selling chametz before Passover represents a socially accommodating and religiously validated maneuver for Jews to maintain full subjection to Jewish law.

Similarly, the halakhic principle of turning a blind eye fosters a permissible "as if" space within religious conduct. It is applied to avoid knowledge about the actions of fellow Jews that, if disclosed, might impinge upon their or others' religious observance. For example, Rabbi Ovadia Yosef, a Sephardic spiritual leader and rabbinic authority, instructed female mikveh attendants to turn a blind eye to their female clients' too-long nails (a condition not in keeping with halakhic requirements for immersion), and synagogue leaders to turn a blind eye to the insufficient religious observance of Jewish men called to read from the Torah during communal prayers. Precisely by acting as if deviations from strict law go unnoticed, religious routines and frameworks as a whole can be preserved. From religious perspectives, such principles are functional adjustments applied to manage otherwise unmanageable situations.

I bring up these principles for two main reasons. First, they provide ready interpretive frameworks for religious Jews involved in conversion. Indeed, they are occasionally raised in public discourses on conversion, as a means for religious Jews to contemplate the conversion problem and negotiate the idea of wink-wink conversion. Second, together with the notion of winking, these principles may explain the logic behind some practical "as if" mechanisms at work in relations between state rabbinic institutions and the Jewish-Israeli public. I will begin with a few examples to demonstrate the first point.

In an attempt to counter Rabbi Brandes's (2008) critique of wink-wink conversion, Rabbi Israel Rosen (2010) juxtaposes the good faith he and his court colleagues place in converts' religious performance with other "as if" traditions religious Jews routinely practice. Writing in *Akademot*, a journal affiliated with liberal religious Zionism, he communicates with a presumably religious Zionist and educated readership: "I assume that Rabbi Brandes, like most of us, sees the value of the Yom Kippur prayers for secular Jews. Many of us take part in the effort to invite such guests to the synagogue on Yom Kippur, to make them like and appreciate the occasion. We all know that only a few of them will actually [repent and] change their ways later in the year. Is all this effort merely deception and self-deceit, devoid of integrity? The comparability to our discussion is clear" (Rosen 2010:212).

In the same journal issue, Arye Edrei (2010), a scholar of Jewish law, counters Brandes's critique from yet another angle. He argues that a great divide lies between turning a blind eye and winking, and that conversion should be understood in terms of the former rather than the latter. While the first principle is based on common sense, decency, and compassion, the other approach lacks integrity and truthfulness and causes religious Jews discomfort. He teases Brandes, asking whether, consistent with his understanding of contemporary conversion as winking, he would also consider selling chametz on the eve of Passover and other normative halakhic arrangements as winking and self-deceit. He contends: "We can bring many other examples from daily halakhic life, in all of which there is some kind of 'winking.' In halakha there are loopholes and legal fabrications, which constitute important institutions in halakhic thought and in how halakha functions. . . . Rabbi Brandes asks halakha to speak in the language of 'either-or' and so take away its ability to speak in an inclusive language of both" (202–203).

Edrei then contends that insisting on the ideal of converts following the law, even if unrealistic, is an important religious and moral statement rather than an empty trick. It is an ideal that converts must be urged to aspire to as part of their initiation into the Jewish world and way of thinking. Edrei further writes: "The fact that the conversion court focuses on the conversion of young women out of care for the next generation, but is less flexible with other converts, is a good example of how we are not talking about abandonment of the principle [of religious observance] but about its weight against other principles" (204).

To give one more example of applying such principles, Elhanan Shilo (2010), a scholar of Jewish philosophy, suggests turning a blind eye to the halakhic status of those applying for marriage in the rabbinate, as a means to solve the conversion problem. He admits his suggestion might be taken as an illegitimate loophole but argues that the conversion courts have undertaken significantly more radical feats. He argues that since the option of conversion is irrelevant for most non-Jewish FSU immigrants, who are unwilling to commit to the religious way of life, a couple registering for marriage should be able to receive authorization so long as they do not disclose their problematic halakhic status. He goes further to propose that because the goal of the rabbi and of the couple is one and the same, there is no reason to regard such a policy as fraudulent but as another step toward what he describes as the absorption of nationally identifying Jews into Jewish tradition and society, even if they are not regarded as Jews according to halakha.

To the extent that Jewish law provides various "as if" mechanisms to address challenging human and communal situations, we can consider how such mechanisms shape the daily, undeniably challenging encounters between representatives of Orthodox state institutions and not only non-Jews but also secular Jews. The idea of winking relations invites us to contemplate a wide array of contexts in which Orthodoxy intervenes in matters of public and personal concern vis-a-vis secular Jews—how unspoken arrangements, collaborations, loopholes, and acts of turning a blind eye constitute political configurations of state religion in Israel. Further research may find value in scrutinizing the dramaturgical dimensions of these configurations.

For example, it may be worthwhile to interrogate the institutional encounters involved in couples getting married as Jews in the rabbinate. Future brides are required to attend a series of meetings with female Orthodox instructors to learn about sexual purity matters. Each bride needs to play along in her assigned role as if she intends to follow these rules and as if she is new to relations with men. The rabbinate's representatives are far from naive, but they act as if they and the brides-to-be maintain an agreement on religious perspectives. Drawing upon my own recollection of getting married in the rabbinate, stories from friends, and seminar papers from my students on the subject, I am inclined to think there is an agreement in this context: to never confront but rather detour around the cultural fissures existing between bride and guide.

The bride is instructed to bring to her wedding ceremony a written confirmation that she both attended the requisite meetings at the rabbinate and immersed in the mikveh on her last night as an unmarried woman, the latter invariably confirming that she is not menstruating on the day of her wedding. Formally, rabbis are supposed to ask for these confirmations, but they tend not to do so in practice.

While secular couples surely determine their wedding dates according to various personal considerations, at the rabbinate they have to act as if they are taking the bride's expected menstrual cycle as a primary consideration. Furthermore, according to the official rules of the wedding ceremony, while under the canopy the bride must not speak or put a marriage ring on the groom's finger; he is to do it himself. I attended several ceremonies in which the rabbi, based on prior agreement with the couple, allowed some degrees of freedom in composing aspects of the wedding ritual. One of my friends shared with me: "Our rabbi basically agreed to turn a blind eye or deaf ear to my more active role. We wanted a more liberal and mutual ritual and without formally admitting it, he was willing to go along with us to some extent." The fact that Tzohar rabbis provide wedding services in the name of the rabbinate, in an attempt to offer friendly and liberalish wedding ceremonies for secular couples, undoubtedly promotes other flexible, off-the-record spaces under the canopy (NRG 2004).

The rabbinate's authorizations of restaurants, coffee houses, caterers, and factories as providers of kosher foods may be another fruitful site for investigating the winking relations framework. Recent developments in this area may be better described as instances of resistance; for example, some businesses aim to take ownership of the process by asserting they work in line with halakhic rules even if they do not hold the rabbinate's stamp of approval. Others have been seeking to establish an independent apparatus to supervise kashrut (Adamker 2015; Barmeli 2014).

These expressions of resistance may be harbingers of more significant waves of public challenge against the rabbinate's monopolies (see also Benn 2016). As important as these developments may be, the great majority of food businesses recognized as kosher remain overseen and certificated by the rabbinate. In light of the microsociological processes taking place between rabbinate supervisors and food business owners, we may wish to ask: What is the role of tacit understandings and double messages in sustaining these potentially explosive encounters? What practices of impression management and passing are implicated in these understandings? What forms of collaboration emerge throughout these processes? Furthermore, which of these dynamics may be motivating efforts toward independent kashrut mechanisms?

Guy Ben-Porat's (2016) study of bargaining over the official public status of the Sabbath provides us with some insights. While the Sabbath is Israel's official day of rest, a symbolic expression of its Jewish character, the state has witnessed a recent expansion of commerce as more and more businesses remain open on this day. Ben-Porat traces how the state's attempt to fight this trend is enacted in a somewhat "as if" fashion. In particular, inspectors from the Ministry of Industry and Trade, authorized to fine businesses employing Jews on the Sabbath, participate in informal but effective games that allow businesses not to be caught and fined. One of his interviewees recalled: "All this enforcement is just a wink to placate the religious groups and nothing more, for if they really wanted to enforce the law then the inspectors would come every Sabbath and all day long. . . . What happens now is only for appearances' sake in order to say that something is being done. . . . Once a single inspector shows up at a site then within seconds everyone at the site knows, and workers vanish into thin air" (343).

Winking Versus Seeing

Seeing is one of the most prevalent organizing metaphors in discussions of the state. It captures the idea that the state exercises power in seeing its citizenry as well as in making aspects of itself markedly visible. Interestingly, even as scholars have grown distant from reified, personified perceptions of the state as a single, coherent thing (with its own wisdom, will, and eyes), the notion that the state can see and be seen still predominates. Likewise, while I endeavor not to succumb to such patterns, referring to those who speak and act in the name of the state rather than simply to the state itself, I still offer an equally anthropomorphizing metaphor of winking.

How can a state wink? Does this notion offer a valuable alternative metaphor to seeing, even if it falls prey to the same personifying, reifying connotations? How can winking help us understand state practice, power, and significance? Addressing these questions requires me to first briefly survey some of the contents and contexts in which the notion of seeing is used. My discussion does not exhaust the relevant literature drawing on this metaphor, though it does flesh out its conceptual utility and variability.

Probably the first work to pioneer the notion of winking is James Scott's (1998) seminal *Seeing Like a State*. Clearly indebted to Michel Foucault's (1980) work linking knowledge to power as well as his analysis of the panopticon and representations of modern disciplining regimes (Foucault [1975] 1977), Scott examines the ways the state renders both society and nature legible.

For Scott, legibility is a mode through which the state reads, and also manipulates, the landscape and its inhabitants, imposing on them a highly synoptic, schematic, top-down logic of scrutinizing and managing. Scott traces an impressively wide historical array of settings in which states have created intelligible, measurable, and manageable objects. When the highly modern state maps, registers, catalogues, and standardizes messy reality on the ground, it imprints visible marks of presence and power upon forests, urban areas, and populations. In so doing, it discards valuable local knowledge emerging from below and suppresses vernacular modes of thinking. In line with his earlier work on resistance, Scott also acknowledges the high social and human costs of such state interventions and the possibility of resistance, such as from communities that render themselves illegible to the state.

Most important for my current purpose is the extent to which Scott's metaphoric conception of seeing has gained wide currency among scholars. It has become a trope for understanding how cities, prisons, and corporations, to name just a few examples, govern by seeing.[3] Several scholars problematize the idea of a monolithic, all-seeing state, pointing to other, less centralized or bird's-eye modes of governing (Herzfeld 2005; Li 2005). However, even these critical accounts do not necessarily erode the seeing metaphor. As James Ferguson suggests, they just describe "a rather different way of seeing" (Ferguson 2005:377).

Another thread of scholarship concerned with the visual nature of state power is surveillance studies, particularly those works addressing the war on terror and the war on crime. This scholarship identifies the ways the state mobilizes cameras placed in public spaces to enforce the law and maintain security and how by utilizing "eyes everywhere" (Doyle, Lippert, and Lyon 2012) the state creates both synoptic and panoptic representations of social truth and public order (Frois 2013; Arteaga Botello 2012). In contexts where the state imposes political terror on its citizens, it uses a "big brother" gaze, enforcing participation in a hypervisible field of conformity and compelling public performances of a faithful-citizen persona (Taylor 1997). Relatedly, states at times use ritualistic, performative, and even grandiose means to make themselves seen (Geertz 1980; Handelman 2004; Mbembe [1992] 2006), with state agents building their authority on the visibility of their roles (Reeves 2014:13–14).

While all these lines of inquiry demonstrate the reach and relevance of thinking about the state through the metaphor of seeing, I want to make a case for the metaphor of winking. Seeing surely resonates with a wide array of practices and experiences implicated in the workings of the state, including in the sites of my research. However, I maintain that the winking metaphor can help us pursue useful complementary lines of inquiry on the state. What we miss when drawing too singularly on the seeing metaphor is an understanding of how things are actually happening on the ground and the kinds of "as if" sensibilities that emerge within relationships between states and subjects. Had I regarded the legible signs conversion candidates learn to project only as mechanisms for being seen without considering the nuanced collaborative work preceding and sustaining them, I would have missed crucial aspects of the conversion dynamics in Israel, such as the ways state representatives go to great lengths to fulfill a challenging national mission. In other words, the seeing metaphor places exclusive emphasis on questions of power, thereby providing insufficient analytical vigor for exposing interactions and transactions held within the institutional semblance of the state.

The idea of winking draws upon scholarly acknowledgment of inherent gaps between formal and informal rules and between idealized bureaucratic schemes and pragmatic handlings (Gupta 2012; Hull 2012). But it extends beyond acknowledging the ways people bend rules and enact off-the-record complicities along the margins of the law, social legitimacy, and ultimately the state (Anjaria 2011; Jusionyte 2015). It points at creative maneuverings made precisely by those who attempt to meet—or give the appearance of meeting—formal rules, while simultaneously tracing the indeterminate and interdependent nature of these efforts. Thomas Szasz's insights about the mechanisms of lying give particular clarity to what I argue about winking:

> The value of lying derives not so much from its direct, communicative meanings as it does from its indirect, meta-communicative ones. By telling a lie, the liar in effect informs his partner that he fears and depends on him and wishes to please him: this reassures the recipient of the lie that he has some control over the liar and therefore need not fear losing him. At the same time, by accepting the lie without challenging it, the person lied to informs the liar that

> he, too, needs the relationship and wants to preserve it. In this way, each participant exchanges truth for control, dignity for security. Marriages and other "intimate" human relationships often endure on this basis.[4]
>
> (cited in Davis 2010:130–131)

As I demonstrate throughout the book, state-subject relations also endure due to similarly metacommunicative bases of interdependency. Rather than imposing a forced analytic uniformity on the notion of winking, this book offers an evocative case for probing possibilities of interdependency—those moments and contexts in which state representatives and state subjects let each other know how much they need their mutual relationship.

Glossary

ALIYAH. Lit. "ascendance." A Hebrew Zionist term used to describe immigration of Jews and descendants of Jews to Israel.

ANUSIM. Lit. "conversos." A term referring to Jewish people who have been forced to convert from Judaism.

ASHER YATZAR. Lit. "He Who Has Formed." The blessing uttered after defecation.

AV BEIT DIN. Lit. "chief of the [Rabbinic] Court."

BALAN. A male mikveh attendant whose role is to govern the immersion ritual (female singular *balanit*; male plural *balanim*; female plural *balaniyot*). See *mikveh*.

BASAD. An acronym in Aramaic for "with the help of heaven." Religious Jews write the acronym at the top of every written document.

BERUR YAHADUT. Lit. "Judaism examination." The clarification of Jewish status.

BIRKON. A booklet containing the grace said over meals.

CHAMETZ. Bread and other leavened foods banned on Passover.

GABBAI. The person responsible for running the synagogue.

GER. Lit. "sojourner" (plural *gerim*). A convert to Judaism. See also *giyyur.*

GIYYUR. Conversion to Judaism. See also *ger.*

GIYYUR MICHAMAT HASAFEK. Lit. "conversion to eliminate doubt." A speedy conversion process. See also *ger, giyyur.*

GOY. Lit. "gentile" (female singular *goya*; plural *goyim*).

HA'AVODAH. Lit. "the Labor." The Israeli Labor Party.

HABAIT HAYEHUDI. Lit. "the Jewish Home." The Israeli religious Zionist party.

HALAKHA. Jewish religious law.

HALAKHIC. According to the halakha. See *halakha.*

HAMIZRACHI. Lit. "the Eastern." A religious Zionist movement, established in 1902 as a faction of the Zionist Federation. See also *Hapoel Hamizrachi.*

HAPOEL HAMIZRACHI. Lit. "the Eastern Worker." A religious Zionist labor movement that adopted the socialist values of secular Zionism within a religious framework. See also *Hamizrachi.*

HARDALI. An acronym in Hebrew for "ultra-Orthodox nationalists." A term referring to religious Zionist communities that began to imitate moral, behavioral, and aesthetic norms associated with the ultra-Orthodox world. See *Hardaliyut.* See also *Haredi.*

HARDALIYUT. An acronym in Hebrew for "ultra-Orthodox nationalism" (*harediut le'umit*). See *Hardali.* See also *Haredi.*

HAREDI. An ultra-Orthodox Jew (plural *Haredim*).

HAṬAFAT DAM. Lit. "drawing a drop of blood." An alternative ritual to Jewish circumcision for males who have been circumcised in a non-halakhic manner or were born circumcised.

HATIKVA. Lit. "the Hope." The Israeli national anthem.

HAVDALAH. Lit. "Separation." A Jewish ceremony that symbolically marks the end of the Sabbath and holidays and signals return to the mundane.

HAZARA BITSHUVA. Return to Orthodoxy.

HITCHAZKUT. Religious intensification.

HUPPAH. Lit. "canopy." The canopy under which the Jewish wedding ritual is preformed.

ITIM. A civic organization dedicated to helping Jews and non-Jews cope with Israel's rabbinic bureaucracy.

KABALAT HAMITZVOTH. Lit. "the acceptance of the commandments." See *ol hamitzvoth.*

KIBBUTZ GALUYOT. Lit. "the ingathering of the exiles." A narrative of historical justice and mythic return of the Jewish people from the diaspora to their homeland, Israel.

KIDDUSH. Lit. "Sanctification." A blessing recited over wine or grape juice to sanctify the Sabbath and Jewish holidays.

KIPPAH. Skullcap (plural *kippot*).

KNESSET. The Hebrew name for the Israeli Parliament.

KOL NIDREI. Lit. "All Vows." A prayer said on Yom Kippur, renouncing vows and oaths. See also *Yom Kippur.*

MA'ARACH HAGIYYUR. A new Conversion Administration (replacing Minhal Hagiyyur) within the Prime Minister's Office. See also *Minhal Hagiyyur; rabbinic courts.*

MAFDAL. An acronym in Hebrew for "the National Religious Party."

MALI. An acronym in Hebrew for "the Institute of Jewish Studies," also known as the Joint Institute, a state-authorized conversion school that is one of the central research arenas of this book.

MAMLAKHTIUT. Lit. "statism" (adj. *mamlakhti*).

MARI'IT 'AYIN. Lit "appearance." The Jewish principle of the matter of impression.

MIKVEH. The ritual bath used for immersion (plural *mikvehs*). See also *tvilah.*

MINHAL HAGIYYUR. The nationwide Conversion Administration, created in 1995. See also *Ma'arach Hagiyyur.*

MITZVAH. One of the Jewish religious commandments (plural *mitzvoh*).

MIZRACHI. Lit. "Eastern." A term that commonly denotes Jews who trace their roots to communities in the Middle East. In colloquial usage, the terms "Mizrachi" and "Sephardic" are often conflated. See *Sephardic.*

MODEH ANI. Lit. "I Thank." The Jewish morning prayer.

MOHEL. A ritual circumciser (plural *mohelim*).

NATLA. A ritual hand-washing cup.

OLEH. Lit. "ascendant" (plural *olim*). A Hebrew Zionist term used to describe Jewish immigrants—and, since the 1970s, their descendants—who are entitled to naturalization and economic benefits. See *aliyah.*

OL HAMITZVOTH. Lit. "yoke of the commandments." See *kabalat hamitzvoth.*

PURIM. A Jewish holiday commemorating the deliverance of the Jews under the ancient Persian Empire.

RABBINICAL COURTS. Jewish religious courts. In Israel the rabbinical courts have a legal standing, as they are part of the judicial system.

SEPHARDIC. Lit. "Spanish." See *Mizrachi.*

SHAS. An acronym for "Sephardic Keepers of the Torah," The Sephardic ultra-Orthodox political party that was founded in 1984.

SHAVUOTH. The Festival of the Pentecost. A Jewish holiday commemorating the giving of the Torah.

SHEHECHEYANU. Lit. "Who Has Given Us Life." A common Jewish prayer marking special occasions and expressing gratitude.

SHIVA. Lit. "seven." A seven-day mourning period observed in Judaism by the relatives of the deceased.

SHMA' YISRAEL. Lit. "Hear O Israel." The name of a crucially important verse from Deuteronomy, appearing in many Jewish prayers, which declares a person's belief in the God of Israel.

SIDDUR. A Jewish prayer book.

SIMCHAT TORAH. Lit. "Joy of the Torah." The holiday of rejoicing with the Torah.

TEFILLIN. A Jewish ritual object made of leather and used by men during the weekday morning prayers. See also *Modeh Ani.*

TVILAH. Lit. "immersion" (plural *tvilot*). A Jewish ritual in which a person immerses him- or herself, or an object, in a bath (*mikveh*) or spring. Among its other purposes, the ritual is the final and decisive act of conversion. See also *mikveh.*

TZAV GIYYUR. Lit. "Conversion Order." A coalition of organizations, rabbis, and religious activists aimed at broadening the scope of halakhic conversion.

TZIZIT. The four-cornered garment worn under a Jewish man's clothes.

ULPAN. An institute or school either for the study of Hebrew or for study toward Jewish conversion.

YESH ATID. Lit. "There Is a Future." An Israeli middle-class party established in 2012.

YESHIVA. A Jewish institution of higher education for Torah study.

YISRAEL BEYTENU. Lit. "Israel Is Our Home." The Israeli Russian-speaking immigrants' party.

YOM KIPPUR. Lit. "the Day of Atonement." See also *Kol Nidrei.*

ZERA YISRAEL. Lit. "the seed of Israel." A halakhic category describing the offspring of Jewish fathers and grandfathers.

Notes

Prologue

1. Here and throughout the book, all translations are mine.

2. By the phrase "shrunken State of Israel," Rabbi Bin-Nun is referring to Israel's internationally recognized 1967 borders, as opposed to "Greater Israel," which includes the occupied territories.

3. All quotes and dialogue from conferences I attended throughout my fieldwork are taken from my field notes. According to Maimonides, an influential medieval Jewish scholar, the distinction between a priori and retrospective judgments about conversion is crucial for determining a conversion's validity. In Maimonides's Code (Sefer Kedusha, Hilkhot Isurei Bi'a 3:17), he argues that even if a Jewish convert returns to his or her evil ways after fulfilling the requirements of conversion (circumcision and ritual immersion for male converts and ritual immersion for female converts), the conversion is still valid and he or she is still considered a Jew.

4. Yom Kippur is considered the most sacred Jewish holiday, and Shavuoth is the commemoration of the giving of the Torah.

5. Female Jews (and hence female converts) are not eligible to testify in rabbinical courts and are not counted in the minyan in halakhically based Jewish communities.

Introduction

1. Throughout the book, I use pseudonyms when referring to conversion candidates and conversion agents whose identities can be concealed (e.g., teachers, rabbinic judges, representatives of the conversion court, and bureaucrats). Because of

the particular concern about anonymity expressed by some rabbinic judges and other conversion court representatives, I use multiple pseudonyms for the same agent. In addition, I also never disclose the areas in which a specific rabbinic panel operates. However, when rabbinic judges publish articles or speak in public, I use their real names. I also employ the real names of public figures (public intellectuals and well-known rabbis or politicians) and of distinctively senior conversion agents whose names are publicly known (or can be easily discovered).

2. From the prestate period through the state's early years, the hebraization of newcomers' names (both first names and surnames) represented an expected, and even enforced, Zionist practice. In contemporary Israel this practice has lost its prescriptive power, and FSU olim are hardly expected to hebraize their names or to adopt Israeli names alongside their original ones. The Russian pseudonyms of conversion candidates appearing throughout the book reflect the fact that most candidates I met during my fieldwork kept their original "Russian" name.

3. The alternative way to achieve Jewish recognition would be the "clarification of Jewish status" (*berur Yahadut*) procedure, which is usually aimed at investigating the halakhic identity of those whose parents wedded outside of Israel (and thus lack documentation of their status). Obviously, this method only applies to those who believe they are halakhically Jewish. See also note 17 in chapter 1.

4. The categories *secular Jews* and *traditional Jews* are worth further clarification. *Secular Jews* is used ubiquitously in both surveys of Jewish-Israeli identity and colloquial public discourses, including those about giyyur. In those discourses *secular* usually designates "nonreligious"; that is, not living according to an Orthodox way of life. In fact, the term *secular Jews* is misleading, as is the argument that Jewish-Israeli society is predominantly secular. As studies have shown, Jewish Israelis observe a great number of Jewish customs, and few of them subscribe to a firm ideology of secularity. Hence, they defy the seemingly dichotomous framework of secular versus religious Jews and problematize the secularization thesis that was once customarily applied to the analysis of Israeli society and nationalism. As an anthropologist I decided to follow the commonly used category despite its analytical drawbacks. For studies that complicate the understanding of Jewish secularity and Jewish religiosity in Israel, see Ben-Porat (2016); Ben-Porat and Feniger (2009); Shoham (2014); Yadgar (2010); Yonah and Goodman (2004). Jews self-described or defined by others as "traditional" (*masorti*) tend to selectively observe some customs associated with religious life without fully committing to an Orthodox, halakhically based way of life. In colloquial Israeli Hebrew this category stereotypically denotes Jews who observe some basic rules of the kosher dietary laws, such as the separation of milk and meat, and mark the Sabbath in ritual ways (e.g., by conducting celebrative and ritualized family meals, sporadically attending services at synagogue, etc.) but also embrace certain secular norms of dress and leisure culture (such as going to the beach or a soccer game on the Sabbath).

5. In fact, contrary to the public image of FSU immigrants as fundamentally atheist, studies reveal how, over the course of their cultural assimilation within Jewish-Israeli society, these olim have shed their distinct antireligious positions and adopted more traditional attitudes toward Jewish practice and state Judaism. See S. Fischer (2012); Hermann (2012); Remennick and Prashizky (2010).

6. *The Presentation of Self in Everyday Life* was published in two editions, one in 1956 and the other in 1959. The sociologist Philip Manning argues in his account of Goffman's work that the first edition reinforces the image of a cynical and manipulative self whose strategically planned performances depart markedly from the "true" self; in the second edition Goffman seems to distance himself from such understandings and to portray a more complicated image of a self whose performances blend in with its self-perceptions (Manning 1992:40–48). My own ethnography draws on the meanings of *presentation* that are emphasized in the second edition.

7. For surveys on conversion, see N. Fisher (2015:33*n*65); Hanin (2014).

8. The definition of Israel as a Jewish state is far from a clear and settled matter. The question "What is Jewish about Israel?" is answered in multiple, and contested, ways (Spektorowsky 2015). Does the state derive its Jewishness from the Jewish values inculcated in citizens within the public education system, from the mundane cultural aspects of Israeli nationalism, or from the requirements of Jewish law that organize public Israeli space? The demographic emphasis—that is, that Israel is a national state of and for Jews—is thus one among many answers.

9. In the biblical period one's Jewish status was based on patrilineal descent. Since the rabbinic period (after 70 CE), Jewish status has been passed down matrilineally (see S. Cohen 1999). In 1983 the Reform Movement expanded its criteria to include patrilineal descent as well, affirming that a child of an interfaith couple is Jewish if one parent is Jewish and the child is raised as a Jew. The Conservative and Orthodox Movements still adhere to the historically dominant matrilineal norm.

10. The conversion of women does not automatically entail the conversion of their children. Often babies, toddlers, and young children accompany their converting mothers to the conversion court. Such children undergo ritual immersion together with their mother. Older children (above thirteen for boys and twelve for girls) must undergo more extensive conversion processes, including learning and explicitly accepting the commandments. For more on the conversion of minors, see chapter 1.

11. During my fieldwork I was exposed to estimates of the proportion of women among converts that ranged from 65 percent to 90 percent. During a session of the Knesset (2013) Committee on the Status of Women and Gender Equality, committee chairperson M. K. Aliza Lavie identified that proportion as 78 percent. In a survey conducted among Orthodox converts in the United States, the figure of 78 percent appeared again; see Heilman (2015).

12. The introduction of the nominal form of giyyur was accompanied by the terms "righteous converts" (*gerei tzedek*, referring to those who entered Judaism through an official gateway) and "resident converts" (*gerei toshav*, referring to those who could assimilate unofficially).

13. Zohar and Sagi emphasize that whereas the first paradigm led some contemporary ultra-Orthodox arbiters to question the finality of giyyur, the second paradigm, equating giyyur with rebirth, stresses that the convert's Jewishness cannot be conditional or revoked retroactively.

14. For elaboration on the controversies surrounding the question of "Who is a Jew?" see A. Cohen and Susser (2000); Corinaldi (2001); Eilam (2000); Gavison and Medan (2003); Landau (1996); Mariner (1999).

15. The status quo is a set of arrangements between religious and secular political parties intended to regulate the relation between state and religious institutes. See Barak-Erez (2009); Barzilai (2010); Levy (2011).

16. The adoption of religious law in the realm of family law was inherited from the Ottoman Empire in Palestine and later from the British Mandatory regime (1917–1948). After the establishment of Israel this arrangement was incorporated into the Israeli legal system and, with some alterations, was applied to all religious communities. See Triger (2012).

17. Civil marriage outside of Israel has become an institutional alternative for those who cannot marry through the rabbinate (e.g., interfaith couples, same-sex couples, and religiously unrecognized individuals) as well as for those Jewish Israelis who seek freedom from religion and more egalitarian marriage arrangements. Those who undergo civil marriage abroad are eligible (though not obliged) to register as married couples in the population registry. Ironically, civil marriage abroad does not allow full freedom from religion, as the rabbinic court system holds jurisdiction over the divorce of such marriages (see Triger 2012). Both civil marriage and nonmarital cohabitation (also known as common-law marriage) vest citizens with the same civil rights as religious marriages. As for burial, over the last two decades, civil burial in Israel has increasingly become an established alternative to religious burial (conducted and endorsed by religious [i.e., Jewish, Muslim, and Christian] burial organizations). Several cemeteries allocate separate space for the burial of those defined as "lacking a religion" (the status that FSU non-Jewish immigrants share) and for those who prefer a civil, rather than a religious, burial.

18. In both cases the Supreme Court deflected the halakhic (i.e., the genealogical) criteria and decided in accordance with how typical Jewish Israelis sociologically address the question of "Who is a Jew?" In the eyes of Jewish Israelis a convert to Christianity cannot be considered Jewish, even if, halakhically speaking, she or he is a Jew.

19. Due to the coupling of the Law of Return and the Citizenship Law, the right to immigrate to Israel under the first law entails rights to citizenship and economic benefits upon immigration, as stated in the latter.

20. For further reading on the debates about the Law of Return, see A. Cohen (2006:63–66); A. Cohen and Susser (2003); Gavison and Medan (2003, 133–147); London (2003); Lustick (1999); Rosen (2003); Sheleg (2004b:8–9, 57–58); Yonah (2005:147–173).

21. The Religious Community (Conversion) Ordinance was legislated by the British Mandatory regime and remained valid in the Israeli legal system.

22. Over the last two decades, the Supreme Court has further complicated the already convoluted legislative arrangements governing conversion. It created distinctions between the entitlement of converts to state recognition and benefits according to the religious denomination (Orthodox, Conservative, or Reform) that conducted the conversion and the location (in or outside of Israel) where it took place. As I write this book, any person who undergoes non-Orthodox conversion in any place, and by any rabbinic authority, is recognized as a Jew by the Israeli Ministry of Interior for the sake of registration in the population registry. A person who undergoes (or even only finalizes) non-Orthodox conversion in any Jewish community outside of Israel is recognized as a Jew for the sake of the Law of Return.

However, a person who undergoes non-Orthodox conversion in Israel cannot be recognized as a Jew for the sake of the Law of Return. Furthermore, as mentioned, for personal status matters any non-Orthodox conversion is invalid.

23. The most well-known claim for an authorized secular form of Jewish conversion was made by former member of the Knesset Yossi Beilin. See Beilin (1999:156–159).

24. For further reading about the political dimensions of religious conversion as an immigration strategy for refugees seeking political asylum, see Koser Akcapar (2006); as an oppositional act against the forces of nationality, see Viswanathan (1998); as a means of achieving economic and family stability, see Luria (1996); or as a conversion to modernity in colonial contexts, see Dirks (1996); Hefner (1993); Van der Veer (1996).

25. It is important to note that even if the government Conversion Administration was established in response to non-Jewish FSU immigration as part of a pro-conversion policy directed selectively at this population, from the administration's beginning Israel utilized it to manage the conversion of people from other backgrounds as well, including the "returnees to Judaism" among the Feres Mura and the marital partners of Israeli citizens.

26. Foucault's writing on biopolitics is vague and inconsistent. The vagueness stems, partially, from the fact that he did not always distinguish clearly between biopolitics and biopower. His inconsistency derives mainly from his continuously shifting understanding of the concept, beginning with his interest in biopolitics in the last part of *The History of Sexuality* ([1976] 1978); in his series of lectures *Society Must Be Defended* ([1976] 2003); *Security, Territory, Population: Lectures at the Collège de France, 1977–78* ([2004] 2007); and, finally, in *The Birth of Biopolitics: Lectures at the Collège de France, 1978–1979* (2008). In his earlier writing on the topic—on which I draw heavily in my usage of the term—he emphasized the emergence of population-related science and administration, as well as the interconnections between political and life-related processes. Some scholars argue that it is through these arguments that Foucault started to shift his focus from the microphysics of power (as in disciplinary power) to more macrophysical mechanisms of state power (Gordon 1991:4; Burchell 1996:19). In his later writings on biopolitics, which are less relevant to my work in this book, Foucault underscored liberal notions of self-governance and the ways in which these notions challenge biopolitical powers. For more on Foucault's various understandings of biopolitics, see Campbell and Sitze (2013); Clough and Willse (2011); Collier (2009); Lemke (2011).

27. Arye Edrei (2010, 2013) shows how central rabbinic authorities took Zionist circumstances into consideration in their halakhic rulings on conversion in Israel. In addition, they implemented a cost-benefit analysis that reflected their realistic approaches to conversion (e.g., preferring conversion to assimilation into Jewish-Israeli society without conversion, even at the cost of compromising the religious criteria).

Relatedly, according to Avi Sagi and Zvi Zohar (2007:60), Ben-Zion Meir Hai Uziel, Israel's first Sephardic chief rabbi, stated that secular non-Jewish wives of secular Jewish men should be accepted for conversion even if the rabbinic court assumes they will maintain their secular habits.

28. For ethnographic studies that expose the decentered, fluid, and labyrinthine nature of state political power, see Hansen and Stepputat (2001); Handelman (2004); Herzfeld (1993); Hull (2012); Sharma and Gupta (2006); Steinmetz (1999).

29. The writing on the performativity of the state often follows Judith Butler's conception of gender and self-making, and it emphasizes the iterative, processual, and generative aspects of statecraft. This literature does not refer to dramaturgical performances by state agents but, rather, to practices that constitute the state and its theatrical effects. See Dunn (2010); Hansen (2001); Sharma and Gupta (2006); Reeves (2014); Taylor (1997); Jusionyte (2015).

30. For further reading on scholarly (including anthropological) discussions about the nature of the state, see Abrams ([1977] 2006); Aretxaga (2003); Mitchell (1991, [1999] 2006); Li (2005); Trouillot (2001); Yang (2005).

31. Much of the scholarship on Jewish conversion, mostly in Israel and the United States, is informed by practical, interventionist agendas. While such scholarship provides tremendously important information and perspectives on various contexts of Jewish conversion, it often focuses (implicitly or explicitly) on how to improve conversion policy. In the American context, see Fishman (2006); Forster and Tabachnik (1991); Huberman (1979). In the Israeli context, see A. Cohen (2004b, 2006); Hanin (2014); Haskin (2012); Fisher (2015); Sheleg (2004b). In contrast to these approaches is an emerging literature of more critically informed scholarship. See Buckser (2003); Goodman (2008a, 2008b); Kravel-Tovi (2012a, 2012b, 2014, 2015); Neiterman and Rapoport (2009); Seeman (2003, 2010).

32. In 2015 Mali changed its name to Nativ, thus adopting the name of its army conversion program. Throughout the book I use *Mali*—the institute's name during my fieldwork.

33. At the beginning of my research I considered including army conversion in my fieldwork. Because this research would have necessarily subjected all of my publications to the authority of the Israeli Military Censor, I decided to avoid this research focus.

34. Rabbinic judges in the regional rabbinic courts derive their authority from the 1955 Law of Rabbinic Judgeship and are nominated for their tenure by the Committee for the Appointment of Rabbinic Court Judges. Unlike them, rabbis in the conversion court are not necessarily certified by the rabbinate as rabbinic judges, and only the chief of the court (*av beit din*) must have *dayyanut* certification (that is, authorized permission to work in the capacity of a rabbinic judge). Most rabbinic judges I met during my fieldwork were never nominated in this kind of official procedure. In general, they were simply recommended by senior officials within the emerging conversion apparatus. In 2009 a search committee in the Prime Minister's Office appointed several new conversion judges.

35. Male converts must undergo circumcision (usually a few weeks) before the ritual immersion. Circumcisions are performed in a number of different medical centers governed by both the rabbinate and the Ministry of Health. Doctors authorized as ritual circumcisers (*mohelim*) conduct the circumcisions, and a rabbinical court panel of three rabbis endorse the ritual. In cases where the convert had previously been circumcised (e.g., for medical reasons) or was born circumcised, he would undergo only a light prick of the penis on the day of the ritual immersion.

36. The Conversion Administration, first established in 1995, changed its name and institutional affiliation a few times. Between 2008 and 2014 the names "Conversion Administration" and "Conversion Department" were often used interchangeably, because the administration was defined as a department in the Prime Minister's Office. Since 2014 it has been known as the Conversion Department. In the book I will use both terms as appropriate, and I will mention the most important details of this institutional trajectory in chapter 1.

37. The garment is designed to float in water to ensure that, as required by Jewish laws of *tvilah*, no barrier exists between the convert's body and the water.

38. As I mentioned at the opening of the introduction, out of respect I adhered to an Orthodox code of dress. But when asked (and I was asked a lot) about myself, I was always straightforward about my secular position.

39. Since 2011 the coordinator of ritual immersion in the department of conversion has been female. This appointment, of course, does not change the patriarchal nature of ritual immersion—that is, the fact that women immerse themselves in front of men.

1. National Mission

1. Interestingly, Rogers Brubaker refers to the rhetoric of a national mission in the American context, emphasizing its religious dimensions and thereby foregrounding the religious nature of American nationalism (Brubaker 2012:10–11).

2. By focusing exclusively on the proconversion policy that emerged in response to mass FSU immigration, this book does not analyze Israel's conversion (or return) policy of Ethiopian immigrants. However, because the Conversion Administration was developed in the context of both immigration waves, a few clarifying comments regarding the Ethiopian case are in order. The conversion of Ethiopian immigrants has never been defined in terms of a national mission. Unlike FSU immigrants who enter Israel through the privileging Law of Return, which grants them immediate citizenship, Ethiopian immigrants enter Israel under the Entry Law. Their conversion is an obligatory component of their immigration and naturalization process; generally speaking, they cannot become citizens without undergoing conversion, which is usually conducted during their time in absorption centers upon their arrival in Israel. The difference between these two conversion policies is sometimes attributed, in critical public discourses, to the state's implicit racial discrimination against "black" populations. While the conversion of non-Jewish FSU olim and immigrants from other backgrounds focuses on individuals (or individual conversion candidates together with their partners), the conversion of Ethiopians usually involves entire families. For further reading on the Ethiopian context and its distinctive features, see Goodman (2008a); Seeman (2010).

3. The chief rabbi's responsibility for conversion is not based on primary legislation but, rather, on legal foundations dating to the British Mandate period as well as on status-quo politics (for further reading on the status quo, see note 15 in the introduction).

4. The term *mamlakhtiut* (lit. "statism"), a central concept in Israeli political life, has various meanings. In one sense, it refers to the historic position advocated by David Ben Gurion, who sought to transfer authority from the institutions that operated during the prestate *Yishuv* period (the years of British Mandate rule) to the newly established state institutions. *Mamlakhti* (as an adjective) may also refer to any institutional entity operated by the state or to public events and behaviors that are considered representative and respectful of the state. In this second sense, Rabbi Goren held a mamlakhti outlook on conversion, and as will become clear later in the chapter, the conversion policy I focus on is based on a mamlakhti apparatus. *Mamlakhti* also refers to an approach that emphasizes both the pannational (rather than sectorial) responsibility of state institutions and the mutual (inter-Jewish) responsibility of citizens in society; this meaning is central to understanding the morality guiding most policy agents I met during my fieldwork (see chapter 2).

5. Leora Batnitzky (2015) argues that Rabbi Goren's religious approach to conversion and Ben Gurion's secular approach to conversion resemble each other in that both are Zionist at their core.

6. The wave of immigration from the Soviet Union in the 1970s comprised 150,000 immigrants (cited in Peled and Shafir 2005:361; see end of note for original source), most of whom were Jews who had experienced a national awakening, especially in the wake of the Six-Day War in 1967, and managed to acquire exit permits from the Soviet government. The arrival of hundreds or thousands of non-Jewish volunteers on kibbutzim is also tied to the admiration Israel earned after what was perceived as a heroic victory in 1967. The original source is Ari M. Paltiel, Eitan Sabatello, and Dorith Tal 1997. "Immigrants from the Former USSR in Israel in the 1990s: Demographic Characteristics and Socio-economic Absorption." In *Russian Jews on Three Continents: Migration and Resettlement*, ed. Noah Lewin-Epstein, Yaacov Ro'i, and Paul Ritterband, 284–321 (London: Routledge, 1997).

7. Between the state's establishment in 1948 and 1968, 2,288 out of 4,010 candidates underwent conversion in Israel (Rosenbloom 1978:136).

8. During the first waves of FSU immigration in the late 1980s and early 1990s, the immigrating population was considered to possess high "human capital" and advanced professional skills. This positive socioeconomic profile possibly enhanced the state's motivation to invest in the absorption of these immigrants. The later immigration waves (from the late 1990s and onward) were not deemed as economically valuable as the first. Some attribute this socioeconomic difference to ethnicity. The first waves, unlike the later ones, were characterized by higher percentages of people raised as Jews and known to have belonged to the Soviet Union's more highly educated classes (Shapiro 2005).

9. The estimates by Dr. Ze'ev Hanin (2014), the chief scientist of the Ministry of Absorption, stand at 270,000–280,000 non-Jewish Russian-speaking immigrants. The media sometimes reference a figure of 330,000. Ian Lustick (2011:36) cites the Central Bureau of Statistics' 2010 report, according to which the number ranges between 330,000 and 350,000. As I will show later, the number 300,000 has captured the imagination within bureaucratic and public discourse.

10. There are halakhic Jews who converted to Christianity before immigrating to Israel—an act that was supposed to have prevented them from immigrating under

the Law of Return. This prohibition, though, was only rarely enforced. Other immigrants converted to Christianity in Israel, usually under the influence of negligible messianic Jewish groups who are frequently active in Russian-speaking neighborhoods (relatedly, see Seeman 2015b on messianic Judaism among the Feres Mura). Either way, these Christian groups constitute a minority among the Russian-speaking population. For further reading on Christian FSU immigrants, see Raijman and Pinsky (2011).

11. This is why non-Jewish olim are categorically different from non-Jewish spouses of Israeli Jews, whose legal status as immigrants is governed by the Citizenship Law. Whereas olim are entitled to citizenship upon their arrival in Israel, non-Jewish spouses of Israeli citizens are required to undergo a lengthy bureaucratic procedure before they can apply for citizenship, and only after a period of time spent as permanent residents.

12. For a more extensive discussion of the political and cultural dynamics of the Russian-speaking immigrant population, see Al-Haj and Leshem (2000); Lerner (2011); Lerner and Feldhai (2012); Leshem and Lissak (2001); Shumsky (2001).

13. Nationality is also reflected in the documented birth date, because only ID cards held by halakhic Jews include the registration of the Hebrew birth date.

14. The Sephardic ultra-Orthodox political party Shas was founded in 1984 and has since played a significant role in Israeli politics and society. In colloquial usage the terms *Mizrachi* and *Sephardic* are often conflated. Both terms commonly denote Jews who trace their roots to Jewish communities in the Middle East.

15. For the media coverage of this virtual response, see Mizrachi (2013).

16. Though it carries a very different meaning, the category "non-Jewish Jews," in Gauri Viswanathan's account of religious minorities in Britain, refers to enfranchised Jews who could be Jewish in blood and appearance but English in their taste, opinions, morals, and intellect (Viswanathan 1998:5–6). In yet another historical context, Isaac Deutscher's ([1958] 1981) concept of the "non-Jewish Jew" has been used as a marker of identity referring to leftist, secular, and humanist Jewish intellectuals (from Baruch Spinoza through Sigmund Freud to himself) who revolutionized modern thought by going beyond what was understood to be proper (i.e., religiously informed) Jewish life.

17. In addition to the expansion of funding and services supporting conversion, the Conversion Administration has paid, in recent years, increasingly careful attention to the clarification of Jewish status. The number of FSU and other immigrants and immigrants' children required by the rabbinate to undergo such a clarification—usually prior to pursuing marriage through the rabbinate—is increasing. See also note 3 in the introduction.

18. It should come as no surprise that the phrase "Goren's conversion" (*giyyurey Goren*) is a derogatory phrase in the ultra-Orthodox world, relating to those who seemingly violated the sacred rules of halakha and created a system of false conversions. See World Rabbinic Committee on Conversion (1989).

19. Since 2002 the IDF's conversion system has revamped and significantly expanded the framework originally initiated by Rabbi Goren forty years earlier—developing a conversion pipeline that handles hundreds of non-Jewish soldiers every year. See Fisher (2015:46–54).

20. Agamben's (2005) perspective on the state of exception has been applied to the Israeli context, especially in respect to the bureaucracy of the occupation. See for example Berda (2012).

21. Israel has operated under a legal state of emergency since its founding in 1948. The Israeli Parliament periodically decides to extend this legal arrangement. The Association for Civil Rights in Israel has fought against the perpetuation of this status. However, the Parliament opposes abolishing it because doing so would lead to the widespread abrogation of legislation that was undertaken under the aegis of the state of emergency.

22. Eighty-six percent of the Jewish public expressed a desire that their children marry Jews. See Itim (2015).

23. The original source is Sammy Smooha, "Ethnic Democracy: Israel as an Ideal Type," *Zionism: Contemporary Polemics* (Sde-Boker: Ben Gurion Heritage Institute, 1996), 311–277.

24. In addition to these fears, Orthodox rabbis (from diverse positions within Orthodoxy) fear a weakening in the political status of halakha. Specifically, they worry that the intense social pressure to permit civil marriages from a significant minority will cause a major upheaval in relations between state and religion.

25. Such fears are clearly demonstrated in the case of the extremist right-wing Lehava organization (*Lehava*; a Hebrew acronym for "Prevention of Assimilation in the Holy Land"), notorious for its violent objection to any personal relationships between Jews and non-Jews—especially between Jewish Israelis and Palestinians. However, such fears are also reflected in the pedagogic decision enforced by the Israeli Education Ministry in December 2015 not to include the book *Borderlife*, by Dorit Rabinyan, a love story between a Jewish-Israeli woman and a Palestinian man, in the advanced literature curriculum in Israeli high schools, on the grounds that it might encourage intermarriage. See Hay (2015).

26. It is interesting to juxtapose these discourses about non-Jewish olim and those prevalent in Jewish diasporic contexts. While within diasporic communities these discourses serve to concentrate the anxieties of a minority group about its relationship to the non-Jewish majority (Berman 2009; Hart 2000; Kravel-Tovi, 2016), in Israel, in the context of non-Jewish FSU immigration, they refer to a unique situation in which a non-Jewish minority blends into the Jewish majority.

27. For an extended discussion of Jewish demography, see DellaPergola (1999); DellaPergola and Cohen (1992); Kosmin et al. (1991); Ritterband (1981).

28. For extensive discussions, see Leibler and Breslau (2005); Orenstein (2004); Stypinska (2007); Yonah (2005).

29. At Jewish funerals it is customary for the deceased's relatives to rend their garments. After the funeral the relatives of the deceased observe a seven-day mourning period (or "sit *shiva*") with its attendant customs, including staying home, abstaining from work, and receiving visitors. In Israel secular Jews also sit shiva, even if they do not observe all the halakhic particulars of the mourning practices. The phrase "to sit shiva" is widely used and understood.

30. For further reading on Foucault's engagement with biopolitics and the management of population, see Foucault ([1976] 1978, [1976] 2003, [1978] 2006, [2004] 2007, 2008).

31. The use of the slogan "giyyur bar hasaga" drew public criticism from secular, liberal Jews. They argued that the state's use of the housing slogan reflected its distorted

priorities, in which it functions more like a Jewish state than a welfare state. They charged the state with abandoning its citizens with respect to their housing needs, but going to great lengths to convert and Judaize its non-Jewish citizens. See Lustig (2013).

32. The targeting of women also drew fire from civic associations for freedom of religion who labeled it a male chauvinist campaign. See Bender (2014).

33. Their focus is on underage pupils who are already enrolled in the religious education system (provided that their parents are supportive of their conversion). See Ganzel and Rafe (2014).

34. Highlighting the special significance placed on those non-Jewish immigrants who will shape future generations, Netanel Fisher (2015) proposes reducing the unrealistic goal of converting all 300,000 to a more modest goal of 25,000.

35. In addition to the emphasis placed on the national component of Israel's immigration policy (a policy based primarily on the Law of Return), some scholars have argued that Israel's immigration policy also reflects internally Jewish, Eurocentric, and republican tendencies that privilege "white" Jews from strong countries. See Peled and Shafir (2005:362); Yonah (2005:122–176).

36. For a summary of the information collected in surveys regarding the positions and motivations of non-Jewish immigrants with respect to conversion, see Fisher (2015:33n65) and Hanin (2014). For additional data on conversion statistics, see Kaplan and Seri-Levi (2013). For an analysis of how non-Jewish FSU women compensate for their non-Jewish status through social practices of belonging, see Prashizky and Remennick (2012).

37. Out of 584 conversion applications submitted to the Committee for Exceptional Cases of Conversion in 2012, only 74 were permitted to undergo conversion in state conversion institutes (see Knesset 2013). Some of those who were denied permission underwent conversion under the aegis of either the Reform or Conservative Movements. Other converts undergo conversion in one of the very few private Orthodox or ultra-Orthodox conversion courts that operate alongside the state Conversion Administration. Until March 2016 these private Orthodox courts were not recognized by the state or the Chief Rabbinate. In a dramatic ruling, the Supreme Court of Israel (in its capacity as the High Court of Justice) decided that conversions held in these courts would be recognized for defining eligibility for the Law of Return. See Ettinger and Pulwer (2016).

38. On more than one occasion I heard stories about the corruption and bribery that formerly characterized the conversion market. A number of officials maintained that the subsidization policy is intended, among other things, to protect potential converts from price hikes and attempts at bribery.

39. During my fieldwork I heard various numerical figures for cost per student. See also Knesset (2008).

40. For literature on the economic integration of Jewish and non-Jewish FSU immigrants, see Al-Haj and Leshem (2000:15–18, 26); Y. Cohen and Kogan (2007); Haberfeld et al. (2011); Shechory and Ben-David (2010).

41. For more on the chief rabbi's opposition to the conversion reforms, see Ettinger (2015a).

42. Because it is customary on Shavuoth to perform a liturgical reading of the Book of Ruth, a biblical story dealing with Ruth's adhesion, or conversion, to Judaism, the holiday has become linked to the conversion issue.

43. For more on Hiddush and this initiative, see Hiddush (2015).

44. In fact, the argument for an inherent Jewish opposition to missionary tendencies is very much in dispute. One can find contradictory historical evidence for missionizing, for example, in ancient Israel (see Samet 1993), among twentieth-century American Jewry (see Berman 2009), with regard to Judaizing movements (see Parfitt and Trevisan Semi 2002), and with regard to Israel Ben Ze'ev's provocative suggestion in the 1950s to convert Palestinians as a means of addressing the "demographic problem" (see Rosenbloom 1978). One can also find indications in current polemics (see Epstein 1992:2014). Yet the word *missionary* has negative connotations in many other Jewish-Israeli contexts as well. These connotations are evident in the aggressive ultra-Orthodox response to non-Jewish missionary groups who aim to convert Israeli Jews, or in the antagonism publicly expressed by secular Jews toward what is often deemed as "the missionizing" efforts of some ultra-Orthodox groups, especially the Shas and Chabad movements.

45. In this regard Israel has in fact shifted its policy toward the non-Jewish parents of soldiers who immigrate to Israel. This shift took place in 2002–2003, when the state created new regulations stipulating that the non-Jewish parents of immigrant soldiers, who would not otherwise be eligible to immigrate to Israel under the Law of Return, can immigrate to Israel and receive citizenship through a relatively expedited process.

2. State Workers

1. An ultra-Orthodox rabbinic conversion judge told me during an interview that he had been "sent" by an important ultra-Orthodox leader to work in the conversion court and pay close attention to how "religious Zionist conversions" were conducted.

2. Coalition agreements made at the opening of the twentieth Knesset (March 2015) between Prime Minister Benjamin Netanyahu and the ultra-Orthodox parties repealed the Conversion Reform Law—a law that was clearly identified with both the religious Zionist party, Habait Hayehudi, and with religious Zionists politicians, most importantly MK Elazar Stern of the Yesh Atid (lit. "There Is a Future") party.

3. Unsurprisingly, in light of the centrality of the idea of return in Jewish religious ideology, religious Zionists are also the driving force behind Jewish organizations that facilitate the immigration and conversion of the Bnei Menashe of northern India and other "Judaizing groups" (see Parfitt and Trevisan Semi 2002). In addition, informed by messianic scripts about the ingathering of exiles and the return of the lost Israelite tribes, religious Zionist communities, more than any other segment of Israeli society, have embrace the Bnei Menashe. See Egorova (2015).

4. The original source is Thomas Bernhard, *Alte Meister* [Old Masters] (Frankfurt: Suhrkamp Verlag, 1989), 27.

5. The ethnographic text that I sent to the person who I call "Rabbi Cohen" already included an alias, and he knew the name I assigned to him.

6. A comparison between religious Zionism and the ultra-Orthodox world is crucial for understanding the ideological, theological, and sociological orientations of religious Zionism, orientations that constitute the background of my discussion in

this chapter. Even if the topic of subgroups within the ultra-Orthodox world is beyond the scope of this chapter, it is important to emphasize one major internal difference between Ashkenazi and Sephardic ultra-Orthodox groups. While the former tend to blatantly reject civilian and political participation in the Zionist state (even if in practice they demonstrate greater flexibility), the latter have created innovative bridges between Zionism and ultra-Orthodox life. They articulate pannational (though not explicitly Zionist) stances with regard to Israel as a Jewish state and display national responsibility over matters of Jewish identity. In these senses, Mizrachi ultra-Orthodox Jews share basic tenets with religious Zionist Jews, to the extent that they compete with them for resources and institutional power with regard to a range of Jewish and religious issues. For more on the Mizrachi ultra-Orthodox national stance, see Leon (2014a, 2014b).

7. For more on religious Zionist models of the relationships between religion and state, see Neuman (2015:290–342).

8. Religious Zionists were never a majority group in Israeli society. According to the Central Bureau of Statistics in Israel's survey from 2009, 12 percent of Jews in Israel define themselves as "religious" (Stern et al. 2015:8).

9. Beginning in the 1990s, the term "ultra-Orthodox nationalism" became common in religious Zionist and other Israeli discourses. However, prominent figures associated with this radicalizing movement reject that designation (instead simply calling themselves "Torah observant" [*Torani*]) and maintain clear sociological boundaries between themselves and ultra-Orthodox communities.

10. It is true that the silent majority of religious Zionists did not settle in the occupied territories. However, the religious Zionist public is identified politically with right-wing attitudes toward the politics of occupation (see Neuman 2015:374–375). For further readings on bourgeoisifying processes within the new middle class of religious Zionists, see Leon (2010b).

11. For further reading on the history of religious Zionism, see A. Cohen (1998); Schwartz (2004).

12. It is not uncommon for non-Jewish olim to integrate into religious Zionist educational contexts, whether they are aware of their non-Jewish halakhic status or not. Such occasions only increase the likelihood that religious Zionists will meet and get involved with non-Jews.

13. Alongside the central narrative of the national problem, one can find religious Zionist narratives describing non-Jewish immigration as a miracle and a sign of the redemptive ingathering of exiles. See for example the Ami website (Ami 2015).

14. For more on the reflexive soul searching among religious Zionists following the disengagement from Gaza, see Ariel (2004); Ben-Meir (2005); Gilad (2006); Kahan (2005); Tur-Paz (2005).

15. Surveys of the religious Zionist public reveal ambivalent attitudes toward halakhic liberalization concerning conversion. In particular, this public is hesitant about its commitment to conversion and feels the lack of rabbinic support for such a commitment. See Fisher (2015:141–142).

16. For further reading on such trends, see Englander (2005); Bar-Asher (2007); R. Friedman (2005).

17. Arye Edrei (2012) argues convincingly that, upon his arrival in Palestine, Rabbi Abraham Isaac HaCohen Kook created a solid foundation for a religious Zionist

halakhic ruling, one that takes into consideration Jewish modernity and secularization, and treats the Jewish social reality in Palestine as a national revival. With these perspectives in mind, Rabbi Kook strayed from the normative Orthodox halakhic opinion in nineteenth-century Europe.

18. In this context, it is instructive to consider the Tzohar organization's support of Rabbi Shlomo Riskin—a religious Zionist rabbi known for his liberal, Zionist, and nationally responsible halakhic approach to, among other things, conversion; the Chief Rabbinic council had threatened to dismiss him.

19. A similar critique is sometimes raised among religious Zionist rabbis. The argument is that the steps religious Zionists have taken in subjecting halakha to national, Zionist concerns are too extensive—such as in the case of conversion. Rabbi Michael Abraham writes that "Rabbi Brandes' proposal to convert non-Jewish FSU immigrants into 'Israeliness' is grounded in the perception that Jewish law [should] serve the national idea and Jewish society in Israel: [that it is] a Zionist instrument, a tool in the Zionist movement's toolbox" (Abraham 2009:205).

20. The Israeli law (the Defense Service Law, 1949) permits exemption of women from military service for reasons of conscience or religious conviction. But the religious Zionist community remains divided over the appropriateness of using this exemption. Central rabbinic authorities have argued vehemently against the conscription of religious women, often tying the issue to a more general critique of the feminist revolution, which over the past decades has made inroads into the religious Zionist movement. Opposite them stand liberal rabbis who encourage the conscription of religious women in the name of both religious feminism and national responsibility (A. Cohen 1998; Neuman 2015).

21. There is no agreement about the relative size of each group—national ultra-Orthodox and modern Orthodox Jews. According to some estimates, even if national ultra-Orthodoxy was significantly larger during the 1970s and 1980s, the majority of religious Zionists today have adopted lifestyles that more closely approximate the modern Orthodox cultural model (Ben-Meir 2005; Pfeffer 2007:42–43; Sheleg 2000:94–96). According to other estimates, nationalist ultra-Orthodoxy is on the rise. See Hoberman (2011).

22. The appeal included three demands: to invalidate the rabbinical court ruling about the nullification of the divorced woman's conversion; to invalidate the principled, halakhic court ruling against Rabbi Druckman's conversion; and to insist that the marriage registration (in the local religious councils) recognize any conversion certificate signed by the Conversion Administration.

3. Legible Signs

1. For other social scientific studies of contemporary Jewish conversion, see Buckser (2003); Forster and Tabachnik (1991); Homolka, Jacob, and Seidel (1997).

2. See chapter 1 for a discussion of the unique and particularly ironic usage of discourses of assimilation in the Jewish-Israeli context.

3. These glossaries include terms pertaining to Jewish belief and morality (e.g., the thirteen principles of Jewish faith and Israel as a light to the nations), Jewish

history (e.g., the Babylonian exile and First and Second Temples), and Jewish religious practice (e.g., Counting of the Omer [*s'firat haomer*], Mitzvot Dependent on the Land of Israel, and the Amidah prayer).

4. In many, if not most, scholarly works on passing, the concept is understood within Butlerian analytic frameworks of performativity (see Butler 1990), which stress how reiterated acting constructs identity (see Ahmed 1999; Caughie 1999; Renfrow 2004; Sanchez and Shlossberg 2001). I instead ground my analysis in the Goffmanian framework from which the concept of passing originally grew (Goffman [1963] 1986).

5. For further discussion on Jeremy Bentham's panopticon as a model of a control system, see Foucault (1980).

6. Several students in the class were anxious that, even if concealed by clothing throughout the conversion process, their tattoos would ultimately be revealed during the ritual bath that marks conversion completion. Building on popular knowledge that Jewish law forbids tattooing (viewed as marring God's creation), these students were afraid they would be required to remove their tattoos. I heard a few converts asking teachers about the matter and learning that they would not be asked to remove them but would be expected to refrain from additional tattoos. Two students asked for my input on whether rabbinic judges raise the issue during candidates' court hearings.

7. Because Mali employs some Conservative and Reform Jews, I heard several times in pedagogic seminars how these teachers fear having an inferior ability to gain judges' confidence and maintain trusting working relations.

8. Several scholars distinguish between sincerity and authenticity by emphasizing the interactive dimension of the former versus the internal, inherent nature of the latter. For more on this distinction and on authenticity, see Puddephatt, Kelly, and Adorjan (2006); J. Taylor (2001).

9. Indeed, I met many conversion candidates who concealed their partners during the conversion process, in order to disencumber them of the burden of surveillance and performance and also because a halakhic lifestyle precludes premarital sexual relations.

10. The original source is Thomas S. Szasz, *The Myth of Mental Illness: Foundations of a Theory of Personal Conduct*, revised edition (1961; reprinted, New York: Perennial, 1974).

4. Dramaturgical Entanglements

1. For more on trust as an investment in the potentiality of the future, see Govier (1997:24, citing Niklas Luhmann, *Trust and Power* [New York: Wiley, 1979]); Simmel (1906:449); Sztompka (1999).

2. In its form and logic, this process resembles the credibility assessments employed by British asylum courts, as described by Good (2011). Good's rich ethnography is not framed in dramaturgical terms, but he does use dramaturgical metaphors, such as when saying that "legal reps see the taking of the statement as a useful 'dress rehearsal'" (ibid., 101).

3. I observed many procedures in which rabbinic judges disagreed about the importance that should be granted to each of these areas as a locus of critical information about candidates. As a whole, panels tended to vary with regard to the themes they emphasized during investigations. During a number of procedures, candidates attempted to negotiate the issues and boundaries constituting investigations, thus calling into question the means by which the court validated their conversions.

4. Some conversion candidates told me they sometimes felt on trial when they went to visit host families. One remarkable example was of a candidate who told me her host mother asked her whether she had ridden earlier in the week on a particular bus line. The convert told me: "What? Did they see someone wearing pants and they wanted to check if I would admit it? Luckily, it really was not me."

5. This separation between the components of the procedure is a bureaucratic trick court agents sometimes used to encourage candidates (by engendering a sense of hope as well as progress) while maintaining surveillance, with the aim of fostering further religious change.

6. With Motti's marked Mizrachi appearance, Rabbi Ushpiz's question may have stemmed in part from common assumptions linking Mizrachi identity to traditional, rather than to secular, Judaism.

7. The original source is "My Private Intifada: An Interview with Orly Castel-Bloom," by Neri Livne, *Ha'aretz*, April 3, 2002, http://www.haaretz.co.il/misc/1.784160 (in Hebrew), retrieved December 2016.

8. Several scholars have demonstrated the performative, theatrical significance of conversion rituals. See Austin-Broos (2003); Goodman (2004); Harding (2000); Keane (2007).

9. The Hebrew name taken in conversion might be an addition to, rather than a replacement of, the original name. Converts sometimes change their name in state documents, although they are not required to do so.

10. Abraham and Sarah, the first patriarch and matriarch of the Jewish people, are considered the first Jewish converts and the father and mother of all who followed them. Hence, it is customary for converts in ritual occasions to be regarded as the sons and daughters of Abraham and Sarah. This custom demonstrates, once again, the perception that Jewish converts join Jewish kinship lines.

5. Biographical Scripts

1. The original source is Joel Robbins, "What Is a Christian? Notes Toward an Anthropology of Christianity," *Religion* 33 (2003): 191.

2. While scholars of Christianity have indeed shown how, in some contexts, converts learn to organize their conversion testimonies according to dramatic schemes of transformation and rebirth (see Snow and Machalek 1983; Stromberg 1993), in other contexts, more prosaic schemes are also permissible. For example, Webb Keane argues that the oratorical events that mediate the conversion of people in Sumba, Indonesia, from ancestral religion to Calvinism often adhere to a mundane and

rational narrative of change rather than to "startling claims about new insights or lives transformed" (Keane 2007:164).

3. The metaphor of a stamp emerged more than once during my fieldwork at the conversion ulpan. Employed by conversion candidates and agents alike, it was usually brought up (in words or in bodily gestures) to indicate the bureaucratic, and therefore cold and shallow, connotations of the conversion procedure. Sometimes it was used to link these connotations to conversion, and sometimes speakers used it to dissociate themselves from such connotations. See also Kravel-Tovi (2014).

4. Andrew Buckser (2003:73) documented similar ambivalences, or even outright suspicion, in his study of Jewish conversion in Copenhagen, Denmark.

5. Some rabbinic judges were more suspicious of converts from atheist backgrounds, while others expressed more suspicion about those from religious, mostly Christian backgrounds. In both cases, the converts' separation from their previous lifestyles (habits, sentiments, perceptions) was much discussed in court.

6. On the difference between return to Zionist Orthodoxy and to ultra-Orthodoxy, see Doron (2013:65–66).

7. Returnees to Orthodox Judaism often confront ambivalent attitudes within the communities they join. Admired for choosing to become righteous on the one hand, they also endure social exclusion and segregation in terms of marriage arrangements, educational opportunities, and social status.

Epilogue

1. It is customary for religious and traditional Jews to "sell" their chametz to non-Jews before Passover. The sale is only temporary, as Jews "buy" the chametz back from the non-Jews after Passover. In fact, the chametz can remain in Jewish homes during Passover, because once sold it belongs to the non-Jewish buyer, regardless of its physical location. Institutions, factories, and businesses can also keep their chametz on their properties, so long as they sell it to a non-Jew. In most if not all kosher supermarkets in Israel, entire shelves containing sold chametz are covered in plastic sheeting. The chief rabbi of Israel, on behalf of the state, participates in a ritual selling of all of the state's chametz to a non-Jew.

2. See 14:15 of Moni Moshonov, *The Jews Are Coming*, season 2, episode 10, directed by Yoav Gross, aired April 15, 2016.

3. See Ferguson (2005); Geschiere (2007); Schayegh (2010); Schept (2014); Valverde (2011).

4. The original source is Thomas S. Szasz, *The Myth of Mental Illness: Foundations of a Theory of Personal Conduct*, revised edition (1961; reprinted, New York: Perennial, 1974).

References

Abraham, Michael. 2009. "The Gates of Conversion: On Violence and Good Intentions: More on the Renewed Polemics of Conversion Following Rabbi Yehuda Brandes' Article (*Akademot* 21)." *Akademot* 22:197–209. In Hebrew.

Abrams, Philip. (1977) 2006. "Notes on the Difficulty of Studying the State." In *The Anthropology of the State: A Reader*, edited by Aradhana Sharma and Akhil Gupta, 112–130. Malden, MA: Blackwell.

Achituv, Yoske. 2005. "From Religious-Zionist Orthodoxy to Hardali Orthodoxy." *Deot* 24:18–21. In Hebrew.

Adamker, Yaki. 2015. "Revolution: A Private Organization Could Give Restaurants Kosher Certificate." *Walla!*, May 6. Accessed August 23, 2015. http://judaism.walla.co.il/item/2851920. In Hebrew.

Agamben, Giorgio. 2005. *State of Exception*. Chicago: University of Chicago Press.

Ahmed, Sara. 1999. "'She'll Wake Up One of These Days and Find She's Turned Into a Nigger': Passing Through Hybridity." *Theory, Culture and Society* 16:87–106.

——. 2004. "Affective Economies." *Social Text* 22 (2): 117–139.

Al-Haj, Majid, and Elazar Leshem. 2000. *Immigrants from the Former Soviet Union in Israel: Ten Years Later*. Haifa: Center for Multiculturalism and Educational Research, University of Haifa. In Hebrew.

Althusser, Louis. (1971) 2006. "Ideology and Ideological State Apparatuses (Notes Towards an Investigation)." In *The Anthropology of the State*, edited by Aradhana Sharma and Akhil Gupta, 86–111. Malden, MA: Blackwell.

Amar, Shlomo. 2006. "The Discussion Rules Regarding Conversion Applications." February 27. Accessed May 17, 2015. http://index.justice.gov.il/Units/Tmihot/Tavhinim/Tavhinim/138.pdf. In Hebrew.

Ami. 2015. "Ulpan News | Ami: Conversion Classes from a Personal Perspective." Accessed July 30. http://www.ami4u.org/category/news. In Hebrew.

Amir, Merav. 2005. "The Emergence of the Biological Clock of the Female Reproductive System as a Mechanism for Social Regulation." Master's thesis, Tel Aviv University.

Anjaria, Jonathan S. 2011. "Ordinary States: Everyday Corruption and the Politics of Space in Mumbai." *American Ethnologist* 38 (1): 58–72.

Aran, Gideon. 2013. *Kookism: The Roots of the Bloc of the Faithful, Settlers' Sub-culture, Zionist Theology, Current Messianism*. Jerusalem: Carmel. In Hebrew.

Aretxaga, Begona. 2003. "Maddening States." *Annual Review of Anthropology* 32:393–410.

Ariel, Yigal. 2004. "The Spiritual Disengagement Is Already Here." *Eretz Acheret* 24:20–23. In Hebrew.

Arteaga Botello, Nelson. 2012. "Surveillance Cameras and Synopticism: A Case Study in Mexico City." In *Eyes Everywhere: The Global Growth of Camera Surveillance*, edited by Aaron Doyle, Randy Lippert, and David Lyon, 249–261. Abingdon: Routledge.

Asad, Talal. 2004. "Where Are the Margins of the State?" In *Anthropology in the Margins of the State*, edited by Veena Das and Deborah Poole, 279–288. Santa Fe: School of American Research Press.

Austin-Broos, Diane. 2003. "The Anthropology of Conversion: An Introduction." In *The Anthropology of Religious Conversion*, edited by Andrew Buckser and Stephen D. Glazier, 1–14. Lanham, MD: Rowman and Littlefield.

Avineri, Shlomo. 2007. "Stop Searching Jewish Offspring." *Walla!*, October 10. Accessed June 9, 2015. http://news.walla.co.il/item/1175662.

Barak-Erez, Daphne. 2009. "Law and Religion Under the Status Quo Model: Between Past Compromises and Constant Change." *Cardozo Law Review* 30 (6): 2495–2507.

Bar-Asher, Avishai, ed. 2007. "'Between Law and Rabbinical Judge': Changes in the Rabbinic Courts' Status—in Light of the Breaking of the Alliance between Religious Zionism and the Chief Rabbinate." *Deot* 34, special issue. In Hebrew.

Barker, Eileen. 1984. *The Making of a Moonie: Choice or Brainwashing?* Oxford: Blackwell.

Barmeli, Dafna. 2014. "The Restaurateurs Who Were Tired of the Rabbinate's Bullying and Have Established an Independent Apparatus." *Globes*, May 24. Accessed February 18, 2016. http://www.globes.co.il/news/article.aspx?did=1000940094. In Hebrew.

Barnes, John. A. 1994. *A Pack of Lies: Towards a Sociology of Lying*. Cambridge: Cambridge University Press.

Barzilai, Gad. 2010. "Who Is a Jew? Categories, Boundaries, Communities and Citizenship Law in Israel." In *Boundaries of Jewish Identities*, edited by Susan Glenn and Naomi Sokoloff, 27–42. Seattle: University of Washington Press.

Bass, David. 2007. "Giyyur and the Acceptance of the Commandments: Theory and Practice." *Tzohar: A Religious Journal* 30:29–40. In Hebrew.

——. 2008. " I Have Seen in Front of Me, with My Own Eyes." *Nekudah* 313:40–42. In Hebrew.

Batnitzky, Leora. 2015. "Conversion Before the Law: Why Conversion Controversies in Israel Are Not Necessarily About Religion." Paper presented at the Oxford Summer Institute of Modern and Contemporary Judaism Workshop, Oxford, June.

Bauman, Zygmunt. 1991. *Modernity and Ambivalence*. Ithaca: Cornell University Press.

——. 1992. *Intimations of Postmodernity*. London: Routledge.

Beilin, Yossi. 1999. *The Death of the American Uncle: Jews in the 21st Century.* Tel Aviv: Yedioth Ahronoth and Hemed. In Hebrew.

Bender, Arik. 2014. "A Letter to Benet: 'Remove Immediately the Ministry of Religious Services' Chauvinistic Conversion Campaign.'" *Maariv,* September 7. Accessed September 30, 2015. http://www.maariv.co.il/news/new.aspx?pn6Vq =E&0r9VQ=GFDEL. In Hebrew.

Ben-Meir, Yehuda. 2005. "A Cultural Educational Revolution in Religious Zionism." *Mifne* 48:8–11. In Hebrew.

Benn, Aluf. 2016. "Being a Jew Without the Rabbinate." *Haaretz*, April 14. Accessed May 5, 2016. http://www.haaretz.co.il/opinions/editorial-articles/1.2914433. In Hebrew.

Ben-Porat, Guy. 2016. *In Practice: The Secularization of Contemporary Israel.* Haifa: Pardes. In Hebrew.

Ben-Porat, Guy, and Yariv Feniger. 2009. Live and Let Buy: Consumerism, Secularization, and Liberalism. *Comparative Politics* 41 (3): 293–313.

Berda, Yael. 2012. *The Bureaucracy of the Occupation: The Permit Regime in the West Bank.* Tel Aviv: Van Leer Jerusalem Institute and Hakibutz Hameuchad. In Hebrew.

Berkovitch, Nitza. 1997. "Motherhood as a National Mission: The Construction of Womanhood in the Legal Discourse in Israel." *Women's Studies International Forum* 20:605–619.

Berman, Lila C. 2009. *Speaking of Jews: Rabbis, Intellectuals, and the Creation of an American Public Identity.* Berkeley: University of California Press.

Bin-Nun, Yoel. 2003. "Mass Conversion Must Be Carried Out." *Eretz Acheret* 17:68–69. In Hebrew.

——. 2004. "Our Rupture Will Project on the Whole of Israeli Society." *Etetz Acheret* 24:31–33. In Hebrew.

Bourdieu, Pierre. 1998. "Rethinking the State: Genesis and Structure of the Bureaucratic Field." In *Practical Reason: On the Theory of Action*, 35–63. Cambridge: Polity.

Brandes, Yehuda. 2008. "The Renewed Polemics of Conversion." *Akademot* 21:83–95.

Brubaker, Rogers. 1996. *Nationalism Reframed: Nationhood and the National Question in the New Europe.* Cambridge: Cambridge University Press.

——. 2012. "Religion and Nationalism: Four Approaches." *Nations and Nationalism* 18 (1): 2–20.

Buckser, Andrew. 2003. "Social Conversion and Group Definition in Jewish Copenhagen." In *The Anthropology of Religious Conversion*, edited by Andrew Buckser and Stephen D. Glazier, 69–84. Lanham, MD: Rowman and Littlefield.

Burchell, Graham. 1996. "Liberal Government and Techniques of the Self." In *Foucault and Political Reason: Liberalism, Neo-Liberalism, and Rationalities of Government*, edited by Andrew Barry, Thomas Osborne, and Nikolas S. Rose, 19–36. Chicago: University of Chicago Press.

Burns, Tom. 1992. *Erving Goffman.* London: Routledge.

Butler, Judith. 1990. *Gender Trouble.* New York: Routledge.

Buur, Lars. 2001. "The South African Truth and Reconciliation Commission: A Technique of Nation-State Formation." In *States of Imagination: Ethnographic Explorations of the Postcolonial State*, edited by Thomas B. Hansen and Finn Stepputat, 149–181. Durham: Duke University Press.

Campbell, Timothy C., and Adam Sitze, eds. 2013. *Biopolitics: A Reader.* Durham: Duke University Press.

Carr, E. Summerson. 2010. *Scripting Addiction: The Politics of Therapeutic Talk and American Sobriety.* Princeton: Princeton University Press.

———. 2013. "'Signs of the Times': Confession and the Semiotic Production of Inner Truth." *Journal of the Royal Anthropological Institute* 19 (1): 34–51.

Caughie, Pamela L. 1999. *Passing and Pedagogy: The Dynamics of Responsibility.* Urbana: University of Illinois Press.

Cherlow, Yuval. 2008. "It Could Have Been Different." *Eretz Acheret* 46:89–91. In Hebrew.

Chua, Liana. 2012. "Conversion, Continuity, and Moral Dilemma Among Christian Bidayuhs in Malaysian Borneo." *American Ethnologist* 39 (3): 511–526.

Clough, Patricia T., and Craig Willse, eds. 2011. *Beyond Biopolitics: Essays on the Governance of Life and Death.* Durham: Duke University Press.

Cohen, Asher. 1998. *The Tallit and the Flag: Religious Zionism and the Vision of the Torah State in the Early Years of the State.* Jerusalem: Ben Zvi Institute. In Hebrew.

———. 2004a. "The Beginning of the Decline of Our Redemption: The Dwindling of Religious Zionism in the Struggle Over Jewish Identity in the State of Israel and Its Future Influences." In *Religious Zionism: An Era of Change: A Research Collection in Memory of Zevulun Hammer*, edited by Asher Cohen and Israel Harel, 364–385. Jerusalem: Bialik Institute. In Hebrew.

———. 2004b. *Israeli Assimilation: Acculturation of Non-Jewish People in Jewish Society in Israel and Its Consequences for Collective Identity.* Ramat Gan: The Rappaport Center for Assimilation Research and Strengthening Jewish Vitality, Bar Ilan University. In Hebrew.

———. 2006. *Non-Jewish Jews.* Jerusalem: Shalom Hartman Institute. In Hebrew.

Cohen, Asher, and Bernard Susser. 2000. *Israel and the Politics of Jewish Identity: The Secular-Religious Impasse.* Baltimore: Johns Hopkins University Press.

———. 2003. *From Accommodation to Escalation: Secular-Religious Conflict in Israel.* Jerusalem: Schocken. In Hebrew.

———. 2009. "Jews and Others: Non-Jewish Jews in Israel." *Israel Affairs* 15 (1): 52– 65.

Cohen, Martin A. 1982. "The Mission of Israel: A Theologico-Historical Analysis." In *Christian Mission—Jewish Mission*, edited by Martin A. Cohen and Helga B. Croner, 46–79. New York: Paulist Press.

Cohen, Shaye J. D. 1983. "Conversion to Judaism in Historical Perspective: From Biblical Israel to Postbiblical Judaism." *Conservative Judaism* 36:31–45.

———. 1999. *The Beginnings of Jewishness: Boundaries, Varieties, Uncertainties.* Berkeley: University of California Press.

Cohen, Yinon, and Irena Kogan. 2007. "Next Year in Jerusalem . . . or in Cologne? Labour Market Integration of Jewish Immigrants from the Former Soviet Union in Israel and Germany in the 1990s." *European Sociological Review* 23 (2): 155–168.

Collier, Stephen J. 2009. "Topologies of Power: Foucault's Analysis of Political Government beyond 'Governmentality.'" *Theory, Culture and Society* 26 (6): 78–108.

Connolly, Jennifer. 2009. "Forbidden Intimacies: Christian-Muslim Intermarriage in East Kalimantan, Indonesia." *American Ethnologist* 36 (3): 492–506.

Corinaldi, Michael. 2001. *The Question of Jewish Identity: The Law of Return in Practice.* Srigim-Li On: Nevo. In Hebrew.

Davidman, Lynn. 1991. *Tradition in a Rootless World: Women Turn to Orthodox Judaism.* Berkeley: University of California Press.

———. 2015. *Becoming Un-Orthodox: Stories of Ex-Hasidic Jews.* Oxford: Oxford University Press.

Davidman, Lynn, and Arthur L. Grail. 2007. "Characters in Search of a Script: The Exit Narratives of Formerly Ultra-Orthodox Jews." *Journal for the Scientific Study of Religion* 46 (2): 201–216.

Davis, Elizabeth A. 2010. "The Antisocial Profile: Deception and Intimacy in Greek Psychiatry." *Cultural Anthropology* 25 (1): 130–164.

DellaPergola, Sergio. 1999. *World Jewry Beyond 2000: The Demographic Prospects.* Oxford: Oxford Centre for Hebrew and Jewish Studies.

DellaPergola, Sergio, and Leah Cohen, eds. 1992. *World Jewish Population: Trends and Policies: Selected Proceedings of a Conference on World Jewish Population, Jerusalem, October 1987.* Jerusalem: Institute of Contemporary Jewry and the Hebrew University of Jerusalem.

Deutscher, Isaac. (1958) 1981. "The Non-Jewish Jew." In *The Non-Jewish Jew and Other Essays*, 25–41. London: Merlin.

Dirks, Nicholas B. 1996. "The Conversion of Caste: Location, Translation, and Appropriation." In *Conversion to Modernities: The Globalization of Christianity*, edited by Peter van der Veer, 115–136. New York: Routledge.

Don-Yihya, Eliezer. 2005. "Orthodox Jewry in Israel and in North America." *Israel Studies* 10 (1): 157–187.

Doron, Shlomi. 2013. *Shuttling Between Two Worlds: Coming to and Defecting from Orthodox Judaism in Israeli Society.* Tel Aviv: Hakibbutz Hamehuhad. In Hebrew.

Doyle, Aaron, Randy Lippert, and David Lyon, eds. 2012. *Eyes Everywhere: The Global Growth of Camera Surveillance.* Abingdon: Routledge.

Druckman, Haim. 2011. "A Call for Hosting Families and Communities." Conversion Administration, Prime Minister's Office Website. Accessed September 2015.

Dunn, Kevin C. 2010. "There Is No Such Thing as the State: Discourse, Effect and Performativity." *Forum for Development Studies* 37 (1): 79–92.

Edelman, Ofra. 2014. "The Olim Who Left Israel Do Not Miss the Definition 'Lacking Religion.'" *Haaretz*, November 7. Accessed July 6, 2015. http://www.haaretz.co.il/news/education/.premium-1.2479360. In Hebrew.

Edrei, Arye. 2010. "We Are Not Responsible for Them: More Points to the Polemics of Giyyur." *Akademot* 24:178–209. In Hebrew.

———. 2012. "The Roots of Religious-Zionist Halakhah: Rabbi Kook and the Sabbatical Year." In vol. 2 of *On the Public Opinion: Religion and Politics in Jewish Thought: The Jubilee Book in Honor of Aviezer Ravitzky*, edited by Benjamin Braun, Menachem Lorberbaum, Avinoam Rosenak, and Yedidya Z. Stern, 883–896. Jerusalem: Israel Democracy Institute. In Hebrew.

———. 2013. "Conversion Polemics in Their Ideological and Historical Context." *Year Book of Hebrew Law* 27:1–59. In Hebrew.

Egorova, Yulia. 2015. "Redefining the Converted Jewish Self: Race, Religion and Israel's Bene Menashe." *American Anthropologist* 177 (3): 493–505.

Eilam, Yigal 2000. *Judaism as a Status Quo: The 1958 Who-Is-a-Jew Controversy and Some Remarks on Secular-Religious Relations in Israel.* Tel Aviv: Am Oved. In Hebrew.

Ellenson, David, and Daniel Gordis. 2012. *Pledges of Jewish Allegiance: Conversion, Law, and Policymaking in Nineteenth- and Twentieth-Century Orthodox Responsa.* Stanford: Stanford University Press.

Elon, Emuna. 2004. "The State's Leadership Will Be More and More Religious." *Eretz Acheret* 24:70–71. In Hebrew.

El-Or, Tamar. 2006. *Reserved Seats: Gender and Ethnicity in Religious Places.* Tel Aviv: Am Oved. In Hebrew.

Englander, Yakir. 2005. "Tractate Kiddushin: Nice to Meet You: Reut Giat." *Deot* 23: 2–14. In Hebrew.

Epstein, Lawrence J. 1992. *The Theory and Practice of Welcoming Converts to Judaism: Jewish Universalism.* Lewiston, NY: Edwin Mellen.

——. 2004. *Conversion to Judaism: A Guidebook.* Lanham, MD: Rowman and Littlefield.

——. 2014. "An Organization to Welcome Converts." *The Times of Israel*, September 6. Accessed October 7, 2015. http://blogs.timesofisrael.com/an-organization-to-welcome-converts/.

Ettinger, Yair. 2008. "Who Said Strife and Contention and Didn't Get Any." *Haaretz*, May 5. In Hebrew.

——. 2013. "The Conversion Administration Does Not Meet the Goals Set by the Government." *Haaretz*, May 5. Accessed September 9, 2014. http://www.haaretz.co.il/news/mevaker/1.2014764. In Hebrew.

——. 2015a. "The Chief Rabbi Attacks the Conversion Reform: 'I Won't Allow Municipal Rabbis' Conversions Even If the High Court of Justice Obliges Me.'" *Haaretz*, February 19. Accessed July 6, 2015. http://www.haaretz.co.il/news/education/1.2569709. In Hebrew.

——. 2015b. "Religious War: Is the Orthodox World on the Verge of a Historical Split?" *Haaretz*, July 23. Accessed July 25, 2015. http://www.haaretz.co.il/magazine/orthodox/.premium-1.2690140. In Hebrew.

——. 2015c. "Bennett to *Haaretz*: Working to Bring Back the Rabbis Who Left the Rabbinate in Exchange for Applying the Conversion Reform." *Haaretz*, August 13. Accessed November 25, 2015. http://www.haaretz.co.il/news/education/.premium-1.2707421. In Hebrew.

Ettinger, Yair, and Judy Maltz. 2015. "The Agency Bypasses the Rabbinate: It Will Establish an Independent Conversion Court Abroad." *Haaretz*, June 25. Accessed July 20, 2015. http://www.haaretz.co.il/news/education/.premium-1.2668380. In Hebrew.

Ettinger, Yair, and Sharonn Pulwer. 2016. "The High Court of Justice Breaks the Rabbinate's Monopoly: Private Conversions Will Be Acknowledged in Israel." *Haaretz*, March 31. Accessed April 1, 2016. http://www.haaretz.co.il/news/education/.premium-1.2901149. In Hebrew.

Farkash, Tali. 2013. "Holy Water: In a Flowery Robe, in front of Three Rabbis." *Ynet*, April 18. Accessed May 15, 2014. http://www.ynet.co.il/articles/0,7340,L-4369265,00.html. In Hebrew.

Fassin, Didier. 2013. *Enforcing Order: An Ethnography of Urban Policing.* Cambridge: Polity.

Feldman, Gregory. 2005. "Culture, State, and Security in Europe: The Case of Citizenship and Integration Policy in Estonia." *American Ethnologist* 32:676–694.

Feldman, Ilana. 2008. *Governing Gaza: Bureaucracy, Authority, and the Work of Rule, 1917-1967.* Durham: Duke University Press.

Ferguson, James. 2005. "Seeing Like an Oil Company: Space, Security, and Global Capital in Neoliberal Africa." *American Anthropologist* 107 (3): 377–382.

Ferguson, Kathy E. 1984. *The Feminist Case Against Bureaucracy.* Philadelphia: Temple University Press.

Fernandes, Leela. 2011. "Unsettled Territories: State, Civil Society, and the Politics of Religious Conversion in India." *Politics and Religion* 4 (1): 108–135.

Fialkova, Larisa, and Maria N. Yelenevskaya. 2006. "How to Outsmart the System: Immigrants' Trickster Stories." *Studia Mythologica Slavica* 7:279–296.

Finkelstein, Ariel. 2013. "The Conversion Crisis in Israel: An Update." Jerusalem: Institute for Zionist Strategies.

Finkelstein, Menachem. 2006. *Conversion: Halakhah and Practice.* Ramat Gan: Bar Ilan University Press.

Finn, Thomas M. 1997. *From Death to Rebirth: Ritual and Conversion in Antiquity.* New York: Paulist Press.

Fischer, Shlomo. 2012. "Yes, Israel Is Becoming More Religious." *Israel Studies Review* 27 (1): 10–15.

Fisher, Netanel. 2013a. "A Jewish State? Controversial Conversions and the Dispute Over Israel's Jewish Character." *Contemporary Jewry* 33 (3): 217–240.

——. 2013b. "Introduction to the History of Conversion in the IDF." In *Book and Sword—Jubilee Book in Honor of Rabbi Mordechai Piron*, edited by Aviad Hacohen, and Zvi E. Tal, 413–453. Jerusalem: Sapir Institute. In Hebrew.

——. 2015. *The Challenge of Conversion to Judaism in Israel: Policy Analysis and Recommendations:* Policy Research 103. Jerusalem: Israel Democracy Institute. In Hebrew.

——. Forthcoming. "Opposition, Integration, and Ambiguity—The Israeli Chief Rabbinate's Policies Regarding Conversion to Judaism." In *Bastards and Believers: Converts and Conversion Between Judaism and Christianity*, edited by Paweł Maciejko, and Theodor Dunkelgrün. Philadelphia: University of Pennsylvania Press.

Fishman, Sylvia B. 2006. *Choosing Jewish: Conversations About Conversion.* New York, NY: American Jewish Committee.

Fitzpatrick, Sheila. 2005. *Tear Off the Masks! Identity and Imposture in Twentieth-Century Russia.* Princeton: Princeton University Press.

Fogiel-Bijaoui, Sylvie. 2013. "The Spousal Covenant, or the Covenant with the Status Quo." *Israel Studies Review* 28 (2): 210–227.

Forster, Brenda, and Joseph Tabachnik. 1991. *Jews by Choice: A Study of Converts to Reform and Conservative Judaism.* Hoboken: Ktav.

Fortes, Meyer, and Edward E. Evans-Pritchard. 1940. *African Political Systems.* London: Oxford University Press.

Foucault, Michel. (1975) 1977. *Discipline and Punish: The Birth of the Prison.* New York: Pantheon.

——. (1976) 1978. *The History of Sexuality: An Introduction.* New York: Pantheon.

——. (1976) 2003. *Society Must Be Defended.* New York: Picador

——. (1978) 2006. "Governmentality." In *The Anthropology of the State: A Reader*, edited by Aradhana Sharma and Akhil Gupta, 131–143. Malden, MA: Blackwell.

——. 1980. *Power/Knowledge: Selected Interviews and Other Writings, 1972-1977*. Brighton, Sussex: Harvester.

——. (2004) 2007. *Security, Territory, Population: Lectures at the Collège de France, 1977–78*. New York: Picador.

——. 2008. *The Birth of Biopolitics: Lectures at the Collège de France, 1978–1979*. Translated by Burchell Graham. Basingstoke: Palgrave Macmillan.

Friedman, Ronen. 2005. "Religious Zionism as Part of Global Religious Trends." *Mifne* 48:12–18. In Hebrew.

Friedman, Shuki. 2015. "The End of the Chief Rabbinate?" *Haaretz*, August 12. Accessed January 5, 2016. http://www.haaretz.co.il/opinions/.premium-1.2706098 . In Hebrew.

Frois, Catarina. 2013. *Peripheral Vision: Politics, Technology, and Surveillance*. New York: Berghahn.

Galili, Lili. 2003. "Nazis by the Law of Return." *Haaretz*, May 22. Accessed February 5, 2012. http://www.haaretz.co.il/misc/1.883573. In Hebrew.

Ganzel, Uriel, and Eli Rafe, eds. 2014. *Conversion in the State of Israel: The Challenge of the Moment*. Lod: Tzohar. In Hebrew.

Gavison, Ruth. 2010. *The Law of Return at Sixty Years: History, Ideology, Justification*. Translated by Gadi Weber. Position paper. Jerusalem: Metzilah Center.

Gavison, Ruth, and Yaaqov Medan. 2003. *Foundation for a New Social Covenant Between the Observant and the Free in Israel*. Jerusalem: Israel Democracy Institute and Avi Chai Foundation. In Hebrew.

Geertz, Clifford. 1973. "Thick Description: Toward an Interpetive Theory of Culture." In *The Interpretation of Cultures: Selected Essays*, 3–30. New York: Basic Books.

——. 1980. *Negara: The Theatre State in Nineteenth-Century Bali*. Princeton: Princeton University Press.

Gellner, David N. 2005. "The Emergence of Conversion in a Hindu-Buddhist Polytropy: The Kathmandu Valley, Nepal, c. 1600–1995." *Comparative Studies in Society and History* 47: 755–780.

Geschiere, Peter. 2007. "Epilogue: 'Seeing Like a State' in Africa—High Modernism, Legibility and Community." *African Studies* 66 (1): 129–134.

Gilad, Yehuda. 2006. "Is There Still a Place for a Sectoral Religious-Zionist Party." *Deot* 24:4–5. In Hebrew.

Gillespie, V. Bailey. 1979. *Religious Conversion and Personal Identity: How and Why People Change*. Birmingham, AL: Religious Education Press.

Ginsberg, Elaine K. 1996. "Introduction: The Politics of Passing." In *Passing and the Fictions of Identity*, edited by Elaine K. Ginsberg, 1–18. Durham: Duke University Press.

Glenn, Sussan, and Naomi Sokoloff. 2010. "Introduction: Who and What Is Jewish? Controversies and Comparative Perspectives on the Boundaries of Jewish Identity." In *Boundaries of Jewish Identity*, edited by Susan Glenn and Naomi B. Sokoloff, 3–11. Seattle: University of Washington Press.

Goffman, Erving. 1959. *The Presentation of Self in Everyday Life*. Oxford: Doubleday.

——. (1963) 1986. *Stigma: Notes on the Management of Spoiled Identity*. New York: Simon and Schuster.

——. 1971. *Relations in Public: Microstudies of the Social Order*. New York: Basic Books.

——. 1974. *Frame Analysis: An Essay on the Organization of Experience*. New York: Harper and Row.

Good, Anthony. 2011. "Witness Statements and Credibility Assessments in the British Asylum Courts." In *Cultural Expertise and Litigation: Patterns, Conflicts, Narratives,* edited by Livia Holden, 94–122. London: Routledge.

Goodman, Yehuda. 2004. "Repentance and New Religious Identities in Israel in the Beginning of the 21st Century." In *Unbelievable: Another View on Religiosity and Secularism,* edited by Aviad Kleinman, 98–177. Tel Aviv: Tel Aviv University Press. In Hebrew.

——. 2008a. "Citizenship, Modernity and Faith in the Nation State: Racialization and De-racialization in the Conversion of Russian Immigrants and Ethiopian Immigrants in Israel." In *Racism in Israel*, edited by Yehouda Shenhav and Yossi Yonah, 381–415. Tel Aviv: Van Leer Jerusalem Institute and Hakibutz Hameuchad Publishing House. In Hebrew.

——. 2008b. "Conversion of Immigrants: Naturalization, Governmentality and Religionization in 21st Century Israel." In *Citizenship Gaps: Migration, Fertility and Identity in Israel,* edited by Yossi Yonah and Adriana Kemp, 207–238. Tel Aviv: Van Leer Jerusalem Institute and Hakibutz Hameuchad. In Hebrew.

Gooren, Henri. 2014. "Anthropology of Religious Conversion." In *The Oxford Handbook of Religious Conversion*, edited by Lewis R. Rambo and Charles E. Farhadian, 84–116. Oxford: Oxford University Press.

Gordon, Colin. 1991. "Governmental Rationality: An Introduction." In *The Foucault Effect: Studies in Governmentality*, edited by Graham Burchell, Colin Gordon, Peter Miller, and Michel Foucault, 1–52. Chicago: University of Chicago Press.

Govier, Trudy. 1997. *Social Trust and Human Communities*. Montreal, QC: McGill-Queen's University Press.

Gupta, Akhil. 2012. *Red Tape: Bureaucracy, Structural Violence, and Poverty in India*. Durham: Duke University Press.

Gupta, Akhil, and James Ferguson, eds. 1997. *Anthropological Locations: Boundaries and Grounds of a Field Science*. Berkeley: University of California Press.

Gvaryahu, Amit. 2005. "It's Time to Tell the Religious Institution: 'Let's Part Company. If You Go to the Left, I'll Go to the Right; If You Go to the Right, I'll Go to the Left." *Deot* 20:3–4. In Hebrew.

Haberfeld, Yitchak, Yinon Cohen, Frank Kalter, and Irena Kogan. 2011. "Differences in Earnings Assimilation of Immigrants from the Former Soviet Union to Germany and Israel During 1994–2005: The Interplay Between Context of Reception, Observed, and Un-observed Immigrants' Attributes." *International Journal of Comparative Sociology* 52 (1–2): 6–24.

Hacker, Daphna. 2009. "Inter-religious Marriages in Israel: Gendered Implications for Conversion, Children, and Citizenship." *Israel Studies* 14 (2): 178–197.

Halfin, Igal. 1997. "Red Eschatology: Communist Students' Autobiographies." *Zmanim: A Historical Quarterly* 59:66–86. In Hebrew.

——. 2006. *The Stalinist Purges: From Members' Trials to Showcase Trials*. Tel Aviv: Resling. In Hebrew.

——. 2011a. *Red Autobiographies: Initiating the Bolshevik Self*. Seattle: University of Washington Press.

——. 2011b. *Intimate Enemies: Demonizing the Bolshevik Opposition, 1918–1928*. Pittsburgh: University of Pittsburgh Press.

Hameiri, Illan. 1997. "The Israeli Situation: A Struggle for Jewish Identity." In *Not by Birth Alone: Conversion to Judaism*, edited by Walter Homolka, Walter Jacob, and Esther Seidel, 83–88. Herndon, VA: Cassell.

Handelman, Don. 2004. *Nationalism and the Israeli State: Bureaucratic Logic in Public Events*. Oxford: Berg.

Hanin, Zeev. 2014. *Marrying Into the Jewish Faith: Russian-Speaking Olim's Identity in the Post-communist Era*. Jerusalem: Beit Morasha of Jerusalem. In Hebrew.

Hansen, Thomas B. 2001. "Governance and State Mythologies in Mumbai." In *States of Imagination: Ethnographic Explorations of the Postcolonial State*, edited by Thomas B. Hansen and Finn Stepputat, 221–256. Durham: Duke University.

Hansen, Thomas B., and Finn Stepputat. 2001. "Introduction: State of Imagination." In *States of Imagination: Ethnographic Explorations of the Postcolonial State*, edited by Thomas B. Hansen, and Finn Stepputat, 1–40. Durham: Duke University Press.

Harding, Susan F. 2000. *The Book of Jerry Falwell: Fundamentalist Language and Politics*. Princeton: Princeton University Press.

Hart, Mitchell B. 2000. *Social Science and the Politics of Modern Jewish Identity*. Stanford: Stanford University Press.

Haskin, Arie. 2012. "Predicting Factors of Progress in Conversion Processes of Israeli Soldiers from the Former FSU: Identities and Motives." PhD dissertation, Hebrew University of Jerusalem. In Hebrew.

Hay, Shahar. 2015. "Book on Israeli-Palestinian Love Excluded from Schools." *Ynetnews*, December 31. Accessed January 4, 2016. http://www.ynetnews.com/articles/0,7340,L-4746725,00.html. In Hebrew.

Hefner, Robert W. 1993. "World Building and the Rationality of Conversion." In *Conversion to Christianity: Historical and Anthropological Perspectives on a Great Transformation*, edited by Robert W. Hefner, 3–44. Berkeley: University of California Press.

Heilman, Uriel. 2015. "10 Revealing Facts about Orthodox Jewish Converts." *JTA*, July 6. Accessed December 15, 2015. http://www.jta.org/2015/07/06/news-opinion/10-interesting-things-about-the-rcas-report-on-conversion-reform.

Heirich, Max. 1977. "Change of Heart: A Test of Some Widely Held Theories About Religious Conversion." *American Journal of Sociology* 83:653–680.

Henslin, James M. 1968 "Trust and the Cab Driver." In *Sociology and Everyday Life*, edited by Marcello Truzzi, 138–157. Englewood Cliffs, NJ: Prentice Hall.

Hermann, Tamar. 2012. "More Jewish than Israeli (and Democratic)?" *Israel Studies Review* 27 (1): 4–9.

Hermann, Tamar, Gilad Be'ery, Ella Heller, Chanan Cohen, Yuval Lebel, Hanan Mozes, and Kalman Neuman. 2014. *The National-Religious Sector in Israel, 2014*. Jerusalem: Israel Democracy Institute. In Hebrew.

Herzfeld, Michael. 1993. *The Social Production of Indifference: Exploring the Symbolic Roots of Western Bureaucracy*. Chicago: University of Chicago Press.

——. 2005. "Political Optics and the Occlusion of Intimate Knowledge." *American Anthropologist* 107:369–376.

Hiddush. 2015. "Calling the Prime Minister to Open the Gates of Judaism" Accessed December 5. http://hiddush.org.il/ActionLetter.aspx?id=1542. In Hebrew.

Hindmarsh, Bruce. 2014. "Religious Conversion as Narrative and Autobiography." In *The Oxford Handbook of Religious Conversion*, edited by Lewis R. Rambo and Charles E. Farhadian, 343–368. Oxford: Oxford University Press.

Hoberman, Haggai. 2011. "Research: The Power of the National Ultra-Orthodox Is Rising in Religious Zionism." Channel 7. May 19. Accessed July 30, 2015. http://www.inn.co.il/News/News.aspx/220006. In Hebrew.

Homolka, Walter, Walter Jacob, and Esther Seidel, eds. 1997. *Not by Birth Alone: Conversion to Judaism*. Herndon, VA: Cassell.

Huberman, Steven. 1979. *New Jews: The Dynamics of Religious Conversion*. New York: Union of American Hebrew Congregations.

Hull, Matthew S. 2012. *Government of Paper: The Materiality of Bureaucracy in Urban Pakistan*. Berkeley: University of California Press.

Ilan, Shahar. 2005. "Everything Is on the Table, Including The Law of Return." *Haaretz*, May 15. In Hebrew.

——. 2007. "In the Knesset There Is an Agreement: The Operation of Converting FSU Immigrants Has Failed." *Haaretz*, October 29. In Hebrew.

Itim. 2015. "Results of an Omnibus Questionnaire Conducted Among a Representative Sample of Adult Jews in Israel on May 15, 2015." IPSOS. Accessed June 7, 2015. http://infomail.inforumobile.com//uploads/users/536/14327282845565b2dc2e6ff.pdf?utm_source=InforuMail&utm_medium=email&utm_campaign=%D7%9E%D7%90%D7%99+2015. In Hebrew.

Jackson, John L. 2005. *Real Black: Adventures in Racial Sincerity*. Chicago: University of Chicago Press.

James, William (1902) 1985. *The Varieties of Religious Experience: A Study in Human Nature*. Cambridge: Harvard University Press.

Jennings, Theodore W. 1982. "On Ritual Knowledge." *Journal of Religion* 62:111–127.

Jones, Robert K. 1978. "Paradigm Shifts and Identity Theory: Alternation as a Form of Identity Management." In *Identity and Religion: International Cross-Cultural Approaches*, edited by Hans Mol, 59–82. London: Sage.

Joskowicz, Ari, and Ethan B. Katz, eds. 2015. *Secularism in Question: Jews and Judaism in Modern Times*. Philadelphia: University of Pennsylvania Press.

Jusionyte, Ieva. 2015. "States of Camouflage." *Cultural Anthropology* 30 (1): 113–138.

Kahan, Yuval. 2005. "Calling for an Alternative to Arrangement Yeshivas [*Yeshivot Ha'hesder*]." *Deot* 23:8–11. In Hebrew.

Kahat, Hannah. 2004. "Between an Autonomous Mind and a Subordinate Mind." *Eretz Acheret* 24:34–39. In Hebrew.

Kahn, Susan M. 2000. *Reproducing Jews: A Cultural Account of Assisted Conception in Israel*. Durham: Duke University Press.

Kaplan, Danny. 2009. "The Songs of the Siren: Engineering National Time on Israeli Radio." *Cultural Anthropology* 24 (2): 313–345.

Kaplan, Elad, and Naama Seri-Levi. 2013. "The State of Religious Services: Itim Follow-Up." Itim. Accessed June 7, 2014. http://www.itim.org.il/wp-content/uploads/20

13/06/%D7%9E%D7%95%D7%A8%D7%94-%D7%A0%D7%91%D7%95%D7%9B%D7%99%D7%9D-%D7%9C%D7%92%D7%99%D7%95%D7%A8-%D7%91%D7%99%D7%A9%D7%A8%D7%90%D7%9C.pdf. In Hebrew.

Keane, Webb. 2002. "Sincerity, 'Modernity,' and the Protestants." *Cultural Anthropology* 17:65–92.

——. 2007. *Christian Moderns: Freedom and Fetish in the Mission Encounter.* Berkeley: University of California Press.

Kharkhordin, Oleg. 1999. *The Collective and the Individual in Russia: A Study of Practices.* Berkeley: University of California Press.

Kidd, Thomas. 2004. "Passing as a Pastor: Clerical Imposture in the Colonial Atlantic World." *Religion and American Culture* 14:149–174.

Kimmerling, Baruch. 2004. *Immigrants, Settlers, Natives: Israel Between a Plurality of Cultures and Cultural Wars.* Tel Aviv: Am Oved. In Hebrew.

King, Leslie. 2002. "Demographic Trends, Pronatalism, and Nationalist Ideologies in the Late Twentieth Century." *Ethnic and Racial Studies* 25:367–389.

Klein, Menachem. 2004. "Religion and Academia in Israel." In *Religious Zionism: An Era of Change: A Research Collection in Memory of Zevulun Hammer,* edited by Asher Cohen, and Israel Harel, 201–253. Jerusalem: Bialik Institute. In Hebrew.

Knesset. 2005a. Committee for Immigration, Absorption and Diaspora Affairs. *Conversion of Immigrant Soldiers in the IDF.* 16th Knesset, January 11, protocol 193. In Hebrew.

——. 2005b. Committee for Immigration, Absorption and Diaspora Affairs. *Ministry of Interior's Preparation for Acknowledging Reform and Conservative Conversion.* 16th Knesset, May 2, protocol 229. In Hebrew.

——. 2007. Special Committee for Public Petition. *The Public Petitions Relating to Jewish Conversion in Israel.* 17th Knesset, May 16, protocol 43. In Hebrew.

——. 2008. Committee for Immigration, Absorption and Diaspora Affairs. *Reform in the Conversion Administration.* 17th Knesset, March 3, protocol 178. In Hebrew.

——. 2010. Committee for Immigration, Absorption and Diaspora Affairs. *On the Occasion of the Festival of the Pentecost—Conversion in Israel, 2010.* 18th Knesset, May 17, protocol 80. In Hebrew.

——. 2013. Committee on the Status of Women and Gender Equality. *Female Converts and Male Converts: Difficulties in Conversion Procedures in Israel.* 18th Knesset, May 13, protocol 9. In Hebrew.

Knesset Research and Information Center. 2008. *Difficulties in the Conversion Process in Israel and Proposed Ways to Cope with Them,* by Naomi Mi-Ami. January 22. In Hebrew.

Kobelinsky, Carolina. 2015. "In Search of Truth: How Asylum Applications Are Adjudicated." In *At the Heart of the Stat: The Moral World of Institutions,* by Didier Fassin, Yasmin Bouagga, Isabelle Coutant, Jean-Sébastien Eideliman, Fabrice Fernandez, Nicolas Fischer, Carolina Kobelinsky, Chowra Makaremi, Sarah Mazouz, and Sébastien Roux, 67–89. London: Pluto.

Koser Akcapar, Sebnem. 2006. " Conversion as a Migration Strategy in a Transit Country: Iranian Shiites Becoming Christians in Turkey." *International Migration Review* 40 (4): 817–853.

Kosmin, Barry A., Sidney Goldstein, Joseph Waksberg, Nava Lerer, Ariella Keysar, and Jeffrey Scheckner. 1991. *Highlights of the CJF 1990 National Jewish Population Survey.* New York: Council of Jewish Federations.

Kravel-Tovi, Michal. 2012a. "'National Mission': Biopolitics, Non-Jewish Immigration and Jewish Conversion Policy in Contemporary Israel." *Ethnic and Racial Studies* 35 (4): 737–756.

——. 2012b. "Rite of Passing: Bureaucratic Encounters, Dramaturgy, and Jewish Conversion in Israel." *American Ethnologist* 39 (2): 371–388.

——. 2014. "Bureaucratic Gifts: Religious Conversion, Change, and Exchange in Israel." *American Ethnologist* 41 (4): 714–727.

——. 2015. " Corrective Conversion: Unsettling Citizens and the Politics of Inclusion in Israel." *Journal of the Royal Anthropological Institute* 21 (1): 127–146.

——. 2016. "Wet Numbers: The Language of Continuity Crisis and the Work of Care Among the Organized American Jewish Community." In *Taking Stock: Cultures of Enumeration in Contemporary Jewish Life*, edited by Michal Kravel-Tovi and Deborah D. Moore. Indiana University Press.

Kravel-Tovi, Michal, and Deborah D. Moore, eds. 2016. *Taking Stock: Cultures of Enumeration in Contemporary Jewish Life*. Indiana University Press.

Kropkin, Tali. 2015. "I Wish I Had Been Zaguri, Russian Immigrants Shatter Painful Stereotypes." *Haaretz*, April 3. Accessed May 20, 2015. http://www.haaretz.co.il/news/education/.premium-1.2606833. In Hebrew.

Landau, David. 1996. *The "Who Is a Jew" Affair: An Example for American Jews on Israeli Policy*. Ramat Gan: American Jewish Committee and Bar Ilan University. In Hebrew.

Lau, Benjamin. 2008. "Membership: An Arcane Debate Turned Into a Searing Headline," a symposium commentary. *Havruta* 1:24–25. In Hebrew.

Lavie, Aliza. Forthcoming. "Ruth Would Not Have Been Accepted Today." In *Israeli Conversion*, edited by Yedidia Z. Stern and Netanel Fisher. Jerusalem: Israel Democracy Institute. In Hebrew.

Leibler, Anat, and Daniel Breslau. 2005. "The Uncounted: Citizenship and Exclusion in the Israeli Census of 1948." *Ethnic and Racial Studies* 28:880–902.

Lemke, Thomas. 2011. *Biopolitics: An Advanced Introduction*. New York: New York University Press.

Leon, Nissim. 2010a. *Soft Ultra-Orthodoxy: Religious Renewal in Oriental Jewry in Israel*. Jerusalem: Yad Izhak Ben-Zvi. In Hebrew.

——. 2010b. "The Transformation of Israel's Religious-Zionist Middle Class." *Journal of Israeli History* 29 (1) : 61–78.

——. 2014a. "Ultra-Orthodoxy, Ethnicity, and Nationalism in Contemporary Israel: Legitimizing the Participation of Shas in Israeli Governments." In *The Nation State and Religion: The Resurgence of Faith*, edited by Anita Shapira, Yedidia Z. Stern, and Alexander Yakobson, 151–162. Vol. 2 of *Contemporary Challenges to the Nation State: Global and Israeli Perspectives*. London: Sussex Academic.

——. 2014b. "Ethno-religious Fundamentalism and Theo-ethnocratic Politics in Israel." *Studies in Ethnicity and Nationalism* 14(1): 20–35.

Lerner, Julia. 2011. "'Russians' in Israel as a Post-Soviet Subject: Implementing the Civilizational Repertoire." *Israel Affairs* 17 (1): 21–37.

Lerner, Yulia, and Feldhai Rivka. 2012. *Russians in Israel: The Pragmatics of Culture in Migration*. Jerusalem: Van Leer Jerusalem Institute and Hakibutz Hameuchad. In Hebrew.

Leshem, Elazar. 2008. "Being an Israeli: Immigrants from the Former Soviet Union in Israel, Fifteen Years Later." *Journal of Israeli History* 27 (1): 29–49.

Leshem, Elazar, and Moshe Lissak. 2001. "Social and Cultural Formation of the Russian Community in Israel." In *From Russia to Israel: Identity and Culture in Transition*, 27–76. Tel Aviv: Hakibutz Hameuchad. In Hebrew.

Levine, Saul V. 1984. *Radical Departures: Desperate Detours to Growing Up*. San Diego: Harcourt Brace Jovanovich.

Levy, Gal. 2011. "Secularism, Religion and the Status Quo." In *Religion and the State: A Comparative Sociology*, edited by Jack Barbalet, Adam Possamai, and Bryan S. Turner, 93–119. London: Anthem.

Li, Tania M. 2005. "Beyond 'the State' and Failed Schemes." *American Anthropologist* 107 (3): 383–394.

Lichtenstein, Aharon, Emanuel Feldman, and Joel B. Wolowelsky, eds. 1990. *The Conversion Crisis: Essays from the Pages of Tradition*. Hoboken: Ktav.

Lofland, John. 1977. *Doomsday Cult: A Study of Conversion, Proselytization, and Maintenance of Faith*. New York: Irvington.

Lofland, John, and Rodney Stark. 1965. "Becoming a World-Saver: A Theory of Conversion to a Deviant Perspective." *American Sociological Review* 30 (6): 862–875

Lohmann, Roger I. 2003. "Turning the Belly: Insights on Religious Conversion from New Guinea Gut Feelings." In *The Anthropology of Religious Conversion*, edited by Andrew Buckser and Stephen D. Glazier, 109–122. Lanham, MD: Rowman and Littlefield.

London, Yaron. 2003. "Identity and Demography." In *Assimilation and Continuity in the Jewish State—Three Approaches*, by Yaron London, Asher Cohen, and Israel Rosen, 7–18. Jerusalem: Institute of the World Jewish Congress.

Luhrmann, Tanya M. 2004. "Metakinesis: How God Becomes Intimate in Contemporary US Christianity." *American Anthropologist* 106 (3): 518–528.

———. 2012. *When God Talks Back: Understanding the American Evangelical Relationship with God*. New York: Knopf.

Luria, Keith P. 1996. "The Politics of Protestant Conversion to Catholicism in Seventeenth-Century France." In *Conversion to Modernities: The Globalization of Christianity*, edited by Peter van der Veer, 23–46. New York: Routledge.

Lustick, Ian S. 1999. "Israel as a Non-Arab State: The Political Implication of Mass Immigration of Non-Jews." *Middle East Journal* 53:417–433.

———. 2011. "Israel's Migration Balance: Demography, Politics, and Ideology." *Israel Studies Review* 26 (1): 33–65.

Lustig, Dafna. 2013. "What Is Preferable—Conversion or Housing?" *Haaretz*, July 17. Accessed June 9, 2015. http://www.haaretz.co.il/magazine/the-edge/.premium-1.2074624. In Hebrew.

MacCannell, Dean. 1973. "Staged Authenticity: Arrangements of Social Space in Tourist Settings." *American Journal of Sociology* 79:589–603.

Magill, R. Jay, Jr. 2012. *Sincerity: How a Moral Ideal Born Five Hundred Years Ago Inspired Religious Wars, Modern Art, Hipster Chic, and the Curious Notion That We All Have Something to Say (No Matter How Dull)*. New York: Norton.

Maltz, Judy. 2015. "Bringing the Bnei Menashe from India Raises Questions About Their Jewish Origins and Netanyahu's Involvement in This Operation." *Haaretz*, February 21. Accessed August 24, 2015. http://www.haaretz.co.il/magazine/.premium-1.2569164. In Hebrew.

Maltz, Robin. 1998. "Real Butch: The Performance/Performativity of Male Impersonation, Drag Kings, Passing as Male, and Stone Butch Realness." *Journal of Gender Studies* 7:273–286.

Manning, Philip. 1992. *Erving Goffman and Modern Sociology.* Stanford: Stanford University Press.

Mariner, Rodney. 1999. "Conversion to Judaism: A Tale of the Good, the Bad and the Ungrateful." In *Religious Conversion: Contemporary Practices and Controversies*, edited by Christopher Lamb and M. Darrol Bryant, 89–101. London: Cassell.

Marzouki, Nadia. 2013. "Introduction." In *Religious Conversions in the Mediterranean World*, edited by Nadia Marzouki and Olivier Roy, 1–12. Basingstoke: Palgrave Macmillan.

Mbembe, Achille. (1992) 2006. "The Banality of Power and the Aesthetics of Vulgarity in the Postcolony." In *The Anthropology of the State: A Reader*, edited by Aradhana Sharma and Akhil Gupta, 381–400. Malden, MA: Blackwell.

McKnight, Scot. 2002. *Turning to Jesus: The Sociology of Conversion in the Gospels.* Louisville, KY: Westminster John Knox.

Menon, Kalyani D. 2003. "Converted Innocents and Their Trickster Heroes: The Politics of Proselytizing in India." In *The Anthropology of Religious Conversion*, edited by Andrew Buckser and Stephen D. Glazier, 43–54. Lanham, MD: Rowman and Littlefield.

Mitchell, Timothy. 1991. "The Limits of the State: Beyond Statist Approaches and Their Critics." *American Political Science Review* 85 (1): 77–96.

——. (1999) 2006. "Society, Economy, and the State Effect." In *The Anthropology of the State: A Reader*, edited by Aradhana Sharma and Akhil Gupta, 169–186. Malden, MA: Blackwell.

Mizrachi, Aviv. 2013. "Meme, Aren't You Jewish?" *Ynet*, January 13. Accessed April 17, 2015. http://www.ynet.co.il/articles/0,7340,L-4331815,00.html. In Hebrew.

Mozes, Hanan. 2009. "Religious Zionism and the State—State of Affairs." *Deot* 41. Accessed June 20, 2012. http://toravoda.org.il/%D7%9B%D7%AA%D7%91%D7%94/%D7%94%D7%A6%D7%99%D7%95%D7%A0%D7%95%D7%AA-%D7%94%D7%93%D7%AA%D7%99%D7%AA-%D7%95%D7%94%D7%9E%D7%93%D7%99%D7%A0%D7%94-%D7%AA%D7%9E%D7%95%D7%A0%D7%AA-%D7%9E%D7%A6%D7%91-%D7%97%D7%A0%D7%9F-%D7%9E/. In Hebrew.

Nachshoni, Kobi. 2008. "Rabbis' Pettition for Rabbi Druckman." *Ynet*, May 15. Accessed July 28, 2015. http://www.ynet.co.il/articles/0,7340,L-3543678,00.html. In Hebrew.

——. 2010. "A Conversion Judge Snooped in the Cellphone and Decided: The Conversion Isn't Approved!" *Ynet*, May 30. Accessed July 8, 2013. http://www.ynet.co.il/articles/0,7340,L-3896082,00.html. In Hebrew.

——. 2015a. "The Conversion Rebellion: Rabbis from Religious Zionism Established an Alternative Conversion System." *Ynet*, August 10. Accessed September 14, 2015. http://www.ynet.co.il/articles/0,7340,L-4689429,00.html. In Hebrew.

——. 2015b. "The Ultra-Orthodox Attack the Conversion Rebellion: 'Anarchist Rabbis.'" *Ynet*, August 11. Accessed September 14, 2015. http://www.ynet.co.il/articles/0,7340,L-4689724,00.html. In Hebrew.

Nader, Laura. 1969. "Up the Anthropologist: Perspectives Gained from Studying Up." In *Reinventing Anthropology*, edited by D. Hymes. New York: Pantheon.

Navaro-Yashin, Yael. 2002. *Faces of the State: Secularism and Public Life in Turkey.* Princeton: Princeton University Press.

Neiterman, Elena, and Tamar Rapoport. 2009. "Converting to Belong: Immigration, Education and Nationalisation among Young 'Russian' Immigrant Women." *Gender and Education* 21:1–16.

Neuberger, Benyamin. 1998. *Government and Politics in the State of Israel.* Tel Aviv: Open University. In Hebrew.

Neuman, Kelman. 2015. "The State of Israel's Judaism in the Eyes of Secular Intellectuals." In *When Judaism Meets State,* by Yedidya Z. Stern, Benjamin Braun, Kelman Neuman, Gideon Katz, and Nir Kedar, 271–419. Tel Aviv: Yedioth Ahronot Books and the Israel Democracy Institute. In Hebrew.

Norton, Mary Beth. 1997. "Communal Definitions of Gendered Identity in Seventeenth-Century English America." In *Through a Glass Darkly: Reflections on Personal Identity in Early America,* edited by Ronald Hoffman, Mechal Sobel, and Fredrika J. Teute, 40–66. Chapel Hill: University of North Carolina Press.

NRG Judaism. 2004. "Easy Trainings: 'Tzohar's' 'Bridal Training'—Another Possibility for the Future Bride's Encounter with Judaism." *NRG,* December 14. Accessed April 19, 2010. http://www.nrg.co.il/online/11/ART/837/244.html. In Hebrew.

O'Neill, Kevin L. 2010. *City of God: Christian Citizenship in Postwar Guatemala.* Berkeley: University of California Press.

Orenstein, Daniel E. 2004. "Population Growth and Environmental Impact: Ideology and Academic Discourse in Israel." *Population and Environment* 26:41–60.

Özgül, Ceren. 2014. "Legally Armenian: Tolerance, Conversion, and Name Change in Turkish Courts." *Comparative Studies in Society and History* 56 (3): 622–649.

Özyürek, Esra. 2009a. "Convert Alert: German Muslims and Turkish Christians as Threats to Security in the New Europe." *Comparative Studies in Society and History* 51 (1): 91–116.

——. 2009b. "Christian and Turkish: Secularist Fears of a Converted Nation: Comparative Studies of South Asia." *Africa and the Middle East* 29 (3): 398–412.

——. 2014. *Being German, Becoming Muslim: Race, Religion, and Conversion in the New Europe.* Princeton: Princeton University Press.

Parfitt, Tudor, and Emanuela Trevisan Semi. 2002. *Judaizing Movements: Studies in the Margins of Judaism.* London: Routledge.

Peled, Yoav, and Gershon Shafir. 2005. *Being Israeli: The Dynamics of Multiple Citizenship.* Tel Aviv: Tel Aviv University Press. In Hebrew.

Pfefer, Anshel. 2007. "The Origins and Future Course of the National-Haredi Public." Publication no. 4/26. Jerusalem: Floersheimer Insitute for Policy Studies. In Hebrew.

Polish, Daniel. 1982. "Contemporary Jewish Attitudes to Mission and Conversion." In *Christian Mission—Jewish Mission,* edited by Martin A. Cohen and Helga B. Croner, 147–169. New York: Paulist Press.

Porton, Gary G. 1994. *The Stranger Within Your Gates: Converts and Conversion in Rabbinic Literature.* Chicago: University of Chicago Press.

Portugese, Jacqueline. 1998. *Fertility Policy in Israel: The Politics of Religion, Gender, and Nation.* Westport, CT: Praeger.

Prashizky, Anna, and Larissa Remennick. 2012. "'Strangers in the New Homeland?' Gendered Citizenship Among Non-Jewish Immigrant Women in Israel." In *Women's Studies International Forum* 35 (3): 173–183.

——. 2014. "Gender and Cultural Citizenship Among Non-Jewish Immigrants from the Former Soviet Union in Israel." *Citizenship Studies* 18 (3–4): 365–383.

Puddephatt, Antony, Benjamin Kelly, and Michael Adorjan. 2006. "Unveiling the Cloak of Competence: Cultivating Authenticity in Graduate Sociology." *American Sociologist* 37:84–98.

Raijman, Rebeca, and Janina Pinsky. 2011. "'Non-Jewish and Christian': Perceived Discrimination and Social Distance Among FSU Migrants in Israel." *Israel Affairs* 17 (1): 125–141.

Rambo, Lewis R. 1993. *Understanding Religious Conversion*. New Haven: Yale University Press.

——. 2003. "Anthropology and the Study of Conversion." In *The Anthropology of Religious Conversion*, edited by Andrew Buckser and Stephen D. Glazier, 211–222. Lanham, MD: Rowman and Littlefield.

Ratzabi, Shalom. 2001 "The Historic Jewish Identity and the Sojournerism Institution." In *Jewish Identities: Fifty Intellectuals Answer Ben-Gurion*, edited by Eliezer Ben-Rafael, 117–138. Sde Boker: Ben Gurion Heritage Institute. In Hebrew.

Ravitzky, Aviezer. 1993. "The Pressing End: The Messianic Religious Zionism." In *Messianism, Zionism, and Jewish Religious Radicalism*, 111–200. Tel Aviv: Am Oved. In Hebrew.

——. 1996. *Messianism, Zionism, and Jewish Religious Radicalism*. Chicago: Chicago University Press.

Reeves, Madeleine. 2013. "Clean Fake: Authenticating Documents and Persons in Migrant Moscow." *American Ethnologist* 40 (3): 508–524.

——. 2014. *Border Work: Spatial Lives of the State in Rural Central Asia*. Ithaca: Cornell University Press.

Remennick, Larissa, and Anna Prashizky. 2010. "Evolving Attitudes and Practices in the Religious Field Among Former Soviet Immigrants in Israel." *Sociological Papers* 15:1–54.

Renfrow, Daniel. 2004. "A Cartography of Passing in Everyday Life." *Symbolic Interaction* 27 (4): 485–506.

Ritterband, Paul. 1981. *Modern Jewish Fertility*. Leiden: Brill.

Robbins, Joel. 2004. *Becoming Sinners: Christianity and Moral Torment in a Papua New Guinea Society*. Berkeley: University of California Press.

Rosen, Israel. 2003. "An Orthodox Perspective on Conversion in Israel." In *Assimilation and Continuity in the Jewish State—Three Approaches*, by Yaron London, Asher Cohen, and Israel Rosen, 33–51. Jerusalem: Institute of the World Jewish Congress.

——. 2006. "We Will Learn How to Live with a Non-Jewish Significant Minority." *Nekudah* 290:34–37. In Hebrew.

——. 2010. "The Middle Road in Contemporary Conversion." *Akademot* 24:210–219. In Hebrew.

Rosenbloom, Joseph R. 1978. *Conversion to Judaism: From the Biblical Period to the Present*. Cincinnati: Hebrew Union College Press.

Rosenblum, Jonathan. 2006. "A New Conversion Scandal." *Yated Ne'eman*, May 17. Accessed July 5, 2010. http://www.jewishmediaresources.com/956/a-new-conversion-scandal.

Rosnak, Avinoam. 2006. "Before the Abyss: Introspection." *Deot* 25:9. In Hebrew.

Rothenberg, Naftali. 2008. "The Polemics of Giyyur and the Paradox of Religious Zionism." *Ynet*, July 15. Accessed May 15, 2013. http://www.ynet.co.il/articles/0,7340,L-3568328,00.html. In Hebrew.

Roy, Olivier. 2013. "Conclusion: What Matters with Conversions?" In *Religious Conversions in the Mediterranean World*, edited by Nadia Marzouki and Olivier Roy, 175–187. Basingstoke: Palgrave Macmillan.

Rueda, Robert, and Hugh Mehan. 1986. "Metacognition and Passing: Strategic Interactions in the Lives of Students with Learning Disabilities." *Anthropology and Education Quarterly* 17:145–165.

Saba, Mahmood. 2001. " Rehearsed Spontaneity and the Conventionality of Ritual: Disciplines of Şalat." *American Ethnologist* 28 (4): 827–853.

Sagi, Avi, and Zvi Zohar. 2007. *Transforming Identity: The Ritual Transition from Gentile to Jew—Structure and Meaning*. London: Continuum.

Salmela, Mikko. 2005. "What Is Emotional Authenticity?" *Journal for the Theory of Social Behaviour* 35:209–230.

Samet, Moshe. 1992. "Sojournerism and Zionism." In *The Jubilee Book for Rabbi Mordechai Breuer*, edited by Moshe Bar-Asher, 487–507. Jerusalem: Academon. In Hebrew.

———. 1993. "Conversion to Judaism in the First Centuries AD." In *Jews and Judaism During the Second Temple, the Mishnah and Talmud Periods*, edited by Aaron Oppenheimer, Isaiah Gafni, and Menachem Stern, 316–343. Jerusalem: Yad Izhak Ben-Zvi Institue. In Hebrew.

Sanchez, Maria C., and Linda Shlossberg, eds. 2001. *Passing: Identity and Interpretation in Sexuality, Race, and Religion*. New York: New York University Press.

Schayegh, Cyrus. 2010. "'Seeing Like a State': An Essay on the Historiography of Modern Iran." *International Journal of Middle East Studies* 42 (1): 37–61.

Schept, Judah. 2014. "(Un)Seeing Like a Prison: Counter-Visual Ethnography of the Carceral State." *Theoretical Criminology* 18 (2): 198–223.

Schiff, Gary S. 1981. "The Politics of Fertility Policy in Israel." In *Modern Jewish Fertility*, edited by Paul Ritterband, 255–278. Leiden: E. J. Brill.

Schmitt, Carl. (1921) 2014. *Dictatorship: From the Origin of the Modern Concept of Sovereignty to Proletarian Class Struggle*. Cambridge: Polity.

———. (1922) 2005. *Political Theology: Four Chapters on the Concept of Sovereignty*. Chicago: University of Chicago Press.

Schwartz, Dov. 2004. "From the Early Flowering to Fulfillment." In *Religious Zionism: An Era of Change: A Research Collection in Memory of Zevulun Hammer*, edited by Asher Cohen and Israel Harel, 24–134. Jerusalem: Bialik Institute. In Hebrew.

———. 2009. *Religious Zionism: History and Ideology*. Boston: Academic Studies Press.

Scott, James C. 1998. *Seeing Like a State: How Certain Schemes to Improve the Human Condition Have Failed*. New Haven: Yale University Press.

Seeman, Don. 2003. "Agency, Bureaucracy, and Religious Conversion: Ethiopian 'Felashmura' Immigrants to Israel." In *The Anthropology of Religious Conversion*, edited by Andrew Buckser and Stephen D. Glazier, 29–42. Lanham, MD: Rowman and Littlefield.

——. 2010. *One People, One Blood: Ethiopian-Israelis and the Return to Judaism*. New Brunswick, NJ: Rutgers University Press.

——. 2013. "Pentecostal Judaism and Ethiopian Israelis." In *Religious Conversions in the Mediterranean World*, edited by Nadia Marzouki and Olivier Roy, 60–76. Basingstoke: Palgrave Macmillan.

——. 2015a. "Jewish Ethiopian Israelis." *The Wiley Blackwell Encyclopedia of Race, Ethnicity, and Nationalism*. First Edition. Accessed March 20, 2016. doi: 10.1002/9781118663202.wberen321.

——. 2015b. "Coffee and the Moral Order: Ethiopian Jews and Pentecostals Against Culture." *American Ethnologist* 42 (4): 734–748.

Segal, Alan F. 2014. "Conversion to Judaism." In *The Oxford Handbook of Religious Conversion*, edited by Lewis R. Rambo and Charles E. Farhadian, 578–596. Oxford: Oxford University Press.

Seligman, Adam. 2010. "Ritual and Sincerity: Certitude and the Other." *Philosophy and Social Criticism* 36 (1): 9–39.

Shapiro, Ina. 2005. "A Sociologist from Bar Ilan: Immigration Should Not Be Instituted on an Ethnic Basis." *Haaretz*, November 28. In Hebrew.

Sharma, Aradhana, and Akhil Gupta. 2006. "Introduction: Rethinking Theories of the State in an Age of Globalization." In *The Anthropology of the State: A Reader*, edited by Aradhana Sharma and Akhil Gupta, 1–42. Malden, MA: Blackwell.

Shechory, Mally, and Sarah Ben-David. 2010. "A Comparative Analysis of Delinquency Among Youth from the Former Soviet Union and from Ethiopia in Israel." *Journal of Ethnicity in Criminal Justice* 8 (4): 290–311.

Sheleg, Yair. 2000. *The New Religious Jews—Recent Developments Among Observant Jews in Israel*. Jerusalem: Keter Publishing. In Hebrew.

——. 2004a. "The Tragedy of the Knitted Skullcap Wearers." *Eretz Acheret* 24:24–29. In Hebrew.

——. 2004b. *Not Halachically Jewish: The Dilemma of Non-Jewish Immigrants in Israel*. Jerusalem: Israel Democracy Institute. In Hebrew.

——. 2006. "Choosing Anew." *Deot* 25:10–11. In Hebrew.

Shenker, Yael. 2004. "'We Have No Artists'—a Religious National Community Establishes Its Artists: Between a Communal Identity and Religious Literature in the Early Eighties." In *Religious Zionism: An Era of Change: A Research Collection in Memory of Zevulun Hammer*, edited by Asher Cohen, and Israel Harel, 283–322. Jerusalem: Bialik Institute. In Hebrew.

Shilo, Elhanan. 2010. "The Solution for the Conversion Crisis: Presumption of Jewishness in Marriage." *Tzav Pius*, November 8. Accessed July 6, 2012. http://www.tzavpius.org.il/node/5202. In Hebrew.

Shoham, Hizky. 2014. *Let's Celebrate! Festivals and Civic Culture in Israel*. Jerusalem: Israel Democracy Institute. In Hebrew.

Shore, Cris, and Susan Wright. 2011. "Introduction: Conceptualizing Policy: Technologies of Governance and the Politics of Visibility." In *Policy Worlds: Anthropology and the Analysis of Contemporary Power*, edited by Cris Shore, Susan Wright, and Davide Però, 1–25. New York: Berghahn.

Shumsky, Dimitry. 2001. "Ethnicity and Citizenship as Perceived by Russian Israelis." *Theory and Criticism* 19:17–40.

Simmel, Georg. 1906. "The Sociology of Secrecy and of Secret Societies." *American Journal of Sociology* 11 (4): 441–498.

Simmonds, Robert B. 1977. "Conversion or Addiction: Consequences of Joining a Jesus Movement Group." *American Behavioral Scientist* 20:909–924.

——. 1984. "The Sociology of Conversion." *Annual Review of Sociology* 10:167–190.

Snow, David A., and Richard Machalek. 1983. "The Convert as a Social Type." *Sociological Theory* 1:259–289.

Spektorowsky, Alberto. 2015. "Nationalism, Land and Religion in Israel." In *Politics of Religion and Nationalism: Federalism, Consociationalism and Secession*, edited by Ferran Requejo and Klaus-Jürgen Nagel, 66–79. New York: Routledge.

Spyer, Patricia. 1996. "Serial Conversion/Conversion to Seriality: Religion, State, and Number in Aru, Eastern Indonesia." In *Conversion to Modernities: The Globalization of Christianity*, edited by Peter Van der Veer, 171–198. New York: Routledge.

Steinmetz, George. 1999. "Introduction: Culture and the State." In *State/Culture: State-Formation After the Cultural Turn*, edited by George Steinmetz, 1–51. Ithaca: Cornell University Press.

Stern, Yedidya Z. 2011. "One Conversion: Three Routes." *Lawyer* 10:17–20. In Hebrew.

Stern, Yedidya Z., Benjamin Braun, Kelman Neuman, Gideon Katz, and Nir Kedar. 2015. *When Judaism Meets State*. Tel Aviv: Yedioth Ahronot and the Israel Democracy Institute. In Hebrew.

Stern, Yedidia Z., Shaul Farber, and Elad Caplan. 2014. *Proposal for a State Conversion Law*. Vol. 7 of *A Motion for Order*. Jerusalem: Israel Democracy Institute and Itim. In Hebrew.

Stollman, Aviad. 2005. "The Extremism Spread Within the National-Religious Society Won't Be Fixed by Disengagement of Moderate People." *Deot* 20:5. In Hebrew.

Stromberg, Peter G. 1993. *Language and Self-Transformation: A Study of the Christian Conversion Narrative*. Cambridge: Cambridge University Press.

——. 2014. "The Role of Language in Religious Conversion." In *The Oxford Handbook of Religious Conversion*, edited by Lewis R. Rambo and Charles E. Farhadian, 117–139. Oxford: Oxford University Press.

Stypinska, Justyna. 2007. "Jewish Majority and Arab Minority in Israel—Demographic Struggle." *Polish Sociological Review* 1:105–120.

Sztompka, Piotr. 1999. *Trust: A Sociological Theory*. Cambridge: Cambridge University Press.

Taussig, Michael T. 1997. *The Magic of the State*. New York: Routledge.

Taylor, Diana. 1997. *Disappearing Acts: Spectacles of Gender and Nationalism in Argentina's "Dirty War."* Durham: Duke University Press.

Taylor, John P. 2001. "Authenticity and Sincerity in Tourism." *Annals of Tourism Research* 28: 7–26.

Thelen, Tatjana, Larissa Vetters, and Keebet von Benda-Beckmann. 2014. "Introduction to Stategraphy: Toward a Relational Anthropology of the State" *Social Analysis* 58 (3): 1–19.

Tikochinsky, Michal. 2008. "'And the Woman Immerses a Woman': A Woman's Immersion for Conversion in Front of a Rabbinical Court." *Akademot* (21): 65–82. In Hebrew.

Toker, Beny. 2012 "Rabbi Haim Iram: Conversion Is a National Mission." *Channel 7*, February 10. Accesed May 30, 2015. http://www.inn.co.il/News/News.aspx/233318. In Hebrew.

Triger, Zvi. 2012. "Freedom from Religion in Israel: Civil Marriages and Non-marital Cohabitation of Israeli Jews Enter the Rabbinical Courts." *Israel Studies Review* 27 (2): 1–17.

Trilling, Lionel. 1972. *Sincerity and Authenticity*. Cambridge: Harvard University Press.

Trouillot, Michel-Rolph. 2001. "The Anthropology of the State in the Age of Globalization." *Current Anthropology* 42:125–138.

Tur-Paz, Moshe. 2005. "For a Sin We Have Sinned." *Deot* 23:7. In Hebrew.

Tzav Giyyur Facebook page. 2014. April 30, 4:40 a.m., https://www.facebook.com/TzavGiyur/photos/a.743116245739338.1073741828.743067179077578/747609481956681/?type=3&theater. In Hebrew.

Ullman, Chana. 1989. *The Transformed Self: The Psychology of Religious Conversion*. New York: Plenum.

Valverde, Mariana. 2011. "Seeing Like a City: The Dialectic of Modern and Premodern Ways of Seeing in Urban Governance." *Law and Society Review* 45 (2): 277–312.

Van der Veer, Peter. 1996. "Introduction." In *Conversion to Modernities: The Globalization of Christianity*, edited by Peter van der Veer, 1–22. New York: Routledge.

——. 2006. "Conversion and Coercion: The Politics of Sincerity and Authenticity." In *Cultures of Conversions*, edited by Jan M. Bremmer, Vout J. van Bekkum, and Arie N. Molendijk, 1–14. Leuven: Peters.

Verkaaik, Oskar. 2010. "The Cachet Dilemma: Ritual and Agency in New Dutch Nationalism." *American Ethnologist* 37 (1): 69–82.

Villa, Diana, and Izhar Hess. Forthcoming. "Tradition and Change—the Challenge of Conversion and Traditional Judaism in Israel." In *Israeli Conversion*, edited by Yedidia Z. Stern and Netanel Fisher. Jerusalem: Israel Democracy Institute. In Hebrew.

Viswanathan, Gauri. 1998. *Outside the Fold: Conversion, Modernity, and Belief*. Princeton: Princeton University Press.

Waxman, Chaim I. 2013. "Multiculturalism, Conversion, and the Future of Israel as a Modern State." *Israel Studies Review* 28 (1): 33–53.

Wedel, Janine R., Cris Shore, Gregory Feldman, and Stacy Lathrop. 2005. "Toward an Anthropology of Public Policy." *Annals of the American Academy of Political and Social Science* 600:30–51.

Weiss, Bernice K. 1996. *How Should Those Converting to Judaism Be Educated?* Jerusalem: Melton Centre for Jewish Education in the Diaspora, Hebrew University of Jerusalem.

Weiss, Bernice K, and Sheryl Silverman, eds. 2000. *Converting to Judaism. Choosing to Be Chosen: Personal Stories*. Deerfield Beach,. FL: Simcha.

Weiss, Erica. 2014. *Conscientious Objectors in Israel: Citizenship, Sacrifice, Trials of Fealty*. Philadelphia: University of Pennsylvania Press.

Weiss, Yfaat. 2001. "The Monster and Its Creator—or How the Jewish Nation-State Became Multi-ethnic." *Theory and Criticism* 19:45–70. In Hebrew.

Williams, Raymond, and Michael Orrom. 1954. *A Preface to Film*. London: Film Drama.

World Rabbinic Committee on Conversion. 1989. "The Fake Conversions Scandal: On Mass Conversion Tricks Under a Halakhic Guise in the State of Israel." Jerusalem. In Hebrew.

Yadgar, Yaacov. 2010. *Jewish Conservatives in Israel: Modernity Without Secularization.* Jerusalem: Shalom Hartman Institute, Faculty of Law, Bar Ilan University and Keter. In Hebrew.

Yakobson, Alexander. 2010. "Joining the Jewish People: Non-Jewish Immigrants from the Former USSR, Israeli Identity and Jewish Peoplehood." *Israel Law Review* 43:218–239.

Yang, Shu-Yuan. 2005. "Imagining the State: An Ethnographic Study." *Ethnography* 6:487–516.

Yehoshua, Yossi. 2016. "The End of Injustice: Soldiers Whose Judaism Is Uncertain Won't Be Buried Separately." *Ynet*, January 7. Accessed March 1, 2016. http://www.ynet.co.il/articles/0,7340,L-4749759,00.html. In Hebrew.

Yonah, Yossi. 2005. *The Virtue of Difference: The Multicultural Project in Israel.* Tel Aviv: Van Leer Jerusalem Institute and Hakibutz Hameuchad. In Hebrew.

——. 2008. "'Finally a Zionist Decision': The Struggle against USSR Migrants' 'Dropping Out.'" In *Citizenship Gaps: Migration, Fertility and Identity in Israel,* edited by Yossi Yonah and Adriana Kemp, 56–91. Tel Aviv: Van Leer Jerusalem Institute and Hakibutz Hameuchad. In Hebrew.

Yonah, Yossi, and Yehuda Goodman. 2004. "Introduction: Religiosity and Secularity in Israel—Other Perspectives." In *Maelstrom of Identities: A Critical Look at Religion and Secularity in Israel,* edited by Yossi Yonah and Yehuda Goodman, 9–45. Tel Aviv: Van Leer Jerusalem Institute and Hakibutz Hameuchad. In Hebrew.

Yuval-Davis, Nira. 1996. "Women and the Biological Reproduction of 'The Nation.'" In *Women's Studies International Forum* 19:17–24.

——. 2007. "Intersectionality, Citizenship and Contemporary Politics of Belonging." *Critical Review of International Social and Political Philosophy* 10:561–574.

Zaslavsky, Tanya, and Tamar R. Horowitz. 2007. "Immigrants from the Former USSR Not Registered as Jewish: Identity Formation and Integration in Jewish Society in Israel." In *Youth in Israel, 2005,* Giora Rahav, Yohanan Wasner, and Faisel Azaiza, 27–51. Tel Aviv: Tel Aviv University. In Hebrew.

Zhensker, Edi. 2014. "The Ministry for Religious Services: Conversion Will Prevent Problems for Your Future Children." *Local Conversation,* September 4. Accessed November 5, 2015. http://mekomit.co.il/%D7%90%D7%95%D7%9C%D7%99-%D7%92%D7%9D-%D7%90%D7%A0%D7%99-%D7%99%D7%94%D7%95%D7%93%D7%99-%D7%95%D7%96%D7%94-%D7%9C%D7%90-%D7%A2%D7%A0%D7%99%D7%99%D7%A0%D7%9A. In Hebrew.

Zivan, Gilli, and Hagit Bartov. 2005. "Where Did We Go Wrong? A Monologue of Dialogues." *Deot* 23:7. In Hebrew.

Zohar, Zvi, and Avi Sagi. 1995. *Conversion and Jewish Identity: Exploration of the Halakha's Foundations.* Jerusalem: Bialik Institute. In Hebrew.

Zucker, Bat Ami. 1989. "Israeli Immigration Policy and Politics." In *The Gatekeepers: Comparative Immigration Policy,* edited by Michael C. LeMay, 119–154. New York: Praeger.

Zureik, Elia. 2008. "Notes on the Demographic Discourse in Israel." In *Citizenship Gaps: Migration, Fertility and Identity in Israel,* edited by Yossi Yonah and Adriana Kemp, 39–55. Tel Aviv: Van Leer Jerusalem Institute and Hakibutz Hameuchad. In Hebrew.

Index